Praise for
Visual Basic Developer's Guide to E-Commerce

Not only does the author spend the time to make the various tools comprehensible, he spends plenty of time on how to implement the business rules that will make or break a site.

This is the kind of book I wish I'd had the first time I built an e-commerce site—or any Web site, for that matter.

E-commerce is probably the fastest developing vertical slice of the software industry today. With Noel's help, lots of old-fashioned hard work, and a bit of luck, you'll have a good chance of creating the next great e-commerce site.

—From the foreword by Don Kiely, a regular speaker at VBITS, contributor to *Information Week*, and author of *Visual Basic Programmer's Guide to the Windows Registry.*

Visual Basic Developer's Guide to E-Commerce with ASP and SQL Server

Visual Basic® Developer's Guide to E-Commerce with ASP and SQL Server™

Noel Jerke

SYBEX®

San Francisco • Paris • Düsseldorf • Soest • London

Associate Publisher: Richard Mills
Contracts and Licensing Manager: Kristine O'Callaghan
Acquisitions & Developmental Editor: Denise Santoro
Editor: Linda Stephenson
Project Editor: Chad Mack
Technical Editor: Tim Sneath
Book Designer: Kris Warrenburg
Graphic Illustrator: Tony Jonick
Electronic Publishing Specialist: Kris Warrenburg
Project Team Leader: Shannon Murphy
Proofreaders: Molly Glover, Nelson Kim, Kimberly August
Indexer: Ted Laux
Companion CD: Ginger Warner, Kara Schwartz
Cover Designer: Design Site
Cover Illustrator/Photographer: Jack D. Myers

Library of Congress Card Number: 99-67595
ISBN: 0-7821-2621-9

Manufactured in the United States of America
10 9 8 7 6 5 4 3 2

I would like to dedicate this book to the great team at Judd's OnLine. You are tops in my book when it comes to e-commerce and site building! Working with each of you over the past four years helped to make this book possible!

FOREWORD

Microsoft and other tool vendors would have you believe that building profitable e-commerce Web sites is a trivial task, but creating great e-commerce sites is one of the toughest tasks you're likely to undertake. There are a lot of great sites out there aggressively seeking your customer's eyeballs, and most consumers have an amazingly short tolerance for slow or hard to use sites. Success demands that you get a site up and running quickly, with the right balance between ease of use and comprehensive complexity, and that it be interesting enough to get people coming back over and over.

What do you put on the site? A complete catalog? Enough hot selling products to whet the consumer's appetite? How do you build site navigation? How many clicks does it take a consumer to place an order? Too many, and you've lost them forever. Too few, and you may be shortchanging your site and products. How do you present the user with a rich shopping experience? How do you build a robust database that scales to the demands on the system? How will you identify a consumer's tastes and recommend other products to boost sales?

An e-commerce site can quickly become the de facto representative of your company, even if you have a real building somewhere. I find myself resisting companies that don't have a presence on the Web or, worse, have a Web site equivalent to an ancient, rodent-infested warehouse, one that I would never step foot in. The book you have in your hand is a great way to get started on building a great e-commerce site, letting you hang out your shingle with pride, ready to welcome enthusiastic customers who are glad they stopped by, even just to browse.

You can see the topics this book presents by examining the table of contents and flipping through the pages. But you can't necessarily learn about the author, Noel Jerke, from skimming the book. Oh, you'll quickly find that Noel is one of the smartest guys around when it comes to Web technologies and putting them to good use. And you'll probably get a sense of his personality and dedication to his work and writing. But there is a lot to Noel Jerke, something I've come to appreciate over the years.

I've had the great pleasure of working with Noel on two major projects. Both have enjoyed success that just would not have been the same without Noel's experience. He was always the guy with the solid ideas, just when we needed them to get us back on track amid the uncertainty of a poorly defined task on the cutting edge. I'm forever grateful for his tolerance of my sometimes goofy ideas. It was a team project, and he's among the best team members I've ever had the privilege of working with.

Just look through the table of contents to see the thought that Noel has put into the book. He is focusing on Microsoft tools, probably the most widely used. Not only does he spend the time to make the various tools comprehensible, he spends plenty of time on how to implement the business rules that will make or break a site. Take Chapter 11, "Managing Tax and Shipping," as an example. Here you'll find practical ways of implementing complex rules in ways that make the site maintainable over the long term. Not the sexiest topic, but obviously critical. Or Chapter 12, "Managing Orders." Or the chapters in Part IV about promotions. E-commerce sites aren't brick and mortar retail stores, but there is a lot to learn from generations of retail operations.

This is the kind of book I wish I'd had the first time I built an e-commerce site— or any Web site, for that matter. If you've read any of Noel's articles in trade magazines, you'll know that he has a way of explaining complex technologies so they are understandable and, more importantly, comprehensible when used with other tools and technologies.

E-commerce is probably the fastest developing vertical slice of the software industry today. With Noel's help, lots of old-fashioned hard work, and a bit of luck, you'll have a good chance of creating the next great e-commerce site.

Good luck!

Don Kiely

Third Sector Technologies

ACKNOWLEDGMENTS

I would like to thank the editors at SYBEX who believed in this book idea and were willing to support its publication. Thank you Denise Santoro for supporting the idea. Thank you Chad Mack, Linda Stephenson, and Tim Sneath for providing a great editing job and keeping the schedule on track. And thank you Shannon Murphy, Kris Warrenburg, and Molly Glover for handling the book's production process so flawlessly.

I want to thank my wife, Maria, for supporting me through thick, thin, and the writing of this book! I love you! Finally, I thank God for his many blessings.

Noel Jerke

CONTENTS AT A GLANCE

Introduction   *xxiii*

Part I: **Designing an E-Commerce Solution**

Chapter 1:   Defining E-Commerce   3

Chapter 2:   The Microsoft Tool Set   13

Chapter 3:   E-Commerce Database Design   27

Chapter 4:   System Configuration   59

Chapter 5:   Sample Application   77

Part II: **Building the Shopping Experience**

Chapter 6:   Building the User Interface   111

Chapter 7:   Making a Basket Case   161

Chapter 8:   Checking Out   195

Chapter 9:   Order Status and Profile Management   283

Part III: **Managing the Solution**

Chapter 10:   Product Management   339

Chapter 11:   Managing Tax and Shipping   423

Chapter 12:   Managing Orders   453

Part IV: **Promotions**

Chapter 13:   Up-Sell and Cross-Sell   505

Chapter 14:   Featured Products   533

Chapter 15:   On Sale   553

Part V: **Advanced Topics**

Chapter 16:   Introducing Site Server 3, Commerce Edition   593

Chapter 17:   Overview of a Site Server 3 Starter Store   619

Chapter 18:   Best Practices and Scalability   641

Appendix A: Database Tables and Stored Procedures   655

Index   *665*

TABLE OF CONTENTS

Introduction   *xxiii*

PART I   Designing an E-Commerce Solution

    1   Defining E-Commerce   3

        Electronic Commerce Phases   4
          Marketing   5
          Customer/Visitor   6
          Web Site Visit   6
          Product Browsing   7
          Shopping Basket   7
          Checkout   7
          Tax and Shipping   7
          Payment   8
          Receipt   8
          Process Order   9
          Fulfill Order   9
          Ship Order   9
        Managing the Storefront   10
        Summary   11

    2   The Microsoft Tool Set   13

        The Microsoft Tool Set   14
          Microsoft Windows NT Server 4   14
          Internet Information Server (IIS)/Windows NT 4
            Option Pack   15
          Active Server Pages (ASP)/Visual InterDev   16
          SQL Server   17
          Visual Basic 6   18
          Microsoft Site Server 3, Commerce Edition   19
          Secure Sockets Layer (SSL)/Verisign Certificates   21

Miscellaneous Tools   21
Browser Issues   22
Building the Functionality   24
Summary   25

3   E-Commerce Database Design   27

Microsoft SQL Server   28
  SQL Development   28
  Transact-SQL Language   29
Designing the Database   29
  Departments   29
  Products   30
  Shoppers   35
  Shopping Basket   38
  Orders   40
  Order Status   42
  Shipping Tables   44
  Tax Tables   46
  Final Database Design   47
Creating the SQL Scripts   47
Summary   56

4   System Configuration   59

Designing the Server Farm   60
  Web Servers   60
  Database Server   62
  Multiple Server Support   62
  Staging and Development Server Management   63
Server Management   64
  Development Environment   64
  Web Server Setup   65
  Server Backups   71
  Security   71
  Database Setup   73
  Load Planning   75
  Browser Considerations   75
Summary   75

5   Sample Application   **77**

Building the Data Table   78
Building the HTML Form   79
Programming the Script Code   86
Testing the Application   94
Managing the Application   98
Summary   105

PART II   Building the Shopping Experience

6   Building the User Interface   **111**

Designing the Store Foundation   112
   Site Architecture   114
   Project Setup   115
   Loading Data   117
Building the Page Structure   120
   Header and Footer Pages   121
   Building the Home Page   128
Browsing Departments and Products   129
   Departments   130
   Products   140
Searching   150
Summary   158

7   Making a Basket Case   **161**

Designing the Basket   162
Adding Items   163
Displaying the Basket   173
Managing the Basket   182
   Updating the Basket   182
   Deleting from the Basket   186
   Emptying the Basket   190
Summary   193

8   Checking Out   **195**

Defining the Checkout Process   196
Defining the Shopper Profile Process   198
Loading Tax and Shipping Data   201
Shipping Page   202

Validate Shipping Page   220
Calculating Shipping and Tax   225
Payment Page   232
Validate Payment Page   258
Confirmation Page   278
Summary   280

9   Order Status and Profile Management   **283**

Order History Management   284
Profile Interface   286
Order History Interface   316
Summary   335

PART III   Managing the Solution

10   Product Management   **339**

Designing the Store Manager   340
Managing Security   343
Managing Products   350
Managing Departments   403
Summary   421

11   Managing Tax and Shipping   **423**

Managing Tax   424
Managing Shipping   435
Summary   451

12   Managing Orders   **453**

Searching for Orders   454
Deleting an Order and Managing Order Status   471
Reviewing and Updating an Order   476
Summary   500

PART IV   Promotions

13   Up-Sell and Cross-Sell   **505**

Designing the Related Products   506
Building the Relationships   507
Related Cross-Sell Products   508
Related Up-Sell Products   510

Managing Related Products   522
Summary   531

14   Featured Products   533

Building and Designing the Featured Products   534
Programming the User Interface   535
Programming the Manager   544
Summary   551

15   On Sale   553

Designing the Sale Features   554
Building the Shopping Sale Features   556
   Implementing Sale Items   556
   Implementing Free Shipping   565
Building the Sale Management Features   572
   Managing Product Sales   572
   Free Shipping Campaign Management   577
Summary   588

PART V   Advanced Topics

16   Introducing Site Server 3, Commerce Edition   593

Core Site Server Components   594
   Requirements   594
   Core Components   596
   Commerce Edition Components   597
Commerce Tools Overview   598
   Commerce Server Objects   600
   Order Processing Pipeline   603
Installation   609
Starter Stores Overview   614
   Clock Tower   615
   Volcano Coffee   615
   Microsoft Market   616
   Microsoft Press   616
   Trey Research   617
Summary   617

17   Overview of a Site Server 3 Starter Store   **619**

Overview   620
Key Pages   622
SQL Database   624
Use of Commerce Objects   626
   Dictionary   626
   MessageManager   627
   StandardSManager   628
   Data Functions   630
   Page   630
   Order Form   632
Pipeline Utilization   636
Summary   639

18   Best Practices and Scalability   **641**

System Architecture   642
   System Hardware   642
   Load Balancing   643
   Three Tier Architecture   643
   Other Considerations   645
Database Best Practices   645
   Configuring and Utilizing SQL Server   646
   Redundancy and Reliability   646
   Database Design   647
IIS Best Practices   647
Programming   649
Site Server, Commerce Edition   650
Additional Resources   652
Summary   653

A   Database Tables and Stored Procedures   **655**

Tables   656
Stored Procedures   660

Index   *665*

INTRODUCTION

Electronic commerce is a hot topic in just about every industry today. Whether trying to reach consumers directly or trying to work with trading partners, there is something in e-commerce for just about everyone.

This book does not pretend to be the ultimate book on the technical topic of e-commerce. That would take many volumes. What it does do is serve to demonstrate to the programming community how e-commerce storefronts can be built on the Microsoft technology platform.

By way of background, I am writing this book after having spent nearly four years to date on the front lines of the e-commerce battleground working on sites such as Martha Stewart (`http://www.marthastewart.com`), Electronics Boutique (`http://www.ebworld.com`), and Ulla Popken (`http://www.ullapopken.com`). The technology has come a long way in those four short years. Of course, many people describe Internet years like dog years, so one could argue it has been nearly 28 (and at times it feels like it)! I have tried to distill the core development requirements into an easy-to-follow case study example of a CD and T-shirt store. All of the key processes and tools are covered in this store from retail storefront to back end management.

Throughout the book you will find sidebars for more information on specific topics, notes, tips, and warnings. These should be helpful guides to any particular issues surrounding the topic at hand.

Microsoft Tools and E-Commerce

Nearly every core Microsoft development tool is touched on in the book to help you understand how to build great Windows NT/Windows 2000–based solutions. This platform provides a reasonable cost, scalable, rapid development platform for developing and deploying e-commerce solutions.

At times choosing the right Microsoft tool can be a bit confusing. There is Site Server, Commerce Edition; Active Server Pages; Visual Basic with its Internet features; Visual Studio; etc. The beginning chapters of this book will review these tools and how they are utilized in both the development and deployment environments.

Finally, just a brief note on technology alternatives. Certainly options of using Sun technology, the up-and-coming Linux operating system, and many other platforms are available. Certainly there are valid arguments that these solutions may be able to scale faster or better in superscaled sites such as E-Bay and others. But, this author can say from experience, Windows NT and SQL Server can scale to handle significant site traffic if architecture is designed properly.

Structure of the Book

The book is broken into five parts. This is meant to provide a very methodical approach to designing and building an e-commerce store.

Part I

The first two chapters in Part I serve to introduce all of the key concepts of e-commerce. They define much of the terminology and review the processes involved.

The last three chapters in Part I begin the design process for building a business-to-consumer storefront. As with any good development process, a database design is created for our store. Then an analysis is done of the system requirements and issues.

The final chapter of the part kicks off the programming phase by building a simple subscription request form. While this is not a full-fledged e-commerce solution in the *shopping basket* sense, it does provide some of the basics of utilizing the Microsoft tool set for Web development.

Part II

In Part II, we get the storefront development underway. The fundamentals of department browsing, product browsing, managing shopping baskets, and checking out are explored.

Issues such as retrieving order status and managing shopper profiles and product attributes are handled throughout the development of the code.

Part III

In Part III, we tackle the side of the store the shopper doesn't see, the store manager. Certainly there are many ways to approach store management, which may contain a mix of traditional LAN-based client/server tools as well as browser-based tools.

In this part, tools for managing departments, products, tax, shipping, and orders are developed. These will be critical for any business manager to have in order to easily maintain product data and order management.

Part IV

We can't leave the marketing side of the equation out of the nuts and bolts building of the e-commerce shopping and management processes. The Web offers unique opportunities to leverage the medium to promote product and generate sales.

This part will touch on sale products, featured products, and free shipping options. The Web shopper side of the development is reviewed as well as the management issues related to supporting these features.

Part V

The last part of the book deals with advanced topics of utilizing Microsoft Site Server, Commerce Edition, for storefront development. The final chapter also provides a list of best practices and guidelines for building stable and scalable storefronts.

The Companion CD

The CD provided with the book contains most of the code developed in the book. It is provided in a part-by-part format. This will make it easy to follow the code development in each part.

> **NOTE**
> The code reviewed in Part V is NOT provided on the CD. This code is provided as a sample of how the Site Server commerce code works. The actual starter store code can be obtained by purchasing MSDN from Microsoft.

The code primarily consists of four types of formats, as outlined in Table 1.

TABLE 1: Source Code File Formats

Format	Description
SQL DDL scripts (.sql)	Scripts that can be run to create the database structure.
Active Server Pages (.asp)	Active Server Pages code files contain a mix of script and HTML code. These can be edited in Visual InterDev.
Visual Basic 6 project files	The tax and shipping component developed in the book was developed in a Visual Basic 6 project.
Images (.gif, .jpg)	Images for the storefront are provided in the code on the CD.

The complete database structure is provided in the *Database* folder on the CD. This code should be utilized for creating the data structures for the storefront.

Instructions are provided in the text for setting up the IIS storefront. Note that the virtual root reference of the store is as follows:

- Store Front: `http://DOMAINNAME/ecstore/wildwilliescds/`

- Store Manager: `http://DOMAINNAME/ecstore/manager/`

References are contained in the ASP code to this structure. If you wish to change this, these references will have to be changed as well.

Note that the hardware and software requirements for running an NT-based and ASP-based storefront are covered in Part I and should be reviewed before beginning development.

> **NOTE**
> Representing ASP/HTML code on the pages of a book can be challenging because of the difficulty of reproducing long lines of code. Code should therefore be pulled directly from the CD to ensure proper formatting and functioning. The code in the book seldom deviates from the CD and can be followed along closely when loading from the CD.

How to Reach the Author

If you have questions for me or have any difficulties with the book, I would be happy to try to assist. You can reach me at my e-mail address (noelj@juddsonline.com) or visit my online forums at my Web site (http://www.activepubs.com). I will have a full working version of Wild Willie's CD Store up and running on my Web site. You can also find book updates at http://www.activepubs.com.

PART I

Designing an E-Commerce Solution

Before we jump into hard core programming, we need to set the parameters of what we are going to try and accomplish with the technology. In the marketplace and the media, e-commerce has come to mean many different things. In Chapter 1, we will seek to put some boundaries on what e-commerce is and what specific topics we will focus on in this book. An exploration of the Microsoft tools utilized in this book will take place in Chapter 2. In Chapters 3 and 4 we will dive into building an e-commerce solution with a focus on the database and system requirements. In Chapter 5 we will build a small sample application to get started.

CHAPTER
ONE

1

Defining E-Commerce

- ■ Electronic Commerce Phases

- ■ Managing the Storefront

Everywhere you look, electronic commerce, or *e-commerce*, is the buzzword of the day. Ten years ago, mail-order catalogs were all the rage. Now we have this new medium in the Internet for transacting business. And that word "business" may be the most critical aspect of what e-commerce is all about.

Most people think of e-commerce as shopping online. That is typically called consumer-to-business (C-to-B) e-commerce. That is your traditional retail or storefront type of business. On the Web today that would include such sites as Martha Stewart (`http://www.marthastewart.com`), Amazon (`http://www.amazon.com`), and many others. For companies like Dell computers (`http://www.dell.com`), their Web sites are beginning to equal their more traditional retail channels in sales volume. There is no doubt that sites like these are gaining critical market space and will continue to grow.

E-commerce also includes the business-to-business (B-to-B) market space, which accounts for a significant amount of activity on the Internet. Just think of all the supply chain purchasing that takes place to manufacture and support many of the products and services we use every day! Examples of B-to-B e-commerce include wholesale companies selling to end retailers—for example, a PC manufacturer selling to distributors and large retailers. As B-to-B commerce grows, businesses will come to rely on this type of e-commerce as an everyday business solution. That favorite restaurant down the corner will probably purchase from different suppliers using this technology, as will your local grocery store, bookshop, and other traditional businesses. The day will come when the Internet will be a standard place for businesses to communicate with other businesses, and that day is just around the corner.

Electronic Commerce Phases

In this book, we are going to focus on the core concepts of purchasing, which are typically related to retail shopping but are also relevant to business-to-business purchasing. Before we start though, it is important to understand the complete e-commerce food chain to understand where the Internet storefront begins and ends and where more traditional back office technology comes into place.

Figure 1 diagrams phases in the purchasing process. The flat boxes show the customer's activities, and the three-dimensional boxes show business processes not performed by the customer. Note that not all of these steps are necessarily required.

FIGURE 1.1:

E-commerce phases

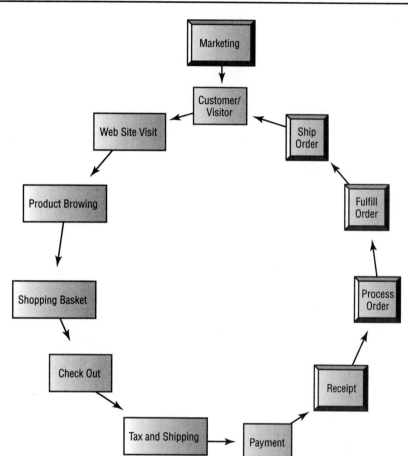

Let's take a look at each of these phases and how they fit into their respective roles in the e-commerce process.

Marketing

There is nothing new about marketing and the need to target consumers. The general goal is to target potential buyers and entice them to give your site a whirl.

What is new is the ability to use the medium of the Internet to target consumers in different ways. While we might not think of banner advertising, targeted e-mails, sweepstakes, etc., as "e-commerce," they can be a critical part of the process in the e-commerce cycle.

Another hot topic on the Net today is the building of community, and creating *sticky* applications. The goal is to provide an environment that will entice the site visitor to come back repeatedly. Examples include discussion forums, polls, surveys, chat, etc.

In this book we will not cover the technology behind using the Internet as a marketing and community building tool, but we will focus on how to use technology to market to the consumer who has found your Web site (see "Promotions," in Part IV).

Customer/Visitor

Of course, what is e-commerce without the customer! In this case our customer is the cyber-surfer who has decided to type in your URL or click on a link to visit your Web site. The biggest distinction we need to make here is the difference between the business-to-business and consumer-to-business customer. Typically when we talk business-to-business, the purchaser is another business entity who will need to have various purchasing options, including credit card, purchase order, and/or credit account (net payment). The seller may need to provide a purchase order number to the buyer. There may be additional requirements for large dollar purchases and mission critical purchases, including authenticated receipt of order, electronic transfer of funds, etc. Many of these issues have been addressed traditionally through Electronic Data Interchange (EDI), which provides agreed upon data interchange standards for businesses.

In the traditional consumer-to-business model the shopper is typically an individual who is going to pay with a credit card and have the item shipped to her home. In this book, we are going to look at the technology behind the core shopping process with a specific focus on consumer-to-business purchasing. But, many of the core processes are equally apropos for business-to-business transactions.

Web Site Visit

Once the individual visits the Web site, the fun begins. Once a business site is downloaded, a number of things can happen to begin building that e-commerce experience for a customer. Immediately we can begin tracking and profiling this consumer. And, based on that information, we can begin to target products that the consumer may be most interested in. This step begins the e-commerce shopping process.

Product Browsing

If the visitor likes what he sees upon entry to the Web site, he will hopefully begin to browse through the site product pages. Typically a visitor will browse through departments and then products within those departments. As a potential customer goes through this shopping experience, he may be enticed with products on sale, promotions, related or upgraded products, etc.

Shopping Basket

The next step is for the shopper to add products into her "shopping basket." The shopping basket is simply a list of products the shopper has selected, the quantities, prices, attributes (color, size, etc.), and anything else related to the potential order. Shopping baskets often offer options to clear the basket, remove items, and update quantities. In Part II we'll be explore the basics of the shopping process, including product browsing, the shopping basket, etc.

Checkout

Once the shopper has all of his items ready for purchase, he will begin the checkout process. On the consumer-to-business side of things, the consumer will typically enter in his shipping and billing address information. The shopper might also add in additional information for a gift greeting, gift wrapping, and other information for ancillary services.

Tax and Shipping

Once the business site knows where the product is going to be shipped and billed, it can execute two important business-rule calculations for taxes and shipping. Taxes can be as easy as simply charging for a state tax if the person lives next to a nexus for the business. Or, in rare cases you may need to provide local tax rate support, usually only where you have local representation such as storefronts in multiple states, etc. If so, then you may need to consider support for local county or city taxes based on the shopper's zip code. Likewise, shipping can be as simple as charging a flat fee or as complicated as calculating charges specific to each product purchased and correlated to distance the product has to be shipped.

Both of these issues can be even more challenging when it comes to handling international ordering. If the business has never supported international orders before, this may represent many challenges and new requirements. But, make no mistake about it, when your site launches, people from other countries will find it one way or another.

Payment

Once we have a subtotal for the product purchase, and tax and shipping are calculated, we are ready for the shopper to present payment. As mentioned above, the options will be quite different for business-to-business and consumer-to-business transactions. In consumer-to-business e-commerce, the typical purchase is via a credit card. Or, depending on the situation, COD or invoice options may be available. In business-to-business e-commerce, all options may need to be available, including purchase orders. Also, for large ticket purchases where inventory, advanced availability, and other issues may come up, a quote or follow-up with final pricing, ship time, etc., may be required as well.

With credit cards, there are options to either clear/transact the credit cards offline or transact them online. Online processing is over the Internet via services such as CyberCash and HP-Veriphone. When using online processing, the credit card data is securely transmitted over the net, and a response is sent back indicating whether the card cleared or not.

Receipt

Once the order has been placed, we might want to return a receipt to the purchaser. For business-to-business e-commerce, the receipt might be a listing to attach to a purchase order. For the consumer, that might be a reprint of the order on the screen or a listing e-mailed to the purchaser. In both cases, this process can be easily automated (as will be demonstrated in this book).

Process Order

At this stage, the customer leaves the picture and we hit the back end of the e-commerce equation. If we did not automatically process the credit card, then the first call to order is to process the financial transaction. In general, standard business rules take over in this phase, just as if the order came in via the phone or mail. The Internet does afford the option to keep the customer informed of the order status. We may want to show that the order has been processed, all items are in stock, etc. To do this, a method will need to be set up on the Web site. This will be explored further in Chapter 8, "Checking Out."

NOTE If you are shipping digital goods over the Internet, you may need to immediately provide fulfillment of the product to the customer once the credit card has been verified. In that case you will need to provide a link and some kind of access to the digital files. Everything would take place in one action.

Fulfill Order

Once we have a valid order, it needs to be fulfilled. This can actually be the most challenging business process to work on. Many different scenarios come into play depending on the type of business you are in.

If you are a traditional retailer with storefronts, there may be an issue of having central inventory to fulfill from. And, even though 90% of the transactions are electronic, there will be those customers who need to make a phone call or send an e-mail to the business.

If you provide fulfillment via a fulfillment house or service, then there might be integration issues with the fulfillment house's system. Even if you do your own fulfillment, there may be integration issues between the Web server and your back end fulfillment systems.

Ship Order

The last step in the process is to get the product to the customer. As in the "Process Order" stage, we can provide order status back to the customer. In this case it may include the UPS or FedEx shipping number for the customer to track their shipment.

Managing the Storefront

There is more to an e-commerce Web site than just the user side of things. There are also all the aspects of managing the store. The right tools to manage the e-commerce Web site are as critical as the right tools to engage the site visitor.

The management tools needed can range from simple order reporting and tracking to full-fledged store database management tools. Table 1 shows an example of some of the sample functionality a solid management interface may need. Keep in mind, all of these can be built on the same technology as the storefront. In fact, the sample stores in Site Server 3, Commerce Edition, come complete with a management interface.

TABLE 1.1:   Storefront Management Tools

Function	Description
Security	High levels of security will be critical for ensuring the right people have the right access to the appropriate functions. The customer too needs to have confidence that his credit card and order details will not be compromised en route to the supplier.
Product Management	The products in the storefront can be managed right on the Web servers if desired. Adding, updating, and deleting of products can be done directly in a Web page environment. An automated process might be necessary to reconcile the online store with a traditional product management system.
Order Tracking and Reporting	There are many opportunities to perform order tracking and general order management. Order data can be downloaded into a database format such as Microsoft Access or a comma delimited ASCII file, perhaps for integration with separate data analysis tools. Various reports can be created to analyze order history, etc.
Department/Category Management	Along with managing products, you can build in functionality to manage product categorization into departments.
Promotion Management	A critical aspect of managing the site might include administrating product promotions, sales, message text, cross sells, up sells, and anything else your marketers can come up with.
Shopper Management	If your e-commerce site has profiling of shoppers and shopper recognition you may need features to manage those profiles.
Business Rule Management	Virtually any aspect of the site should be customizable from a solid management tool. Tax, shipping, and other critical business rules of the Web site could be easily managed from a Web interface.

The technology behind the management interface does not have to be in a Web page. Traditional GUI client server development can also provide all the tools needed to manage the online store. The only potential downside is that remote management via the Web may be difficult to do with Visual Basic when your server farm is not located on the premises. Certainly database connections can be made with technologies such as Remote Data Services (RDS), but that may not be as flexible as a Web browser based interface will be.

Summary

E-commerce can be as simple as a single form online that accepts a credit card. Or it can be as complex as integrating disparate vendor systems to support supply chain purchasing.

In this book we are going to focus on the technology behind the e-commerce process. It is important to point out that underlying e-commerce are the basics of any business—customer service, fulfillment, marketing, inventory management, and much more.

A lot of planning needs to go into a successful e-commerce business. This book will show you how to utilize the products you already know—Visual Basic, SQL Server, Windows NT, and more—to build a successful, feature rich online presence for your business.

CHAPTER

TWO

2

The Microsoft Tool Set

- The Microsoft Tool Set

- Building the Functionality

The Visual Basic language is a key tool in the e-commerce developer's arsenal. But, there are many, many tools in the supporting cast that make up the successful e-commerce deployment. In this chapter we will explore these tools and, of course, take an in depth look at the Visual Basic language and how it will be utilized.

The Microsoft Tool Set

The tools range from server software to programming languages to encryption technology. Each is critical in building the complete solution. An overview of each is given, along with a list of features that are critical for e-commerce.

Microsoft Windows NT Server 4

Windows NT is the foundation for building a Visual Basic programmed solution. It provides the core security, TCP/IP functionality, and other fundamental requirements for a Web server operating system. Table 2.1 discusses the key features for e-commerce.

TABLE 2.1:   NT E-Commerce/Web Features

Feature	Description
Security	As with any Web server, it is critical to provide solid security to protect the network and operating system from the rest of the world.
TCP/IP networking	TCP/IP is, of course, the standard networking protocol used across the Internet that allows computers to communicate with each other.
Component Object Model (COM) support	When using Visual Basic to build the necessary business objects for an e-commerce Web site, COM is a key tool.
Web server	Internet Information Server (IIS) is the server that supports the core Web server functionality (see next section).

There are many excellent references available for setting up and administering Windows NT as a Web server. It is important that NT is set up properly to ensure security integrity, scalability, and other key issues.

NOTE   At the time this book was published, Windows 2000 was nearing completion. There are purported to be significant enhancements in Windows 2000 to the core foundation for Web server functionality. The Active Directory Services will provide an even more robust platform for managing directory level security and file management. The programming in this book is foundational and will work properly in an NT 4 or NT 2000 environment.

Internet Information Server (IIS)/Windows NT 4 Option Pack

IIS is the Web server that is provided with Windows NT 4. The latest version is IIS 4.0 and is provided with the Windows NT Option Pack. A new version of IIS will be released with Windows 2000. Table 2.2 overviews the key features of IIS.

TABLE 2.2: IIS Web Server Features

Feature	Description
Index Server	Site content indexing, including HTML pages, Word documents, etc., is supported with Index Server. This will enable your Web site to have site search functionality.
FTP service	IIS provides the basic functionality to support the File Transfer Protocol (FTP).
HTTP service	IIS provides the basic HTTP service.
SMTP service	IIS also provides the support for SMTP mail protocol for sending e-mail from the Web server.
NNTP service	Internet Newsgroups can also be set up and supported in IIS.
Certificate server	Certificate server allows you to manage your own set of certificates to enable authentication between the server and the client.
Message Queue Server	Microsoft Message Queue Server (MSMQ) is a fast store-and-forward service for Microsoft Windows NT Server.
Transaction server	The Option Pack also comes with Microsoft Transaction Server for developing high performance, mission critical applications.

Continued on next page

TABLE 2.2 CONTINUED: IIS Web Server Features

Feature	Description
Management console	The management console is the interface for managing the Web server.
Active Server Pages	Active Server Pages represent the foundation for Web server development. The ASP engine provides a hosting environment for a number of scripting languages, with integrated support for VBScript and JavaScript (JScript).
FrontPage extensions	The FrontPage extensions are a key tool for supporting site development in Microsoft FrontPage and Microsoft Visual InterDev. These extensions allow InterDev and FrontPage 98 to manage the Web site over a standard TCP/IP connection.

Active Server Pages (ASP)/Visual InterDev

The heart of the tool set for building our applications is the Active Server Pages component of IIS. Combine that with the Visual InterDev development tool for creating Web pages, working with SQL Server, and building e-commerce applications. Table 2.3 reviews the key features of ASP.

TABLE 2.3: ASP Key Features

Feature	Description
VBScript language	Active Server Pages provide the ability to combine client-side HTML code with server side VBScript, a slightly cut-down version of the popular Visual Basic programming language. This code will allow us to access our database, control the code being sent to the client browser, and much more.
Built in objects	IIS has several key objects built in that provide the core functionality for programming from ASP. For example the Response and Request objects (among others). Through these objects we can manage cookies, maintain session state, access other server functions, etc.
COM components	There are a number of COM components that come with ASP, including ADO for accessing data from a range of remote sources, and browser capabilities for checking the user's browser capabilities, managing ad rotation, and much more.

Visual InterDev will be a key tool throughout this book. It will be our primary development environment for building our Active Server Pages online store. It will also be the tool we will utilize to insert COM objects created in Visual Basic 6 into our Active Server Pages.

In the last section of the book, when we work with Site Server Commerce Edition, Visual InterDev will also be utilized for working with the starter stores ASP code. Table 2.4 provides an overview of the key features of Visual InterDev.

TABLE 2.4: Visual InterDev Features

Feature	Description
SQL database tools	Visual InterDev provides an excellent interface to working with remote database environment. Queries can be built, tables managed, stored procedures worked with, and all of the critical functions for building data driven e-commerce applications can be accomplished.
Remote server site management	Through the use of FrontPage server extensions, with Visual InterDev you can manage your server based Web projects remotely.
Active Server Pages development	Of course, the key use of the tool is for Active Server Pages programming.
Team project development/ Visual Source Safe integration	In conjunction with Visual Source Safe and the FrontPage server extensions, team project development can easily be done on the same set of pages. Pages that are "checked out" can be locked from use by anyone else.
Client side HTML/script editor	Not only can you work on server side script development, but you can also work on client side scripts, DHTML development, cascading style sheets, etc.
Debugging tools	As is good practice with any development tool, debugging tools are provided for that occasional error that a programmer may make.

SQL Server

As critical to e-commerce as programming is, even more critical is the database. Without a database to store products, baskets, orders, and much more, there would be no e-commerce at all. Microsoft SQL Server provides a robust development platform for building multi-tier Web applications. You can place as much or as little logic in the database tier as needed. If you are running a multi-server Web farm, then partitioning the client, Web server, and database tier become critical to ensuring solid performance and balancing server load.

SQL Server can be completely configured for different security levels, segmentation with replication, programming logic in stored procedures, etc. With Microsoft's ActiveX Data Objects (ADO) and an OLE DB provider (or ODBC) you can connect from nearly any Microsoft development tool and interface with the underlying e-commerce database.

Visual Basic 6

While Active Server Pages provides a powerful environment for server-based Web applications in itself through the scripting languages it exposes, it can be further enhanced by the use of compiled code written in a language such as Visual Basic. There are multiple ways in which we can interface from Visual Basic to the Internet, as explored in Table 2.5.

TABLE 2.5:   Visual Basic 6 Internet Features

Feature	Description
IIS applications	With Version 6, a new feature has been added to Visual Basic. IIS applications let you create Visual Basic programs with a standard HTML based browser as their interface. These applications allow the programmer to utilize all of the familiar tools in VB, such as classes, database programming, etc. The only difference is that the interface is a browser instead of a standard form. And, these applications run centrally on a Web server and can be accessed on your Intranet or Internet Web site.
COM objects	A key tool for e-commerce development is the creation of Component Object Model (COM) business objects. For example, in our e-commerce process outlined in Chapter 1, we might build objects for tax and shipping calculations encapsulating existing logic. These COM objects could then be called from our ASP script code.
WIN INET tools/browser control	Of course, there is a traditional capability to create Web applications in a standard Visual Basic forms interface. Visual Basic contains an ActiveX control that can be placed on a form and provides a subset of Internet Explorer. This may be attractive for building management tools for the online store.
ActiveX controls	For use in the Internet Explorer browser interface, ActiveX controls can be created in Visual Basic that will run on the client's computer. Again, this may be attractive for encapsulating functionality on the management side of the store.

Continued on next page

TABLE 2.5 CONTINUED: Visual Basic 6 Internet Features

Feature	Description
DHTML applications	In conjunction with IIS applications, DHTML applications were also introduced in version 6. DHTML applications allow the Visual Basic programmer to create DHTML interfaces in Internet Explorer, but the language is full-fledged Visual Basic instead of JScript or VBScript. Note that DHTML runs on the client side whereas IIS applications run on the server side.

In this book we are going to focus on building business objects in Visual Basic 6. We could explore the use of IIS Applications for storefront programming as well as adding DHTML features to the management interface. But the standard development for e-commerce is ASP with the use of COM objects. A good example of this is the Commerce Server component of Site Server 3, Commerce Edition.

Microsoft Site Server 3, Commerce Edition

Microsoft's Site Server 3, Commerce Edition (SSCE), is the big gun in Microsoft's arsenal for developing extended e-commerce applications. Site Server provides a number of tools, including the core programming environment for directory level security, site personalization, membership tracking, site log file analysis, staging and development server support, and much more. With this tool set, built on an ASP programming foundation and SQL Server high end, feature rich Web sites can be built. Sample sites include the Dell Computers (`http://www.dell.com`), Martha Stewart (`http://www.marthastewart.com`), and Ulla Popken (`http://www.ullapopken.com`).

In Part V of this book, we will explore the commerce tools provided with Site Server, Commerce Edition. In reality, it is important to point out that the Commerce tools are actually a framework of COM objects that support the purchasing process, as outlined in Chapter 1. These COM objects are built on an ASP foundation with Microsoft providing several starter stores encompassing traditional retail selling, business purchasing, internal purchasing, and selling online content. Table 2.6 overviews the key feature set of Site Server, Commerce Edition. Also, Microsoft has just announced the next release of their commerce technology, called "Commerce Server."

The Commerce Interchange Pipeline (CIP)

The Commerce Interchange Pipeline enables businesses of all sizes to exchange information electronically. The CIP packages and transports business data objects from one application to another, over a LAN, WAN, Value-Added Network (VAN), or the Internet. While it certainly supports business-to-consumer purchasing, it has the flexibility to tie together disparate systems for business-to-business ordering. The CIP integrates with existing protocols such as e-mail and HTTP, Distributed Component Object Model (DCOM), and Microsoft Message Queue (MSMQ).

The CIP exposes COM interfaces for developers, and third-party vendors can create compatible components and easily link them together into any desired configuration. The architecture of the CIP allows components to be developed independently of transport protocols and of specific data formats. Those components can be created in languages such as Visual Basic and Visual C++.

The CIP provides a way for any business class application to utilize its capabilities. The pipeline is easily executed and provides a method of executing e-commerce transactions that is independent of data format and transport format. And, there is a rich offering of third party vendor components for the CIP. Examples include components for tax, shipping, and credit card authorization. In the future Microsoft will also be releasing BizTalk tool set.

If your goal is to start out developing in Site Server, it is still a good idea to review Parts II, III, and IV. These will provide a solid foundation for developing on ASP and SQL Server. Understanding how to utilize this foundation will make it much easier to begin learning the commerce tools in Site Server.

TABLE 2.6:   Site Server 3, Commerce Edition, Key Features

Feature	Description
Membership Server	Membership Server provides a way to create a membership based site with appropriate security and tracking. Security can be based on a database or on the Lightweight Directory Access Protocol (LDAP) used by the Windows 2000 Active Directory among others.
Personalization Server	Personalization Server provides a way to provide targeted content to the user based on the user's membership profile.

Continued on next page

TABLE 2.6 CONTINUED: Site Server 3, Commerce Edition, Key Features

Feature	Description
Commerce Server (SSCE Only)	Commerce Server is the key tool set for building e-commerce applications. The Commerce Interchange Pipeline (CIP) provides a series of COM objects to manage the purchasing process and can support business-to-business integration as well.
Ad Server (SSCE Only)	Ad Server provides the ability to manage banner ad campaigns on a Web site. A complete Web based management interface is provided for adding, updating, and deleting ad campaigns and, in particular, tracking the success of a campaign.

Secure Sockets Layer (SSL)/Verisign Certificates

Security on an e-commerce Web site is crucial for securing private data, especially credit card data. On the management side of things, passwords and other business critical data should be encrypted between the browser and the server.

IIS 4 supports SSL 3. There is a simple process for requesting a certificate on the server and then submitting the certificate request to an authority, such as Verisign (http://www.verisign.com). Once the certificate request is made, the keys will be sent back and will be installed on the server.

Miscellaneous Tools

There are many other tools available for Internet development as well. Certainly many non-Microsoft tools are available for development on Windows NT or on any other operating system. Table 2.7 reviews other Microsoft tools.

TABLE 2.7: Microsoft's Web-Enabled Tools

Feature	Description
Microsoft Exchange Server	If you want to build extended e-mail capabilities to e-mail targeting, provide e-mail boxes for customer support, and other related functions, Exchange Server provides a robust e-mail platform.

Continued on next page

TABLE 2.7 CONTINUED: Microsoft's Web-Enabled Tools

Feature	Description
Microsoft FrontPage 2000	While Visual InterDev does provide WYSIWYG editing, FrontPage 98 is an excellent WYSIWYG HTML editing tool for creating static content on the Web site.
Microsoft Office	Microsoft Office provides extended tools for working with the Web. Microsoft Word can also be utilized for creating and editing Web page documents. Microsoft Access can be an excellent tool to use in conjunction with Microsoft SQL Server.
Internet Explorer	Internet Explorer provides much more than standard Web page display. There are a number of tools provided along with the browser itself. Remote Data Service (RDS) objects are provided for interfacing with data on the Web server via HTTP; ActiveX controls can run in the browser interface; and there is the ability to create client side scripting in VBScript and JScript.
Visual Source Safe	Visual Source Safe provides a source code control tool set for storing source code and related files in a source database. It provides source code version management, and also provides an infrastructure for checking code in and out; this is particularly useful for avoiding version conflicts in team-based environments.
Remote Data Services (RDS)	RDS provides a tool set for querying databases across the Internet via HTTP. It provides a direct link between the browser and the database without having to make a trip to the server to work through ASP or some other server side development tool.
Microsoft Visual Studio	We have already mentioned two tools included in Visual Studio: Visual InterDev and Visual SourceSafe. Also included are Visual C++ and Visual J++, along with other development tools such as Visual Modeler. All of these may be useful at various points in the development process.

Browser Issues

There are two primary browsers utilized on the Internet. The first is Internet Explorer 4.*x* and the second is Netscape Navigator (or Communicator) 4.*x*; Figures 2.1 and 2.2 show the two browsers respectively. Even though Internet Explorer has seen strong growth in utilization, Netscape is still a significant player in the marketplace.

Internet Explorer 4

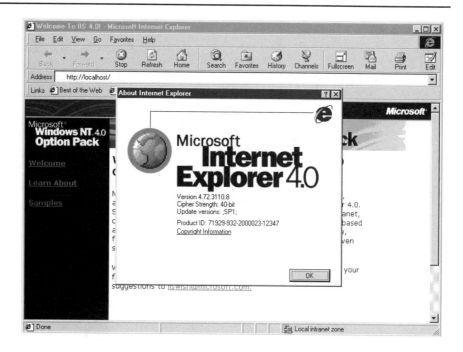

Netscape Navigator 4

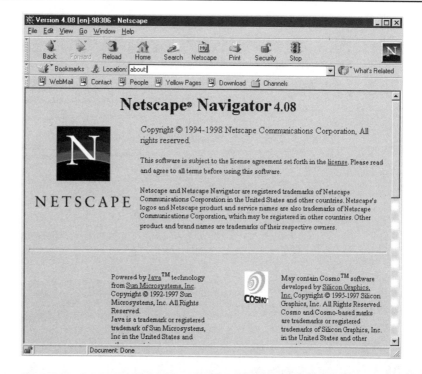

Both browsers support standard HTML and some extended features such as cascading style sheets, dynamic HTML, and JavaScript. But the only thing you can be sure will work in both is standard HTML, and even then the visual rendering might be a little different in each.

Trying to design a truly unique and advanced interface on the client side can be very tricky when trying to ensure support in both browsers. Even if you decide to build two different interfaces for those two browsers, you still have issues of supporting smaller segment browsers, such as earlier versions, specialized browsers, etc.

In this book, we will not explore the difficult issues of cross-browser development of client side JavaScript, etc. In certain cases, we will do some very specific development with VBScript on the client side in Internet Explorer to enhance the ability to maintain the e-commerce storefront.

For more information on building client side browser based applications, see the following books:

- *Mastering JavaScript and JScript*
- *VB Developer's Guide to ASP*
- *Mastering Visual Basic*

Building the Functionality

So, how will all of these tools be utilized to build the e-commerce functionality laid out in this book? Table 2.8 breaks down the process as outlined in Chapter 1.

TABLE 2.8:   Using Microsoft Tools to Build an E-Commerce Solution

Feature	Description
Marketing	ASP, VB6, SQL
Customer/Visitor	ASP, SQL
Web Site Visit	ASP, SQL
Product Browsing	ASP, SQL

Continued on next page

TABLE 2.8:   Using Microsoft Tools to Build an E-Commerce Solution

Feature	Description
Shopping Basket	ASP, SQL
Checkout	ASP, SQL
Tax and Shipping	ASP, VB6, SQL
Payment	ASP, VB6, SQL
Receipt	ASP, SQL
Process Order	ASP, SQL (order status)
Fulfill Order	ASP, SQL (order status)
Ship Order	ASP, SQL (order status)
Managing the Storefront	ASP, VB6, SQL, IE

In the last section we will explore the use of the Site Server tool set for building the complete e-commerce functionality. In that case we are relying on the built-in functionality to support the purchasing process.

Summary

In this book we are going to focus on the technology behind the e-commerce process. It is important to point out that underlying e-commerce are the basics of any business—customer service, fulfillment, marketing, inventory management, and much more. In the next chapter we will begin the exploration of the database requirements underlying an e-commerce solution.

CHAPTER
THREE

3

E-Commerce Database Design

- ■ Microsoft SQL Server

- ■ Building the Database

- ■ Creating the SQL Scripts

At the core of any interactive Web site is a well-designed database. Before we jump into programming the Web site, we need to know the core design for all of the key components of the Web site.

For the purposes of this book, the database system we will use is Microsoft SQL Server. Oracle and other databases supporting ODBC or OLE DB interfaces could be utilized instead. Throughout this book, the SQL code and related development will be as server-agnostic as possible so it can be utilized on different database platforms.

Microsoft SQL Server

SQL Server is Microsoft's enterprise level database offering. Microsoft Access is its entry level offering for basic application development. In the fall of 1998, SQL Server version 7 was released, which was a significant upgrade from version 6.5.

SQL Server provides a robust relational database architecture for building high transaction e-commerce Web sites. It is the server technology behind such high profile e-commerce Web sites as Martha Stewart Catalog site (`www.marthabymail .com`), Electronics Boutique (`www.ebworld.com`), and 1-800-Flowers (`www. 1800flowers.com`).

TIP
The databases created in this book, while developed on Microsoft SQL Server, could be utilized on Oracle or even Microsoft Access. Some of the SQL queries, stored procedures, etc., may have to be retargeted at those database platforms.

SQL Development

The primary tools utilized for interfacing with SQL Server will be Visual Studio and specifically the data tools included with Visual InterDev and Visual Basic 6.0. Both products provide query development tools, table management, etc.

For direct development, SQL Enterprise Manager will be utilized. It provides powerful administration tools that you can use to manage multiple servers. With SQL Enterprise Manager you can configure, start, pause, and stop SQL Servers, monitor current server activity, and view the SQL Server error log. You can create and manage devices, databases, etc. You can manage security, including logins, database users, and permissions. SQL Enterprise Manager and the SQL Executive service provide a way to set alerts for various server events and to schedule server tasks. SQL Enterprise Manager also provides a graphical way to set up and manage replication, and enables you to execute and analyze queries, back up and restore databases, and generate SQL scripts.

It is out of the scope of this book to delve into the inner depths of setting up and configuring SQL Server. In the next chapter we will explore the issues surrounding utilizing SQL Server.

Transact-SQL Language

Microsoft SQL Server supports the Transact-SQL language, which is a superset of Structured Query Language (SQL), a leading standard for querying relational databases. T-SQL has been certified as compliant with the ANSI SQL-92 standard, but any code taking advantage of proprietary extensions will of course not be easily portable. As much as possible, SQL code written in this book will be ANSI compliant.

Designing the Database

Our online store is going to sell CDs and a few T-shirts. We are going to need an appropriate database that will define music departments/ genres, products, basket storage, and order data. We will first develop the high-level relational data schema for each of these departments. Then we will take an in-depth look at the field structure for each table.

Departments

The top-level categorization of products will be departments. For example, we might have rackets and tennis balls in the Tennis department, whereas the hoop, backboard, and net would be in the Basketball department. In the case of our CD store, CDs will be classified into music categories such as Jazz and Country.

Conceivably we could also have multi-level departments, as shown in Figure 3.1. In that case we could have a top-level department, such as sporting goods, with several departments below it, such as Tennis and Basketball.

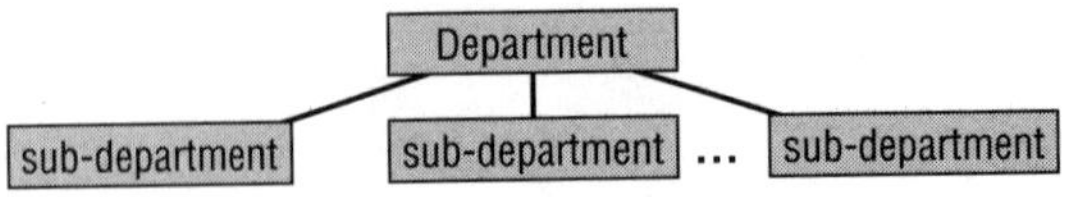

FIGURE 3.1:

Multi-level department diagram

In the sample store there will be a flat department model. Table 3.1 outlines the key fields in the database table.

TABLE 3.1:   Department table fields

Field	Description
idDepartment	The ID will be auto-incremented to give a unique identifier for the department table.
chrDeptName	The name will be the displayed name in the store.
txtDeptDesc	The department description can be utilized for internal business use or external display.
chrDeptImage	Included in our database might be a pointer to an image that is representative of the department.

Next we will define the products that will be categorized into the departments.

Products

Offering products in our store would seem pretty simple. But, when you begin to think about defining a generic product, it can get pretty complicated. For example, a computer will have many attributes, including processor speed, drive size, RAM, etc., whereas a simple paper clip might not have any specific attributes.

Sample Database Tables

In our sample store for the Web site, we will assume that our products (such as T-shirts) can have only two specific attributes—size and color. But our relational table structure will allow for more attribute types. Figure 3.2 shows the product diagram for our database.

FIGURE 3.2:

Sample database products diagram

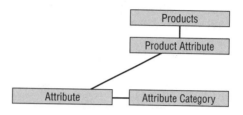

In this diagram we have four tables.

The Products table   This table stores the primary product data.

The Attribute table   This table stores all of the attributes (e.g., red, green, X, XL).

The Product Attribute table   This table is the link between the attributes a product has and the product itself.

The Attribute Category table   This table categorizes each attribute (e.g., size, color, weight).

Two other key relationships to note are that our products are categorized into departments and we need to depict a relationship between products. For example, a red skirt may be related to the red blouse that goes with it. That would be a *cross-sell*. Another type of relationship would be the *up-sell*. In that case we might want to tempt the customer from a lower cost product to a more expensive one. Figure 3.3 shows the core products table related to departments and other products. Each product can be in multiple departments and can have multiple related products.

FIGURE 3.3:

Product relationships diagram

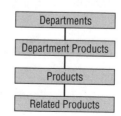

The Product Table   Each product is categorized into at least one department. In our case we are allowing a product to be categorized into multiple departments. Thus, we have the lookup table and Department Products. And, we have a relationship table of products related to other products in Related Products. In the subsequent chapters, SQL statements will be provided creating products and tables, and building the relationships between them. Table 3.2 details the fields for the top-level product table.

TABLE 3.2:   Product Table Fields

Field	Description
idProduct	The ID will be auto-incremented to give a unique identifier for the product.
chrProductName	The name of the product as displayed to the shopper.
txtDescription	A description of the product. The information will be stored as text, but HTML tagging can be placed in the text for display purposes.
chrProductImage	The name of the image to be displayed. Typically there is a presumed reference to a location on the Web server and just the image file name is stored. Or this might just be a hyperlink to the file.
intPrice	The price of the product. To avoid rounding issues with decimal numbers, the price is stored as an integer with the cents stored in the 1s and 10s digit positions.
dtSaleStart	Date the sale price of the product is available.
dtSaleEnd	Date the sale price of the product ends.
intSalePrice	Sale price of the product.
intActive	Flag to indicate if the product is active or not.

The Attribute Table   Now that we have the product table fields defined, we can take a look at the fields in the attribute table. Table 3.3 shows the fields.

TABLE 3.3:   Attribute Table Fields

Field	Description
idAttribute	The ID will be auto-incremented to give a unique identifier to each attribute.
chrAttributeName	The name of the attribute as displayed to the shopper.
idAttributeCategory	Link to the category that this attribute is assigned to.

This simple table will assign the attribute an ID and store a description. Example data would include an ID of *1* and a name of *red*.

The Product Attribute Table   The product attribute table is what ties the particular product's attributes to the list in the attribute table. Table 3.4 shows the fields.

TABLE 3.4:   Product Attribute Table Fields

Field	Description
idProductAttribute	The ID will be auto-incremented to give a unique identifier for each combination.
idAttribute	The ID of the attribute.
idProduct	The ID of the product the attribute is related to.

As you can see, this table is a simple cross-reference listing of what attributes a product has. Note that at this level we are not assigning any type of categorization to the attributes.

The Attribute Category Table   Finally, we can assign a categorization to the attributes in the attribute list. Table 3.5 shows the fields.

TABLE 3.5:   Attribute Category Table Fields

Field	Description
idAttributeCategory	The ID will be auto-incremented to give a unique identifier for each category.
chrCategoryName	The name of the category.

This table is a simple lookup table of attribute categories.

NOTE   If we wish to list the attributes of a product by category, we will simply need to build a query that returns a unique list of categories based on the set of attributes assigned to a product.

Categorizing Products into Multiple Departments

As previously mentioned, each product will be assigned to at least one department, although we want our database to be flexible enough to support categorizing products into multiple departments. For example, although a blouse may be categorized in the Blouses department, it can also be part of the Spring Collection department. A CD might fall into a Jazz category as well as a Blues category. Table 3.6 shows the fields for the DepartmentProducts table.

TABLE 3.6:   DepartmentProducts Table Fields

Field	Description
idDepartmentProduct	The ID will be auto-incremented to give a unique identifier for each relationship.
idDepartment	The ID of the department.
idProduct	The ID of the product categorized into the department.

As with the product attribute table, this table simply has a listing of relationships between products and departments.

Linking Two Products Together

Finally, with regards to products, we need a way to link two products together. To the shopper this may show up as a listing of *related* products, or it may show up as a suggestion to *upgrade* to a better product. These will be items that the shopper will be interested in or need to know about when purchasing another product. Table 3.7 shows the fields for the table that accomplishes this task.

TABLE 3.7:   RelatedProducts Table Fields

Field	Description
idRelatedProduct	The ID will be auto-incremented to give a unique identifier for each relationship.
idproductA	The ID of the product.
idProductB	The ID of the product related to the other product.
idRelationType	Indicates if the product relation is an up-sell or a cross-sell.

Again, this table is simply a listing of relationships between products.

Reporting inventory availability to the user can be critical if the shopping site will have a high level of order volume or limited inventory at any time. Our product definitions may require an inventory field or a link to an inventory database to keep track of availability. And, in the ordering process, we will need to decrement the inventory availability to keep an accurate count.

Defining the proper product definitions and relationships is critical to properly presenting the shopper with your product line. The structure outlined here for products will mostly likely work for very simple products with minimal attribute requirements. In more complex stores, the data diagram for products can become much more complex.

In particular, most established companies will already have a product database. While this may not be in the right form to use as part of an online store, a close link between the two databases will be necessary to ensure that the two are reconciled.

Shoppers

Next we need to think about shoppers. Obviously we are going to have to store some information about them, especially when they order products from our store. The options in this area range quite a bit from the storing of minimal shopper data to a complete shopper profile. A complete profile would include the ability to do one-click shopping (a la Amazon.com). On the simplest of ends, only the shipping, billing, and payment information would be stored per order.

It is important to understand that stores can be as different and complex as people. We all share the same elements (head, heart, body), but the character and nature of each is quite different. Thus, it will be important to have a thorough understanding of your store's requirements and how the template provided in this book will be best applied.

If we store shopper information on an ongoing basis, we then have many options available to customize the Web site. If we have a bit of profile data on the shopper, we can begin to target product offerings and other types of promotions at them when they log on to the site. Also, we can provide extended customer service information, such as order status, shipping tracking numbers, etc.

For the purposes of this book, we will store shopper information and allow the shopper to retrieve it at a later date by setting a cookie or entering a username and password.

Our shopper data is going to be a fairly straightforward table. It will primarily store the shipping and billing information of the shopper. Since each order will have the ID of the shopper stored in it long term, we could do some correlation between what the shopper has been ordering and how we present the site to the shopper (personalization). Table 3.8 shows the fields for the table.

WARNING   Because of the increased threat of theft, you need to be aware of the security concerns surrounding long-term storage of credit card data. Storage of credit card data can be an issue for your shoppers, and forcing that option on shoppers might turn them away. The shopper table in this scenario does not enable long-term storage of payment information in shoppers' records.

TABLE 3.8:   Shopper Table Fields

Field	Description
idShopper	The ID will be auto-incremented to give a unique identifier for each shopper.
chrFirstName	The shopper's first name.
chrLastName	The shopper's last name.
chrAddress	Address of the shopper.
chrCity	City of the shopper.
chrState	State of the shopper.
chrProvince	International province location of the shopper.
chrCountry	Country of the shopper.
chrZipCode	Zip code of the shopper.
chrPhone	Phone number of the shopper.

Continued on next page

TABLE 3.8 CONTINUED: Shopper Table Fields

Field	Description
chrFax	Fax number of the shopper.
chrEmail	E-mail address of the shopper.
dtEntered	Date the shopper information was entered.
chrUserName	User name of the shopper. This will be utilized in accessing the shopper's profile, order status, etc.
chrPassword	Password used by the shopper to access their profile and order status.
intCookie	Flag indicating if the shopper wishes to have no username/password access requirement to their profile. This will allow the shopper to be immediately recognized when they log on from their computer.

In our example, the shopper data will be the typical billing information for the shopper. Shoppers can choose to ship the product to different locations. In some instances, the profile data may be the shipping address, and the shopper will want to enter in billing information that may change. And, in many cases, the shipping and billing address information will be the same regardless.

NOTE   In our example, we are not storing any payment information with the shopper profile. Instead, we store this information on a per-order basis in a separate table. We could have a secondary table of credit card types, expiration dates, etc. Keep in mind that a shopper may utilize different payment methods. In the business-to-business environment, payment methods such as COD, Invoice, PO, etc. may need to be stored in the profile.

Keep in mind that in many cases a shopper profile will be created with each order even though the shopper may order more than once. The shopper may simply choose to not participate in utilizing her or his profile. There is no real way to limit the consumer from doing this without severely locking down the Web site, which may only be prudent if you are trying to promote impulse shopping.

NOTE   We are not accounting for international orders and appropriate address fields in this example.

Shopping Basket

As the shopper is maneuvering through the Web site, we will need to store the items they are selecting in their shopping basket. Ultimately this task acts as a type of storage of the product data selected by the shopper. We then have to keep a few *state* items in mind.

If the shopper selects a product to be added to his/her basket and it is on sale, we don't want them to be shocked if the sale ends while they are shopping and the price suddenly jumps up. Or, for that matter, if the store manager initiates a pricing update, we don't want the prices changing on the fly for the shopper.

Figure 3.4 shows the basket tables in relation to the shopper table.

FIGURE 3.4:

Basket tables diagram

In our diagram, each shopper has a basket. In fact, if the shopper is returning and pulling up her profile, she may have several baskets. Each basket will then have either one or a series of items in it. Table 3.9 defines the basket table fields.

TABLE 3.9:   Basket Table Fields

Field	Description
idBasket	The ID will be auto-incremented to give a unique identifier for each basket.
intQuantity	The total quantity of items on the shopping basket.
dtCreated	The date the basket was created.
idShopper	The ID of the shopper for whom the basket was created.
intOrderPlaced	Flag that will indicate if the basket was ordered by the shopper.
intSubTotal	Subtotal cost of the basket without any shipping, tax, handling, or other charges.

Continued on next page

TABLE 3.9 CONTINUED: Basket Table Fields

Field	Description
intTotal	Total cost of the order with all costs included.
intShipping	Shipping cost of the order. This will be calculated based on the appropriate business logic.
intTax	Tax cost of the order. This will be calculated based on the appropriate business logic.

Note that the basket totals store the different costs and totals of the order. These will be stored at the time of the order in case the business logic behind any of the costs changes or there are any promotions that happen based on the type of order.

With each basket there will be a listing of items that have been added. This will store the basic information about the product, and this table will be used to receipt the items for the order. Table 3.10 defines the basket items.

TABLE 3.10:   Basket Items Table Fields

Field	Description
idBasketItem	The ID will be auto-incremented to give a unique identifier for each basket
idProduct	ID of the product added to the basket.
intPrice	Price of the product when added to the basket. Note that this price may be a sale price.
chrName	Name of the product.
intQuantity	Quantity of the product ordered.
idBasket	ID of the basket that these items belong to.
chrSize	Stores the size value.
chrColor	Stores the color value.

TIP

A key issue related to database management is managing the basket and basket item tables. On high volume Web sites, the number of baskets that are generated can be far more than just the number of orders placed. It will be important to put in place a process to clear out baskets that are older than a specified amount of time (e.g., 24 or 48 hours).

The basket tables for each shopper will be managed as the shopper browses through the Web site. Functionality will be built to add, update, and delete items in the basket. Next we will look at storing orders placed on the site.

Orders

This is the good part that every businessperson likes to deal with—the collection of money. We will need to store the order data when the person checks out from the store. We need to store basic order information including shipping and billing addresses, payment data, items ordered, etc.

The order data relates to the shopping basket and specifically the items in the shopping basket. Figure 3.5 shows the relationship between the order table, basket tables, and the shopper data (if present).

FIGURE 3.5:

Order tables diagram

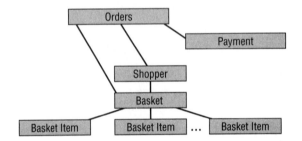

In this case the order will be related to the shopping basket and the shopper. Each basket, and each order, must have a shopper assigned to it.

The payment data will be stored in a separate table in case we wish to easily delete this data on a frequent basis and yet keep the primary contact information on the order for later reference. Table 3.11 defines the fields for the table.

TABLE 3.11:   OrderData Table Fields

Field	Description
idOrder	The ID will be auto-incremented to give a unique identifier for each order.
idShopper	The ID of the shopper placing the order.

Continued on next page

TABLE 3.11 CONTINUED: OrderData Table Fields

Field	Description
chrShipFirstName	First name of the person the product will be shipped to.
chrShipLastName	The last name of the person the product will be shipped to.
chrShipAddress	Address where the product will be shipped.
chrShipCity	City where the product will be shipped.
chrShipState	State where the product will be shipped. This will also potentially have a bearing on tax and shipping calculations.
chrShipProvince	The Province for an international order.
chrShipCountry	Country where the order will be shipped.
chrShipZipCode	Zip code to which the product will be shipped. In complex tax situations, tax may be calculated down to the zip code local.
chrShipPhone	Phone number at the ship to location.
chrShipFax	Fax number at the ship to location.
chrShipEmail	E-mail address for the person the product is being shipped to.
chrBillFirstName	First name of the billing contact.
chrBillLastName	Last name of the billing contact.
chrBillAddress	Address of the billing contact.
chrBillCity	City of the billing contact.
chrBillState	State of the billing contact.
chrShipProvince	The province of the billing contact.
chrCountry	The country of the billing contact.
chrBillZipCode	Zip code of the billing contact.
chrBillPhone	Phone number of the billing contact.
chrBillFax	Fax number of the billing contact.
chrBillEmail	E-mail address of the billing contact.
dtOrdered	Date the order was placed.

In many cases the shipping and billing address information will be the same. But, we will store it twice in case there is a need to update one or the other if they change. In the interface, an option should be provided to enter the address information only once if the billing and shipping address are the same.

Next we need to define the table to store the payment data for the shopper. We will need to store the key three items of credit card data to facilitate payment authorization. Those items include the type of credit card used, credit card number, and the expiration date. Table 3.12 reviews the fields for the payment data.

TABLE 3.12: PaymentData Table Fields

Field	Description
idPayment	The ID will be auto-incremented to give a unique identifier for each payment.
idOrder	ID of the order that the payment is related to.
chrCardType	The type of credit card (Visa, American Express, etc.)
chrtCardNumber	The credit card number.
chrExpDate	The expiration date of the credit card.
chrCardName	The name of the card owner.

Again, it is critical to securely manage this data and ensure it is deleted after it has been processed. Now that we have our order data, it will go into an order processing stage. In order to provide good customer service, we will want to provide a way for the customers to see their order status.

Order Status

For the purposes of this book, we will provide three types of status.

1. The first will be that the order has been received and is in process to be fulfilled.

2. In the second stage the order will be fulfilled and the status will be indicated if the order is fulfilled.

3. The final stage will be the shipping stage. The status will indicate that the order was shipped and what the shipping number is.

Each order will have a specific order status table, as shown in Figure 3.6. Table 3.13 shows the definitions for the order status table.

FIGURE 3.6:

Order status diagram

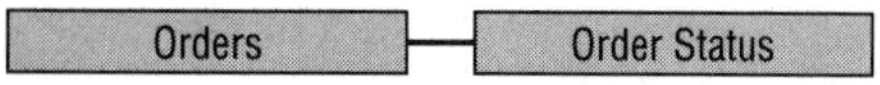

TABLE 3.13:   OrderStatus Table Fields

Field	Description
idOrderStatus	The ID will be auto-incremented to give a unique identifier for each payment.
idOrder	ID of the order that the payment is related to.
idStage	The type of credit card (Visa, American Express, etc.)
dtShipped	Date the order was shipped (stage 3).
dtFulfilled	Date the order was fulfilled from inventory (stage 2).
dtProcessed	Date the order was processed from the Web (stage 1).
txtNotes	Any notes related to the order status. For example, if there is a problem with the order, notes could be placed here.
chrShippingNum	The shipping number for when the order is shipped to the customer.
intProcessed	Indicates whether the order has been processed for fulfillment or not.

The order status table could be much more complicated than what is represented above. We could have multiple stages and ideally this status data would be directly plugged into a back end order processing system.

Shipping Tables

Shipping can be calculated in a number of ways. There tend to be several different models. Each is outlined as follows in Table 3.14.

TABLE 3.14: Shipping Models

Shipping calculation	Description
Item Quantity	The shipping total will be based on the number of items in the order. The variations can include a per item fee or a fee based on ranges. Examples would include 1 to 5 items costs $3, 6 to 10 items costs $6, etc.
Order Total	Instead of the quantity of items in the order, the shipping would be based on the total amount of the order. If the order total is $0 to $5, the shipping cost would be $1. If the total is from $6 to $10, the shipping cost would be $3.
Weight	Weight can also be a factor in situations where the products are unusually large or vary in size. Weight calculations will need to be related to the product table where, presumably, weight of the product would be stored.
Shipping Distance	Perhaps the most complicated of the shipping models is calculating the cost based on shipping distance. If you use zip codes to determine distance, the calculations can become complex. A simpler model would specify costs for shipping within a region and costs for shipping between regions. Often this shipping model will be combined with a weight calculation as well.

These are just four examples of how shipping can be calculated, but there are any number of combinations depending on the business requirements. For example, we might want to combine shipping distance with the weights of the products to come up with the final charges.

For the example in this book, we will use a simple table of shipping rates based on order item quantities. The table will list the rate range and the cost. Table 3.15 shows the shipping table fields.

TABLE 3.15: Shipping Table Fields

Field	Description
idQuantityRange	The ID will be auto-incremented to give a unique identifier for each rate range.
intLowQuantity	The low-end number of products for this range.
intHighQuantity	The high-end number of products for this range.
intFee	Shipping fee for cost range.

When the shopper checks out, the number of items ordered will be checked against the data in the table to find the appropriate rate. Example data for our sample code in this book is as follows in Table 3.16.

TABLE 3.16: Shipping Rates

Low Quantity	High Quantity	Fee
0	5	$5.00
6	10	$7.50
11	20	$10.00
21	99,999	$15.00

In most cases, we will have a high range and maximum fee. In this case, we have a quantity range of 21 to 99,999. Another variation on this shipping option would be to simply have a fee formula based on the quantity above 20.

NOTE Options for handling two-day and next-day shipping options are often available. For example, if the customer wants the product shipped within two days, then $5 might be added to the order. For next-day shipping, $10 might be added.

Tax Tables

Similar to shipping, we also need to be able to calculate tax. Figuring tax can be fairly complicated or quite simple. It all depends on the state tax requirements and location of nexus points for shipping the product. For purposes of this book, we are going to calculate tax based on simple state tax requirements. We will assume that we have shipping nexus locations in only two or three states.

Based on this requirement, Table 3.17 simply defines storing tax rates by state.

TABLE 3.17:   Tax Table Fields

Field	Description
idState	The ID will be auto-incremented to give a unique identifier for each state.
chrState	The state abbreviation.
intTaxRate	The tax rate for the state.

The sample tax data for our purposes will be as follows in Table 3.18.

TABLE 3.18:   Tax Rate Sample Data

State	Tax Rate
TX	5% (.05)
VA	10% (.10)
DC	25% (.25)

In the order process, we will simply check the state entered as the shipping address against the tax table to compute our tax for the store.

Final Database Design

Now that we have our database tables defined, we can produce a final relationship diagram. Figure 3.7 shows the final set of tables and their relationships.

FIGURE 3.7:

ECStore database diagram

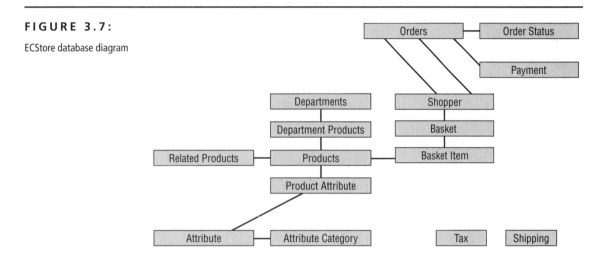

Putting it all together provides the complete data picture needed for our e-commerce store. Next we will take a look at the script programming needed to create our tables.

Creating the SQL Scripts

Now that we have our database fields designed, we are ready to create the SQL scripts behind all of the tables. These will be utilized in setting up the database. And, we will need to see the appropriate tables with data (e.g., tax, shipping).

> **WARNING**   All the code presented in this chapter was tested on a SQL Server 7 SP1 environment. While it should run identically on SQL Server 6.5, you could possibly run into glitches with other builds.

Note that we are not creating all of the necessary stored procedures and other database objects necessary to utilize the tables. That will be created throughout the rest of the book.

Our first script is for the Attribute table. The idAttribute field is the primary key.

LISTING 3.1   Attribute Table

```
CREATE TABLE dbo.Attribute (
    idAttribute int IDENTITY (1, 1) NOT NULL ,
    chrAttributeName varchar (255) NULL ,
    idAttributeCategory int NULL
)
```

Next is the Attribute Category table. Note that the primary key for the table is the idAttributeCategory field.

LISTING 3.2   Attribute Category Table

```
CREATE TABLE dbo.AttributeCategory (
    idAttributeCategory int IDENTITY (1, 1) NOT NULL ,
    chrCategoryName varchar (255) NULL
)
```

In the Basket Table, the idBasket field is the primary key. The dtCreated field will be defaulted with the GetDate() statement call. All of the monetary fields will also be defaulted to a value of 0. Be sure to apply these defaults in your database setup.

LISTING 3.3   Basket Table

```
CREATE TABLE dbo.Basket (
    idBasket int IDENTITY (1, 1) NOT NULL ,
    intQuantity int NULL CONSTRAINT DF_Basket_intQuantity_1__13
DEFAULT (0),
    idShopper int NULL ,
    intOrderPlaced int NULL CONSTRAINT DF_Basket_intOrderPlaced11__12
DEFAULT (0),
    intSubTotal int NULL CONSTRAINT DF_Basket_intSubTotal_13__12
DEFAULT (0),
```

```
        intTotal int NULL CONSTRAINT DF_Basket_intTotal_15__12 DEFAULT
(0),
        intShipping int NULL CONSTRAINT DF_Basket_intShipping_12__12
DEFAULT (0),
        intTax int NULL CONSTRAINT DF_Basket_intTax_14__12 DEFAULT (0),
        dtCreated datetime NULL CONSTRAINT DF_Basket_dtCreated_1__12
DEFAULT (getdate()),
        intFreeShipping int NULL CONSTRAINT DF_Basket_intFreeShipping1__13
DEFAULT (0),
        CONSTRAINT PK___9__12 PRIMARY KEY  CLUSTERED
        (
                idBasket
        )
)
```

In the BasketItem table, the idBasketItem is the primary key. The intQuantity field will be defaulted to 0.

LISTING 3.4   **BasketItem Table**

```
CREATE TABLE dbo.BasketItem (
        idBasketItem int IDENTITY (1, 1) NOT NULL ,
        idProduct int NULL ,
        intPrice int NULL ,
        chrName varchar (255) NULL ,
        intQuantity int NULL CONSTRAINT DF_BasketItem_intQuantity1__12
DEFAULT (0),
        idBasket int NULL ,
        chrSize varchar (50) NULL ,
        chrColor varchar (50) NULL ,
        CONSTRAINT PK___10__12 PRIMARY KEY  CLUSTERED
        (
                idBasketItem
        )
)
```

Our next two tables define the Department and the Department Products, which defines how the department products are assigned. In each case, our primary key is defined as the Identity column.

LISTING 3.5   Department Table

```
CREATE TABLE dbo.Department (
    idDepartment int IDENTITY (1, 1) NOT NULL ,
    chrDeptName varchar (255) NULL ,
    txtDeptDesc text NULL ,
    chrDeptImage varchar (255) NULL ,
    CONSTRAINT PK___1__12 PRIMARY KEY  CLUSTERED
    (
        idDepartment
    )
)
```

LISTING 3.6   Department Products Table

```
CREATE TABLE dbo.DepartmentProducts (
    idDepartmentProduct int IDENTITY (1, 1) NOT NULL ,
    idDepartment int NULL ,
    idProduct int NULL ,
    CONSTRAINT PK___6__12 PRIMARY KEY  CLUSTERED
    (
        idDepartmentProduct
    )
)
```

The OrderData table defines idOrder as its primary key field. The dtOrdered table is defaulted with the GetData() function call. Thus, the order insertion date will be set to the server time when the customer completed the order.

LISTING 3.7   OrderData Table

```
CREATE TABLE dbo.OrderData (
    idOrder int IDENTITY (1, 1) NOT NULL ,
    idShopper int NULL ,
    chrShipFirstName varchar (50) NULL ,
    chrShipLastName varchar (50) NULL ,
    chrShipAddress varchar (150) NULL ,
    chrShipCity varchar (150) NULL ,
    chrShipState varchar (50) NULL ,
    chrShipZipCode varchar (15) NULL ,
    chrShipPhone varchar (25) NULL ,
```

```
        chrShipFax varchar (25) NULL ,
        chrShipEmail varchar (100) NULL ,
        chrBillFirstName varchar (50) NULL ,
        chrBillLastName varchar (50) NULL ,
        chrBillAddress varchar (150) NULL ,
        chrBillCity varchar (100) NULL ,
        chrBillState varchar (50) NULL ,
        chrBillZipCode varchar (15) NULL ,
        chrBillPhone varchar (25) NULL ,
        chrBillFax varchar (25) NULL ,
        chrBillEmail varchar (100) NULL ,
        dtOrdered datetime NULL CONSTRAINT DF_OrderData_dtOrdered_12__12
        DEFAULT (getdate()),
        chrShipProvince varchar (150) NULL ,
        chrShipCountry varchar (150) NULL ,
        chrBillProvince varchar (150) NULL ,
        chrBillCountry varchar (150) NULL ,
        idBasket int NULL ,
        intFreeShipping int NULL CONSTRAINT DF_OrderData_intFreeShipp1__13
        DEFAULT (0),
        CONSTRAINT PK___11__12 PRIMARY KEY  CLUSTERED
        (
                idOrder
        )
)
```

In the Order Status field, we default the idStage value to 0. This will indicate the order has not yet been processed. The intProcessed field is also defaulted to 0. It will be set to 1 as soon as the order is received and put into the fulfillment process. The idOrderStatus field is the primary key. Following the Order Status table is the Payment Data table. The idPayment field is the primary key.

LISTING 3.8   **OrderStatus Table**

```
CREATE TABLE dbo.OrderStatus (
    idOrderStatus int IDENTITY (1, 1) NOT NULL ,
    idOrder int NULL ,
    idStage int NULL CONSTRAINT DF_OrderStatu_idStage_14__12 DEFAULT
(0),
    dtShipped datetime NULL ,
    dtFulfilled datetime NULL ,
    dtProcessed datetime NULL ,
```

```
        txtNotes text NULL ,
        chrShippingNum varchar (30) NULL ,
        intProcessed int NULL CONSTRAINT DF_OrderStatu_intProcesse1__12
DEFAULT (0),
        CONSTRAINT PK___13__12 PRIMARY KEY  CLUSTERED
        (
                idOrderStatus
        )
)
```

LISTING 3.9   **PaymentData Table**

```
CREATE TABLE dbo.PaymentData (
    idPayment int IDENTITY (1, 1) NOT NULL ,
    idOrder int NULL ,
    chrCardType varchar (50) NULL ,
    chrCardNumber varchar (30) NULL ,
    chrExpDate varchar (25) NULL ,
    chrCardName varchar (150) NULL ,
    CONSTRAINT PK___12__12 PRIMARY KEY  CLUSTERED
    (
            idPayment
    )
)
```

The Product Attribute table links up the products with their assigned attributes. The idProductAttribute will be the primary key for the table.

LISTING 3.10   **Product Attribute Table**

```
CREATE TABLE dbo.ProductAttribute (
    idProductAttribute int IDENTITY (1, 1) NOT NULL ,
    idAttribute int NULL ,
    idProduct int NULL ,
    CONSTRAINT PK___4__12 PRIMARY KEY  CLUSTERED
    (
            idProductAttribute
    )
)
```

The Products table defines the product data for the store with the `idProduct` field as the primary key. The `intPrice` and `intSalePrice` fields will default to 0. The `dtSalestart` and `dtSaleEnd` fields will be defaulted to 1/1/1980 to ensure no sales prices are read.

LISTING 3.11   Products Table

```
CREATE TABLE dbo.Products (
    idProduct int IDENTITY (1, 1) NOT NULL ,
    chrProductName varchar (255) NULL ,
    txtDescription text NULL ,
    chrProductImage varchar (255) NULL ,
    intPrice int NULL CONSTRAINT DF_Products_intPrice_3__12 DEFAULT
(0),
    dtSaleStart datetime NULL CONSTRAINT DF_Products_dtSaleStart_2__12
DEFAULT ('1 / 1 / 80'),
    dtSaleEnd datetime NULL CONSTRAINT DF_Products_dtSaleEnd_1__12
DEFAULT ('1 / 1 / 80'),
    intSalePrice int NULL CONSTRAINT DF_Products_intSalePrice_4__12
DEFAULT (0),
    intActive int NULL CONSTRAINT DF_Products_intActive_3__12 DEFAULT
(0),
    intFeatured tinyint NULL CONSTRAINT DF_Products_intFeatured_3__10
DEFAULT (0),
    dtFeatureStart datetime NULL CONSTRAINT DF_Products_dtFea-
tureStar2__10 DEFAULT ('1/1/80'),
    dtFeatureEnd datetime NULL CONSTRAINT DF_Products_dtFea-
tureEnd_1__10 DEFAULT ('1/1/80'),
    CONSTRAINT PK___2__12 PRIMARY KEY  CLUSTERED
    (
        idProduct
    )
)
```

The Related Products table defines the relationship between products. The primary key is the `idRelatedProduct` field and the rest of the fields are all defaulted to 0.

LISTING 3.12   RelatedProducts Table

```
CREATE TABLE dbo.RelatedProducts (
    idRelatedProduct int IDENTITY (1, 1) NOT NULL ,
    idProductA int NULL CONSTRAINT DF_RelatedPro_idProductA_1__12
DEFAULT (0),
    idProductB int NULL CONSTRAINT DF_RelatedPro_idProductB_2__12
DEFAULT (0),
    idRelationType int NULL CONSTRAINT DF_RelatedPro_idRelationT3__12
DEFAULT (0),
    CONSTRAINT PK___7__12 PRIMARY KEY  CLUSTERED
    (
            idRelatedProduct
    )
)
```

The shipping table defines the shipping rates for the store. The idQuantityRange is the primary key and the rest of the fields are defaulted to 0.

LISTING 3.13   Shipping Table

```
CREATE TABLE dbo.Shipping (
    idQuantityRange int IDENTITY (1, 1) NOT NULL ,
    intLowQuantity int NULL CONSTRAINT DF_Shipping_intLowQuantit3__12
DEFAULT (0),
    intHighQuantity int NULL CONSTRAINT DF_Shipping_intHighQuanti2__12
DEFAULT (0),
    intFee int NULL CONSTRAINT DF_Shipping_intFee_1__12 DEFAULT (0),
    CONSTRAINT PK___14__12 PRIMARY KEY  CLUSTERED
    (
            idQuantityRange
    )
)
```

The Shopper table defines the shopper data for the store. The dtEntered field is defaulted to the current date with the getdate() function to indicate when the shopper record was created. Also, the intCookie field is defaulted to 0 to indicate that a cookie should *not* be set to store the shopper's ID. The idShopper field is the primary key.

LISTING 3.14   Shopper Table

```
CREATE TABLE dbo.Shopper (
      idShopper int IDENTITY (1, 1) NOT NULL ,
      chrFirstName varchar (50) NULL ,
      chrLastName varchar (50) NULL ,
      chrAddress varchar (150) NULL ,
      chrCity varchar (100) NULL ,
      chrState varchar (2) NULL ,
      chrZipCode varchar (15) NULL ,
      chrPhone varchar (30) NULL ,
      chrFax varchar (30) NULL ,
      chrEmail varchar (150) NULL ,
      chrUserName varchar (25) NULL ,
      chrPassword varchar (25) NULL ,
      intCookie tinyint NULL CONSTRAINT DF_Shopper_intCookie_1__12
DEFAULT (0),
      dtEntered datetime NULL CONSTRAINT DF_Shopper_dtEntered_1__12
DEFAULT (getdate()),
      chrProvince varchar (150) NULL ,
      chrCountry varchar (150) NULL ,
      CONSTRAINT PK___8__12 PRIMARY KEY  CLUSTERED
      (
            idShopper
      )
)
```

The tax table defines our tax rates by state. The primary key is the idState field
and the intTaxRate field is defaulted to 0.

LISTING 3.15   Tax Table

```
CREATE TABLE dbo.Tax (
      idState int IDENTITY (1, 1) NOT NULL ,
      chrState varchar (50) NULL ,
      fltTaxRate float NULL CONSTRAINT DF_Tax_fltTaxRate_1__13 DEFAULT
(0),
      CONSTRAINT PK___15__12 PRIMARY KEY  CLUSTERED
      (
            idState
      )
)
```

With that, our core tables are created with all of the appropriate primary keys set and default values set for specific fields. You're now ready to create the tables in your database.

Summary

A solid fundamental database design is the key to any successful e-commerce Web site. In this chapter we have defined the core tables that will be utilized in building our e-commerce solution. In the next chapter we will explore the system design required for our e-commerce solution. Then, following that we will begin the core programming process to build the store.

CHAPTER
FOUR

4

System Configuration

- Designing the Server Farm

- Server Management

Properly configuring the systems for running an e-commerce Web site is crucial to the site's success. Setting up the server farm properly is crucial whether the e-commerce store is simple and meant to sell just a few products or complex and intended for prime time e-commerce retailing.

Also, issues such as backups, development environment, product staging, source code control, etc., become critical in a 24x7x365 real-time production environment where any downtime may mean real loss of dollars.

NOTE   For purposes of this book, we presume that from a business perspective your organization is ready to begin selling its products and/or services online.

Designing the Server Farm

The server *farm* will consist of all the servers required to run the site. That may include only one server or many servers with different roles such as database management, Web site serving, etc. Many aspects of setting up the server farm need to be considered when developing an e-commerce system. Often there will be multiple servers playing different roles. While it is possible to run all of the functions on one server, doing this could compromise security. Let's explore the options for building a server farm.

Web Servers

The e-commerce store will need to run on a Windows NT Web server. For our ASP and Visual Basic based example, you will also need Internet Information Server 4.0. For the Site Server Commerce Edition examples at the end of the book, Site Server Commerce Edition will be required on the Web server.

TIP   Typically a Web site will encompass more than just an e-commerce store. Other features might be more content focused and not necessarily commerce related.

Typically the e-commerce Web server will be set up separately from the database server and the Web server. Only in cases of very simple minimal traffic sites should all three be combined. There are some key requirements to consider, as shown in Table 4.1.

TABLE 4.1: E-Commerce Configuration Requirements

Requirement	Description
E-Commerce management interface	A management interface will be built during the store's design process. Security is essential, so the management interface URL should be distinct (for example, `https://admin.ecstore.com`) from that of the user shopping site (for example, `http://www.ecstore.com`). Security can be implemented in a number of ways. NT Challenge and Response authentication can be required with directory level security. Or, as will be explored later in the book, a database driven security system can be implemented.
SSL security	Secure Sockets Later security will be required for encrypting private data between the browser and the server.
Database connection	Presuming the database server is not on the same machine, we will need an ODBC link to the database on the e-commerce Web server. That also presumes that the database server is easily accessible on the network.

The e-commerce Web server is like any other Web server. But, unlike a server that is primarily serving static pages, this Web server will be delivering primarily template and data driven Web pages.

Web Server

If a Web server that is separate from the e-commerce server is required, it will be configured in much the same way as the e-commerce Web server. The primary requirement will be an appropriate link to the Web store. An excellent example of how this type of server management is done can be found on the American Diabetes Association Web site. The primary Web site is at `http://www.diabetes.org`. The e-commerce store is hosted at `http://merchant.diabetes.org`.

Database Server

Typically you do not want the database server to be accessible to the outside world. It should sit behind a firewall and not be directly accessible to the Internet. In that case it will be accessible via the LAN environment behind the firewall. If the Web server and the database server are on the same machine, then the database is exposed to outside access. This has the potential of permitting access to private data such as credit cards, etc. While certainly SQL Server does provide login access security and other means of locking down the database, making the database publicly inaccessible helps to ensure security.

Multiple Server Support

As mentioned, the simplest of Web sites would be one single Web server with all functionality on that Web server (as shown in Figure 4.1). The next level of division, as shown in Figure 4.2, is to separate any Web server support from database support. This would require two servers in the data farm. The next challenge is when multiple Web servers and database servers are needed to support transaction volume, as shown in Figure 4.3. While the fundamental coding and database functionality is the same, there are issues of data synchronization, content synchronization, load balancing, etc., that will need to be addressed. Specifically tackling those issues is beyond the scope of this book, but careful consideration should be given to these issues before launching a potential high transaction volume Web site to the public.

FIGURE 4.1:

Single server farm

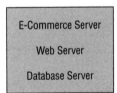

FIGURE 4.2:

Multiple server farm

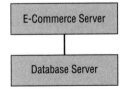

FIGURE 4.3:

FIGURE 4.3:

High transaction volume
server farm

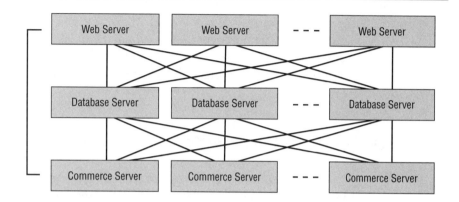

TIP

For development purposes, there is no problem having all of the functionality on a single server. But it is important to stage the full server farm to ensure that all items are linking up properly.

WARNING

When the requirement for load balancing comes into play in a multiple-server environment, additional functionality will be needed to handle serving the Web requests to the different servers. It is also important to ensure that the server the Web visitor is sent to initially is the same server the visitor continues to interact with during his visit. If the site visitor ends up going to different Web servers, tracking his shopping basket and other vital data will be next to impossible.

It is also important to point out that as Web sites grow and different levels of traffic spiking occur, the server farm configuration may change. Ensuring up front that the foundation development of the store is done properly for future growth is critical.

Staging and Development Server Management

While much of the attention is given to the production Web server farm, consideration should also be given to development server and staging server management. The development server is where ongoing development will take place for new functionality on the e-commerce Web server.

The staging server will be utilized for staging Web site updates into the Web server farm to ensure all is working. This phase is especially critical if updates will be ongoing and frequent, especially in a multi-server production environment. If the updates to the site are significant, it may be critical to do proper load testing to ensure the changes will not fail under a full production load.

Server Management

Many of the traditional challenges of managing a client/server server farm environment are also inherent in managing a Web server farm. Key aspects of any good development and production management process include source code control, backups, etc. In this section we will review some of those requirements. Also, we will review the basics of setting up the Web site so we can kick off our development in the next chapter.

Development Environment

Building an e-commerce store is not significantly different than building an internal client/ server application. Good development techniques and tools are critical.

Visual SourceSafe is an excellent tool for managing source code for a project. And, it does an excellent job of managing code checkin and checkout in a group project development environment. The SourceSafe database can reside on the development server, or preferably on a separate server on the network.

A development requirement unique to an electronic commerce Web server development environment is that all of the source code files must be worked on in a central development server. Figure 4.4 shows the basic development process for working in Visual InterDev on the development Web server.

The developer in this environment will connect to the Web server via Visual InterDev. The FrontPage extensions will need to be installed on the Web server for the IP address of the development Web site. InterDev then connects via that IP address.

FIGURE 4.4:

Active Server Pages development environment

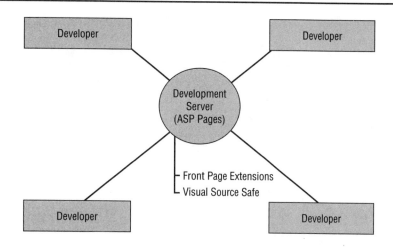

Web Server Setup

To create our development environment, let's go through the steps to configure Internet Information Server and FrontPage Extensions, and then connect via Visual InterDev.

1. First start up Internet Information Server. The Microsoft Management Console (MMC) is utilized for managing processes on the server. In this case, the snap-ins are for configuring the Internet services including FTP, Web, and SMTP. Figure 4.5 shows the MMC.

2. Our next task is to configure the Web site. In the example in this book, the Web site is simply going to run off the default Web site installed with IIS. You can create a new Web site and apply an IP address to it. Figure 4.6 shows the configuration panel for the Web site. For a local Web site on the machine use the Localhost IP of 127.0.0.1.

3. We also need to configure the home directory to ensure that we have the proper settings for our Web site. The home directory pane is shown in Figure 4.7. The *FrontPage* Web option must be checked to ensure the site supports FrontPage extensions. The rest of the defaults should be fine.

FIGURE 4.5:

The Microsoft Management Console with IIS snap-ins loaded

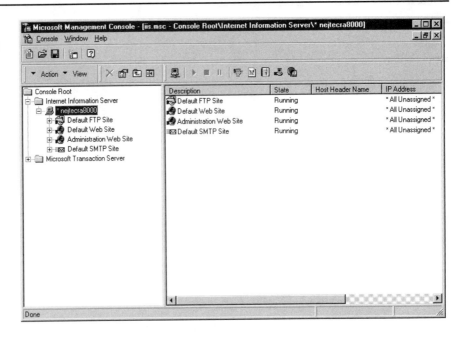

FIGURE 4.6:

The Web site configuration pane for our Web site

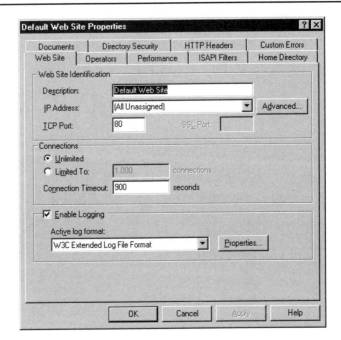

FIGURE 4.7:

The Web site configuration pane for our Web site's home directory

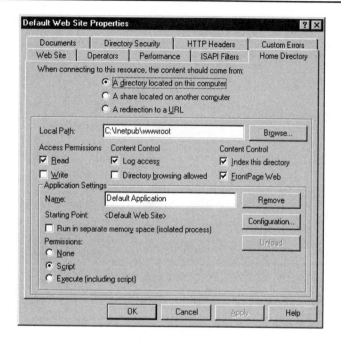

4. That gets the basics of our Web site set up. Now we need to install the Front-Page extensions on the site. Start up the FrontPage Server Administrator, which is found in the Windows NT 4 Option Pack program group. Figure 4.8 shows the administrator.

    From the list box select the new Web site you have created. Then select *Install* to create the extensions on that Web server.

5. Now we are ready to connect to the Web site in Visual InterDev. Figure 4.9 shows InterDev at startup. To create our new project, select the *New* tab and *Visual InterDev Projects*. Then give the project a name.

6. Visual InterDev will next prompt us for the IP address of the Web site we want to connect to. If it is the local site on the Web server, then the IP is 127.0.0.1 or Localhost. Figure 4.10 shows the dialog box.

FIGURE 4.8:

Configuring the Web site
FrontPage extensions

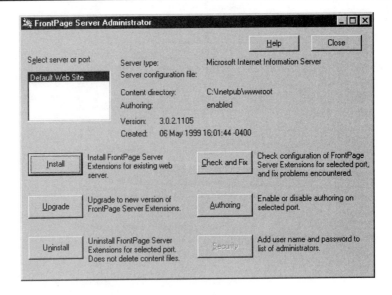

FIGURE 4.9:

Visual InterDev at startup

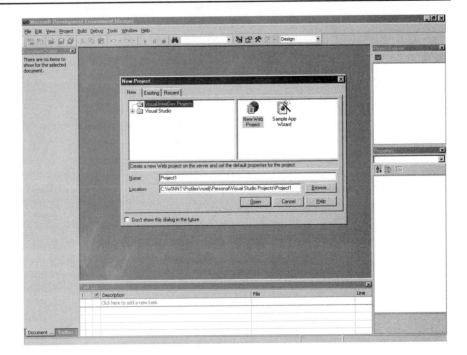

FIGURE 4.10:

Prompt for the IP address
of the Web site we want
our Web project to work on

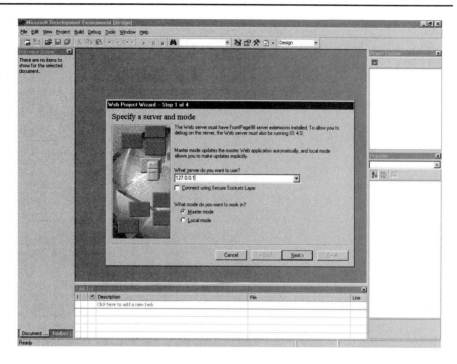

FIGURE 4.10:

Prompt for the IP address
of the Web site we want
our Web project to work on

7. Once we have selected the Web site we want to connect to, it will then ask what *virtual* Web or Web *application* we wish to connect to. In our case, let's create a new one called *ECStore*. Figure 4.11 shows the settings.

8. And with that, we are connected to our Web site. When the new Web application is created, a new global.asa file is created. The global.asa file will contain global settings for application and session level actions for our Web application. At this stage we are ready to begin developing our Web site (see Figure 4.12).

FIGURE 4.11:

Specifying the Web application to connect with

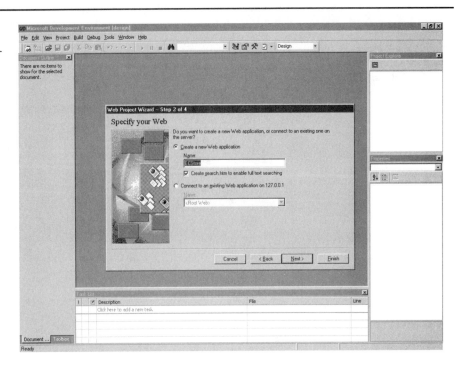

FIGURE 4.12:

New Web project created in Visual InterDev

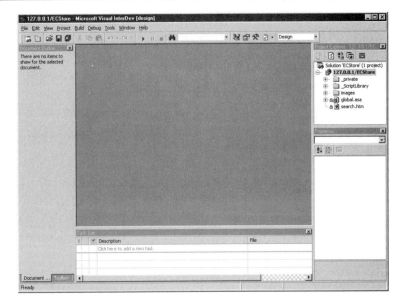

Server Backups

Backing up server data is of course critical. Perhaps on the Web backups are even more crucial due to the transactional nature of the Web site and the need to have 24x7x365 capability. Table 4.2 overviews key items to back up.

TABLE 4.2: Server Backup Considerations

Requirement	Description
ASP and other key Web files	Of course the code, images, HTML pages, and other files on the Web site should be backed up frequently. Keeping backups over time may be important as well in case past content needs to be resurrected.
COM objects	Business objects we will be creating in Visual Basic 6 will also need to be backed up on a frequent basis. Of course, the source code for these objects (stored in Visual SourceSafe) should be backed up as well.
SSL certificates	Often missed in the backup process is the requirement to store the SSL certificates in a backed up location. If the certificates are lost, there is no choice but to request a new set of certificates.
ODBC DSNs	Another oft-missed item is backing up the settings of ODBC DSNs on the Web server. If you are using File DSNs, the actual DSN can be backed up.
IIS configuration settings	If you are making changes to the default IIS configuration settings, those should also be noted and saved in case the Web server needs to be rebuilt.
SQL Server configuration settings	The same goes for the SQL Server configuration settings as with the IIS configuration settings.
Operating system and other server files	As with any good standard backup and for a quick recovery, the full system should be backed up frequently.

Security

As mentioned earlier in the chapter, security is a key issue for configuring the Web site. We can secure our Web site directly at the Web level in IIS. This is opposed to implementing database security and not allowing access to content via ASP coding.

Figure 4.13 shows the Directory Security Pane of IIS for the Web site. In general, anonymous access is the setting for providing public access to a Web site. If a particular virtual root or directory needs to be locked down further, you can implement basic authentication and Windows NT Challenge/Response. Basic Authentication sends passwords across the Internet in clear text. In Windows NT Challenge/Response, you have to use Internet Explorer to gain access to the Web site. In either case, the user is prompted with a username and password dialog box.

FIGURE 4.13:

Security settings for the Web site

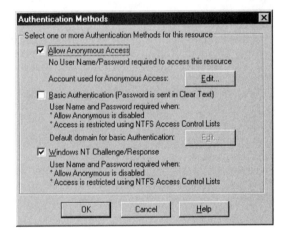

Also on the security front, management of SSL certificates is also critical. On the primary management interface of the IIS management console is the Key Manager icon. Clicking on that will bring up the Key Manager interface, as shown in Figure 4.14.

In the Key Manager you can create a new key, install certificates from a certificate authority (e.g., Verisign), import certificates, and back up certificates.

FIGURE 4.14:

Key Manager

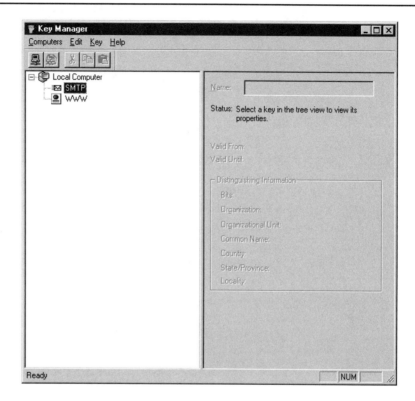

Database Setup

Configuring the database is as important as setting up the Web server. While it is out of the scope of this book to go through all of the ins and outs of database configuration, here are a few items to consider, as shown in Table 4.3.

TABLE 4.3: Database Configuration Considerations

Configuration	Description
Peak loading	Unlike the business environment where the peak *spike* load may be a moderate blip on the radar, Web sites can often have peaks at unusual times that will require far more resources than day to day loading. Holidays, sales promotions, and other events can provide significant loading requirements. Ensure the Web server can support extended connections and data objects. Each of these will impact the server configuration requirements, etc.

Continued on next page

TABLE 4.3 CONTINUED: Database Configuration Considerations

Configuration	Description
Drive space	Transaction logs and other space requirements, including sheer data storage of information collected from the Web, can impact drive storage requirements. Continuing to monitor the drive utilization, etc., is critical.
Multiple server support	If multiple database servers are in place, ensuring synchronization of product data, orders, customer profiles, and other issues must be addressed up front in the basic system design.

Backup and replication is also a critical issue. There are several different scenarios that should be considered when building in redundancy and backup for the database server. Table 4.4 reviews the different options.

TABLE 4.4: Database Backup and Replication Scenarios

Configuration	Description
Device backup	Simple device backup with backup to tape nightly can provide basic backup capabilities. The only downside is that there is no real-time backup to ensure the Web site will stay up without significant down time.
Warm backup	There are possible *warm* backup scenarios where the database data is transferred or replicated on an infrequent basis (perhaps hourly or less). If the database server should go down, a simple reconfiguration of ODBC settings to point at the warm backup will keep the Web site up and functioning.
Real-time replication	The best of all worlds is real-time replication between database servers. Putting this kind of requirement on the database server calls for significant planning for resource loading, depending on the different transaction levels.

Another critical issue is supporting database development that ensures live site synchronization and updates go smoothly. Any time updates are made to the production database server from the development server, issues such as ensuring peak loading will not be affected and providing security become critical to the Web site's success.

Load Planning

As illustrated throughout many of the discussions in this chapter on system design, load planning is a critical issue. Coding of the e-commerce platform for core functionality may have a minimal impact, but if significant load is being planned for, ensuring the code is solid and is planned to handle multiple server requirements will be important.

There are excellent load planning tools to be found on the Web. If you are working with an ISP to run and manage the server farm, the ISP will typically have load-testing capabilities to assist in planning for different traffic loads. In these tests, it is important to ensure that key *code heavy* sections of the site are properly tested.

Browser Considerations

Finally, a key part of system planning is understanding the browser requirements that the system will need to support. While much of this relates to design, in some cases the type of browser may be dictated if certain parts of the site are coded to use extended browser features (such as ActiveX or DHTML). An example of this could include a store manager that is developed to use a specific browser for extended functionality. In some cases Internet Explorer may be required for NT Challenge/Response. Or perhaps in rare cases Internet Explorer Remote Data Services (RDS) may be needed.

Summary

System design for a Web site is critical to ensuring success of all that hard work that goes into the code development of the Web site. In some respects the issues are not all that different than designing a client/server server farm. The primary differences are in planning for different server loads, a somewhat different set of tools, different clients, and the potential for the environment to change rapidly.

CHAPTER
FIVE

5

Sample Application

- Building the Data Table

- Building the HTML Form

- Programming the Script Code

- Testing the Application

- Managing the Application

Before we go full bore into an online store development process based on the database design in Chapter 3, we are going to build a very simple e-commerce application based on Active Server Pages and SQL Server. This will help to get our feet wet with the ASP development environment.

Our sample application will be a simple form to purchase a subscription to a publication. This form will take in name and address information and credit card data.

Building the Data Table

The first thing we will need is a simple database table that we can insert our subscriptions into. The obvious fields are in the table for the subscriber's name, address, credit card information, etc., as shown in Listing 5.1.

LISTING 5.1   **Subscription Database Table**

```
CREATE TABLE dbo.Subscriptions (
    idSubscription int IDENTITY (1, 1) NOT NULL ,
    chrFirstName varchar (100) NULL ,
    chrLastName varchar (100) NULL ,
    chrAddress varchar (150) NULL ,
    chrCity varchar (100) NULL ,
    chrState varchar (10) NULL ,
    chrZipCode varchar (15) NULL ,
    chrPhone varchar (25) NULL ,
    chrEmail varchar (100) NULL ,
    chrCardName varchar (150) NULL ,
    chrCardType varchar (50) NULL ,
    chrCardNumber varchar (25) NULL ,
    chrExpDate varchar (50) NULL ,
    intProcessed tinyint NULL DEFAULT 0,
      /* Default to 0 */
    dtEntered datetime NULL
      DEFAULT GETDATE(),
      /* Default to current date */
    intLength tinyint NULL
  )
```

A couple of status fields are included in the table. The *intProcessed* field would be used to flag the order as processed so an indication of what subscriptions have been retrieved can be easily tracked. This field should be defaulted to 0, to indicate "unprocessed." The next status field is the *dtEntered* field. This defines the date the subscription was entered into the database. It should be defaulted to the current date.

Building the HTML Form

Open up the project created in the last chapter (found in the Section I folder of the CD). Right click on the project in the Project Explorer window. Then select *Add* on the menu. On the sub-menu select *Active Server Page*, as shown in Figure 5.1. In the dialog box enter the name of the subscription Active Server Page, *subscription.asp*.

FIGURE 5.1:

Creating the *subscription.asp* page

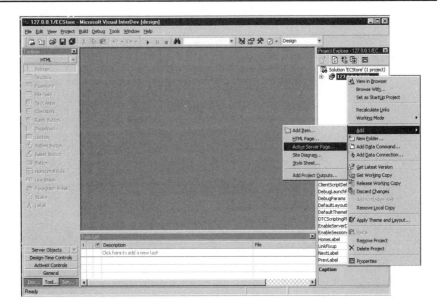

Once that is done, a new file is created on the Web server. We are now ready to begin building the HTML structure of the page. A basic template for the page is created when the ASP page is created. We can begin editing in Visual InterDev. We have three options—*Design*, *Source* and *Quick View*. In general, the Source view will be utilized for all development. The Design View is used for WYSIWYG HTML building. Quick View is utilized for viewing the HTML in a browser interface, but note that no ASP code is processed.

To build the HTML page, we will need to create an HTML form and HTML elements on the page. Then we will build a script page to process the data entered by the user.

The first part of the page is straightforward, as shown in Listing 5.2. The standard HTML headers for the page are created. We also start out the form by setting it to post results to the *ProcessSub.asp* page, which will process the subscription.

Session Variables

In standard Web technology there is no simple way of remembering *state* data between Web pages. For example, if the shopper enters in their zip code and then starts browsing through the rest of the site, we would have to do a lot of work to track that data on the URL or through the use of Hidden HTML elements. Fortunately, in IIS/ASP, Microsoft built in the Session variable capability. This allows us to save data in a variable that stays active for the user's entire visit to the Web site. All we do is set the variable on one page and then retrieve the value as needed on subsequent pages. Note that sessions have a timeout setting that is defaulted to 30 minutes. In reality, we never know when the visitor has left the site, so we want the session data to disappear if there is no activity for that session for the specified timeout period.

LISTING 5.2   **Subscription.asp Page**

```
<%@ Language=VBScript %>
<HTML>
<HEAD>
<META NAME="GENERATOR" Content="Microsoft Visual Studio 6.0">
</HEAD>
<BODY>

<BR><BR>

<center>

<!-- Setup the Header -->
<font size="4" color="blue"><b>
```

```
XYZ Publication
</b></font>

<!-- Start the form that will post to the
     ProcessSub.asp page. -->
<form method="post" action="ProcessSub.asp">
```

The next section of the page is the table that contains the form for displaying the input fields of the subscription page. There are several key actions on the page. First, if the user enters invalid data, we want to be able to send him back to this form and have the data he entered repopulated into the form.

The repopulation is done by reading session variables set in the *ProcessSub.asp* page when the data is in error. Our first challenge is the length of the subscription (set in *intLength*). If the user selected two-year or three-year subscriptions, then we will want to set the proper radio button. If not, then the one-year option will be set.

LISTING 5.3   Subscription.asp continued

```
<!-- Next the table starts that will layout the
     data entry form -->
<table border=1>

<!-- Subscription Length -->
<tr>
  <td align="right">Subscription Length:</td>
  <td>
<%
     ' Check to see if a length was set. If so
     ' then default the radio button selected.
     if session("intLength") = "1" then
         CheckOne = "Checked"
         Flag = 1
     end if

     if session("intLength") = "2" then
         CheckTwo = "Checked"
         Flag = 1
     end if

     if session("intLength") = "3" then
         CheckThree = "Checked"
         Flag = 1
```

```
        end if

          '  If this is the first time the form is
          '  displayed in the session then default to
          '  a length of one year.
          if Flag <> 1 then CheckOne = "Checked"

    %>
      <!--  Radio buttons for selecting the length -->
      <input type="radio" value="1" name="intLength" <%=CheckOne%>>One Year
      <input type="radio" value="2" name="intLength" <%=CheckTwo%>>Two Year
      <input type="radio" value="3" name="intLength" <%=CheckThree%>>Three
                                                                    Year
    </td>
  </tr>

  <!--  First Name -->
  <tr>
    <td align="right">First Name:</td>
    <!--  Input field for the first name -->
    <td><input type="text" value="<%=session("chrFirstName")%>"
            name="chrFirstName"></td>
  </tr>

  <!--  Last Name -->
  <tr>
    <td align="right">Last Name:</td>
    <!--  Input field for the last name -->
    <td><input type="text" value="<%=session("chrLastName")%>"
            name="chrLastName"></td>
  </tr>

  <!--  Address -->
  <tr>
    <td align="right">Address:</td>
    <!--  Input field for the address -->
    <td><input type="text" value="<%=session("chrAddress")%>"
            name="chrAddress"></td>
  </tr>

  <!--  City-->
  <tr>
    <td align="right">City:</td>
```

```
        <!-- Input field for the city -->
        <td><input type="text" value="<%=session("chrCity")%>"
                name="chrCity"></td>
    </tr>

    <tr>
      <td align="right">State:</td>
      <td><input type="text" value="<%=session("chrState")%>"
                name="chrState" size=2></td>
    </tr>

    <!-- Zip Code -->
    <tr>
      <td align="right">Zip Code:</td>
      <!-- Input field for the zip code -->
      <td><input type="text" value="<%=session("chrZipCode")%>"
                name="chrZipCode"></td>
    </tr>

    <!-- Phone Number -->
    <tr>
      <td align="right">Phone:</td>
      <!-- Input field for the phone number -->
      <td><input type="text" value="<%=session("chrPhone")%>"
                name="chrPhone"></td>
    </tr>

    <!-- Email Address -->
    <tr>
      <td align="right">Email Address:</td>
      <!-- Input field for the email address -->
      <td><input type="text" value="<%=session("chrEmail")%>"
                name="chrEmail"></td>
    </tr>

    <!-- Name on Card -->
    <tr>
      <td align="right">Name on Card:</td>
      <!-- Input field for the email address -->
      <td><input type="text" value="<%=session("chrCardName")%>"
                name="chrCardName"></td>
    </tr>
```

A process similar to the length of subscription logic needs to take place for the card type. If the user selected Master Card or American Express, then we want to reselect those options when the user is returned to the form.

LISTING 5.4   **Subscription.asp continued**

```asp
<!-- Input field for the credt card type -->
<tr>
  <td align="right">Card Type:</td>
  <td>

<%

    ' Check to see which card was selected previously
    ' if there was an error.
    if session("chrCardType") = "Visa" then
        SelVisa = "Selected"
    end if

    if session("chrCardType") = "MasterCard" then
        SelMC = "Selected"
    end if

    if session("chrCardType") = "AmEx" then
        SelAmEx = "Selected"
    end if
%>

    <!-- Select box for the type of cards -->
    <select name="chrCardType">
        <option value="Visa" <%=SelVisa%> >Visa
        <option value="MasterCard" <%=SelMC%>>Master Card
        <option value="AmEx" <%=SelAmEx%>>American Express
    </select>

  </td>
</tr>

<!-- Credit Card Number -->
<tr>
  <td align="right">Card Number:</td>
```

```
<!--  Input field for the credit card number -->
<td><input type="text" value="<%=session("chrCardNumber")%>"
name="chrCardNumber"></td>
</tr>

<!--  Credit card expiration date -->
<tr>
  <td align="right">Expiration Date:</td>
  <!--  Input field for the expiration date -->
  <td><input type="text" value="<%=session("chrExpDate")%>"
            name="chrExpDate"></td>
</tr>
```

The last section of our page is the HTML submit button for sending the form data to the server. Then the form and the page are closed out.

LISTING 5.5   The end of subscription.asp

```
<!--  Submit button -->
<tr>
  <td colspan="2" align="center">
  <input type="submit" value="Subscribe!" name="submit">
  </td>
</tr>


</table>

</center>

<!--  Closing tag for the end of the form -->
</form>

</BODY>
</HTML>
```

The input page is fairly straightforward. If you are new to ASP coding, then mixing script code and HTML tags in the same page might take some getting used to. But it is precisely this powerful integration that makes ASP such a rich development environment for building e-commerce Web applications.

Programming the Script Code

Now the real programming fun begins on the processing of the subscription request. Our goal in this page is several-fold. First, we want to retrieve the data from the user and validate it. We want to ensure that she has entered in values for all required fields, and when possible we want to validate that the data is correct.

Second, we want to then give feedback to the user if there is an error. A message will be displayed telling the user certain fields are incorrect. And, we will provide a link back to the subscription page for the user. That is where the session variables and repopulating the subscription form come into play.

Third, if the data is valid, we want to thank the user. In this case, we are going to re-display the input data for good customer service feedback. And of course, we need to be sure to insert the subscription data into the database for later retrieval.

As with the *subscription.asp* page, the *processsub.asp* page opens up with basic HTML tagging. Listing 5.6 shows the page code.

LISTING 5.6   **ProcessSub.asp Page**

```
<%@ Language=VBScript %>

<HTML>

<BODY BGCOLOR="WHITE">
```

Our first task is to retrieve the data from the form. We utilize the Request object to retrieve the data and reference the field names on the form. The data is stored in variables for later use.

NOTE   Variables do not have to be used to store the form data. The Request object could be used throughout the page. But, the variable use makes for easier manipulation of the data later.

LISTING 5.7   **ProcessSub.asp continued**

```
<%

'   Retrieve all of the data that the user entered
'   by using the request object.
intLength = Request("intLength")
chrFirstName = Request("chrFirstName")
chrLastName = Request("chrLastName")
chrAddress = Request("chrAddress")
chrCity = Request("chrCity")
chrState = Request("chrState")
chrZipCode = Request("chrZipCode")
chrPhone = Request("chrPhone")
chrEmail = Request("chrEmail")
chrCardName = Request("chrCardName")
chrCardType = Request("chrCardType")
chrCardNumber = Request("chrCardNumber")
chrExpDate = Request("chrExpDate")
```

The next step is to check each field and validate it. For most of the fields we are simply going to ensure the field is not blank. For the state field, we do a little more validation to ensure that the length is not more than two characters. On the credit card expiration date we can use the IsDate function to validate that it is a valid date.

LISTING 5.8   **ProcessSub.asp continued**

```
'   Check to see if the first name was entered.
if chrFirstName = "" then

    '   Give an error if not.
    strError = "You did not enter in your first name.<BR>"

end if

'   Check to see if a last name was entered.
if chrLastName = "" then

    strError = strError & "You did not enter in your last name.<BR>"
```

```
        end if

        '  Check to see if an address was entered
        if chrAddress = "" then

            strError = strError & "You did not enter in your address.<BR>"

        end if

        '  Check to see if a city was entered.
        if chrCity = "" then

            strError = strError & "You did not enter in your city.<BR>"

        end if

        '  Check to see if the state was entered of if the length
        '  is more than two characters.
        if chrState = ""  or len(chrState) > 2 then

            strError = strError & "You did not enter in a valid state.<BR>"

        end if

        '  Check to see if a zip code was entered.
        if chrZipCode = "" then

            strError = strError & "You did not enter in your zip code.<BR>"

        end if

        '  Check to see if the card name was entered.
        if chrCardName = "" then

            strError = strError & "You did not enter in the name on your credit
                                " & _ "card.<BR>"

        end if

        '  Check to see if the card number was entered
        if chrCardNumber = "" then
```

```
        strError = strError & "You did not enter in your credit card
                          " & _ "number.<BR>"

end if

'   Check to see if the card expiration date was entered
if (chrExpDate = "") or (isdate(chrExpDate) = false) then

        strError = strError & "You did not enter in a valid credit card
                          " & _ "expiration date.<BR>"

end if
```

Now that the data is validated, we are ready to take appropriate action. We can check the *strError* variable to see if it is set. If it is, then there was an error. If not, then there was no error.

```
'   Now we check to see if there are any errors.
if strError <> "" then

%>
```

If there is an error, we simply display the appropriate message and write out the error string. The key though is ensuring we have the data from the form stored so that it can be retrieved and displayed when the user returns to the form. The best way to do this is with session variables, which will stay *alive* while the user's session is still in progress. Then on the subscription form we can retrieve those values and display them.

LISTING 5.8   **ProcessSub.asp continued**

```
        <!-- Note the error -->
        <B><font color="red">
            There is an error in your subscription request:<BR><BR>
        </b></font>

<%


'   Write out the error messages
        Response.Write strError

%>
```

```
<!-- Link back to the subscription page -->
<BR>
Click <a href="subscription.asp">here</a> to update.

<%

'  Set session variables to the subscription form can be
'   re-populated
Session("intLength") = request("intLength")
Session("chrFirstName") = request("chrFirstName")
Session("chrLastName") = Request("chrLastName")
Session("chrAddress") = Request("chrAddress")
Session("chrCity") = Request("chrCity")
Session("chrState") = Request("chrState")
Session("chrZipCode") = Request("chrZipCode")
Session("chrPhone") = Request("chrPhone")
Session("chrEmail") = Request("chrEmail")
session("chrCardName") = Request("chrCardName")
Session("chrCardType") = Request("chrCardType")
Session("chrCardNumber") = Request("chrCardNumber")
Session("chrExpDate") = Request("chrExpDate")

else

%>
```

If the data was all valid then we are ready to process the subscription form. An appropriate thank you message is displayed and then a recap of the form data is displayed.

LISTING 5.9   **ProcessSub.asp continued**

```
<!-- Thank the customer for the ordedsr -->
<font size="4" color="blue">Thank you for your order!
 It will be processed immediately.</font>

 <!-- Redisplay the data entered into the subscription -->
<BR><BR>
<Table>
<tr><td align="right"><B>Name:</b></td>
```

```
<td><i>  <% = chrFirstName & " " & chrLastName %></i></td></tr>

 <tr><td align="right"><B>Address:</b></td>
<td><i>  <% = chrAddress %></i></td></tr>

 <tr><td align="right"><B>City:</b></td>
<td><i>  <% = chrCity %></i></td></tr>

 <tr><td align="right"><B>State:</b></td>
<td><i>  <% = chrState %></i></td></tr>

 <tr><td align="right"><B>Zip Code:</b></td>
<td><i>  <% = chrZipCode %></i></td></tr>

 <tr><td align="right"><B>Phone:</b></td
><td><i>  <% = chrPhone %></i></td></tr>

 <tr><td align="right"><B>Email:</b></td>
<td><i>  <% = chrEmail %></i></td></tr>

 <tr><td align="right"><B>Card Name:</b></td>
<td><i>  <% = chrCardName %></i></td></tr>

 <tr><td align="right"><B>Card Type:</b></td>
<td><i>  <% = chrCardType %></i></td></tr>

 <tr><td align="right"><B>Card Number:</b></td>
<td><i>  <% = chrCardNumber %></i></td></tr>

 <tr><td align="right"><B>Expiration Date:</b></td>
<td><i>  <% = chrExpDate %></i></td></tr>

 </ul>
```

Now we are ready to do the important step of inserting the data into the database. The first step is to create an ADO connection object to the database. You will need an ODBC DSN to connect to the database. Be sure to create the DSN. Note in this case a file DSN is being utilized, but a system DSN could be created instead. Be aware that user DSNs operate only under the context of the user for which they were created, rendering them unsuitable for use within IIS.

Next we have to sanitize the data for insertion into the database. We have to ensure that any single quotes that may be entered are doubled up so they can be inserted and not confused as delimiters. Examples of this problem would include last names (e.g., O'Brien), cities, addresses, etc. Using the Replace command makes it easy to replace these single quotes with doubles. In this case we will check the First Name, Last Name, Address, Card Name, and City.

TIP

SQL server will interpret two single quotes together ('') as only one single quote. We will need to double up all single quotes that are part of the data to be stored in a field. Our values that are being inserted should start with a single quote and end with one as well.

Once the data is ready, we can build a SQL statement for inserting the data into the database. And then we are ready to execute the SQL statement.

LISTING 5.10   **ProcessSub.asp continued**

```
<%

    '  Create an ADO database connection
    set dbSubs = server.createobject("adodb.connection")

    '  Open the connection using our ODBC file DSN
    dbSubs.open("filedsn=SubForm")

    '  If any of our names have a single quote, we will
    '  need to double it to insert it into the database
    chrFirstName = replace(chrFirstName, "'", "''")
    chrLastName = replace(chrLastName, "'", "''")
    chrAddress = replace(chrAddress, "'", "''")
    chrCardName = replace(chrCardName, "'", "''")
    chrCity = replace(chrCity, "'", "''")

    '  SQL insert statement to insert the subscription
    '  data into the database
    sql = "insert into subscriptions(" & _
          "chrFirstName, " & _
          "chrLastname, " & _
          "chrAddress, " & _
          "chrCity, " & _
```

```
            "chrState, " & _
            "chrZipCode, " & _
            "chrPhone, " & _
            "chrEmail, " & _
            "chrCardName, " & _
            "chrCardType, " & _
            "chrCardNumber, " & _
            "chrExpDate, " & _
            "intLength) " & _
            "values (" & "'" & _
            chrFirstName & "', '" & _
             chrLastName & "', '" & _
             chrAddress & "', '" & _
             chrCity & "', '" & _
             chrState & "', '" & _
             chrZipCode & "', '" & _
             chrPhone & "', '" & _
             chrEmail & "', '" & _
             chrCardName & "', '" & _
             chrCardType & "', '" & _
             chrCardNumber & "', '" & _
             chrExpDate & "', " & _
             intLength & ")"

    '   Execute the SQL statement
    dbSubs.execute(sql)

end if

%>

</body>
</html>
```

That is it for the user side programming. In Part III, we will explore how we can utilize Web based reporting to retrieve the subscriptions.

Testing the Application

Now we are ready to begin testing. Calling the *subscription.asp* page from your Web server accesses the Web page shown in Figure 5.2.

FIGURE 5.2:

The *subscription.asp* page

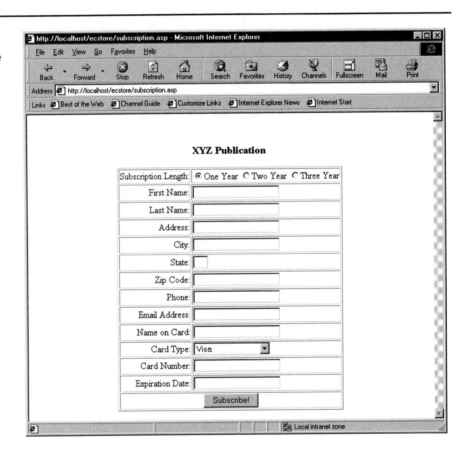

Now we need to go ahead and enter data into the form. We will want to enter in some invalid data so that we can test the error handling. Figure 5.3 shows the form filled out with sample data. Note that the expiration date is invalid. When done, we need to submit the form to the *ProcessSub.asp* page.

FIGURE 5.3:

Entering invalid data into
the subscription page

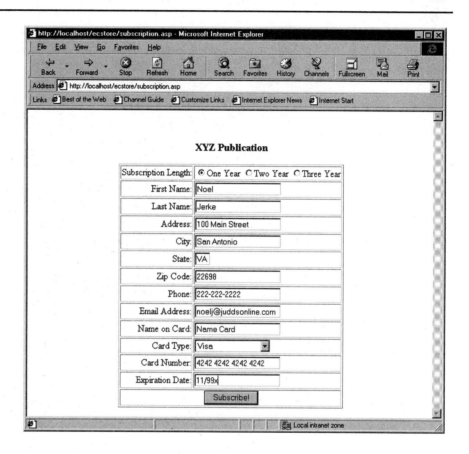

The *ProcessSub.asp* page will process the data. And, in fact, if all is working
properly we should see an error message indicating the expiration date is invalid.
Figure 5.4 shows the error message.

FIGURE 5.4:

Error page with invalid expiration date

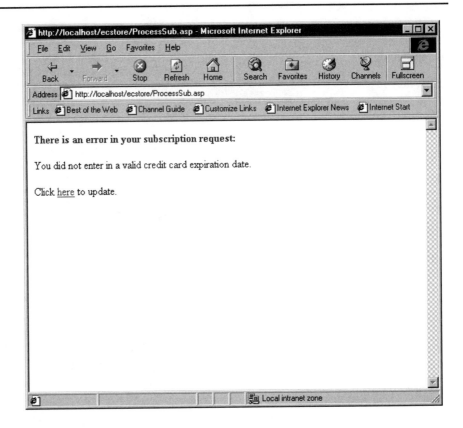

Now we can click on the error link and go back to the subscription page. When we do so, the data form should be re-populated with our subscription data, error messages, and all. Figure 5.5 shows a correctly entered subscription.

TIP   You may want to have the field name highlighted in red to help indicate on the subscription form which field is invalid.

FIGURE 5.5:

Entering valid data into the subscription page

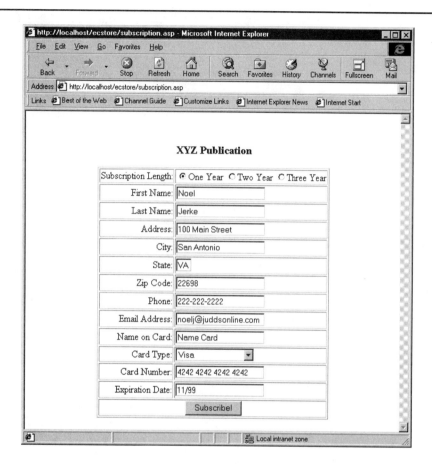

Now we can correct the data and then resubmit the subscription data. When we do, the thank you response is displayed with a recap of the data. Figure 5.6 shows the thank you page. And, we should also be able to verify that the data went into the database.

FIGURE 5.6:

Thank you message after a successful subscription

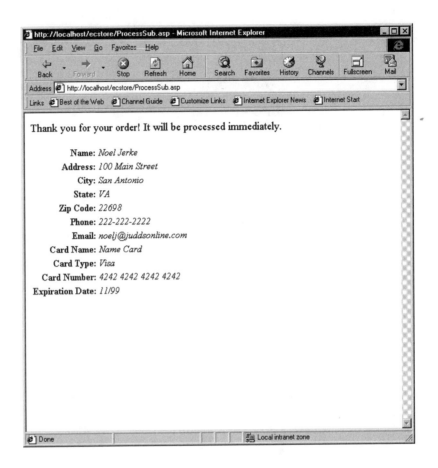

Now that we have completed the user experience, we need to worry about the back end management of the subscription data. We will need a way to retrieve the subscriptions.

Managing the Application

The last piece of our e-commerce sample application is the reporting form. The purpose of the form is to report out the subscription data entered since the last subscriptions were processed. And, it will give an option for the user to mark the

current listing of subscriptions as processed. Listing 5.11 shows the code for the
SubReport.asp page.

LISTING 5.11   SubReport.asp

```
<%@ Language=VBScript %>
<HTML>
<HEAD>
<META NAME="GENERATOR" Content="Microsoft Visual Studio 6.0">
</HEAD>
<BODY>
```

The first step is to create our database connection. Then we need to check and
see if we are to mark subscriptions as processed. If so, then there will be an *idSubscription* parameter on the URL. This is set later in the code when the clear option
is selected. If the parameter is set, then all subscriptions that have ID less than or
equal to the subscription ID will be cleared. Anything above that will remain
unprocessed and be displayed.

LISTING 5.12   SubReport.asp continued

```
<%

    ' Create an ADO database connection
    set dbSubs = server.createobject("adodb.connection")
    set rsSubs = server.CreateObject("adodb.recordset")

    ' Open the connection using our ODBC file DSN
    dbSubs.open("filedsn=SubForm")

    ' Retrieve any subscription IDs on the URL
    idSubscription = Request("idSubscription")

    ' Check to see if there is a value.
    if idSubscription <> "" then

        ' Built an SQL update statement to process the subs.
        sql = "update subscriptions set intProcessed = 1 where " & _
            "idSubscription <= " & _
        idSubscription
```

```
          '  Execute the SQL statement
      dbSubs.execute sql

  end if
```

Next we are ready to retrieve all of the subscriptions in the system that have not been processed. A SQL statement is built with the appropriate *where* clause and then the SQL statement is executed with a record set returned.

```
      '  Create a SQL statement to retrieve any unprocessed
  subscriptions
      sql = "select * from subscriptions where intProcessed = 0"

      '  Execute the statement and retrieve the record set
  set rsSubs = dbSubs.Execute(sql)

%>
```

Next we are ready to begin the structure of the table that will be utilized to display the unprocessed subscriptions. The formatting is fairly simple, with field names on the left and the data on the right.

TIP   You might want to put some logic in place to have the subscriptions listed out in several columns instead of just one. If you are processing many subscriptions, that will reduce the number of pages that will be displayed.

LISTING 5.13   SubReport.asp continued

```
<!--  Start the table to display the subs. -->
<Table border="1">

<%

      '  Check to see if no subs are returned
  if rsSubs.EOF then

          '  If so, then write
      Response.Write "No subscriptions to report."
```

LISTING 5.14   **SubReport.asp continued**

```
<%

    '   Store the last subscription id
    idSubscription = rsSubs("idSubscription")

    '   Move to the next sub
    rsSubs.MoveNext

     loop

    end if

%>

</table>

<BR><BR>
```

Finally we build a link back to this page with the ID of the last subscription so this report can be cleared. Note that the ID of the subscription is stored on the URL with the *idSubscription* parameter.

LISTING 5.15   **SubReport.asp continued**

```
<!-- Link to this page with the last subscription ID -->
Click <a
href="SubReport.asp?idSubscription=<%=idSubscription%>">here</a>
 to clear this report.

</BODY>
</HTML>
```

The page is then ready to be run. Make sure the database is seeded with some sample subscriptions. Figure 5.7 shows the report page with the sample data. Note the link to clear the report.

FIGURE 5.7:

Subscriptions report page

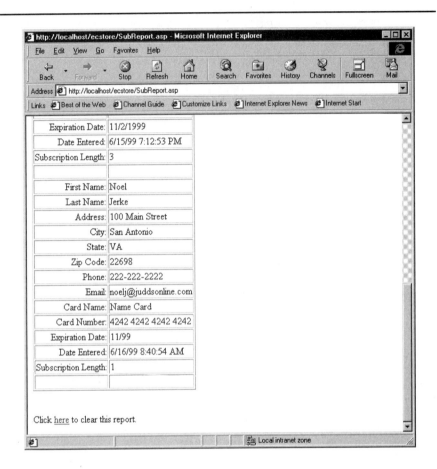

Go ahead and click on the link to clear the subscriptions. When you do so, the page is re-called with the ID of the last subscription on the URL. Then the section of code is run to mark these subscriptions as processed. You should be able to check the processed fields in the database to verify they are set to 1. Any new subscriptions will be displayed or a message is displayed indicating no more subscriptions are available to be displayed. Figure 5.8 shows the processed page.

FIGURE 5.8:

Cleared subscriptions
report page

We might want to provide a richer interface for searching for subscriptions, processed and unprocessed. Date entered, length of subscription, etc., may be offered as options to search by.

Summary

Our sample application hits on the key tools we will be utilizing for development—ASP, SQL Server, HTML, and a browser. For a site that needs a simple way to request subscriptions, memberships, or other data, this type of form will be more than adequate.

A couple of things should be considered when implementing this type of form. First is security. Certainly the form should be encrypted with Secure Sockets Layer (SSL) to ensure the data cannot be easily *sniffed* on the Internet. And, make sure your usernames and passwords to access the database are not readily guessed or easily found out. And, the manager page should not be readily accessible to just anyone. You will want to secure it either with a password-protected form using SQL, or else by using Windows NT Authentication and an Access Control List (ACL) on the directory where the manager page exists.

Second, you may want to provide an order number back to the person who has just ordered so they can make any queries referencing that number. The best way to implement that would be to build a stored procedure that inserts the subscription data and returns a parameter that is the ID of the identity column in the table. That can then be displayed in the thank you message to the user.

Finally, if you want to provide immediate processing of the credit card data you might want to consider using tools such as CyberCash or HP/Veriphone. Then, if the user's order is cleared, you can immediately give them online access to content, etc.

With that we have ended the first section of the book. We are now well positioned to move to the next phase of beginning the development of our full-blown e-commerce store.

PART II

Building the Shopping Experience

In Part I we defined e-commerce, took a look at the Microsoft tools involved, worked on the basics of database design and system design, and built a sample application.

The database designed in Chapter 3 will be utilized as the basic database underlying the chapters in this section. We will take those fundamentals and begin building the shopping experience for the user. Chapter 6 will focus on the basics of navigation, the store home page, and the general infrastructure of the web site.

In Chapter 7 the core process of the shopping basket will be built. Chapter 8 will take it to the next step to manage the checkout process for the user. And finally, Chapter 9 will explore providing customer service functionality with an order status section of the Web site.

Building the User Interface

- Designing the Store Foundation

- Building the Home Page

- Browsing Departments and Products

- Searching

There are some fundamental aspects of an e-commerce store we assess when designing the user interface. How these are approached will have a significant impact on the shopper's experience. In this chapter we will work on building the core foundation of the store including navigation, site structure, and product data.

Designing the Store Foundation

Our store is going to be made up of multiple ASP pages combined with a Visual Basic application for business rule management. These pages will be working against the database design we defined in Chapter 3, "E-Commerce Database Design." Table 6.1 defines the pages in our store and the function of each. Also noted is the chapter in which the code is reviewed.

T A B L E 6 . 1 : ECStore Web Pages

Page	Description	Chapter
Footer.asp	Included at the bottom of every display page on the site. It provides the closing structure for the navigation and primary content area.	Chapter 6
Header.asp	Included at the top of every display page on the site. It provides the navigation structure	Chapter 6
AddItem.asp	Adds items to the shopping basket when the user selects a product.	Chapter 7
Basket.asp	Displays all of the items in the users shopping basket.	Chapter 7
Confirmed.asp	Provides a confirmation message and thank you when the shopper has completed an order.	Chapter 8
Default.asp	Home page for the store.	Chapter 6
DeleteItem.asp	Deletes an item from the shopping basket.	Chapter 7
Dept.asp	Lists all of the departments in the store.	Chapter 6
EmailPassword.asp	E-mails the profile password related to the specified profile e-mail address.	Chapter 9

Continued on next page

TABLE 6.1 CONTINUED: ECStore Web Pages

Page	Description	Chapter
EmptyBasket.asp	Empties all items from the shopping basket.	Chapter 7
Global.asa	Application level file that is executed each time a new application or session is started.	Chapter 6
OrderHistory Display.asp	Displays the order history of the shopper.	Chapter 9
OrderReceipt.asp	Displays an on-screen order receipt.	Chapter 8
OrderStatus.asp	Login in page for the the shopper order history.	Chapter 9
Payment.asp	Provides data input for the shopper's billing information.	Chapter 8
Product.asp	Displays information on the specified product.	Chapter 6
Products.asp	Displays all of the products in the specified department.	Chapter 6
Profile.asp	Login in page for the shopper to retrieve and edit their profile.	Chapter 9
ProfileDisplay.asp	Displays the profile data for the specified shopper.	Chapter 9
Search.asp	Provides search capabilities for finding products in the database.	Chapter 6
Shipping.asp	Provides data input for the shipping information of the order.	Chapter 8
UpdateBasket.asp	Updates the shopper basket items with the specified new quantities.	Chapter 7
UpdateProfile.asp	Updates the shopper's profile.	Chapter 9
ValidatePayment.asp	Validates the payment data entered by the shopper.	Chapter 8
ValidateShipping.asp	Validates the shipping data entered by the shopper.	Chapter 8

NOTE   In Part III, "Managing the Solution," we will build tools for managing the data in the store. In Part IV, "Promotions," we will add functionality supporting different promotional functions.

It is these core pages that will provide the environment for facilitating the shopping experience. There is an expected shopping process that we are trying to facilitate through the navigation and the various pages.

Site Architecture

When the shopper enters the store, they will typically follow one of several steps for beginning their shopping process. Ideally they will look at department and product data through browsing the store. Or they may search for something specific.

We hope this browsing phase culminates in items added to the shopping basket and ready for purchase. The shopper then has the opportunity to manage their shopping basket and then check out. The checkout process will collect all of their key data like shipping and billing information. Once processed, they then can check their order history through a profile they set up online. Figure 6.1 diagrams the shopping process:

The navigation we design into the system certainly needs to provide a way to jump between any state that is appropriate. But, for example, we cannot allow someone to go to the payment page if there are no items in their shopping basket. Likewise, if we go to the shopping basket before adding any items to it, we need to provide appropriate feedback to the user.

Finally, it is going to be critical that we maintain *state* throughout the entire process. We will need to be able to track the current shopper ID so we can maintain their basket. Also, we will need to be able to maintain state on data entered into the various forms. For example, if the shopper gets to the payment page and decides they want one more item, we don't want them to have to enter their shipping information all over again.

To make this happen, we will be utilizing session variables throughout the site to track data.

FIGURE 6.1:

Shopping process

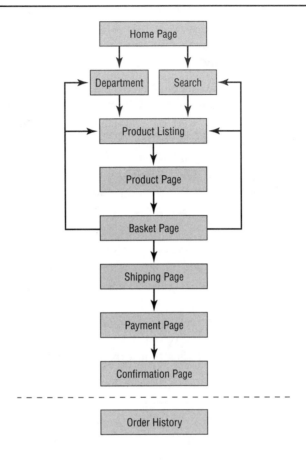

Project Setup

As shown in Chapter 5, "Sample Application," we will need to set up a new development project on our Web server. Our sample store for this demonstration is called Wild Willie's CD Store. The store is going to sell some very unusual CD titles, some that even the biggest of Internet retailers would probably not carry (or want to carry).

The sample CD contains SQL scripts for populating department and product data into the database structure and will be reviewed below. The CD also contains all of the graphics for our store. If you actually want to see the store running live, go to www.activepubs.com.

From the coding side of the store, we are going to keep things fairly simple in our ASP code. And, as you will see, good solid page-level development and breakout of code will more than meet our needs for the store development. The naming conventions in the code are straightforward and easy to understand.

One of the first pages we need to develop is the global.asa file, as shown in Listing 6.1. Functions from within this file are called every time a new application is started (when the Web site is started/restarted) or a new user session is started. It contains specific functions that are fired off depending on the request. For example the `Application_OnStart` function will be executed when the Web site application is started. This is useful for initializing any parameters or settings upon startup. There is also a corresponding `Application_OnEnd` function. While we don't use these two in our sample store, they might be useful for storing global data such as statistical counts across the store, variable data related to the specific server, etc.

We do use the `Session_OnStart` function. Remember it was noted that we will need to track the ID of the shopper throughout the store. Well, when the shopper first visits, there is no shopper ID, and we will eventually need to see if they have their profile set as a cookie on their machine. To ensure that this key variable is initialized properly, the *IDShopper* variable is initially set to 0. It will later get set to either a new shopper ID or an existing one from a stored profile on the user's machine. There is also a corresponding `Session_OnEnd` function, which is not utilized.

LISTING 6.1   **Global.asa**

```
<SCRIPT LANGUAGE=VBScript RUNAT=Server>

'    *********************************************************
'    Global.ASA - Fired off when each new session is
'    started for a new shopper.
'    *********************************************************

'    Subroutine is fired off when the session starts.
Sub Session_OnStart

'    Start the shopper ID at 0.
session("idShopper") = 0

End Sub

</SCRIPT>
```

The last little item we are going to need is an ODBC Data Source Name (DSN) to connect to the database. In this case we are using a File DSN, WildWillieCDs. Next we will be ready to prep the store with some sample data so the coding can begin.

NOTE   You may also consider using OLE DB as a connection. For building and testing purposes, using the SA username and the corresponding password makes the development process simpler. But be sure to lock down the security in production.

Loading Data

Since we haven't built the management side of the store yet, we need to go ahead and populate the store with some sample data. On the CD are provided SQL scripts for inserting the data. But let's go ahead and review the data inserts to ensure it is clear how the tables are being populated.

First we will need to load the department table with department data. This will include the department name, the description, and the corresponding image. Listing 6.2 shows a sample insert.

LISTING 6.2   Loading Departments

```
insert into department(chrDeptName, txtDeptDesc,
        chrDeptImage)
values('Funky Wacky Music',
    'The craziest music you have ever seen. Is it even
    music?','funk.gif')
```

Next we will need to load product data and then designate which department the products are assigned to. The first SQL insert shown below builds the product information. One sample CD, *Joe Bob's Thimble Sounds*, is added into the products table.

TIP   Be sure to check for single quotes and double them for proper insert into the database. Chapter 5, "Sample Application," demonstrated this technique.

The next sample SQL code, in Listing 6.3, ties our new product with one of the departments. In this case, we are tying together the first product inserted with the first department inserted by building the relationship in the DepartmentProducts table.

NOTE Be sure to run the LoadDepts.sql script first and then the LoadProducts.sql script. The second depends on the departments being in place and in the specified order.

LISTING 6.3   **Loading Products**

```
insert into products(chrProductName, txtDescription,
                     chrProductImage, intPrice,
                     intActive)
values('Joe Bob''s Thimble Sounds',
       'Great thimble music that you will love!',
       'thimble.gif', 1000, 1)
insert departmentproducts(idDepartment, idProduct) values(1,1)
```

Some of our products will have attributes that we need to load. For example, in Listing 6.4, we will have T-shirts that the shopper selects from among different colors and sizes. The following two SQL statements insert our two attribute types, Size and Color, for our sample store.

LISTING 6.4   **Adding Product Attributes**

```
insert into attributecategory(chrCategoryName)
          values('Size')
insert into attributecategory(chrCategoryName)
          values('Color')
```

Next we need to load in the names of the attributes in these categories. For example, in the Size category we will have Small, Medium, Large, and X-Large. The following SQL insert statements in Listing 6.5 create the attributes for the different categories.

LISTING 6.5   Creating Attribute Categories

```
insert into attribute(chrAttributeName,
                      idAttributeCategory)
        values('Small', 1)
insert into attribute(chrAttributeName,
                      idAttributeCategory)
        values('Medium', 1)
insert into attribute(chrAttributeName,
                      idAttributeCategory)
        values('Large', 1)
insert into attribute(chrAttributeName,
                      idAttributeCategory)
        values('X-Large', 1)

insert into attribute(chrAttributeName,
                      idAttributeCategory)
        values('Red', 2)
insert into attribute(chrAttributeName,
                      idAttributeCategory)
        values('Blue', 2)
insert into attribute(chrAttributeName,
                      idAttributeCategory)
        values('Green', 2)
insert into attribute(chrAttributeName,
                      idAttributeCategory)
        values('White', 2)
```

Finally, we have to hook up our products to the different attributes. In this case it will be the two T-shirts in Wild Willie's store. The following SQL statements in Listing 6.6 build the combination.

LISTING 6.6   Assigning Attributes

```
insert into productattribute(idAttribute, idProduct)
        values(1, 9)
insert into productattribute(idAttribute, idProduct)
        values(2, 9)
insert into productattribute(idAttribute, idProduct)
        values(3, 9)
```

```
insert into productattribute(idAttribute, idProduct)
            values(4, 9)
```

This initial load of data will take care of the data requirements in this chapter. We will be loading additional data throughout this section.

Building the Page Structure

A good store design should provide consistent navigation throughout the shopping experience. Key navigational elements include a link to the department page, the shopping basket, the checkout process, and product searching.

In addition, we will provide a link to retrieve order status and to manage the shopper's profile, which will be retrievable between visits. Figure 6.2 shows the page layout.

FIGURE 6.2:

The store's navigation interface

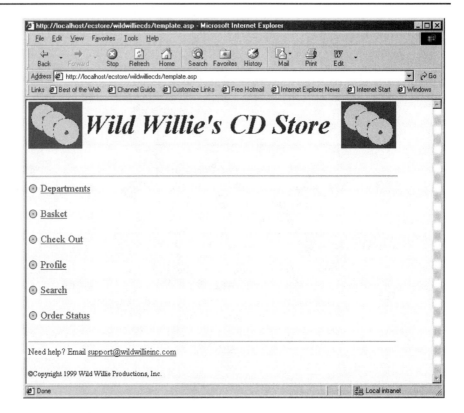

Also note the elements at the bottom of the page. We will want to wrap our pages in a navigational structure that will be easy to manage. For example, perhaps down the road we will want to add in a link to specials on the site. We do not want to have to change all of the pages in the store to have this new link. Instead, we want to encapsulate the header and footer into include files that will build the page structure.

Header and Footer Pages

The Header.asp page shown in Listing 6.7 will build the structure of the site. It will also handle some key logic for setting up the shopper. The first section of the page handles checking to see if the ID of the shopper is set to 0 in the session (*idShopper*) variable.

If so, then we have to do a couple of tasks. The first is to see if there is a cookie set on the user's machine that contains a previous shopper ID. To check this, the WWCD cookie value is checked. If it is blank then we know we need to create a new shopper tracking record. If not, then we will read the ID from the cookie.

LISTING 6.7   Header.asp

```
<!--   Header.asp - This page should be included at the
       top of all pages in the store to define the
       navigation and layout of the pages. -->

<%


'  Check to see if the shopper session is 0. If so
'  then we will need to create a shopper ID for tracking
'  the shopper.
if session("idShopper") = "0" then

      '  Next we look to see if a Wild Willie cookie
      '  has been set with the shopper ID.
      if Request.Cookies("WWCD") = "" then
```

To create the shopper record we open a database connection and execute the sp_InsertShopper stored procedure. That stored procedure returns the new ID of the shopper. We then set the session variable and continue. Note that we do not write the ID of the shopper out to a cookie. We will give the shopper that option in the checkout process.

LISTING 6.8   **Header.asp Continued**

```
    '  Create an ADO database connection
set dbShopper = _
        server.createobject("adodb.connection")

    '  Create a record set
set rsShopper = _
    server.CreateObject("adodb.recordset")

    '  Open the connection using our ODBC file DSN
dbShopper.open("filedsn=WildWillieCDs")

    '  Call the stored prodecure to insert a new
    '  shopper since there is no cookie.
sql = "execute sp_InsertShopper"

    '  Execute the SQL statement
set rsShopper = dbShopper.Execute(sql)

    '  Set the shopper ID in the session variable.
session("idShopper") = rsShopper("idShopper")

else
```

If there is a cookie, then we will retrieve the shopper ID from the cookie. But that is not all we need to do. We also want to ensure that we retrieve the last open basket if there is one so the shopper can continue where they left off. The shopper ID is stored in the session variable. We then execute the sp_RetrieveLastBasket stored procedure to return the last basket. If a basket is returned, then the ID is stored in the session variable.

LISTING 6.9   **Header.asp Continued**

```
    '  Retrieve the shopper ID from the cookie
session("idShopper") = Request.Cookies("WWCD")

    '  Create an ADO database connection
set dbShopperBasket =
    server.createobject("adodb.connection")
```

```
'  Create a record set
set rsShopperBasket =
  server.CreateObject("adodb.recordset")

'  Open the connection using our ODBC file DSN
dbShopperBasket.open("filedsn=WildWillieCDs")

'  Retrieve the last basket that the shopper
'  utilized. Note that only baskets that are not
'  completed will be returned.
sql = "execute sp_RetrieveLastBasket " & _
    session("idShopper")

'  Execute the SQL statement
set rsShopperBasket = dbShopperBasket.Execute(sql)

'  Checck to see if a basket has been returned.
if rsShopperBasket.EOF <> true then

    '  Set the session ID of the basket
    session("idBasket") = _
        rsShopperBasket("idBasket")

end if

'  Indicate that a profile has NOT been retrieved.
session("ProfileRetrieve") = "0"

end if

end if

%>
```

Now that we have taken care of business on setting up the shopper and the basket, we are ready to format the header of the page. Several tables are created that will hold the key sections of the page.

The first section of the page is the top row where the CD logo and the title of the page are shown. Following that table is the table that structures the navigation section of the page. The first column in the first row builds out the navigation links for each of the key sections. The second column is where the core content of the page will be displayed. Note that the footer.asp will contain the appropriate closing tags for the column, row, and table.

LISTING 6.10   Header.asp Continued

```
<!-- Set the default body tag for all of the pages -->
<body bgcolor="lightgoldenrodyellow"
      topmargin="0" leftmargin="0">

<!-- This table defines the header for the page -->
<table width="680" border="0">
<tr>
    <td align="right" valign="center"><img
    src="images/cdlogo.gif"></td>
    <td><font size="7" color="blue">
        <b><i>Wild Willie's CD Store</i></b></font></td>
    <td align="right" valign="center"><img
    src="images/cdlogo.gif"></td>
</tr>
</table>

<br><br>
<!-- Dividing line -->
<hr width="680" align="left">

<!-- This table defines the navigation for the page and the
     structure for placing the page content.-->
<table width="680" border="0">
<tr>
    <!-- Navigation column -->
    <td width="130" valign="top">
        <img src="images/cdbullet.gif" border="0"
            align="center">
        <font color="blue" size="4">
        <a href="dept.asp">Departments</a></font>
        <br><br>

        <img src="images/cdbullet.gif" border="0"
            align="center">
        <font color="blue" size="4">
```

```
<a href="basket.asp">Basket</a></font>
<br><br>

<img src="images/cdbullet.gif" border="0"
    align="center">
<font color="blue" size="4">
<a href="shipping.asp">Check Out</a></font>
<br><br>

<img src="images/cdbullet.gif" border="0"
    align="center">
<font color="blue" size="4">
<a href="profile.asp">Profile</a></font>
<br><br>

<img src="images/cdbullet.gif" border="0"
    align="center">
<font color="blue" size="4">
<a href="search.asp">Search</a></font>
<br><br>

<img src="images/cdbullet.gif" border="0"
    align="center">
<font color="blue" size="4">
<a href="OrderStatus.asp">Order Status</a></font>
<br><br>

</td>

<!-- Spacing column between navigation and core
    content area    -->
<td width="10"> <td>

<!-- Start the column for the main page content -->
<td valign="top" width="540">

<!-- Note that the footer.asp include must
    close out any page that has the header include.
    The table will be closed out    -->
```

We utilized two stored procedures in this page. The first, sp_InsertShopper, creates a new row in the shopper table. A new value is set in the identity column.

We return that by referencing the @@*identity* system variable, which contains the last value.

LISTING 6.11   **sp_InsertShopper Stored Procedure**

```
/*  Utilized to insert a new shopper
    into the database.
*/
CREATE PROCEDURE sp_InsertShopper AS

/*  Insert the shopper into the database and
    set the first and last name to blank */
insert into shopper(chrusername, chrpassword)
            values('', '')

/*  Return the identity column ID of the shopper */
select idShopper = @@identity
```

The second stored procedure, sp_RetrieveLastBasket, will return the last active basket the shopper was utilizing. It checks to ensure that only baskets that are not part of a completed order are returned. And, to return the last basket at the top of the record set, the DESC syntax returns them in reverse order.

LISTING 6.12   **sp_RetrieveLastBasket Stored Procedure**

```
/*  Stored Procedure to retrieve the last
    basket for the shopper. */
CREATE PROCEDURE sp_RetrieveLastBasket

/*  Pas in the ID of the shopper */
@idShopper int

AS

/*  Select the basket data for all baskets
    assigned to the shopper and where the
    order was never finished. We sort the
    data in descending order so that the
    last basket is returned first. */
select * from basket
where idShopper = @idShopper and
```

```
        intOrderPlaced =0 and intTotal = 0
    order by dtCreated DESC
```

Following the header, we will need to include the footer.asp in the bottom of the page. This page closes out the tags started in the header. And in this case, it gives us an opportunity to show a copyright notice, support e-mail, etc. Listing 6.13 shows the footer.asp page.

LISTING 6.13   Footer.asp

```
<!--
    Footer.asp - This page should be included at the
    bottom of all pages in the store to close out the
    structure of the page.
-->
    <!-- Close out the content column
        started in the header -->
    </td>

<!-- Close out the row -->
</tr>

<!-- Start a new row to display the
    footer information -->
<tr>
    <!-- Start a column, note the display across
        the four columns -->
    <td colspan="4" width="680">
    <HR>
    <!-- Display the help email -->
    Need help?  Email
    <a href="mailto:support@wildwillieinc.com">
    support@wildwillieinc.com</a>
    <BR><BR>
    <!-- Show the copy right -->
    <font size="2">&copy;Copyright 1999 Wild Willie
    Productions, Inc.</font>
    </td>
</tr>
</table>
```

It is important that on all pages that display content to the user, these two pages are included at the top and bottom of the page. If only one or the other is included, then the page will not build properly because they contain opening and closing tags that relate to one another.

Building the Home Page

The home page for the store puts our header and footer into place and gives an entry point for the shopper. Right after the opening tags for the page, we include the header.asp page by using the ASP include syntax.

Then we put in the core information on the page, which in this case is just a welcome message. Following that we close out the page with the footer.asp include. The home page code is shown in Listing 6.14.

LISTING 6.14   **Default.asp**

```
<%@ Language=VBScript %>
<HTML>
<!--
    Default.asp - Home page for the store and provides
    a welcome message.
-->

<!-- #include file="include/header.asp" -->

    <!-- Opening screen text -->
    Welcome to <font color="blue"><B>Wild Willie's CRAZY CD</b></font>
    store!  We have some
    of the wildest CDs that not even the biggest of the CD stores have.
<br><br>

    Select departments on the left to start your shopping experience!

<!-- #include file="include/footer.asp" -->

</BODY>
</HTML>
```

Figure 6.3 shows the store home page in all of its glory. The sample code on the CD has all of the images appropriately linked, etc., to make everything pop up in the right place. Next we will move on to exploring the interactive functionality of the store.

FIGURE 6.3:

Default page for the store

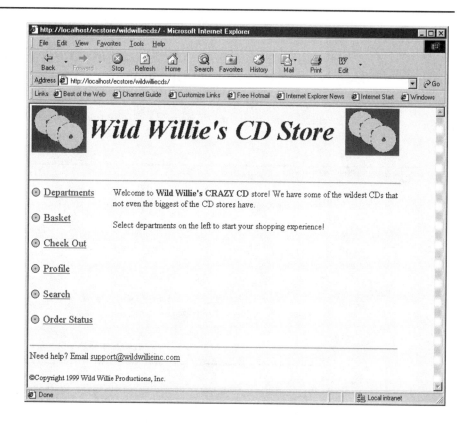

Browsing Departments and Products

The core experience to be built in this chapter is the browsing of departments and products. Now that we have the core page structure and the database loaded, we are ready to get started.

From a marketing standpoint this can be the most critical aspect of enticing the consumer to spend some time window-shopping and maybe coming in. What is represented here is the core functionality that is underlying any "skin" that may be on the store. Yes, that may mean one even better than Wild Willie's.

Departments

The department page is built to display a list of departments in the store. In this case we are going to show the department name and a corresponding image that represents the department. Listing 6.15 is the code for our department page.

The page starts out with our standard structure that will have the header included.

LISTING 6.15   **Dept.asp**

```
<%@ Language=VBScript %>
<HTML>
<!--
    Dept.asp - Displays the departments in the
    stores.
-->

<!-- #include file="include/header.asp" -->

<b>Select from a department below:</b><BR><BR>
```

Next we create a database connection and retrieve all of the departments in the database with the sp_retrieveDepts stored procedure. Then we are ready to begin looping through the departments and displaying the data.

LISTING 6.16   **Dept.asp Continued**

```
<%

'   Create an ADO database connection
set dbDepts = server.createobject("adodb.connection")

'   Create a record set
set rsDepts = server.CreateObject("adodb.recordset")
```

```
' Open the connection using our ODBC file DSN
dbDepts.open("filedsn=WildWillieCDs")

' Call the stored procedure to retrieve
' the departments in the store.
sql = "execute sp_RetrieveDepts"

' Execute the SQL statement
set rsDepts = dbdepts.Execute(sql)

' We will use a flag to rotate images
' from left to right
Flag = 0
```

To make the listing visually interesting, we will rotate the department image display from left to right in relation to the text. With each pass we retrieve the department name, the department image, and the ID of the department.

In each case we are linking the image and name to the products.asp page where the products for the department will be listed. With each loop we check a flag and build the link appropriately.

Finally the page is closed out with the footer.asp link and the closing end tags.

LISTING 6.17   Dept.asp Continued

```
' Loop through the departments
do until rsDepts.EOF

' Retrieve the field values to display the
' name, image and link to the ID of the
' department
chrDeptName = rsDepts("chrDeptName")
chrDeptImage = rsDepts("chrDeptImage")
idDepartment = rsDepts("idDepartment")

' Check the flag
If Flag = 0 then

    ' Flip the flag
    Flag = 1
```

```
%>

    <!-- Display the image and the name of the department
         In this case the image is on the left and the
         name on the right.
    -->
    <a href="products.asp?idDept=<%=idDepartment%>">
        <img src="images/<%=chrDeptImage%>" align="middle" border=0>
        <%=chrDeptName%></a><BR><BR>

<% else %>

    <!-- Display the image and the name of the department
         In this case the image is on the right and the
         name on the left.
    -->
        <a href="products.asp?idDept=<%=idDepartment%>">
        <%=chrDeptName%>
        <img src="images/<%=chrDeptImage%>" align="middle" border=0>
    </a><BR><BR>

<%

    '  Reset the flag
    Flag = 0

end if

'  Move to the next row.
rsDepts.MoveNext

loop

%>

<!-- #include file="include/footer.asp" -->

</BODY>
</HTML>
```

In this page we utilize one stored procedure, sp_RetrieveDepts, to return the products in the department. In this case we have a simple select statement that returns the data.

LISTING 6.18 **sp_RetrieveDepts Stored Procedure**

```
/*  Stored procedure to retrieve all of
    the departments in the database */
CREATE PROCEDURE sp_RetrieveDepts AS

/*  Select all of the departments data */
select * from department
```

With that, we have our first interactive display page built for the store. Figure 6.4 shows the page with the sample data populated. Note that the images rotate from left to right around the product name. And each department is linked to display the products in the department.

FIGURE 6.4:

Department page

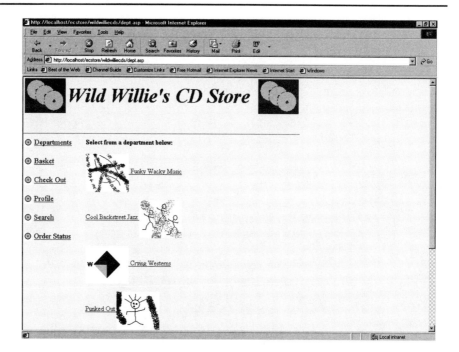

TIP
A couple of tips on designing the department page: If you have a large number of departments, you may want to list them in multiple columns instead of in a direct top to bottom list. This would simply require a bit of logic to rotate back and forth between columns in a table.

Next we move to the page that will display the products in the department that was selected from the dept.asp page. The ID of the department is passed on the URL to the products.asp page, as shown in Listing 6.19.

The first thing we do in the page is create a record set, by which we can query the database. The sp_RetrieveDept stored procedure is utilized to return the department data for the specified department. The ID passed on the URL is passed into the stored procedure.

LISTING 6.19   Products.asp

```
<%@ Language=VBScript %>
<HTML>
<!--
    Products.asp - This page displays the products in a
    department.
-->

<!-- #include file="include/header.asp" -->

<%

'  Create an ADO database connection
set dbDepartment = server.createobject("adodb.connection")

'  Create the record set
set rsDepartment = server.CreateObject("adodb.recordset")

'  Open the connection using our ODBC file DSN
dbDepartment.open("filedsn=WildWillieCDs")

'  Build the SQL statement. We are calling the
'  stored procedure to retrieve the department
'  information and passing in the ID of the
'  department
sql = "execute sp_RetrieveDept " & request("idDept")
```

Once we have the SQL statement built we are ready to retrieve the department data and display it as the header of the page. We will show the department image, name, and description. This will help to serve as a visual placeholder to indicate where the shopper has navigated to.

For future use, we store the ID of the department requested in a session variable. That way when the shopper goes to the basket page, a link can be built back to the department they were shopping in. Thus, in this case if the shopper is really interested in Jazz music, they can quickly jump back to the Jazz department and keep shopping.

LISTING 6.20   **Products.asp Continued**

```
'  Retrieve the departments
set rsDepartment = dbDepartment.Execute(sql)

'  Retrieve the product information
txtDescription = rsDepartment("txtDeptDesc")
chrDeptImage = rsDepartment("chrDeptImage")
chrDeptName = rsDepartment("chrDeptName")

'  Store the ID of the deparment being referenced in
'  the LastIDDept session variable. This will allow us
'  to build a link on the basket back to the department
'  for further shopping.
session("LastIDDept") = request("idDept")

%>

<!-- Display the department image and name -->
<CENTER>
    <img src="images/<%=chrDeptImage%>" align="middle">
    <FONT size="4"><B><%=chrDeptName%></b></font><BR><BR>
</CENTER>

<!-- Display the description -->
<%=txtDescription%> Select a product:<BR><BR>
```

Next we are ready to retrieve the products in the department. We once again create a new database connection and prepare a stored procedure to return all of the products. The ID of the department is passed to the stored procedure.

LISTING 6.21   **Products.asp Continued**

```
<%

'   Create an ADO database connection
set dbProducts = server.createobject("adodb.connection")

'   Create the record set
set rsProducts = server.CreateObject("adodb.recordset")

'   Open the connection using our ODBC file DSN
dbProducts.open("filedsn=WildWillieCDs")

'   Build the sql statement to retrieve the products in
'   the department. The ID of the department is passed in.
sql = "execute sp_RetrieveDeptProducts " & request("idDept")

'   Execute the SQL statement and retrieve the record set
set rsProducts = dbProducts.Execute(sql)
```

As with the department page, we are ready to display the images of the products in a rotating from-left-to-right fashion. As we loop through the products, a flag keeps track of the position of the last image.

With each product we are displaying the product name and the product image. As with the department, we link the image and name. In this case we are linking to the product page and passing on the URL the ID of the product. Following that we close out the page with the standard include and tags.

LISTING 6.22   **Products.asp Continued**

```
'   We are going to rotate the images from left
'   to right.
Flag = 0

'   Loop through the products record set
do until rsProducts.EOF

'   Retrieve the product information to be displayed.
chrProductName = rsProducts("chrProductName")
chrProductImage = rsProducts("chrProductImage")
idProduct = rsProducts("idProduct")
```

```
'  Check the display flag. We will rotate the
'  product images from left to right.
If flag = 0 then

    '  Set the flag
    flag = 1

%>

    <!-- Build the link to the product information. -->
    <a href="product.asp?idProduct=<%=idProduct%>">
        <img src="images/products/sm_<%=chrProductImage%>"
            align="middle" border="0">
    <%=chrProductName%></a><BR><BR>

<% else %>

    <!-- Build the link to the product information. -->
    <a href="product.asp?idProduct=<%=idProduct%>">
        <%=chrProductName%>
        <img src="images/products/sm_<%=chrProductImage%>"
            align="middle" border="0"></a><BR><BR>
<%

    '  Reset the flag
    Flag = 0

end if

'  Move to the next row
rsproducts.movenext

loop

%>

<!-- #include file="include/footer.asp" -->

</BODY>
</HTML>
```

We are utilizing two stored procedures in this page. The first stored procedure retrieves the department by the ID passed into it.

LISTING 6.23   sp_RetrieveDept Stored Procedure

```
/*  Retrieve the department data */
CREATE PROCEDURE sp_RetrieveDept

/*  Pass in the ID of the department */
@idDepartment int

AS

/*  Select all of the data on the
    department */
select * from department
where idDepartment = @idDepartment
```

The second stored procedure returns the products assigned to the department. In this case we have to join together the Department table, the DepartmentProducts table, and the Products table. We are going to return all products where there is a matching department ID in the DepartmentProducts table.

LISTING 6.24   sp_RetrieveDeptProducts Stored Procedure

```
/*  Stored Procedure to retrieve the products
    assigned to the specified department */
CREATE PROCEDURE sp_RetrieveDeptProducts

/*  Pass in the ID of the department */
@idDept int

AS

/*  Select the product data from the
    related products */
select * from products, departmentproducts

where products.idproduct = departmentproducts.idproduct and
      departmentproducts.iddepartment = @idDept
```

Now we can click on any department listed on dept.asp and go to a listing of the products on the products.asp page. We can surf through each of the departments quickly by clicking on the departments link on the navigation bar. Figure 6.5 shows the Funky Wacky music department in our store.

FIGURE 6.5:

Department page

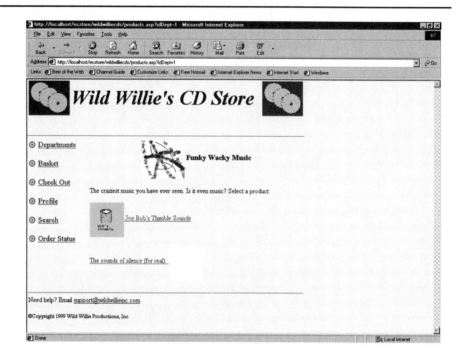

In this case we have two products tied to that department, *Joe Bob's Thimble Sounds* and *The Sounds of Silence* (for real). Note the department information display right below the header for the page.

If we click back to the department listing, we can select a new department such as the Crying Westerns. Again, in Figure 6.6 we see the left to right positioning of the product images.

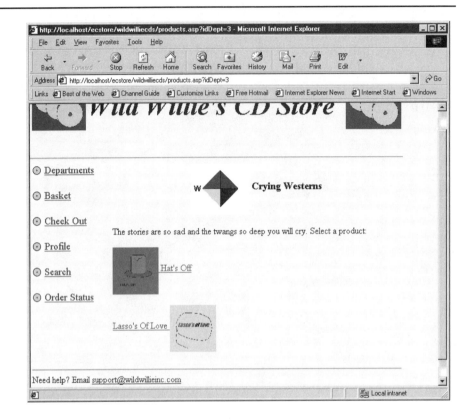

Now we are ready to actually look at some product data, the ultimate goal of the shopper.

Products

The product page, as shown in Listing 6.25, displays the data on the product selected from the products.asp page. This is where the shopper will be able to peruse the data in more detail and make a purchasing decision.

The page starts out in the usual fashion with the header include and creates a database connection so we can retrieve the product data.

LISTING 6.25   Product.asp

```
<%@ Language=VBScript %>
<HTML>
<!--
    Product.asp - Displays the product information.
-->

<!-- #include file="include/header.asp" -->

<%

'  Create an ADO database connection
set dbProduct = server.createobject("adodb.connection")

'  Create a record set
set rsProduct = server.CreateObject("adodb.recordset")

'  Open the connection using our ODBC file DSN
dbProduct.open("filedsn=WildWillieCDs")
```

The SQL statement utilizes the sp_RetrieveProduct stored procedure to retrieve the product data specified by the ID pass on the URL to the page. When the data is returned, we pull out the key product information including the description, product image, product name, product price, and the ID of the product.

LISTING 6.26   Product.asp Continued

```
'  Execute the stored procedure to retrieve
'  the product and pass in the id of the product.
sql = "execute sp_RetrieveProduct " & request("idProduct")

'  Execute the SQL statement
set rsProduct = dbProduct.Execute(sql)

'  Retrieve the product data
txtDescription = rsProduct("txtDescription")
chrProductImage = rsProduct("chrProductImage")
chrProductName = rsProduct("chrProductName")
intPrice = rsProduct("intPrice")
idProduct = rsProduct("idProduct")
%>
```

We create a form that will post to the additem.asp page. When the form is posted, it will pass the key data to add the item to the shopping basket and track it until order completion.

We then start the table to display the product data. The image is on the left with the name, description, and price in the right column. We also provide input for the user to specify the quantity they wish to purchase.

You will also notice a series of hidden fields are built. These fields are utilized to make basic basket data quickly available in the additem.asp page.

LISTING 6.27   Product.asp Continued

```
<!-- The additem.asp page will be called to
     add the product to the basket -->
<form method="post" action="additem.asp">

<!--  The table will provide the layout
      structure for the product. -->
<table border="0" cellpadding="3" cellspacing="3">

<!--  Row to display the product image, name and
      description.  -->
<TR>
    <!--  Display the image -->
    <td><img src="images/products/<%=chrProductImage%>"></td>

    <!--  Show the product name and description -->
    <td valign="top">
        <CENTER><b><font size="5">
        <%=chrProductName%></font></b></center>
        <BR><BR>
        <%=txtDescription%><BR><BR>
    </td>
</TR>

<!--  Show the product price. An input quantity box is
      created. Also, several hidden variables will hold
      key data for adding the product to the database. -->
<TR>
    <TD align="center"><B>Price:
        <%=formatcurrency(intPrice/100, 2)%></b>
    </td>
```

```
<TD align="center">
   <B>Quantity:
   <input type="text" value="1"
       name="quantity" size="2"></b>
    <input type="hidden" value="<%=idProduct%>"
       name="idProduct">
   <input type="hidden" value="<%=chrProductName%>"
       name="ProductName">
   <input type="hidden" value="<%=intPrice%>"
       name="ProductPrice">
</td>
</TR>
```

Next we have to check to see if there are attributes for the product. Remember that for the T-shirts we loaded color and size attributes. The code below makes an assumption that we have two attributes of color and size. The database certainly will support many different variations of attributes.

We utilize the sp_Attributes stored procedure to retrieve the attributes. The ID of the product is passed into the query. We then check to see whether any attributes are returned.

LISTING 6.28   Product.asp Continued

```
<%

'  Create an ADO database connection
set dbAttributes = server.createobject("adodb.connection")

'  Create a record set
set rsAttributes = server.CreateObject("adodb.recordset")

'  Open the connection using our ODBC file DSN
dbAttributes.open("filedsn=WildWillieCDs")

'  Execute the stored procedure to retrieve the attributes
'  for the products.
sql = "execute sp_Attributes " & request("idProduct")

'  Execute the SQL statement
set rsAttributes = dbProduct.Execute(sql)
```

```
'  Loop through and display the attributes for the product.
if not rsAttributes.EOF then

%>
<TR>
    <!--  Color column -->
    <TD>
```

We first process the color attribute. An option box is built that will list all of the different options. The value of each option will be the actual name of the attribute. Long term, we want to simply store the attribute names.

Handling Product SKUs

Different businesses handle product SKUs differently. Some will have the core *product ID* as the primary SKU, with attributes just part of the order data. That is how we are handling attributes in this store. But many store SKUs will be combinations of the product ID, any attributes, etc. There are a couple of considerations to keep in mind when storing attribute data and product data in general. First, if the product mix changes frequently, then storing prices, attributes, etc., in the order may be critical. We would not want a price change to happen (or a color change, etc.) right after a shopper orders and then have them charged the new price. In general the tack taken in this store is to take a *snapshot* of the product information at purchase. In the context of a much larger inventory management system, this may not be necessary.

As we are looping through all of the attributes for the product, we watch for a change from the color attribute to the size attribute. When that happens, we are ready to move on to building the next select box of size attributes.

Building the size attributes follows the same pattern as building the color attributes. That pretty much ends the display of our product data. Now the user can make their selections.

LISTING 6.29   **Product.asp Continued**

```
Color:
<!--  Select box for display the color options -->
<SELECT name="color">
```

```
<%

    '  Loop through the attributes.
    do until rsAttributes.EOF

    '  Check to see if we have moved beyond the
    '  color attribute in the list..
    if rsAttributes("chrCategoryName") <> _
       "Color" then

        '  Exit the do loop
        exit do

    end if

%>

<!-- Build the option value for the color. The
     value will be the ID of the color -->
<option value="
   <%=rsAttributes("chrAttributeName")%>">
   <%=rsAttributes("chrAttributeName")%>

<%

    '  Move to the next row
    rsAttributes.MoveNext

    loop

%>

    </select>
</TD>

<!-- Site column -->
<TD>
    Size:

    <!-- Start the size select box -->
    <SELECT name="size">
```

```
<%

'   Loop through the size attributes
do until rsAttributes.EOF

%>

<!-- Display the options -->
<option value="
    <%=rsAttributes("chrAttributeName")%>">
    <%=rsAttributes("chrAttributeName")%>

<%

'   Move to the next row
rsAttributes.MoveNext

loop

%>

        </select>

    </TD>

</TR>

<%

end if

%>
```

Finally, the page closes out with a Submit button, the closing form tag, the footer include, and the end of the page.

LISTING 6.30   **Product.asp Continued**

```
<!-- Show the submit button -->
<TR>
    <td colspan="2" align="center">
        <input type="submit" value="Order" name="Submit">
```

```
        </td>
    </tr>

    </table>

    </form>

    <!-- #include file="include/footer.asp" -->

    </BODY>
</HTML>
```

The first stored procedure utilized is `sp_RetrieveProduct`. This simply returns the product data based on the ID of the product passed to it.

LISTING 6.31   sp_RetrieveProduct Stored Procedure

```
/*  Retrieve the product data */
CREATE PROCEDURE sp_RetrieveProduct

/*  Pass in the ID of the product */
@idProduct int

AS

/*  Select the product data */
select * from products
where idProduct = @idProduct
```

The `sp_Attributes` stored procedure returns all of the attributes for the specified product. To do this we have to join four tables, including Products, ProductAttribute, Attribute, and AttributeCategory. The AttributeCategory table stores the Size and Color categories. The AttributeName table defines the color and size names in the categories. And the ProductAttribute table is a lookup of which attributes apply to the specific product.

The data returned from the stored procedure is ordered by the category name. That way in our loops above we can go down the list of all attributes and build select boxes with each break in category.

LISTING 6.32   **sp_Attributes Stored Procedure**

```
/*  Returns the attributes in the database for the
    specific product.
*/
CREATE PROCEDURE sp_Attributes

/*  Pass in the ID of the product */
@idProduct int

AS

/*  select statement to return attributes for the product. */
select products.idproduct,
       attribute.idattribute,
       attribute.chrattributename,
       attributecategory.chrcategoryname

from products, productattribute, attribute, attributecategory

where

products.idproduct = @idProduct and
productattribute.idproduct = @idProduct and
productattribute.idattribute = attribute.idattribute and
attribute.idattributecategory =
         attributecategory.idattributecategory
order by chrcategoryname
```

That does it for the development of the product page. Primarily the page is created for display of the product data. The real magic begins to happen when the user decides to add the item to their basket.

Figure 6.7 shows one of our sample product pages. The product image is placed on the left with the product data on the right. The price shows directly below the image. To order the product, the shopper would click on the Order button. That would then fire off the additem.asp page.

FIGURE 6.7:

Product page—Alley Jazz

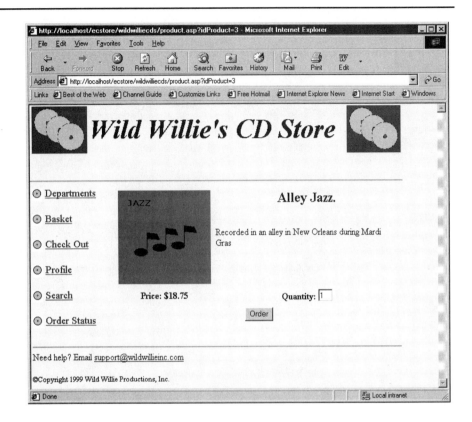

Figure 6.8 shows a product that has attributes. In this case it is the lovely and unique undershirt that costs $20. And, much to every shopper's delight, it comes in four different colors and four different sizes. The user will select a size and color combination and then add it to the basket.

FIGURE 6.8:

Product page—Undershirt

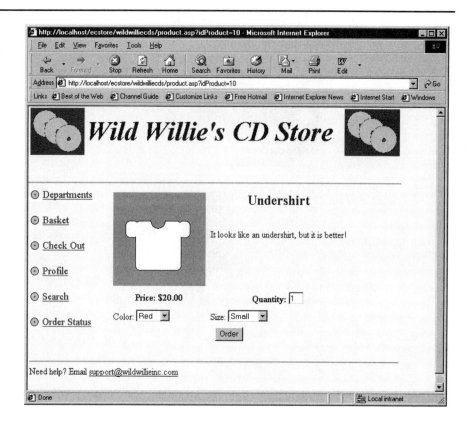

The shopper can now accomplish basic navigation through departments and products. Next we will take a look at how the shopper can find products through the search feature.

Searching

The search feature on the Web site is critical for allowing users to find products that meet their specific needs. In this case we are going to provide two basic kinds of searches. The first is the standard keyword search. This search will be executed against the name and description fields using SQL syntax.

The second search option will be a search for products that fall into a certain price range. For example, I could search for products in the $10 to $20 price range that have "jazz" in the title or description.

The page begins in the standard fashion, as shown in Listing 6.33. The form for submitting the search has a bit of a different twist. Instead of posting to another page to process the results, it posts to the search.asp page itself. A check is done in the page to see if results have been posted.

LISTING 6.33   Search.asp

```
<%@ Language=VBScript %>
<HTML>
<!--
    Search.asp - Provides searching capabilities for finding
    products.
-->

<!-- #include file="include/header.asp" -->

<BR>

<!--  Build the search form. Note we post
      to this page. -->
<form method="post" action="search.asp">
```

The first thing we display is the search table. This will be shown even if a search has been executed. That way the shopper can easily begin a new search after reviewing the results of the recent search. Note that we default the values to any previously input data.

LISTING 6.34   Search.asp Continued

```
<!--  Table to display the search options -->
<table border="0">

<!--  Display the text search option -->
<tr>
    <td align="right"><b>Enter your search text:</b></td>
    <!--  Input text box -->
    <td align="right"><input type="text"
```

```
            value="<%=request("search")%>" name="Search">
      </td>
   </tr>

   <!-- Provide a product price range search -->
   <tr><td><b>Price Range:</b></td>
      <td align="right">Low:
      <input type="text" value="<%=request("low")%>" name="Low"></td>
   </tr>

   <!-- High price search option -->
   <tr><td></td>
      <td align="right">High: <input type="text"
      value="<%=request("high")%>" name="High"></td>
   </tr>

   <!-- Break column -->
   <tr><td colspan="2"> </td></tr>

   <!-- Submit button -->
   <tr><td colspan="2" align="center">
      <input type="submit" value="Submit" name="Submit">
   </td></tr>

</table>

</form>
```

Our next set of code on the page checks to see if a search request was posted to the page. We check out three post variables—search, low, and high. Following that we go ahead and open our database connection in preparation for the search.

LISTING 6.35   Search.asp Continued

```
<%

'   Check to see if a search request was posted to
'   page.
if request("search") <> "" or _
   request("low") <> "" or _
   request("high") <> "" then
```

```
' Create an ADO database connection
set dbSearch = server.createobject("adodb.connection")

' Create a result set
set rsSearch = server.CreateObject("adodb.recordset")

' Open the connection using our ODBC file DSN
dbSearch.open("filedsn=WildWillieCDs")
```

First the *low* value is checked to see if anything has been entered and to ensure that what was entered is a number. If nothing was entered, we default the lower value to 0. If something was entered, the value is retrieved and multiplied by 100.

The value has to be multiplied to provide a search against the prices in the database, which are stored in whole number values.

LISTING 6.36   Search.asp Continued

```
' Check to see if the low search was set and is a
' number.
If request("Low") = "" or _
    isnumeric(request("low")) = false then
      ' Default to 0
      Low = 0
else
      ' Set value to the data entered. Note that
      ' prices are stored in whole number so we must
      ' mulitply the value times 100.
      Low = request("Low") * 100
end if
```

A similar check is done against the *high* value entered. If nothing was entered, then the value is defaulted to a very large dollar amount. If it was entered, as with the low price, the value is multiplied by 100.

LISTING 6.37   Search.asp Continued

```
' Check to see if the high search was set and is a
' number.
if request("High") = "" or _
```

```
        isnumeric(request("High")) = false then

            '  Default to a very high number
            High = 99999999

    else

            '  Get the value and multiply times 100
            High = Request("High") * 100

    end if
```

The SQL query that searches for the results is based on the `sp_SearchProducts` stored procedure. The search key works as low and high prices are passed into the query. The query is then executed against the database and a result set is returned.

LISTING 6.38   **Search.asp Continued**

```
'  Build a SQL query that will return the requested
    '  products. The search text and price range
    '  is passed in.
    sql = "execute sp_SearchProducts '" & _
        request("search") & "', " & Low & ", " & High

    '  Execute the SQL statement
    set rsSearch = dbSearch.Execute(sql)

%>

<!-- Start the list -->
<UL>
```

The results are returned from the query. We simply loop through the results and list the products in a bulleted list. If there are no products returned, then nothing is listed. Finally, the page is ended in the usual fashion.

LISTING 6.39   **Search.asp Continued**

```asp
<%

'  Loop through the record set
do until rsSearch.eof

%>

    <!-- Display the List -->
    <li><a href="product.asp?idProduct=
        <%=rsSearch("idProduct")%>">
        <%=rsSearch("chrProductName")%></a></li>

<%

    '  Move to the next record set
    rsSearch.MoveNext

'  Loop back
Loop

'  End the check
End If

%>

</UL>

<!-- #include file="include/footer.asp" -->

</BODY>
</HTML>
```

The search products stored procedure takes in three parameters including the search text, the low price, and the high price. The SQL query uses the *like* capability to check the product name and the description to see if the key words are found in the text. And finally, the price is checked against the low and high price.

Site Searching

Searching is an interesting topic when it comes to Web sites. There are two types of searches typically found on a Web site. The first is the unstructured type of search that a typical site search accomplishes. Tools such as Index Server crawl content files and index key words in the content into a specialized database. Then a special query language can be used to query the database. The second is the database search, which typically can be done through languages such as SQL. The database search is like the database product search in the electronic commerce store.

In an e-commerce Web site, especially with a lot of products, the search may be one of the most popular pages on the site. Special focus can be given to features such as tracking key words that shoppers are searching on, and building special *key word* fields into the database to enhance the possibility of search hits. You can even get as sophisticated as to use recommendation engines like some of the major Web retailers (such as Amazon, CD Now, EBWord, and others).

Special focus should be given on the site search features of an electronic commerce store. While the traditional method of shopping through departments, department products, etc., is critical, don't overlook the important nature of the search. A good product database search can help site visitors find exactly what they are looking for, especially while the urge to buy is hot.

LISTING 6.40　sp_SearchProducts Stored Procedure

```
/*  Stored procedure to search for products based
    on passed in parameters. */
CREATE PROCEDURE sp_SearchProducts

/*  Pass in the search text, low price and
    high price */
@SearchText varchar(255),
@Low int,
@High int

AS


/*  Select products from the data base where the
```

```
                        product name or description contain the search
                        text. And where the price falls in the given
                        parameters. The products are ordered by the
                        product name. */
                  select * from products
                  where (chrProductName like '%' + @SearchText+ '%' or
                          txtDescription like '%' + @SearchText + '%') and
                          (intPrice >= @low and intPrice <= @High)
                  order by chrProductName
```

Figure 6.9 shows the site search screen. Note the three input fields. To build a sample search, put **jazz** into the search text box, **10** into the low price box, and **20** into the high price box.

FIGURE 6.9:

Search screen

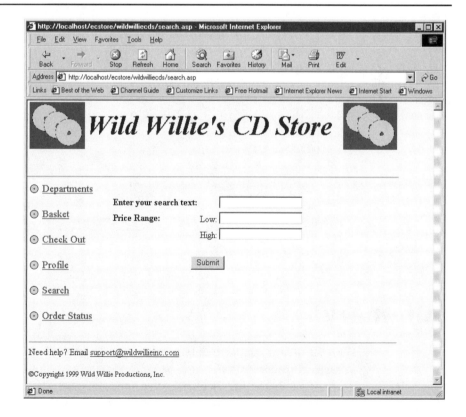

Figure 6.10 shows the search results. In this case we have one product that is returned, *Alley Jazz*. The shopper can then just click on the link and they are ready to buy.

FIGURE 6.10:

Search results

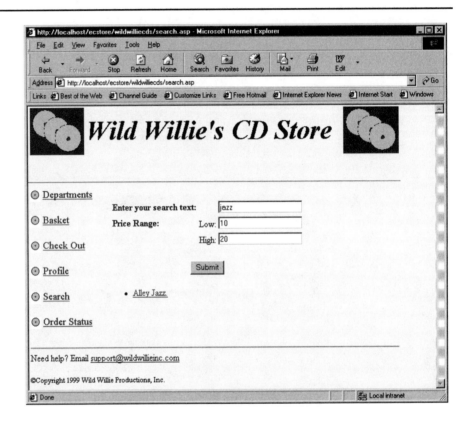

Summary

With the default, departments, products, and search pages, we have built the core infrastructure for presenting the store to the shopper. This is also typically where much of the marketing focus of a Web site is targeted. In Part IV, "Promotions," we will focus on how to work promotions into the Web site.

There are a few key concepts to note about the build of these pages. The first is the use of the include files to provide the overall framework of the pages. By using the include files, we build a very encapsulated approach to the user interface that is changeable and easily scalable down the road.

Second is the implementation of the database structure. Through the use of the stored procedures we have implemented the core department and product structure, including the product attributes, etc.

Finally, we have a platform for which we are ready to build the other half of the store, which supports the basket and checkout process. In the next chapter we will tackle the basket management phase of the store.

CHAPTER

SEVEN

7

Making a Basket Case

- Designing the Basket

- Adding Items

- Displaying the Basket

- Managing the Basket

In the last chapter shoppers were able to browse and search for products at their leisure. Now we are ready to begin the basket management process.

The shopping basket is the foundational element of making the e-commerce store functional. This is where we want the shopper to *park* products they are interested in, allowing them to decide later what they ultimately want to purchase.

Designing the Basket

The shopping basket is made up of several key functions that make it a very dynamic aspect of the Web site. Table 7.1 shows the core functions we will be adding into the shopping basket section of the Web site.

TABLE 7.1: Basket Functionality

Core Function	Description
Add item to basket	When the shopper is on the product page and hits the Order button, some magic needs to happen to add the product to the basket. There are a few key business rules we need to keep in mind.
Display basket	When the user actually hits the basket page, we need to be able to list all of the items they have added to their basket and display the quantities.
Update basket items	If the user wishes to change the quantity ordered of any item in the basket, we need to provide a capability of changing the item quantities.
Remove item	If the user decides they don't want a certain item in their shopping basket, we need to provide a method for removing a selected item.
Empty basket	If for some reason the user decides they just want to dump the whole thing, we can provide a function to empty the basket completely.

Figure 7.1 shows how the functions of the basket interact dynamically. On the top of the diagram, items are added into the basket. The shopper can empty the basket, adjust quantities, and remove items. So, without further ado, let's jump into the programming that makes all of this work.

FIGURE 7.1:

Basket functions interact dynamically.

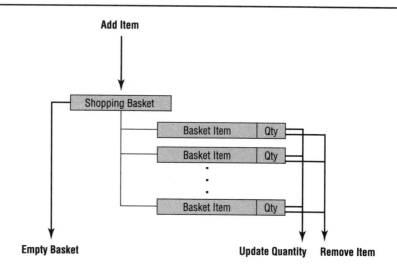

Adding Items

The first step in the process is adding items to the basket. This page is called when the user selects the Order button on the product page. Note that this page performs processing only. There is no information displayed directly to the user and it redirects immediately to a view of the basket produced by basket.asp.

The first step in the page is to check and see if there is a shopper ID assigned yet. If not, then we default the shopper ID to 0 so we can continue processing. Listing 7.1 begins the AddItem.asp code.

LISTING 7.1 AddItem.asp

```
<%@ Language=VBScript %>
<%
'    **********************************************************
'    AddItem.asp - This page is utilized to add a selected
'    product into the shopping basket.
'    **********************************************************
```

```
'  Check to see if a shopper variable has been set. If not
'  then default to 0.
if session("idShopper") = "" then

    '  Default to 0
    session("idShopper") = 0

end if
```

Next we check to see if the quantity of product ordered was 0. We do not want to add the product to the basket if that is the case. If so, then we send the shopper back to the product page. The link is set with the ID of the product to ensure the proper one is pulled up.

LISTING 7.2   AddItem.asp Continued

```
'  Check to ensure that the quantity is not 0.
if request("quantity") = "0" then

    '  Send the user back to the product page.
    Response.Redirect("product.asp?idProduct=" & _
    request("idProduct"))

End If
```

Next we retrieve the values from the product page. Remember that the key product values are stored in hidden values on that page. Now we are able to retrieve them for our use here. On the product name, we are going to ensure that single quotes are doubled so we can insert the name into the database.

LISTING 7.3   AddItem.asp Continued

```
'  Retrieve the quantity
intQuantity = request("quantity")

'  Retrieve the id of the product
idProduct = request("idProduct")

'  Retrieve the product name
chrName = replace(request("productname"), "'", "''")
```

```
'  Retrieve the product price
intPrice = request("productprice")

'  Retrieve the size
chrSize = request("size")

'  Retrieve the color
chrColor = request("color")
```

Next we have to ensure that there is a basket for this order session. We can't insert a basket item without a basket. The *idBasket* session variable is checked to see if it has been initialized.

If it hasn't, then we open up a database connection to create the new basket. The **sp_CreateBasket** stored procedure is executed. In order to create a new basket, we have to assign a shopper ID, so that it is passed into the stored procedure.

Once the basket is inserted, we retrieve the new basket ID returned from the database (through an identity column). That value is then stored in our session variable.

LISTING 7.4   **AddItem.asp Continued**

```
'  Check to see if a basket has been created
if session("idBasket") = "" then

    '  Create an ADO database connection
    set dbBasket = server.createobject("adodb.connection")

    '  Create a record set
    set rsBasket = server.CreateObject("adodb.recordset")

    '  Open the connection using our ODBC file DSN
    dbBasket.open("filedsn=WildWillieCDs")

    '  Execute the create basket stored procedure
    '  to create a new basket for the shopper
    sql = "execute sp_CreateBasket " & session("idShopper")

    '  Execute the SQL statement
    set rsBasket = dbBasket.Execute(sql)

    '  Retrieve the id of the basket returned from the
```

```
'  insert
idBasket = rsBasket("idBasket")

'  Set the basket id in the session variable
session("idBasket") = idBasket

else
```

If a basket already existed, then we would need to check and see if this item is already in the basket. We don't want duplicate entries in the basket. What we really want is to simply increment the quantity based on whatever is in the basket.

We open a connection to the database and execute the sp_CheckBasketItem-Quantity stored procedure, passing in the ID of the product and the ID of the basket to ensure we check the right item.

LISTING 7.5   AddItem.asp Continued

```
'  Create an ADO database connection
set dbBasket = server.createobject("adodb.connection")

'  Create a record set
set rsBasket = server.CreateObject("adodb.recordset")

'  Open the connection using our ODBC file DSN
dbBasket.open("filedsn=WildWillieCDs")

'  Call the stored procedure to check the basket
'  item quantity. The id of the product to check
'  and the ID of the basket is sent in.
sql = "execute sp_CheckBasketItemQuantity " & _
      idProduct & ", " & _
      session("idBasket")

'  Execute the SQL statement
set rsBasket = dbBasket.Execute(sql)
```

If nothing is returned then we know that the item does not exist in the basket. If something is returned then we need to update the basket item quantity for the existing item.

To do the update, the sp_UpdateBasketItemsQuantity stored procedure is called. We pass in the ID of the basket and the ID of the product. Also, we pass in the new quantity. This is done by accessing the current quantity returned from our previous query combined with the quantity the shopper just selected for the product. Then the user is redirected to the basket page.

LISTING 7.6   AddItem.asp Continued

```
'  Check to see if the item is in the basket. If
'  it is then we are going to update the quantity
'  instead of updating it.
if rsbasket.eof = false then

    '  If so, then we are going to update the basket
    '  quantity instead of adding a new item.
    sql = "execute sp_UpdateBasketItemsQuantity " & _
        session("idBasket") & ", " & _
        intQuantity + rsBasket("intQuantity") & _
        ", " & idProduct

    '  Execute the SQL statement
    set rsBasket = dbBasket.Execute(sql)

    '  Go to the basket
    Response.Redirect "basket.asp"

    end if

end if
```

If we get to this point on the page, we are ready to actually add a new item into the BasketItems table. We call the sp_InsertBasketItem stored procedure to add the item to the basket.

All of the key values are passed into the stored procedure including the ID of the basket, the quantity, the price, the product name, Id of the product, size, and color. When the insert is finished, the shopper is sent to the basket page.

NOTE   Many of our sample products do not include the size and color attributes. If these attributes do not exist, then nothing is returned from the Request and the fields are blank in the database.

LISTING 7.7 **AddItem.asp Continued**

```
'  Create an ADO database connection
set dbBasketItem = server.createobject("adodb.connection")

'  Create a record set
set rsBasketItem = server.CreateObject("adodb.recordset")

'  Open the connection using our ODBC file DSN
dbBasketItem.open("filedsn=WildWillieCDs")

'  Call the stored procedure to insert the new
'  item into the basket.
sql = "execute sp_InsertBasketItem " & _
      session("idBasket") & ", " & _
      intQuantity & ", " & _
      intPrice & ", '" & _
      chrName & "', " &  _
      idProduct & ", '"& _
      chrSize & "', '" & _
      chrColor & "'"

'  Execute the SQL statement
set rsBasketItem = dbBasketItem.Execute(sql)

'  Send the user to the basket page
Response.Redirect "basket.asp"

%>
```

The `sp_InsertBasketItem` stored procedure handles the insert of the new item in the basket. The appropriate fields are passed in and then the SQL insert is executed.

LISTING 7.8 **sp_InsertBasketItem Stored Procedure**

```
/*  Stored procedure to insert a new basket
    item */
CREATE PROCEDURE sp_InsertBasketItem

/*  Pass in the id of the basket, quantity, price
    product name, product price, ID of the product,
```

```
      size of the product and the color.
*/
@idBasket int,
@intQuantity int,
@intPrice int,
@chrName varchar(255),
@idProduct int,
@chrSize varchar(50),
@chrColor varchar(50)

AS


/*  Insert the item into the table */
insert into basketitem(idBasket, intQuantity,
                       intPrice, chrName,
                       idProduct, chrSize,
                       chrColor)

            values(@idBasket, @intQuantity,
                   @intPrice, @chrName,
                   @idProduct, @chrSize,
                   @chrColor)
```

The sp_CreateBasket stored procedure creates a new basket for the shopper. This happens when a shopper visits the store and is a new shopper in the database or an existing shopper who has completed orders for all existing shopping baskets.

The ID of the shopper is passed into the stored procedure. The insert is then executed to add the basket. The ID of the basket is returned from the stored procedure by using the @@*Identity* variable, which is set to the last value returned from the Insert.

LISTING 7.9   sp_CreateBasket Stored Procedure

```
/*  Creates a new basket and returns the ID */
CREATE PROCEDURE sp_CreateBasket

/*  Pass in the ID of the shopper
    the basket will belong to.
*/
@idShopper int

AS
```

```
/*  Insert a new role into the basket and
    set the shopper ID
*/
insert into basket(idShopper) values(@idShopper)

/*  Retrieve the ID of the basket which will be in the
    @@identity variable value
*/
select idbasket = @@identity
```

The sp_CheckBasketItemQuantity stored procedure will return the basket item quantity for the specified product in the specified basket.

LISTING 7.10   **sp_CheckBasketItemQuantity Stored Procedure**

```
/*  Checks the quantity of items in the basket for
    the specified product.
*/
CREATE PROCEDURE sp_CheckBasketItemQuantity

/*  Pass in the ID of the product and
    the ID of the basket
*/
@idProduct int,
@idBasket int

AS

/*  Retrieve the quantity value */
select intQuantity from basketitem
where idProduct = @idProduct and
      idBasket = @idBasket
```

The sp_UpdateBasketItemsQuantity stored procedure handles updating the basket item quantity to the new value passed into the stored procedure. The item is identified by the ID of the basket and the IDof the product.

LISTING 7.11   **sp_UpdateBasketItemsQuantity Stored Procedure**

```
/*  Stored procedure to update the
    basket item quantity. */
```

```
CREATE PROCEDURE sp_UpdateBasketItemsQuantity

/*  Pass in the ID of the basket, the quantity
    and the ID of the product (basket item). */
@idBasket int,
@intQuantity int,
@idProduct int

as

/*  Update the basketitem table wit the new
    quantity for the product. */
update basketitem set intQuantity = @intQuantity
where idBasket = @idbasket and
      idProduct = @idProduct
```

Figure 7.2 shows a product page with *Joe Bob's Thimble Sounds*. When you click on Order, the item will be added into the basket and displayed.

FIGURE 7.2:

Product page to add to basket

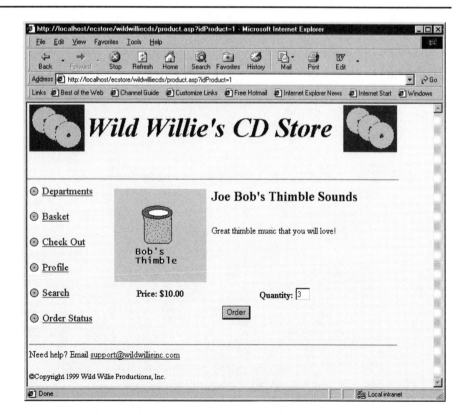

Figure 7.3 shows the basket when the product is added (we will review the basket in the next section). Note that the quantity shown is 1 since that is what was selected when the product was added.

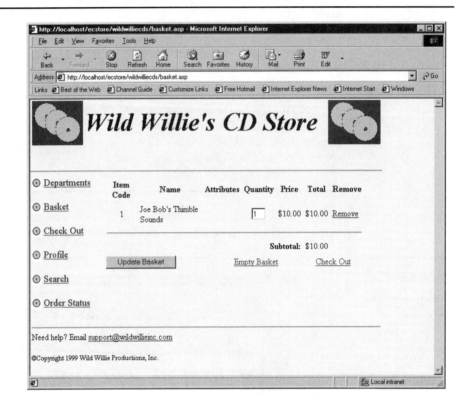

Figure 7.4 shows the effect when *Joe Bob's Thimbles* are added again. This time the quantity to be added is three items. Since that product is already loaded, a new item is not added to the basket. The quantity of the existing order is simply updated to reflect the total quantity of 4.

FIGURE 7.4:

The basket page with the quantity updated

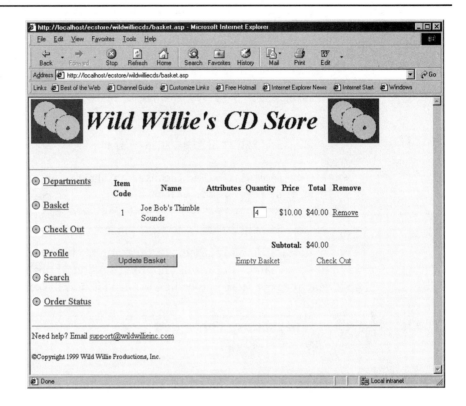

Well, now that you have seen that the basket works, let's dive into the code behind the basket.

Displaying the Basket

The shopping basket is a list of items that needs to be displayed on the page. The page starts in the standard fashion with the appropriate header file included. The page starts out with a form that will be utilized for updating the quantities on the page. Listing 7.12 shows the basket.asp page and its corresponding stored procedures.

LISTING 7.12   **Basket.asp**

```
<%@ Language=VBScript %>
<HTML>
<!--
    Basket.asp - Displays the items in the shoppers basket.
-->

<!-- #include file="include/header.asp" -->

<!-- This form will allow the user to update the quantity
     of the items in the basket  -->
<form method="post" action="UpdateBasket.asp">
```

As on the AddItem.asp page, we are going to check and see if the shopper has a basket created yet for this shopping session. If not, then we utilize the sp_CreateBasket stored procedure to have the new basket added to the database.

LISTING 7.13   **Basket.asp Continued**

```
<%

'  Check to see if the ID of the basket is blank
if session("idBasket") = "" then

    '  Create an ADO database connection
    set dbBasket = server.createobject("adodb.connection")

    '  Create a record set
    set rsBasket = server.CreateObject("adodb.recordset")

    '  Open the connection using our ODBC file DSN
    dbBasket.open("filedsn=WildWillieCDs")

    '  Create a new shopping basket
    sql = "execute sp_CreateBasket " & session("idShopper")

    '  Execute the SQL statement
    set rsBasket = dbBasket.Execute(sql)

    '  Retrieve the id of the basket returned from the
```

```
   '   insert
   idBasket = rsBasket("idBasket")

   '   Set the basket id in the session variable
   session("idBasket") = idBasket

end if
```

Next we are ready to retrieve the basket items for the current basket. The `sp_RetrieveBasketItem` stored procedure is used to pull out all of the basket items for the current basket for the current shopper.

LISTING 7.14   Basket.asp Continued

```
'   Create an ADO database connection
set dbBasketItem = server.createobject("adodb.connection")

'   Create a record set
set rsBasketItem = server.CreateObject("adodb.recordset")

'   Open the connection using our ODBC file DSN
dbBasketItem.open("filedsn=WildWillieCDs")

'   Execute the stored procedure to retrieve the basket
'   items for the shopper.
sql = "execute sp_RetrieveBasketItem " & session("idBasket")

'   Execute the SQL statement
set rsBasketItem = dbBasketItem.Execute(sql)
```

If the basket is empty then we will display an appropriate message to the shopper. If not, then we are ready to loop through the items and display them.

LISTING 7.15   Basket.asp Continued

```
'   Check to ensure a basket has been created and that
'   there are items in the basket
if session("idBasket") = "" or rsBasketItem.EOF = true then

%>

    <!-- Show the empty basket message -->
```

```
<center>
<BR><BR>
<font size="4">Your basket is empty.</font>
</center>

<%

else
```

E-Commerce Store Navigation

We have built into the core a navigation structure that allows the shopper to navigate to the shopping basket, departments, searching, and checking out.

Building in the link back to the department on the basket page helps facilitate the shopping process they were following. In a real physical store, we would not make the shopper go to a basket somewhere else and then have to walk all the way back to the department they were in. This link helps to facilitate the continuation of their shopping process.

There are some other elements of the shopping navigation process that we might want to consider. Many stores implement a forward/back feature on the product page to allow the shopper to move back and forth between products without navigating back to the department page.

Other considerations would include selling products in groups. For example, if we are selling a selection of bedding, in many cases the shopper would buy a complete set (e.g.,. pillowcases, sheets, etc.). In that case we might have other product templates that would allow multiple products to be displayed on one page and purchased in one group.

Considering these navigational issues is key to ensuring that your shoppers have the best experience navigating the store. The type of navigational requirements is somewhat dependent upon the type of product being sold, but many of the principles outlined here are universal in utilization.

Before we begin the loop we will display a link back to the department of the product they just purchased. Remember on the products.asp page that we stored a session variable that indicated the last department viewed.

In this case we check that session variable to see if it is set. If it is, then we build a link to that department for easy navigation back to the department in which the shopper was browsing.

LISTING 7.16   Basket.asp Continued

```
'   Check to see if the last department is set
'   based on where they ordered from.
if session("LastIDDept") <> "" then

%>

<!--   Show the link to go back to the department to
       make navigation easier.
-->
<BR>
Click <a href="products.asp?idDept=<%=session("LastIDDept")%>">
here</a> to continue shopping.
<BR><BR>

<%end if%>
```

Next on the page we will create a table structure for displaying the products in the basket. The header is displayed first that shows the columns of data we will display in the basket.

LISTING 7.17   Basket.asp Continued

```
<!--   Build the basket table -->
<table border="0" cellpadding="3" cellspacing="2" width="500">

<!--   Build the header row -->
<tr>
    <th>Item Code</th>
    <th>Name</th>
    <th>Attributes</th>
    <th>Quantity</th>
    <th>Price</th>
    <th>Total</th>
    <th>Remove</th>
</tr>
```

Next we will loop through the items in the basket. With each iteration the product ID, product name, and any attributes are displayed. Following that we display the product quantity currently selected to be purchased.

When the product quantity is displayed, the value of the text box is set to the product ID. That way, on the update page we can determine what product the shopper is changing the quantity on.

Following the quantity, we display the product price and the purchase price. Remember that the prices are stored in the database in an integer format. To display the proper price, we have to divide the stored value by 100 to show the decimals properly. To display the price formatted properly, the `FormatCurrency` function is utilized to add the dollar signs, etc. The purchase price is calculated by multiplying the quantity by the product price.

Finally, the Remove option is built into the form. In this case we are linking to the deleteitem.asp page. The ID of the product is passed on the URL to the page to indicate which item should be removed from the basket.

With each iteration the subtotal is calculated, to be displayed after all of the basket items are displayed. At the end, the record set is moved to the next row and we loop back to show the next item.

LISTING 7.18   **Basket.asp Continued**

```asp
<%

'   Loop through the basket items.
do until rsBasketItem.EOF

%>

<!--  Show the row -->
<tr>
    <!--  Show the product id -->
    <td align="center"><%=rsBasketItem("idProduct")%></td>
    <!--  Show the product name -->
    <td><%=rsBasketItem("chrName")%></td>
    <!--  Show the product attributes -->
    <td>
        <% if rsBasketItem("chrColor") <> " " then %>
        <%=rsBasketItem("chrSize")%>,
```

```
        <%=rsBasketItem("chrColor")%>
        <% end if %>
    </td>
    <!-- Show the product quantity -->
    <td align="center">
        <input type="text"
         value="<%=rsBasketItem("intQuantity")%>"
         name="<%=rsBasketItem("idProduct")%>"
         size="2">
        </td>
    <!-- Show the product price -->
    <td><%=formatcurrency(rsBasketItem("intPrice")/100,↵
        2)%></td>

    <!-- Show the product total cost -->
    <td>
    <%=formatcurrency(rsBasketItem("intPrice")/100 * ↵
        rsBasketitem("intQuantity"), 2)%>
    </td>
    <!-- Show the remove option. -->
    <td>
    <a href="deleteitem.asp? ↵
    idBasketItem=<%=rsBasketItem("idBasketItem")%>"> ↵
    Remove</a>
    </td>
    <!-- Continue to calculate the subtotal -->
    <% subtotal = subtotal + (rsBasketItem("intPrice") * _
        rsBasketitem("intQuantity")) %>

</tr>

<%

'  Move to the next row
rsBasketItem.MoveNext

'  Loop back
loop

%>
```

After the products in the basket are displayed, we will show the current subtotal of the basket. Note that in the table there is a break row put in and then in the next row the subtotal is displayed lined up under the purchase price column.

LISTING 7.19   Basket.asp Continued

```
<!--  Build a break -->
<tr>
    <td colspan="7"><HR></td>
</tr>

<!--  Show the sub total of the basket -->
<tr>
    <td colspan="5" align="right"><b>Subtotal:</b></td>
    <td><% = formatcurrency(subtotal/100, 2) %></td>
    <td> </td>
</tr>

</table>
```

TIP

To make the look of the basket more consistent, you might want to have images displayed instead of a Submit button and text links. A form can be submitted with a graphic image as the button. And, of course, the images can be linked as well. That will provide more consistency in the interface.

The Submit button is displayed for submitting any quantity changes for the basket. Following that we have links to the emptybasket.asp page and the shipping.asp page. Finally the page is ended with the proper include and tags.

LISTING 7.20   Basket.asp Continued

```
<!--  Show the submit button for the quantity update action -->
<table width="100%">

<td><input type="submit" value="Update Basket" name="Submit"></td>
```

```
</form>

<!-- Show the empty basket and check out links -->
<td><a href="emptybasket.asp">Empty Basket</a></td>
<td><a href="shipping.asp">Check Out</a></td>

</tr>

</table>

<% end if %>

<!-- #include file="include/footer.asp" -->

</BODY>
</HTML>
```

Now we have our basket functional. Figure 7.5 shows the basket with several items displayed on the basket. Note the different quantities for each item and the *Total* column showing the multiplied price. And at the bottom, the entire basket is subtotaled. Also note the link *Click here to continue shopping*. That will take the shopper back to the department in which they were shopping.

NOTE   We are only showing the subtotal in the basket. The shipping and tax will be done in the checkout process. If your store has large shipping costs or unusual tax requirements, it may be prudent to show these charges at the basket level. But in many cases this will require the shopper to enter at least a shipping and/or billing zip code.

FIGURE 7.5:

Basket page

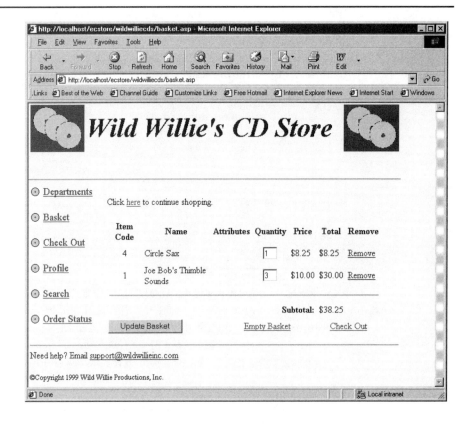

That takes care of displaying the basket, and we have all of the proper links set to provide the shopper with the tools to manage the basket.

Managing the Basket

Now the shopper has been able to add items in the basket and see their choices displayed. Next we will look at the tools to manage the basket. These will include the UpdateBasket.asp page, DeleteItem.asp page, and the EmptyBasket.asp page.

Updating the Basket

With our first page, updatebasket.asp, we will be building a non-display page that will do the process of the update request. The first thing we do when the page is started is to open up a database connection.

With the database connection, we will retrieve the shopper's basket items. The basket will be looped through with an update done on each product. A second record set is created to provide us with a connection to update each basket item as we loop through the basket items. Listing 7.21 is the code for the Update-Basket.asp page we will review next.

LISTING 7.21   UpdateBasket.asp

```asp
<%@ Language=VBScript %>
<%
'   ****************************************************
'   UpdateBasket.asp - This page will read in new
'   quantity for items in the basket and set them
'   appropriately.
'   ****************************************************

'   Create an ADO database connection
set dbBasketItem = server.createobject("adodb.connection")


'   Create a record set
set rsBasketItem = server.CreateObject("adodb.recordset")


'   Open the connection using our ODBC file DSN
dbBasketItem.open("filedsn=WildWillieCDs")


'   Retrieve the basket items
sql = "execute sp_RetrieveBasketItem " & session("idBasket")


'   Execute the SQL statement
set rsBasketItem = dbBasketItem.Execute(sql)


'   Create an ADO database connection
set dbUpdateItem = server.createobject("adodb.connection")


'   Create a record set
set rsUpdateItem = server.CreateObject("adodb.recordset")


'   Open the connection using our ODBC file DSN
dbUpdateItem.open("filedsn=WildWillieCDs")


'   Loop through the basket items
do until rsBasketItem.EOF
```

In each loop, we retrieve the quantity value by accessing the ID of the product from our open record set. Remember that each quantity text field on the basket page has as its name the ID of the product. Thus, when we do the request call, we have to pass in the ID of the product we are currently looping through.

Next the stored procedure, sp_UpdateBasketItemQuantity, is called to update the item with the new quantity. Note that the ID of the basket and the ID of the product are passed as well into the stored procedure.

Once the loop is completed the shopper is sent back to the basket page. On the basket page the quantities will be updated and the new line item totals and subtotal will be displayed.

LISTING 7.22   UpdateBasket.asp Continued

```
'  Retrieve the quantity. We use the ID of the
'  basket item from the database to retrieve the
'  datan from the correct input box.
intQuantity = request(cstr(rsBasketItem("idProduct")))

'  Call the stored procedure to update the quantity
sql = "execute sp_UpdateBasketItemsQuantity " & _
session("idBasket") & ", " & intQuantity & ", " & _
rsBasketItem("idProduct")

'  Execute the SQL statement
set rsUpdateItem = dbUpdateItem.Execute(sql)

'  Move to the next item
rsBasketItem.MoveNext

loop

'  Send the user to the basket page
Response.Redirect "basket.asp"

%>
```

The sp_RetrieveBasketItem stored procedure is utilized to get the basket items from the database for the specified shopping basket. The ID of the basket is passed into the stored procedure.

sp_RetrieveBasketItem Stored Procedure

```
/*  Stored Procedure to retrieve the
    basket item from the database */
CREATE PROCEDURE sp_RetrieveBasketItem

/*  Pass in the ID of the basket */
@idBasket int

AS

/*  Retrieve the items for the specified basket */
select * from basketitem where idBasket = @idBasket
```

Figure 7.6 shows our basket page. We have two items, *Circle Sax* and *Joe Bob's Thimble Sounds*. The first has a quantity of 6 items purchased and the second has 9 items purchased. Now let's change the quantities to 3 each.

FIGURE 7.6:

Preliminary basket

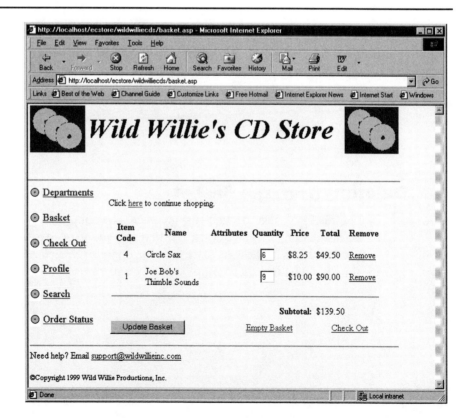

Figure 7.7 shows the updated basket. Note that the quantities are updated, the line item totals are updated, and the overall basket subtotal is updated.

FIGURE 7.7:

Updated basket

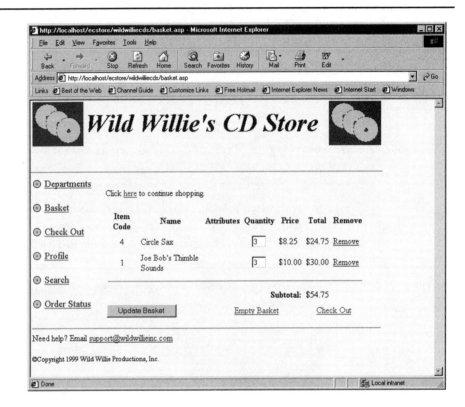

Deleting from the Basket

Our next page is also a non-display page. It is going to handle the processing of basket-item removal requests. The first step in the page is to open a database connection that will allow us to execute the remove request. The Active Server Page shown in Listing 7.24 accomplishes this task for us.

LISTING 7.24 **DeleteItem.asp**

```
<%@ Language=VBScript %>
<%

'    **********************************************************
'    DeleteItem.asp - Deletes the specified item from the
'    shopping basket.
'    **********************************************************

'    Create an ADO database connection
set dbBasketItem = server.createobject("adodb.connection")

'    Create a record set
set rsBasketItem = server.CreateObject("adodb.recordset")

'    Open the connection using our ODBC file DSN
dbBasketItem.open("filedsn=WildWillieCDs")
```

The ID of the basket item to be removed is passed on the URL to this page. The sp_RemoveBasketItem stored procedure is called with the ID of the basket and the ID of the basket item passed into it. The stored procedure is executed and then the shopper is directed back to the basket.asp page.

LISTING 7.25 **Deleteitem.asp Continued**

```
'    Call the delete item SQL statement and
'    pass in the ID of the basket and the id of
'    the item.
sql = "execute sp_RemoveBasketItem " & _
      session("idBasket") & _
      ", " & request("idBasketItem")

'    Execute the SQL statement
set rsBasketItem = dbBasketItem.Execute(sql)

'    Send the user back to the baket page
Response.Redirect "Basket.asp"

%>
```

The sp_RemoveBasketItem stored procedure handles removing the basket item from the table. The ID of the basket and the ID of the basket item is passed into the stored procedure. Then the delete statement is executed to remove the row.

LISTING 7.26   **sp_RemoveBasketItem Stored Procedure**

```
/*  Stored Procedure to remove an item from
    the basket */
CREATE PROCEDURE sp_RemoveBasketItem

/*  Pass in the ID of the basket and
    the ID of the basket item to be
    removed.
*/
@idBasket int,
@idBasketItem int

AS

/*  Delete the item from the database */
delete from basketitem
where idBasket = @idBasket and
      idBasketItem = @idBasketItem
```

To test our functionality, Figure 7.8 shows a preliminary shopping basket with 5 items in it. Click on the Remove option next to the *T-Shirt Rip* product.

FIGURE 7.8:

Preliminary basket

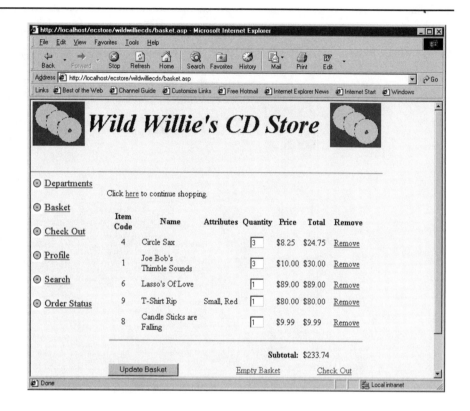

FIGURE 7.8:

Preliminary basket

Figure 7.9 shows the item removed from the basket. Note that the subtotal is updated and the rest of the basket is still intact.

FIGURE 7.9:

Item removed from basket

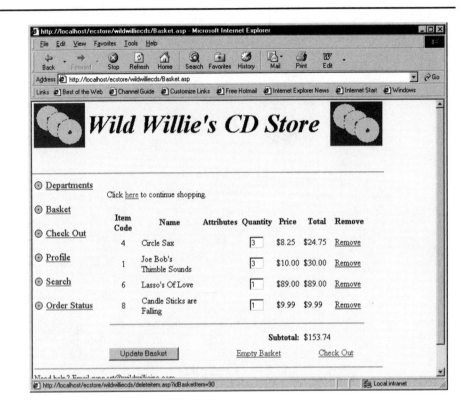

The last functionality we will look at is the emptying of the basket in empty-basket.asp.

Emptying the Basket

The last functionality is the ability for the shopper to completely empty the shopping basket. Listing 7.27 shows the code for the emptybasket.asp page. Of course, we hope that the shopper will not use this function, but it can provide a sense of peace for the shopper to know the items they have selected are cleared if they are not interested in ordering.

The first thing we do is open a database connection. In this case, we don't pass anything into the page from the basket. All we need to know is the ID of their basket. Then the `sp_ClearBasketItems` stored procedure is executed with the ID of the basket passed in. Once that is done, the shopper is sent back to the basket.asp page.

LISTING 7.27   EmptyBasket.asp Stored Procedure

```
<%@ Language=VBScript %>
<%
'   ********************************************************
'   EmptyBasket.asp - This empties the items in the
'   basket.
'   ********************************************************

'   Create an ADO database connection
set dbBasketItem = server.createobject("adodb.connection")

'   Create a record set
set rsBasketItem = server.CreateObject("adodb.recordset")

'   Open the connection using our ODBC file DSN
dbBasketItem.open("filedsn=WildWillieCDs")

'   Call the clear basket items stored procedure
sql = "execute sp_ClearBasketItems " & session("idBasket")

'   Execute the SQL statement to empty
'   the basket
set rsBasketItem = dbBasketItem.Execute(sql)

'   Send the user to the basket page
Response.Redirect "basket.asp"

%>
```

The sp_ClearBasketItems stored procedure takes in the ID of the basket and then executes a delete statement to remove all basket items related to that basket.

LISTING 7.28   sp_ClearBasketItems Stored Procedure

```
/*  Clear the items in the basket */
CREATE PROCEDURE sp_ClearBasketItems

/*  Pass in the ID of the basket */
@idBasket int
```

```
AS

/*  Delete all items in the specified basket */
delete from basketitem where idBasket = @idBasket
```

Figure 7.10 shows a standard shopping basket with multiple items. Click on the Empty Basket option.

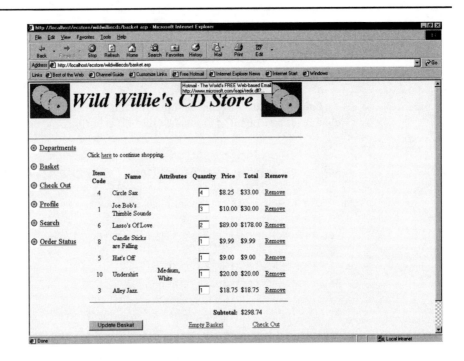

Figure 7.11 shows that all of the items have been removed from the basket. In this case we just get the standard error message indicating the basket is empty.

FIGURE 7.11:

Basket cleared of all items

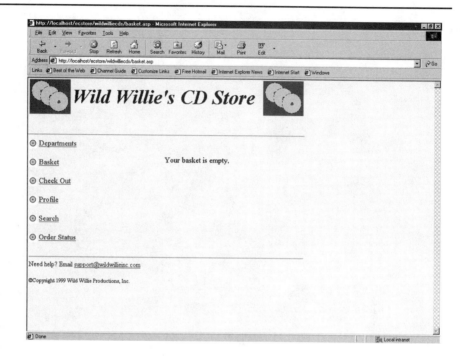

Summary

In the last chapter we explored the basic functionality of browsing through departments, products, and executing searches. This was the key focus for the initial entry of the shopper into the store.

In this chapter we explored the shopping basket and its role in the e-commerce process. The shopping basket is the key tool in the online shopping experience. This is the tool that the shopper will utilize to keep track of her interests and allow her to manage what she will ultimately purchase. It is also the stepping off point to making the final purchase.

In the next chapter we will explore the process of checking out once shoppers have selected the products they are interested in. We will be dealing with validation issues, calculating shipping and tax, and generally ensuring the order is executed properly.

CHAPTER

EIGHT

8

Checking Out

- Defining the Checkout Process

- Defining the Shopper Profile Process

- Loading Tax and Shipping Data

- Shipping Page

- Validate Shipping Page

- Calculating Shipping and Tax

- Payment Page

- Validate Payment Page

- Confirmation Page

We have finally come to the stage where the shopper is ready to check out and place their order. It is important at this stage to make the process as smooth and seamless as possible and ensure all data is captured correctly.

Defining the Checkout Process

We will have several pages involved in this process. The user is essentially going to see three pages, but there is a lot happening behind the scenes. Table 8.1 outlines the checkout functions.

TABLE 8.1: Checkout Process

Core Function	Description
Shipping	The first step is for the shopper to enter in the shipping information for the order. When the shopper enters this data, this is what the shipping fees will be calculated from.
Validate Shipping	As soon as the shopper submits their data, we will need to validate it. We need to ensure that all of the appropriate data has been entered to have a complete order.
Payment	The payment page is where the shopper will enter in their billing information as well as the credit card data. Also shown on the page will be the shipping and tax for the order.
Validate Payment	As with the validation of the shipping data, we will need to validate the billing data.
Confirmation	Once the shopper has successfully completed the order, the confirmation page will give an order number to the new customer.

The checkout process is fairly straightforward, but it also contains the core of the business rule logic behind the e-commerce store. Figure 8.1 shows the checkout process.

FIGURE 8.1:

Checkout process

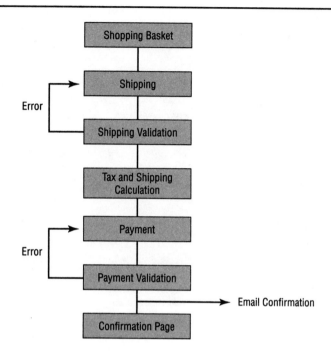

The checkout process starts with the basket. As indicated, the shipping is the next step and then the validation is done on the shipping data. If there is an error on the shipping information, the shopper is sent back to the shipping page with an indication of an error.

When the user jumps to the payment process, we will calculate the tax and shipping. In this case we are going to be building a Visual Basic COM object that we will call from our ASP pages.

Following that, the payment process follows in the same fashion as the shipping process. The user will enter in their payment data and it will then be validated. If the validation is successful, an e-mail receipt is sent to the shopper and the confirmation page is shown.

Checkout Page Approaches

The processes modeled in our sample store are pretty standard. But, there are many different variations on the theme. In our example, we are going to be supporting just a couple of international options, but many stores will provide different checkout processes based on whether they are serving an international customer or domestic.

Another approach is to combine the shipping and billing pages into one page. In that case, it is important to give the shopper an option of making the billing data the same as the shipping data so the shopper doesn't have to re-key data. If this approach is taken it is still important to show the shipping and tax calculations at some point in the checkout process.

Some stores, such as amazon.com, provide sophisticated checkout processes where multiple addresses and payment options are remembered to facilitate easy purchasing. Also, stores such as amazon.com provide features such as one-click shopping to provide as simple as possible purchasing options.

Defining the Shopper Profile Process

Another key part of the shopping process is storing the shopper information in a profile. The basic idea behind the profile is to remember the shopper data down the road to save re-keying in the checkout process and to facilitate the shopper retrieving an order status once their order is paced. Also, if the shopper wishes to keep a cookie on their system, the shopper's previous basket will be retrieved (if not a completed order).

If you will remember, the navigation bar contains an option link *profile*. That will allow the shopper to edit an existing profile. The profiles are created when the shopper first places an order. They have the option of saving their profile. Table 8.2 shows the key profile pages.

TABLE 8.2: Profile Functions

Core Function	Description
Edit Profile	When a user has a profile created, they can edit by selecting the option on the navigation bar. They also will be editing their profile every time they place an order.

Continued on next page

TABLE 8.2 CONTINUED: Profile Functions

Core Function	Description
E-mail Password	If the user wishes to retrieve the profile (or order history), they will need to enter in their username and password. If they have forgotten their password, they can have it e-mailed to them.
Create Profile	A shopper profile is created when the shopper places an order. On the payment page, they will have the option of creating a profile or updating an existing profile.
Retrieve Profile	If the shopper has a cookie set, their profile will be automatically retrieved upon return to the store. And, if they enter in their username and password, the profile will be retrieved as well.

Figure 8.2 shows the connection points in the shopping process where the shopper profile is interacted with.

FIGURE 8.2:

Profile data interaction

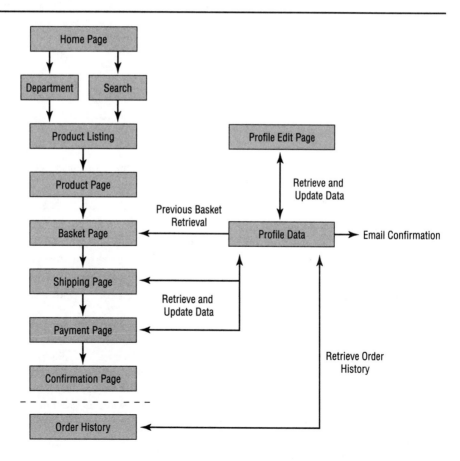

As depicted, the profile data is interacted with in the shopping process in a number of ways. We have direct pages for editing the profile data. The basket page will retrieve a previous in-process basket if the shopper has one. The checkout pages will provide a vehicle for retrieving and updating the data. And, finally, the shopper will be able to retrieve their order history through their profile as well.

We will see in the code that the profile data is touched in about the same places in the code as depicted in the diagram. The header.asp page (as noted in the previous chapters) will look for a shopper cookie to retrieve shopper data. To help clarify the different scenarios for how profile data is retrieved in the process, Table 8.3 outlines the key interaction scenarios.

TABLE 8.3: Profile Retrieval Scenarios

Scenario	Description
No cookie	If there is no cookie, the user can complete the shopping process and in essence will create a new profile if they don't retrieve the old one with a username and password.
Cookie	The header.asp page will retrieve the ID of the shopper from the cookie. Then a check is done to see if an existing unfinished basket is available.
No cookie—user-name and pass-word entered	If the shopper has no cookie set, but retrieves a previous profile, that is all that will be retrieved. We don't want to overwrite any basket they may have in progress by retrieving a previous basket that was unfinished.
No previous profile	If there was no previous profile, when the shopper checks out a profile will be created regardless of whether they enter in a password for later retrieval. They will only be able to retrieve the profile if they enter in a password.

The profiling done in our example store in this book is really just the beginning of what is possible. By being able to track order history, shopping history, etc. there are many options available to target the shopper with additional data down the road and do extensive analysis on shopping patterns.

TIP

If you wish to test different scenarios for how shopper profile data is retrieved, be sure to look in the local cookies folder for the Wild Willie cookie. That can be deleted to clear any automatic retrieval. The way cookies are stored varies between browsers and browser versions—for specific instructions, refer to the documentation or help files that came with your browser.

Loading Tax and Shipping Data

For the checkout process, we are going to need to set up our data for tax and shipping calculations. Recall that we have two tables in the database for storing this data.

For shipping data the Shipping table is utilized. Shipping is calculated based on a low item quantity and a high item quantity. Each quantity range will have a specific price. The following SQL statements handle the insert of the data.

In our sample shipping data, we have four levels of shipping costs. Note that the last range essentially is a set price for all orders with 31 items or more.

LISTING 8.1   **Creating Shipping Costs**

```
insert into shipping(intLowQuantity,
                     intHighQuantity,
                     intFee)
          values(1, 10, 200)

insert into shipping(intLowQuantity,
                     intHighQuantity,
                     intFee)
          values(11, 20, 400)

insert into shipping(intLowQuantity,
                     intHighQuantity,
                     intFee)
          values(21, 30, 600)


insert into shipping(intLowQuantity,
                     intHighQuantity,
                     intFee)
          values(31, 999999, 800)
```

For the tax data, we have a table named *Tax*. This stores values for each state. In this case we are setting up two states, Virginia and Texas, that will have specific tax rates.

LISTING 8.2   **Creating Tax Rates**

```
insert into tax(chrState, fltTaxRate)
        values('VA', .045)

insert into tax(chrState, fltTaxRate)
        values('TX', .08)
```

As noted in Chapter 3, "E-Commerce Database Design," there are many options for calculating tax and shipping. For example, when we hit more than 31 items in the basket, we may wish to instead calculate the shipping costs based on a percentage of the order total or some other method.

In this chapter, we will build a COM object in Visual Basic 6. This COM object will encapsulate the rules for calculating tax and shipping. The idea is that down the road we may need to change how our tax and shipping business rules work. We will be able to change our underlying database structure and our Visual Basic code without having to worry about changing our front line shopper code.

Now that we have good overview of all the facets of the checkout process, shopper profiling, and the tax/shipping business rules, we are ready to dive into the code to see how all of this will work.

Shipping Page

The first step in our checkout process is collecting the shipping information from the shopper. There are a number of checks we need to do at the beginning of the page to ensure the shopper should be at this stage.

LISTING 8.3   **Shipping.asp**

```
<%@ Language=VBScript %>
<%
```

```
'  ******************************************************
'  Shipping.asp - Provides for the user to enter in
'  shipping data for the store.  It will check to
'  see if a profile can be retrieved.
'  ******************************************************
```

The first check is to ensure there is a basket created in this session. If there isn't then obviously we cannot allow the shopper to continue, and instead must direct them to the basket.asp page. When they hit that page, they will get the message that their basket is empty. Following this check, we begin the standard page building.

LISTING 8.4   Shipping.asp Continued

```
'  Check to ensure a basket has been created.
if session("idBasket") = "" then

    '  Redirect to the basket page
    Response.Redirect "basket.asp"

end if
%>

<HTML>

<!-- #include file="include/header.asp" -->

<BR>
<center>
<font size="5"><b>Shipping Information</b></font>
</center>
```

The next check we perform is to see if a profile has been retrieved. The *Profile-Retrieve* session variable is checked. Note that we only want to retrieve a shopper's profile once each session (unless they retrieve it themselves through the navigation link). The reason we want to do this is that the shopper may be updating their shipping and billing information; we don't want to overwrite the changes should they return to the shipping page for some reason (like an error).

If no profile has been retrieved, then we will provide a link to the profile.asp page for the shopper to retrieve a past profile. This link will typically only show up if there is no cookie for a past profile or they simply have no previous profile.

LISTING 8.5   **Shipping.asp Continued**

```
<%

' Check to see if a profile has been retrieved
' or not.
if session("ProfileRetrieve") = "" then

' If not then we will create a link to retrieve an existing profile.
%>
    <BR>
    <B><i>Click <a href="profile.asp">here</a>
        to retrieve an existing profile.</i></b>
    <BR>

<%

else
```

Next we check to see if the *ProfileRetrieve* session variable does not equal 1. It will be set to 0 when the shopper's basket is retrieved in the header.asp based on a cookie. Here we will now retrieve the address data now for that shopper from their profile.

If it not set to 1 then we create a database connection. The `sp_Retrieve-ProfileById` stored procedure will retrieve the profile based on the ID of the shopper set in our session variable.

Once the profile is retrieved, the values are read into our session variables that will track the ship-to data for the shopper. Then we set the *ProfileRetrieve* session variable to 1, which indicates that the address information had been retrieved once and should not be retrieved again.

LISTING 8.6   **Shipping.asp Continued**

```
' Check to see if the ProfileRetrieve value is 1.  If
' not then the profile will be retrieved if possible.
' Note the ProfileRetrieve value will be 0 when a
```

```
'  new shopper ID is created from the Header.
if session("ProfileRetrieve") <> "1" then

    '  Create an ADO database connection
    set dbProfile = server.createobject("adodb.connection")

    '  Create the record set
    set rsProfile = server.CreateObject("adodb.recordset")

    '  Open the connection using our ODBC file DSN
    dbProfile.open("filedsn=WildWillieCDs")

    '  Build the SQL stored procedure to retrieve
    '  the profile based on the id of the shopper
    '  (which would be retrieved by the cookie).
    sql = "execute sp_RetrieveProfileByID " & _
        session("idShopper")

    '  Execute the statement
    set rsProfile = dbProfile.Execute(sql)

    '  Set the shipping variables
    session("chrShipFirstName") = rsProfile("chrFirstName")
    session("chrShipLastName") = rsProfile("chrLastName")
    session("chrShipAddress") = rsProfile("chrAddress")
    session("chrShipCity") = rsProfile("chrCity")
    session("chrShipState") = rsProfile("chrState")
    session("chrShipProvince") = rsProfile("chrProvince")
    session("chrShipCountry") = rsProfile("chrCountry")
    session("chrShipZipCode") = rsProfile("chrZipCode")
    session("chrShipPhone") = rsProfile("chrPhone")
    session("chrShipEmail") = rsProfile("chrEmail")
    session("chrPassword") = rsProfile("chrPassword")
    session("intCookie") = rsProfile("intCookie")

end if

'  Set the session so we don't retrieve the data again.
'  This will ensure we don't pull the profile again.
session("ProfileRetrieve") = "1"

end if
```

The next check is to see if there is an error set in our global Error session variable. This session variable is set in the ValidateShipping.asp page when there is an error in the shipping data that has been entered. If the variable is set, then the error string stored in the variable is displayed to the user. This indicates to the shopper what the problems were with the shipping data. Following the error message display, the session variable is cleared.

LISTING 8.7   **Shipping.asp Continued**

```
'   Check to see if an error was returned if the form
'   was submitted
if session("Error") <> "" then

'   Show the error data.
%>
<BR>
<b>You have an error in your shipping form, please correct the
data:</b><BR><BR>

<!--  Build out a table to display the error. -->
<table>
<tr>
  <td width="70"> </td>
  <td><i><%=Response.Write(session("Error"))%></i></td>
</tr>
</table>
<BR><BR>
<%

'   Clear the error variable.
session("Error") = ""

else

%>
```

Now we are ready to get to the shipping address form for the shopper's data entry. With each row in the shipping table, we build a data entry field for the shopper to enter in their data.

Note that the value fields for each text box are defaulted to whatever is in the corresponding session variable. This allows the shipping data to be repopulated based on any previous data entry. And, if the profile has been retrieved, the session variables set above will be displayed already for them. This simplifies the shopping process if the shopper is shipping to the same address as a previous order.

LISTING 8.8   Shipping.asp Continued

```asp
<BR>
<b>Enter your shipping address:</b>
<BR><BR>

<%

end if

%>

<!--  This form will post to the validate page to ensure
      the shipping data has been entered properly.   -->
<center>

<!--  Form to post the shipping data. -->
<form method="post" action="ValidateShipping.asp">

<!--  The table will display the shipping form.
      Note that the values will be defaulted to
      any session variables.   -->
<table>
<!--  Shipping First Name -->
<tr>
    <td align="right">First Name:</td>
    <td><input type="text" value="<%=session("chrShipFirstName")%>"
        name="chrShipFirstName" size="30"></td>
</tr>
<!--  Shipping Last Name -->
<tr>
    <td align="right">Last Name:</td>
    <td><input type="text" value="<%=session("chrShipLastName")%>"
        name="chrShipLastName" size="30"></td>
</tr>
```

```
<!-- Shipping Address -->
<tr>
    <td align="right">Address:</td>
    <td><input type="text" value="<%=session("chrShipAddress")%>"
        name="chrShipAddress" size="30"></td>
</tr>
<!-- Shipping City -->
<tr>
    <td align="right">City:</td>
    <td><input type="text" value="<%=session("chrShipCity")%>"
        name="chrShipCity" size="30"></td>
</tr>
```

The select options boxes have to be handled a bit differently than the standard text boxes. We need to be able to default to any previously selected or profile value. To do this the *selected* HTML keyword must be placed in the <option> tag for the appropriate value.

To accomplish this we use a series of IF statements (or a select case statement) to see which state has been set and then set a corresponding variable with the *selected* text. Then in the building of our option box, we can insert each variable into the corresponding <option> tag.

LISTING 8.9   Shipping.asp Continued

```
<!-- Shipping State -->
<tr>
    <td align="right">State:</td>
    <td>

    <%

    ' Check to see which state was selected previously
    ' if there was an error.  We then set a variable to
    ' put in the appropriate 'SELECTED' HTML tag.
    if session("chrShipState") = "AL" then
        SelAL = "Selected"
    end if

    if session("chrShipState") = "AK" then
        SelAK = "Selected"
    end if
```

```
if session("chrShipState") = "AZ" then
    SelAZ = "Selected"
end if

if session("chrShipState") = "AR" then
    SelAR = "Selected"
end if

if session("chrShipState") = "CA" then
    SelCA = "Selected"
end if

if session("chrShipState") = "CT" then
    SelCT = "Selected"
end if

if session("chrShipState") = "CO" then
    SelCO = "Selected"
end if

if session("chrShipState") = "DC" then
    SelDC = "Selected"
end if

if session("chrShipState") = "DE" then
    SelDE = "Selected"
end if

if session("chrShipState") = "FL" then
    SelFL = "Selected"
end if

if session("chrShipState") = "GA" then
    SelGA = "Selected"
end if

if session("chrShipState") = "HI" then
    SelHI = "Selected"
end if

if session("chrShipState") = "ID" then
    SelID = "Selected"
end if
```

```
if session("chrShipState") = "IL" then
    SelIL = "Selected"
end if

if session("chrShipState") = "IN" then
    SelIN = "Selected"
end if

if session("chrShipState") = "IA" then
    SelIA = "Selected"
end if

if session("chrShipState") = "KS" then
    SelKS = "Selected"
end if

if session("chrShipState") = "KY" then
    SelKY = "Selected"
end if

if session("chrShipState") = "LA" then
    SelLA = "Selected"
end if

if session("chrShipState") = "ME" then
    SelME = "Selected"
end if

if session("chrShipState") = "MA" then
    SelMA = "Selected"
end if

if session("chrShipState") = "MD" then
    SelMD = "Selected"
end if

if session("chrShipState") = "MI" then
    SelMI = "Selected"
end if

if session("chrShipState") = "MN" then
    SelMN = "Selected"
end if
```

```
if session("chrShipState") = "MS" then
    SelMS = "Selected"
end if

if session("chrShipState") = "MO" then
    SelMO = "Selected"
end if

if session("chrShipState") = "MT" then
    SelMT = "Selected"
end if

if session("chrShipState") = "NE" then
    SelNE = "Selected"
end if

if session("chrShipState") = "NV" then
    SelNV = "Selected"
end if

if session("chrShipState") = "NH" then
    SelNH = "Selected"
end if

if session("chrShipState") = "NJ" then
    SelNJ = "Selected"
end if

if session("chrShipState") = "NM" then
    SelNM = "Selected"
end if

if session("chrShipState") = "NY" then
    SelNY = "Selected"
end if

if session("chrShipState") = "NC" then
    SelNC = "Selected"
end if

if session("chrShipState") = "ND" then
    SelND = "Selected"
end if
```

```
if session("chrShipState") = "OH" then
    SelOH = "Selected"
end if

if session("chrShipState") = "OK" then
    SelOK = "Selected"
end if

if session("chrShipState") = "OR" then
    SelOR = "Selected"
end if

if session("chrShipState") = "PA" then
    SelPA = "Selected"
end if

if session("chrShipState") = "RI" then
    SelRI = "Selected"
end if

if session("chrShipState") = "SC" then
    SelSC = "Selected"
end if

if session("chrShipState") = "SD" then
    SelSD = "Selected"
end if

if session("chrShipState") = "TN" then
    SelTN = "Selected"
end if

if session("chrShipState") = "TX" then
    SelTX = "Selected"
end if

if session("chrShipState") = "UT" then
    SelUT = "Selected"
end if

if session("chrShipState") = "VT" then
    SelVT = "Selected"
end if
```

```
if session("chrShipState") = "VA" then
    SelVA = "Selected"
end if

if session("chrShipState") = "WY" then
    SelWY = "Selected"
end if

if session("chrShipState") = "WI" then
    SelWI = "Selected"
end if

if session("chrShipState") = "WV" then
    SelWV = "Selected"
end if

if session("chrShipState") = "WA" then
    SelWA = "Selected"
end if

%>
```

Now that we have our variables set, we can build the option box of states. Each state is listed in the select box. And in each case we are inserting the corresponding *VBScript* variable. The one that has been set to *Selected* will insert that keyword tag. Thus, that option will be selected as the default on that page.

LISTING 8.10   Shipping.asp Continued

```
<!--  Option box for the shipping states.  Note that
      the past default will be selected   -->
<select name="chrShipState">
    <option value="">Select a State
    <option value="AL" <%=SelAL%>>Alabama
    <option value="AK" <%=SelAK%>>Alaska
    <option value="AZ" <%=SelAZ%>>Arizona
    <option value="AR" <%=SelAR%>>Arkansas
    <option value="CA" <%=SelCA%>>California
    <option value="CT" <%=SelCT%>>Connecticut
    <option value="CO" <%=SelCO%>>Colorado
    <option value="DC" <%=SelDC%>>D.C.
    <option value="DE" <%=SelDE%>>Delaware
```

```
            <option value="FL" <%=SelFL%>>Florida
            <option value="GA" <%=SelGA%>>Georgia
            <option value="HI" <%=SelHI%>>Hawaii
            <option value="ID" <%=SelID%>>Idaho
            <option value="IL" <%=SelIL%>>Illinois
            <option value="IN" <%=SelIN%>>Indiana
            <option value="IA" <%=SelIA%>>Iowa
            <option value="KS" <%=SelKS%>>Kansas
            <option value="KY" <%=SelKY%>>Kentucky
            <option value="LA" <%=SelLA%>>Louisiana
            <option value="ME" <%=SelME%>>Maine
            <option value="MA" <%=SelMA%>>Massachusetts
            <option value="MD" <%=SelMD%>>Maryland
            <option value="MI" <%=SelMI%>>Michigan
            <option value="MN" <%=SelMN%>>Minnesota
            <option value="MS" <%=SelMS%>>Mississippi
            <option value="MO" <%=SelMO%>>Missouri
            <option value="MT" <%=SelMT%>>Montana
            <option value="NE" <%=SelNE%>>Nebraska
            <option value="NV" <%=SelNV%>>Nevada
            <option value="NH" <%=SelNH%>>New Hampshire
            <option value="NJ" <%=SelNJ%>>New Jersey
            <option value="NM" <%=SelNM%>>New Mexico
            <option value="NY" <%=SelNY%>>New York
            <option value="NC" <%=SelNC%>>North Carolina
            <option value="ND" <%=SelND%>>North Dakota
            <option value="OH" <%=SelOH%>>Ohio
            <option value="OK" <%=SelOK%>>Oklahoma
            <option value="OR" <%=SelOR%>>Oregon
            <option value="PA" <%=SelPA%>>Pennsylvania
            <option value="RI" <%=SelRI%>>Rhode Island
            <option value="SC" <%=SelSC%>>South Carolina
            <option value="SD" <%=SelSD%>>South Dakota
            <option value="TN" <%=SelTN%>>Tennessee
            <option value="TX" <%=SelTX%>>Texas
            <option value="UT" <%=SelUT%>>Utah
            <option value="VT" <%=SelVT%>>Vermont
            <option value="VA" <%=SelVA%>>Virginia
            <option value="WA" <%=SelWA%>>Washington
            <option value="WY" <%=SelWY%>>Wyoming
            <option value="WI" <%=SelWI%>>Wisconsin
            <option value="WV" <%=SelWV%>>West Virginia
        </select>
```

Since we do want to support international shipping, we will need to take in a province value as well for those countries that don't have states. The idea is for the shopper to select one or the other and we will need to validate that in the ValidateShipping.asp page.

Following the province, we give the shopper a country selection option. In this example, we are only supporting shipping to Canada and Mexico. As with the state select box, we need to build the logic to handle defaulting a previously selected option. As before we set a corresponding *VBScript* variable corresponding to each option. If one was previously selected or set in the profile, then it will be defaulted in the select option box.

LISTING 8.11   Shipping.asp Continued

```
<!--  Province option -->
or Province:<input type="text"
            value="<%=trim(session("chrShipProvince"))%>"
            name="chrShipProvince" size="15">

    </td>
</tr>
<!--  Shipping Country -->
<tr>
    <td align="right">Country:</td>
    <td>

    <%
    '  Check to see which country was selected previously
    '  if there was an error.  We then set a variable to
    '  set the 'Selected' tag.
    if session("chrShipCountry") = "US" then
        SelUS = "Selected"
    end if

    if session("chrShipCountry") = "CA" then
        SelCA = "Selected"
    end if

    if session("chrShipCountry") = "MX" then
        SelMX = "Selected"
    end if
```

```
%>

<!-- Option box for the country with the past
     country defaulted  -->
<select name="chrShipCountry">
    <option value="">Select a Country
    <option value="US" <%=SelUS%>>United States
    <option value="CA" <%=SelCA%>>Canada
    <option value="MX" <%=SelMX%>>Mexico
</select>
</td>
</tr>
```

The rest of the table is set as the rest of the text fields. Each will be defaulted to any previous values. The table ends with a Submit button for the form, the ending form tag, and the closing of the Web page.

LISTING 8.12   Shipping.asp Continued

```
<!-- Shipping Zip Code or Postal Code -->
<tr>
    <td align="right">Zip/Postal Code:</td>
    <td><input type="text" value="<%=session("chrShipZipCode")%>"
        name="chrShipZipCode" size="30"></td>
</tr>
<!-- Shipping Phone -->
<tr>
    <td align="right">Phone:</td>
    <td><input type="text" value="<%=session("chrShipPhone")%>"
        name="chrShipPhone" size="30"></td>
</tr>
<!-- Shipping Email -->
<tr>
    <td align="right">Email:</td>
    <td><input type="text" value="<%=session("chrShipEmail")%>"
        name="chrShipEmail" size="30"></td>
</tr>
<!-- Submit Button -->
<tr>
    <td colspan="2" align="center">
```

```
            <input type="Submit" value="Submit" name="Submit">
        </td>
    </tr>
    </table>

    </form>

    </center>

    <!-- #include file="include/footer.asp" -->

    </BODY>
    </HTML>
```

In this page, we use the sp_RetrieveProfileByID stored procedure to retrieve the data in a previous profile. The ID of the shopper is passed into the stored procedure and the query pulls the data from the shopper table.

LISTING 8.13   sp_RetrieveProfileByID Stored Procedure

```
/*  Retrieve the shopper profile */
CREATE PROCEDURE sp_RetrieveProfileByID

/*  Pass in the shopper ID */
@idShopper int

AS

/*  Select the shopper data by shopper
    ID */
select * from shopper
where idShopper = @idShopper
```

To test out the page, let's first begin with an option where no previous profile has been retrieved. To do this, be sure to delete any profile cookies you may have had set for working with sample code.

Then hit the shipping page after adding several items into the shopping basket. Figure 8.3 shows the blank shopping page. Note the text indicating where to click to retrieve a previous profile.

FIGURE 8.3:

Blank shipping page

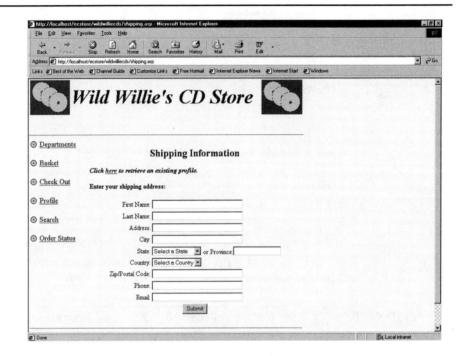

Now let's enter some data into the page. Fill everything out but don't select a state and don't enter in a province. Finish everything else out as appropriate. Figure 8.4 shows a sample data entry input.

Once submitted, the ValidateShipping.asp page is engaged. It will show that there is an error in our page because no state was selected (see Figure 8.5). Now fill in a state as appropriate and continue to shop.

FIGURE 8.4:

Shipping page filled out with an error

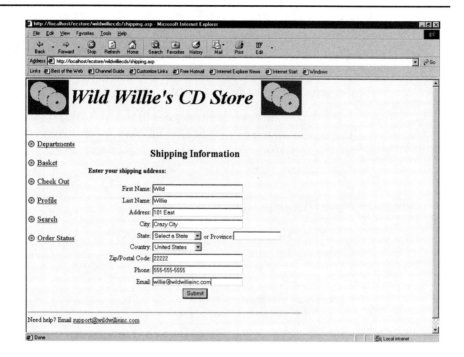

FIGURE 8.5:

Shipping page with error message

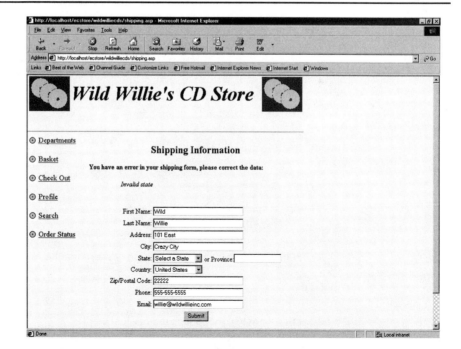

Validate Shipping Page

Now that we have seen the valid shipping page in action, let's take a look at the code. This primary role of this page is to ensure that whatever is entered in the shipping page is valid for completing an order.

The first thing done in the page is to retrieve the data entered into the form. Then we launch into a series of validation checks on each field. Most of the checks are done to ensure that some data was entered into the form fields. We cannot fully validate items like name, last name, etc.

LISTING 8.14   **ValidateShipping.asp**

```
<%@ Language=VBScript %>
<%

'   Retrieve the submitted items.
chrShipFirstName = request("chrShipFirstName")
chrShipLastName = request("chrShipLastName")
chrShipAddress = request("chrShipAddress")
chrShipCity = request("chrShipCity")
chrShipState = request("chrShipState")
chrShipProvince = request("chrShipProvince")
chrShipCountry = request("chrShipCountry")
chrShipZipCode = request("chrShipZipCode")
chrShipPhone = request("chrShipPhone")
chrShipEmail = request("chrShipEmail")

'   Check to ensure a first name was entered.
if chrShipFirstName = "" then

    strError = strError & "Invalid first name<BR>"

end if

'   Check to ensure a last name was entered.
if chrShipLastName = "" then

    strError = strError & "Invalid last name<BR>"

end if

'   Check to ensure an address was entered.
```

```
if chrShipAddress = "" then

    strError = strError & "Invalid address<BR>"

end if

'  Check to ensure a city was entered.
if chrShipCity = "" then

    strError = strError & "Invalid city<BR>"

end if
```

We have to do some extra checking on the state, province, and country fields. We don't want to allow the shopper to select a U.S. state and then select shipping to Canada. Likewise, we don't want the user to enter in a province and then select the U.S. as a shipping country.

Our code checks to see which country was selected. Then based on that we check to ensure either the province or state field was selected appropriately.

LISTING 8.15   ValidateShipping.asp Continued

```
'  Check to see if a US country was entered.
if chrShipCountry = "US" then

    '  If the state field is empty then build the
    '  appropriate error message.
    if chrShipState = "" then

        strError = strError & "Invalid state<BR>"

    end if

else

    '  If it is an international country is entered
    '  then a province must be entered.
    if chrShipProvince = "" then

        strError = strError & "Invalid province<BR>"

    end if
```

```
end if

'   Check to see if a country was entered.
if chrShipCountry = "" then

    strError = strError & "Invalid country<BR>"

end if

'   Check to ensure a zip code was entered.
if chrShipZipCode = "" then

    strError = strError & "Invalid zip code<BR>"

end if

'   Check to ensure a phone number was entered.
if chrShipPhone = "" then

    strError = strError & "Invalid phone number<BR>"

end if
```

We also can do some additional validation on the e-mail address field. We know that every e-mail address must have an @ symbol, as well as a dot (.). We can utilize the *Instr* function in VBScript to check to ensure these characters appear in the e-mail address.

LISTING 8.16   **ValidateShipping.asp Continued**

```
'   Next we validate the email address.  The email address
'   must have a @ symbol or period.
if (instr(1, chrShipEmail, "@") = 0) or _
   (instr(1, chrShipEmail, ".") = 0) then

    strError = strError & "Invalid email address<BR>"

end if
```

One additional check we need to do on the state and province fields is to ensure that both fields are not filled out. The above check just ensures that one or the other is filled out based on the country selected, but that would still allow the shopper to enter in both.

LISTING 8.17   ValidateShipping.asp Continued

```
'  Check to ensure that both the state and province fields
'  are filled in.
if (chrShipState <> "") and (chrShipProvince <> "") then

    strError = strError & _
      "You can not fill in both the " & _
      "state and province fields<BR>"

end if
```

Once we have done all of our validation, we are ready to store the values into the session variables corresponding to each field. This will ensure that whatever the shopper entered will be available for entry either into the payment page or back on the shipping page if there was an error.

LISTING 8.18   ValidateShipping.asp Continued

```
'  Copy the shipping values to session variables
session("chrShipFirstName") = request("chrShipFirstName")
session("chrShipLastName") = request("chrShipLastName")
session("chrShipAddress") = request("chrShipAddress")
session("chrShipCity") = request("chrShipCity")
session("chrShipState") = request("chrShipState")
session("chrShipProvince") = request("chrShipProvince")
session("chrShipCountry") = request("chrShipCountry")
session("chrShipZipCode") = request("chrShipZipCode")
session("chrShipPhone") = request("chrShipPhone")
session("chrShipEmail") = request("chrShipEmail")
```

We next check to see if there was an error set in our *strError* variable. If so, then we store the error in our session variable and send the shopper back to the shipping page to start again.

LISTING 8.19   ValidateShipping.asp Continued

```
' Check to see if an error was generated.
if strError <> "" then

    ' Store the error in a session variable and then direct
    ' the shopper back to the shipping page.
    session("Error") = strError
    Response.Redirect "shipping.asp"

else
```

If there were no errors, we are ready to continue. Since in many cases the shipping and billing information will be the same, we are going to set our session variables for the billing data to be the same as the shipping data. Then we send the user to the payment.asp page to continue the shopping process.

LISTING 8.20   ValidateShipping.asp Continued

```
' All of the data is correct, so we copy the shipping
' data to billing variables to default the data on the
' payment form.  That way the user does not have to
' retype their billing information if it is the same.
session("chrBillFirstName") = _
        request("chrShipFirstName")
session("chrBillLastName") = request("chrShipLastName")
session("chrBillAddress") = request("chrShipAddress")
session("chrBillCity") = request("chrShipCity")
session("chrBillState") = request("chrShipState")
session("chrBillProvince") = request("chrShipProvince")
session("chrBillCountry") = request("chrShipCountry")
session("chrBillZipCode") = request("chrShipZipCode")
session("chrBillPhone") = request("chrShipPhone")
session("chrBillEmail") = request("chrShipEmail")

' Send the user to the payment page.
Response.Redirect "Payment.asp"

end if

%>
```

The primary purpose of this page is to ensure that the shopper has the correct data entered for shipping information. We do some fairly basic validation on most of the fields to ensure that proper data has been entered.

Data Validation

In our sample application, we simply check to ensure a province or state is entered in conjunction with a proper country. And, we ensure that a zip code of some kind has been entered. But if we are dealing in volume orders to many international locations, potential costs of receiving bad data could be quite high. There are more options. For example, zip code loop-up data is available for validating zip codes against states selected. And, data is available for providing province selection options based on country selected. If needed, this level of validation could be performed as well.

Calculating Shipping and Tax

Now that we have valid shipping data, the shopper is moved to the next step. Before we jump into the payment page, we are going to diverge into the world of Visual Basic 6. As mentioned above, we want to build our line of business logic like tax and shipping into an encapsulated COM object that will be accessible from our ASP pages.

We are going to follow basic steps in building the COM object. The following list touches on each step.

1. Creation of a New Visual Basic 6 Project

2. Creation of a Class Object that will contain two functions for calculating tax and shipping

3. Programming of our business logic for accessing the database and calculating the appropriate values

4. Building of the DLL object that will contain the COM object

5. Implementing the COM object in our ASP Pages

To get started, we will need to open up Visual Basic and create a new project. Figure 8.4 shows the development tool at startup.

FIGURE 8.6:

Visual Basic 6 at startup

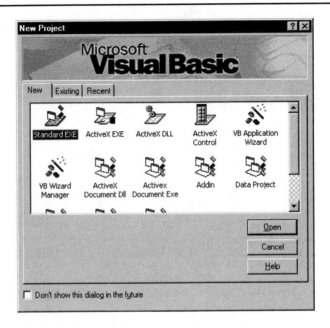

You have several options for the type of project to create. In this case, we are going to create an ActiveX DLL. This DLL will be installed on our server where the Web site is run. The DLL will be callable as a COM object in our ASP code.

Go ahead and create the new project. Save the project as ECStoreBizLogic. You will want to edit the project properties to ensure several settings are set up properly. From the Project menu select <Project> Properties where <Project> indicates ECStoreBizLogic. Figure 8.7 shows the properties dialog box.

On the General tab, be sure and set the Project Name to ECStoreBizLogic. Now click on the Make tab. We also want to set the Application Title to be ECStoreBizLogic. That will ensure that we can properly call the COM object from our ASP pages. Click OK and we are ready to continue in our project.

Since we will be using ADO as our database connectivity, we are going to ensure we have a reference for ADO in our Visual Basic project. To do this, select the Project menu again and select the References option. Figure 8.8 shows the dialog box.

FIGURE 8.7:

FIGURE 8.7:

Project Properties
dialog box

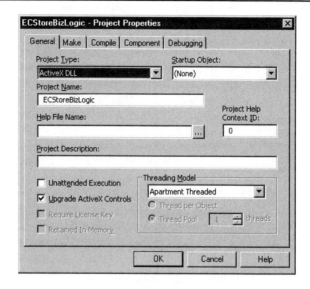

FIGURE 8.8:

References dialog box

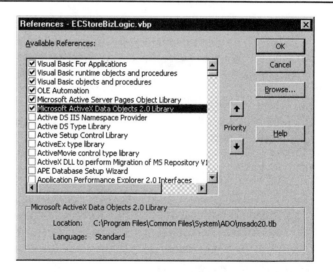

In the dialog box, select the Microsoft ActiveX Data Objects 2 Library. Click on
the OK button and the ADO objects will now be referenced in your project.

The next step is to work with the class object that is created in the project for us. We will need to rename it from `Class1` to `TaxShip`. In our ECStoreBizLogic COM object, we will call the `TaxShip` object specifically for the tax and shipping functions.

Now we are ready to begin working on our code in the class object. Be sure to double-click on the `TaxShip` class to open it up for editing. We are going to create two functions in our class, Tax and Shipping. The following are the declarations for each:

```
Public Function Tax(strState As String,
                    intOrderTotal As Long) As Long


Public Function Shipping(intQuantity As Long) As Long
```

For the Tax function, we will pass in the state and the order total to calculate the tax for the order. The return value to the calling application is a number representing the tax amount.

For the Shipping function we pass in the quantity of items in the order. Remember that shipping is based on the number of items in the basket. The value returned is the shipping total for the order.

Our class code starts out with the Option Explicit statement, as shown in Listing 8.21, indicating that all variables must be declared within the code. In the more robust and powerful Visual Basic development environment, this is a good practice.

Our first function, Tax, is started with our declaration. We then open a database connection using ADO. This is essentially the same connection code we are using in our ASP code.

The `sp_GetTaxRate` stored procedure is utilized to get the tax rate for the state that is passed into the function. We then check to see if any value was returned. If not then the tax charge is 0. If a rate is returned, the order total passed into the function is multiplied times the tax rate. The value is then returned to the calling application.

LISTING 8.21   **TaxShip.cls**

```
Option Explicit

'   This function will return the appropriate tax calculation
'   based on the order total and the ship to state.
```

```
Public Function Tax(strState As String, intOrderTotal As Long) As Long

'  Declare our variables
Dim dbTax As New ADODB.Connection
Dim rsTax As New ADODB.Recordset
Dim strSQL As String

'  Open the connection
dbTax.Open "filedsn=WildWillieCDs"

'  Creat the SQL statement and pass in the
'  state to get the appropriate rate
strSQL = "execute sp_GetTaxRate '" & strState & "'"

'  Get the record set.
Set rsTax = dbTax.Execute(strSQL)

'  See if a rate was returned.
If rsTax.EOF = False Then

    '  Set the amount of tax.
    Tax = (rsTax("fltTaxRate") * intOrderTotal)

Else

    '  Return no tax.
    Tax = 0

End If

End Function
```

Our next function is the shipping calculation. In this case we open an ADO data connection to retrieve the shipping rate structure from the database.

The sp_GetShippingRate stored procedure is utilized to retrieve the rate structure. The rates are looped through and checked against the quantity passed into the function. If the quantity falls within the low and high quantity values then the shipping rate is set.

LISTING 8.22   **TaxShip.asp Continued**

```
'  The shipping function will calculate the appropriate shipping
'  rate based on the quantity of items in the order.
Public Function Shipping(intQuantity As Long) As Long

'  Declare our variables.
Dim dbShipping As New ADODB.Connection
Dim rsShipping As New ADODB.Recordset
Dim strSQL As String

'  Open the connection
dbShipping.Open "filedsn=WildWillieCDs"

'  Declare the SQL statement
strSQL = "execute sp_GetShippingRate"

'  Retrieve the record set
Set rsShipping = dbShipping.Execute(strSQL)

'  Start out with a shipping rate of $0
Shipping = 0

'  Loop through the quantity settings
Do Until rsShipping.EOF

    '  Check to see if the quantity is between the
    '  current low and high values
    If intQuantity >= rsShipping("intLowQuantity") And _
       intQuantity <= rsShipping("intHighQuantity") Then

        '  If so set the shipping fee.
        Shipping = rsShipping("intFee")

    End If

    '  Move to the next row
    rsShipping.MoveNext

Loop

End Function
```

The sp_GetShippingRate stored procedure retrieves all of the shipping rate values from the Shipping table.

LISTING 8.23   **sp_GetShippingRate Stored Procedure**

```
/* Retrieve the shipping rates for the store */
CREATE PROCEDURE sp_GetShippingRate

AS

/* Return all of the shipping values */
select * from shipping
```

The sp_GetTaxRate stored procedure has the state abbreviation sent into it. It returns the rate for the specified state if it is set in the database.

LISTING 8.24   **sp_GetTaxRate Stored Procedure**

```
/* Return the tax rate setting for the store. */
CREATE PROCEDURE sp_GetTaxRate

/* Pass in the state */
@chrState varchar(2)

AS

/* Retrieve the tax rate for the specified state */
select fltTaxRate from tax where chrState = @chrState
```

That is it for our code. As you can see, it is fairly straightforward in terms of building the basic code for implementing tax and shipping. Now we are ready for deployment.

TIP   To test the code before deployment, it would be wise to start a second Visual Basic project with a standard form interface (Standard EXE). The DLL can be referenced in the references dialog box as EcStoreBizLogic. Then we can call the Tax and Shipping functions in our Visual Basic interface to ensure all is working properly before deployment.

To deploy the COM object, we need to compile the application into a DLL. Once a DLL is created, if it has been compiled on the server on which it will be deployed, then all we need to do is call the COM object appropriately. If it needs to be packaged up into a deployment package, the *Package and Deployment Wizard* provided in Visual Basic 6 can be utilized to deploy the DLL through a number of methods. See the Visual Basic 6 documentation on the appropriate steps to make this happen.

Once the DLL is deployed we can implement it within our ASP pages. As with creating an ADO connection, we will use the `server.createobject` syntax to implement our `EcStoreBizLogic` COM object. The following code example shows how the COM object would be utilized.

```
set EC = _
    server.CreateObject("ECStoreBizLogic.TaxShip")

Tax = EC.tax('VA', 10000)

Shipping = EC.Shipping(10)
```

In the first line of code, we are creating an instance of our `TaxShip` object. It will be referenced as *EC*. In the next line, we are calling the Tax function and passing in Virginia as the state and $100.00 as the order total. In the next line we are calling the Shipping function and passing in a quantity of 10 items.

Now that we have the business logic created for tax and shipping, we are ready to move on to the payment page for the final form the shopper will use to provide data entry.

Payment Page

The next page the shopper will see is the payment.asp page, as shown in Listing 8.25. This is the page where the shopper will enter in their credit card data and their billing address information.

This page is the critical last step in the process. The first thing we do is check to see if the shopper has come to this page from an appropriate route. We utilize the *HTTP_REFERER* variable of the ServerVariables collection of the request object. The *HTTP_REFERER* variable tells us what page the shopper linked from to get to this page. If that is not one of the shipping.asp, ValidatePayment.asp, or payment.asp (in other words, as a result of a refresh) pages then we know we need to send the user back to the shopping basket.

LISTING 8.25   Payment.asp

```
<%@ Language=VBScript %>
<%
'   ********************************************************
'   Payment.asp - The shopper will enter in their
'   payment information including credit card data.
'   ********************************************************

'   Check to ensure that the user only came to this page
'   from the shipping page, payment page (back button or
'   error), or a refresh of this page.  We utilize the
'   ServerVariables to read the HTTP header.
if instr(lcase(Request.ServerVariables("HTTP_REFERER")), _
        "shipping.asp") = 0 and _
    instr(lcase(Request.ServerVariables("HTTP_REFERER")), _
        "validatepayment.asp") = 0 and _
    instr(lcase(Request.ServerVariables("HTTP_REFERER")), _
        "payment.asp") = 0 then

    '   Send the user back to the basket
    Response.Redirect "basket.asp"

end if
```

Next we move onto the display of the shopper's final charges for the order. A database connection is opened and the sp_BasketSubtotal stored procedure is executed to retrieve the current subtotal for the shopping basket. Following that we execute the sp_BasketQuantity stored procedure to retrieve the current number of items in the basket. Note that both are stored in session variables for later reference when we go to store the order in the database.

LISTING 8.26   Payment.asp Continued

```
'   Create an ADO database connection
set dbBasket = server.createobject("adodb.connection")
```

```
'  Create the record set
set rsBasket = server.CreateObject("adodb.recordset")

'  Open the connection using our ODBC file DSN
dbBasket.open("filedsn=WildWillieCDs")

'  Build the SQL stored procedure to retrieve the basket
'  subtotal
sql = "execute sp_BasketSubtotal " & session("idBasket")

'  Execute the statement
set rsBasket = dbBasket.Execute(sql)

'  Retrieve the subtotal and store in a session variable.
SubTotal = rsBasket("subtotal")
session("Subtotal") = Subtotal

'  Now build a query to retrieve the basket quantity
sql = "execute sp_BasketQuantity " & session("idBasket")

'  Execute the statement
set rsBasket = dbBasket.Execute(sql)
```

Now we are ready to work with our Visual Basic COM object to calculate the tax and shipping for the store. An instance of our TaxShip object is created using the server.createobject syntax.

A check is done to ensure that the quantity returned was not 0 for some reason. If it is, the shopper is sent back to the basket. If not, then we execute the Shipping method and the shipping charge is returned for the basket. That value is then stored in a session variable.

| LISTING 8.27 | **Payment.asp Continued** |

```
'  Next we create our Bussiness Logic component to
'  calculate our tax and shipping.
set BizLogic = _
    server.CreateObject("ECStoreBizLogic.TaxShip")

'  Check the quantity returned from the database
if rsBasket("quantity") > 0 then
```

```
'  Call the shipping function of our component.  The
'  quantity is passed in and must be in a long data type
'  format.  The Shipping fee is returned.
     Shipping = BizLogic.Shipping(clng(rsBasket("quantity")))

else

     '  Redirect to the basket page since the quantity is 0
     Response.Redirect("Basket.asp")

end if

'  Store the shipping value in a session variable
session("Shipping") = Shipping

'  Store the quantity in a session variable
session("Quantity") = rsBasket("quantity")
```

Next we execute the Tax method of our COM object and pass in the current subtotal of the basket. The tax charges for the order are then stored in a session variable. Following that we calculate the total based on the subtotal, shipping, and tax.

LISTING 8.28   Payment.asp Continued

```
'  Calculate the tax by calling the Tax function of
'  our component.  We pass in the shipping state and the
'  order subtotal.  The value is also stored in a session
'  variable.
Tax = BizLogic.tax(session("chrShipState"), clng(subtotal))
session("Tax") = Tax

'  Calculate the total and store in a session variable.
Total = SubTotal + Shipping + Tax
session("Total") = Total

%>
```

Once we have all the checking and calculations out of the way, we are ready to begin building the payment page. It starts out in the usual fashion with the appropriate header include. We then first show the order recap based on the calculations we have just performed.

A simple table is created with each row displaying the appropriate values. First the subtotal is shown, followed by the shipping charge, then the tax charge, and finally the total for the basket. This will provide the shopper with a final charge that will be placed on their credit card.

LISTING 8.29   Payment.asp Continued

```
<HTML>

<!-- #include file="include/header.asp" -->

<BR>

<center>
<font size="5"><b>Billing Information</b></font>
</center>

<BR>
<b>Order Recap:</b>
<BR><BR>

<!-- Build a table to display the order total -->
<table>

<!--  Display the Subtotal -->
<tr>
    <td align="right">Subtotal:</td>
    <td><%=formatcurrency(Subtotal/100, 2)%></td>
</tr>

<!--  Display the Shipping Value -->
<tr>
    <td align="right">Shipping:</td>
    <td><%=formatcurrency(Shipping/100, 2)%></td>
</tr>

<!--  Display the Tax Value -->
<tr>
    <td align="right">Tax:</td>
    <td><%=formatcurrency(Tax/100, 2)%></td>
</tr>
```

```
<!--  Display the Total  -->
<tr>
    <td align="right"><B>Total:</b></td>
    <td><b><%=formatcurrency(Total/100, 2)%></b></td>
</tr>

</table>
```

The next section of the page builds the form fields for entering in the credit card data for the shopper. The form is going to post to the ValidatePayment.asp page.

The fields on the form include chrCCName for the name on the credit card, chrCCNumber for the credit card number, chrCCType for the type of credit card, chrCCExpMonth for the expiration month, and finally chrCCExpYear for the expiration year.

TIP

The first time the payment page is accessed, we may want to default the name on the credit card to the name in the profile. The only danger here is that if the name in the profile is something like *John Doe* and the name on the card is *John E. Doe* then the shopper may not think to put in the middle initial. This could be a problem when validating the credit card.

LISTING 8.30   Payment.asp Continued

```
<!--  Enter in the credit card information  -->
<BR>
<b>Enter your Credit Card information:</b>
<BR><BR>

<!--  The form will post the data to the validate payment page  -->
<form method="post" action="ValidatePayment.asp" id=form1 name=form1>

<!--  Table to display the credit card data  -->
<table>

<!--  Name on credit card  -->
<tr>
    <td align="right">Name on Card:</td>
    <td><input type="text" value="<%=session("chrCCName")%>"
               name="chrCCName" size="55"></td>
```

```
    </tr>

    <!--  Number on credit card -->
    <tr>
        <td align="right">Card Number:</td>
        <td><input type="text"
                   value="<%=session("chrCCNumber")%>"
                   name="chrCCNumber" size="25"></td>
    </tr>
```

In the credit card payment section, we have three option selection boxes. There is always the possibility that the shopper will make an error on this page and we will redirect the shopper back to this page. In that event, we want to be sure to make the default selections in each option box match what they previously selected.

As we saw on the shipping.asp page, we need to check to see what was selected previously through a series of check statements. If that option was previously selected then we set a matching variable name with the *Selected* text. Thus, when the options of the selection box are being built on the page, the variable that is set to the *Selected* value will show the *Selected* text in the appropriate option. The first selection box is for the card type.

LISTING 8.31   Payment.asp Continued

```
    <!--  Type of credit card -->
    <tr>
        <td align="right">Card Type:</td>
        <td>
        <!--  Check to see which card was previously selected  -->
        <%

        '  Check to see which card was selected previously
        '  if there was an error.
        if session("chrCCType") = "Visa" then
            SelVisa = "Selected"
        end if

        if session("chrCCType") = "MasterCard" then
            SelMasterCard = "Selected"
        end if

        if session("chrCCType") = "Amex" then
```

```
            SelAmex = "Selected"
      end if

      %>

      <!-- Select box with the selected card defaulted  -->
      <select name="chrCCType">
          <option value="Visa" <%=SelVisa%>>Visa
          <option value="MasterCard"
                  <%=SelMasterCard%>>Master Card
          <option value="Amex" <%=SelAmex%>>American Express
      </select>
```

The next selection box is for the expiration month for the card. Note that we are storing integers to represent the card month instead of month abbreviations. But, in the selection box, we are showing the full month name.

LISTING 8.32   **Payment.asp Continued**

```
      <%

      '  Check to see which month was selected previously
      '  if there was an error.
      if session("chrCCExpMonth") = "1" then
          SelJan = "Selected"
      end if

      if session("chrCCExpMonth") = "2" then
          SelFeb = "Selected"
      end if

      if session("chrCCExpMonth") = "3" then
          SelMar = "Selected"
      end if

      if session("chrCCExpMonth") = "4" then
          SelApr = "Selected"
      end if

      if session("chrCCExpMonth") = "5" then
          SelMay = "Selected"
      end if
```

```
if session("chrCCExpMonth") = "6" then
    SelJun = "Selected"
end if

if session("chrCCExpMonth") = "7" then
    SelJul = "Selected"
end if

if session("chrCCExpMonth") = "8" then
    SelAug = "Selected"
end if

if session("chrCCExpMonth") = "9" then
    SelSep = "Selected"
end if

if session("chrCCExpMonth") = "10" then
    SelOct = "Selected"
end if

if session("chrCCExpMonth") = "11" then
    SelNov = "Selected"
end if

if session("chrCCExpMonth") = "12" then
    SelDec = "Selected"
end if

%>

<!-- Select option box to allow the user to
     select a card expiration month -->
Month:
<select name="chrCCExpMonth">
    <option value="1" <%=SelJan%>>January
    <option value="2" <%=SelFeb%>>February
    <option value="3" <%=SelMar%>>March
    <option value="4" <%=SelApr%>>April
    <option value="5" <%=SelMay%>>May
    <option value="6" <%=SelJun%>>June
    <option value="7" <%=SelJul%>>July
```

```
            <option value="8" <%=SelAug%>>August
            <option value="9" <%=SelSep%>>September
            <option value="10" <%=SelOct%>>October
            <option value="11" <%=SelNov%>>November
            <option value="12" <%=SelDec%>>December
        </select>
```

Our final selection box is for the expiration year. The same logic is followed for building the default.

NOTE   Note that we are in a sense hard coding expiration years into the code. That means when it is no longer 1999, we will need to remove that option and probably tack a new option year onto the end. VBScript code could be written to automate building the list of years starting from the current year for X years. That would make the code logic for defaulting a previous selection a bit more complicated.

LISTING 8.33   Payment.asp Continued

```
<%

'   Check to see which year was selected previously
'   if there was an error.
if session("chrCCExpYear") = "1999" then
    Sel1999 = "Selected"
end if

if session("chrCCExpYear") = "2000" then
    Sel2000 = "Selected"
end if

if session("chrCCExpYear") = "2001" then
    Sel2001 = "Selected"
end if

if session("chrCCExpYear") = "2002" then
    Sel2002 = "Selected"
end if
```

```
%>

<!--  Option box to select the card expiration year -->
Year:
    <select name="chrCCExpYear">
    <option value="1999" <%=Sel1999%>>1999
    <option value="2000" <%=Sel2000%>>2000
    <option value="2001" <%=Sel2001%>>2001
    <option value="2002" <%=Sel2002%>>2002
</select>

    </td>
</tr>

</table>
```

The next step is to show any error messages that may have occurred during the validation process. In this case, as with the shipping.asp page, the Error session variable will be set to the appropriate error messages. We simply do a check to ensure that the variable is set and if so then it is displayed on the page. Once the error is displayed, the Error session variable is cleared.

LISTING 8.34   **Payment.asp Continued**

```
<%

'  Check to see if there was an error.
if session("Error") <> "" then

%>
<!--  Display the error message  -->
<BR>
<b>You have an error in your billing form,
please correct the data:</b><BR><BR>

<!--  Write out the error.   -->
<table>
<tr>
  <td width="70"> </td>
  <td><i><%=Response.Write(session("Error"))%></i></td>
</tr>
```

```
</table>
<BR><BR>
<%

'  Show the error.
session("Error") = ""

else

%>
```

Next we move to the billing address form for the page. Note that the fields either are going to be defaulted with the data received from the shipping page or they are going to be defaulted to values previously entered on this page.

TIP

It may be wise, given the type of shoppers visiting the store, to provide the shopper with an option on the shipping page of whether that data will be automatically copied over to this page. If you have a lot of business purchasers, then the shipping and billing addresses more often than not may be different. In that case, it could get tedious for the shopper to always have to overwrite the defaulted data. And, in that case as well, the profile data may need to be defaulted only on this page (if the shopper desires).

LISTING 8.35   Payment.asp Continued

```
<BR>
<b>Enter your billing address:</b>
<BR><BR>

<%

end if

%>

<center>
```

A table is constructed with each row representing one of the address fields. As with the shipping form, most of the fields are utilizing text boxes for data entry. The values of these text boxes are defaulted to the billing address session variables.

LISTING 8.36   **Payment.asp Continued**

```
<!-- Table that will diplay the billing information -->
<table>
<!-- Billing first name -->
<tr>
    <td align="right">First Name:</td>
    <td><input type="text" value="<%=session("chrBillFirstName")%>"
            name="chrBillFirstName" size="30"></td>
</tr>
<!-- Billing last name -->
<tr>
    <td align="right">Last Name:</td>
    <td><input type="text" value="<%=session("chrBillLastName")%>"
            name="chrBillLastName" size="30"></td>
</tr>
<!-- Billing address -->
<tr>
    <td align="right">Address:</td>
    <td><input type="text" value="<%=session("chrBillAddress")%>"
            name="chrBillAddress" size="30"></td>
</tr>
<!-- Billing city -->
<tr>
    <td align="right">City:</td>
    <td><input type="text" value="<%=session("chrBillCity")%>"
            name="chrBillCity" size="30"></td>
</tr>
```

The billing address state is handled the same way as the shipping address state is. It is even more important to ensure a previously selected state is defaulted since we are trying to match up what was selected on the shipping form. The same method applies for setting a corresponding variable with *Selected* to default the appropriate option.

LISTING 8.37   Payment.asp Continued

```asp
<!-- Billing state -->
<tr>
    <td align="right">State:</td>
    <td>

    <%

    '  Check to see which state was selected previously
    '  if there was an error.
    if session("chrBillState") = "AL" then
        SelAL = "Selected"
    end if

    if session("chrBillState") = "AK" then
        SelAK = "Selected"
    end if

    if session("chrBillState") = "AZ" then
        SelAZ = "Selected"
    end if

    if session("chrBillState") = "AR" then
        SelAR = "Selected"
    end if

    if session("chrBillState") = "CA" then
        SelCA = "Selected"
    end if

    if session("chrBillState") = "CT" then
        SelCT = "Selected"
    end if

    if session("chrBillState") = "CO" then
        SelCO = "Selected"
    end if

    if session("chrBillState") = "DC" then
        SelDC = "Selected"
```

```
end if

if session("chrBillState") = "DE" then
    SelDE = "Selected"
end if

if session("chrBillState") = "FL" then
    SelFL = "Selected"
end if

if session("chrBillState") = "GA" then
    SelGA = "Selected"
end if

if session("chrBillState") = "HI" then
    SelHI = "Selected"
end if

if session("chrBillState") = "ID" then
    SelID = "Selected"
end if

if session("chrBillState") = "IL" then
    SelIL = "Selected"
end if

if session("chrBillState") = "IN" then
    SelIN = "Selected"
end if

if session("chrBillState") = "IA" then
    SelIA = "Selected"
end if

if session("chrBillState") = "KS" then
    SelKS = "Selected"
end if

if session("chrBillState") = "KY" then
    SelKY = "Selected"
end if
```

```
if session("chrBillState") = "LA" then
    SelLA = "Selected"
end if

if session("chrBillState") = "ME" then
    SelME = "Selected"
end if

if session("chrBillState") = "MA" then
    SelMA = "Selected"
end if

if session("chrBillState") = "MD" then
    SelMD = "Selected"
end if

if session("chrBillState") = "MI" then
    SelMI = "Selected"
end if

if session("chrBillState") = "MN" then
    SelMN = "Selected"
end if

if session("chrBillState") = "MS" then
    SelMS = "Selected"
end if

if session("chrBillState") = "MO" then
    SelMO = "Selected"
end if

if session("chrBillState") = "MT" then
    SelMT = "Selected"
end if

if session("chrBillState") = "NE" then
    SelNE = "Selected"
end if

if session("chrBillState") = "NV" then
    SelNV = "Selected"
```

```
end if

if session("chrBillState") = "NH" then
    SelNH = "Selected"
end if

if session("chrBillState") = "NJ" then
    SelNJ = "Selected"
end if

if session("chrBillState") = "NM" then
    SelNM = "Selected"
end if

if session("chrBillState") = "NY" then
    SelNY = "Selected"
end if

if session("chrBillState") = "NC" then
    SelNC = "Selected"
end if

if session("chrBillState") = "ND" then
    SelND = "Selected"
end if

if session("chrBillState") = "OH" then
    SelOH = "Selected"
end if

if session("chrBillState") = "OK" then
    SelOK = "Selected"
end if

if session("chrBillState") = "OR" then
    SelOR = "Selected"
end if

if session("chrBillState") = "PA" then
    SelPA = "Selected"
end if
```

```
if session("chrBillState") = "RI" then
    SelRI = "Selected"
end if

if session("chrBillState") = "SC" then
    SelSC = "Selected"
end if

if session("chrBillState") = "SD" then
    SelSD = "Selected"
end if

if session("chrBillState") = "TN" then
    SelTN = "Selected"
end if

if session("chrBillState") = "TX" then
    SelTX = "Selected"
end if

if session("chrBillState") = "UT" then
    SelUT = "Selected"
end if

if session("chrBillState") = "VT" then
    SelVT = "Selected"
end if

if session("chrBillState") = "VA" then
    SelVA = "Selected"
end if

if session("chrBillState") = "WY" then
    SelWY = "Selected"
end if

if session("chrBillState") = "WI" then
    SelWI = "Selected"
end if

if session("chrBillState") = "WV" then
    SelWV = "Selected"
```

```
    end if

    if session("chrBillState") = "WA" then
        SelWA = "Selected"
    end if
%>
```

Once we have the appropriate option set for defaulting the right state, we can then build our state option box. Again note that the contents of each corresponding state variable will be displayed. Only the one that was previously selected will be set to the *Selected* keyword tag.

LISTING 8.38   **Payment.asp Continued**

```
<!-- Option box to select the billing state -->
<select name="chrBillState">
    <option value="">Select a State
    <option value="AL" <%=SelAL%>>Alabama
    <option value="AK" <%=SelAK%>>Alaska
    <option value="AZ" <%=SelAZ%>>Arizona
    <option value="AR" <%=SelAR%>>Arkansas
    <option value="CA" <%=SelCA%>>California
    <option value="CT" <%=SelCT%>>Connecticut
    <option value="CO" <%=SelCO%>>Colorado
    <option value="DC" <%=SelDC%>>D.C.
    <option value="DE" <%=SelDE%>>Delaware
    <option value="FL" <%=SelFL%>>Florida
    <option value="GA" <%=SelGA%>>eorgia
    <option value="HI" <%=SelHI%>>Hawaii
    <option value="ID" <%=SelID%>>Idaho
    <option value="IL" <%=SelIL%>>Illinois
    <option value="IN" <%=SelIN%>>Indiana
    <option value="IA" <%=SelIA%>>Iowa
    <option value="KS" <%=SelKS%>>Kansas
    <option value="KY" <%=SelKY%>>Kentucky
    <option value="LA" <%=SelLA%>>Louisiana
    <option value="ME" <%=SelME%>>Maine
    <option value="MA" <%=SelMA%>>Massachusetts
    <option value="MD" <%=SelMD%>>Maryland
    <option value="MI" <%=SelMI%>>Michigan
    <option value="MN" <%=SelMN%>>Minnesota
    <option value="MS" <%=SelMS%>>Mississippi
```

```
        <option value="MO" <%=SelMO%>>Missouri
        <option value="MT" <%=SelMT%>>Montana
        <option value="NE" <%=SelNE%>>Nebraska
        <option value="NV" <%=SelNV%>>Nevada
        <option value="NH" <%=SelNH%>>New Hampshire
        <option value="NJ" <%=SelNJ%>>New Jersey
        <option value="NM" <%=SelNM%>>New Mexico
        <option value="NY" <%=SelNY%>>New York
        <option value="NC" <%=SelNC%>>North Carolina
        <option value="ND" <%=SelND%>>North Dakota
        <option value="OH" <%=SelOH%>>Ohio
        <option value="OK" <%=SelOK%>>Oklahoma
        <option value="OR" <%=SelOR%>>Oregon
        <option value="PA" <%=SelPA%>>Pennsylvania
        <option value="RI" <%=SelRI%>>Rhode Island
        <option value="SC" <%=SelSC%>>South Carolina
        <option value="SD" <%=SelSD%>>South Dakota
        <option value="TN" <%=SelTN%>>Tennessee
        <option value="TX" <%=SelTX%>>Texas
        <option value="UT" <%=SelUT%>>Utah
        <option value="VT" <%=SelVT%>>Vermont
        <option value="VA" <%=SelVA%>>Virginia
        <option value="WA" <%=SelWA%>>Washington
        <option value="WY" <%=SelWY%>>Wyoming
        <option value="WI" <%=SelWI%>>Wisconsin
        <option value="WV" <%=SelWV%>>West Virginia
    </select>
```

The province option is also provided. This option is for all non-U.S. purchasers. Note that the billing addresses could feasibly be an international location and the shipping address be a domestic location or vice versa.

Following the province, we have the country for the billing address. Again, this operates in the same fashion to ensure the original country was defaulted.

LISTING 8.39   **Payment.asp Continued**

```
<!--  Or allow the user to select a billing province -->
or Province:<input type="text"
                    value="<%=session("chrBillProvince")%>"
                    name="chrBillProvince" size="15">
```

```
        </td>
    </tr>
    <!-- Country selection -->
    <tr>
        <td align="right">Country:</td>
        <td>

        <%

        ' Check to see which country was selected previously
        ' if there was an error.
        if session("chrBillCountry") = "US" then
            SelUS = "Selected"
        end if

        if session("chrBillCountry") = "CA" then
            SelCA = "Selected"
        end if

        if session("chrBillCountry") = "MX" then
            SelMX = "Selected"
        end if

        %>

        <!-- Option box for the billing country -->
        <select name="chrBillCountry">
            <option value="">Select a Country
            <option value="US" <%=SelUS%>>United States
            <option value="CA" <%=SelCA%>>Canada
            <option value="MX" <%=SelMX%>>Mexico
        </select>
        </td>
    </tr>
```

The rest of the address information defaults appropriately into text boxes.

LISTING 8.40   Payment.asp Continued

```
    <!-- Billing postal code -->
    <tr>
        <td align="right">Zip/Postal Code:</td>
```

```
<td><input type="text" value="<%=session("chrBillZipCode")%>"
            name="chrBillZipCode" size="30"></td>
</tr>
<!--  Billing phone number -->
<tr>
    <td align="right">Phone:</td>
    <td><input type="text" value="<%=session("chrBillPhone")%>"
            name="chrBillPhone" size="30"></td>
</tr>
<!--  Billing email address -->
<tr>
    <td align="right">Email:</td>
    <td><input type="text" value="<%=session("chrBillEmail")%>"
            name="chrBillEmail" size="30"></td>
</tr>
```

Now we hit the option where the shopper can work with their profile. We want to provide the option for the shopper to do two things. The first is to have their profile saved as a cookie on their machine. That way it will be automatically accessed next time they return. The second option is to have a password saved with the profile so they can retrieve their order status, or retrieve their profile from another machine where the cookie is not set.

NOTE The shopper could have the cookie set and have their profile retrieved on the next visit. But, if they do not have a password set, they will not be able to access the order status portion of the site. Even if a cookie is set, we are still requiring the e-mail address and password be entered to retrieve their order status.

We need to treat the default selection of the cookie option buttons the same as we treated the option select boxes. If the shopper has indicated in a previous visit, or by coming back to this page on an error, that one or the other option is preferred, we want to be sure to default to that value. In this case, we need to have the *Checked* keyword tag in the radio element. We follow the same logic as the option select boxes, but insert *Checked* instead of *Selected*.

LISTING 8.41   Payment.asp Continued

```
<!--  Cookie option to save the profile -->
<tr>
    <td align="right">Save Profile Cookie?</td>
```

```
<td>
<%
'  Check to see if a previous setting was selected.
if session("intCookie") = 1 then

    YesChecked = "CHECKED"

else

    NoChecked = "CHECKED"

end if
%>

<!--  Radio boxes to select the cookie setting  -->
<input type="radio" value="1" name="intCookie"
       <%=YesChecked%>> Yes
<input type="radio" value="0" name="intCookie"
       <%=NoChecked%>> No

</td>
</tr>
```

For the password field, we use a password HTML element type to ensure that the password is not directly displayed on the screen. The original password entered by the shopper is defaulted. But, note that the shopper also has an opportunity here to change their password by entering in a new one.

LISTING 8.42   **Payment.asp Continued**

```
<!--  Password field -->
<tr>
    <td align="right">Password for Shopper Profile:</td>
    <td><input type="password" value="<%=session("chrPassword")%>"
              name="chrPassword" size="10"></td>
</tr>
```

The page finally finishes out with a Submit button for our form and the appropriate form ending tag followed by the closing include for the page and ending page tags.

LISTING 8.43   **Payment.asp Continued**

```
<!--  Submit button -->
<tr>
    <td colspan="2" align="center">
        <input type="Submit" value="Submit" name="Submit">
    </td>
</tr>

</table>

</form>

</center>

<!-- #include file="include/footer.asp" -->

</BODY>
</HTML>
```

The sp_BasketQuantity stored procedure is used to retrieve the total number of basket items in the shopper's order. The ID of the basket is passed into the stored procedure. The SQL Sum function is utilized to total the intQuantity column of the BasketItem table.

LISTING 8.44   **sp_BasketQuantity Stored Procedure**

```
/*  Procedure to get the quantity of items
    in the basket */
CREATE PROCEDURE sp_BasketQuantity

/*  Pass in the ID of the basket */
@idBasket int

AS

/*  Select statement to sum up the quantity of items
    in the basket */
select quantity=sum(intQuantity)
from basketitem
where idBasket = @idBasket
```

The sp_BasketSubTotal stored procedure operates in much the same way. But in this case it is totaling the quantity times the price of each item in the BasketItem table for the specified shopper's basket.

LISTING 8.45   **sp_BasketSubTotal Stored Procedure**

```
/* Stored procedure to total the prices of the
   items in the basket. */
CREATE PROCEDURE sp_BasketSubTotal

/*  Pass in the ID of the basket */
@idBasket int

AS

/*  Retrieve the price and quantity of the items
    in the basket.  The sum is then calculated.
*/
select subtotal=sum(intQuantity * intPrice)
from basketitem where idBasket = @idBasket
```

Figure 8.9 shows our payment page defaulted with the data entered from our last interaction with the basket on the shipping page. Note that the payment data is not entered since this is our first visit to the page. Also, the appropriate state and country are defaulted as well.

At the top of the page we have our order recap displayed. In this case there is a tax amount since the shipping address is to Virginia and we charge 4.5% tax in Virginia. Our shipping fee is $2.00 since we had between 1 and 10 items in the shopping basket.

Next let's enter in our payment data. To test our payment validation, which we will explore next, enter in a credit card expiration date that is prior to the current date. Then finish filling out the rest of the data. Figure 8.10 shows the sample bad data.

FIGURE 8.9:

Payment page

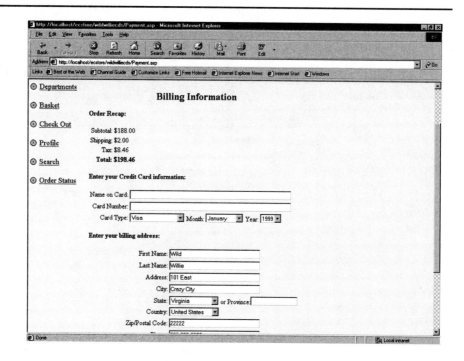

FIGURE 8.10:

Payment page with
bad data

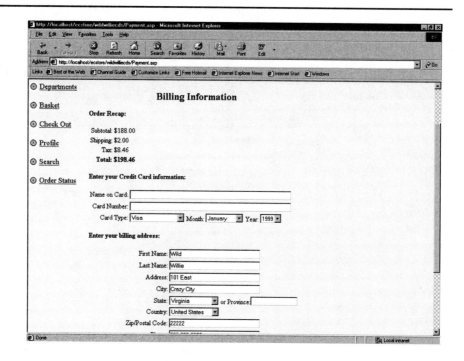

When we submit the page for validation, the payment page comes back with an error indicating that we have an invalid expiration date for our credit card.

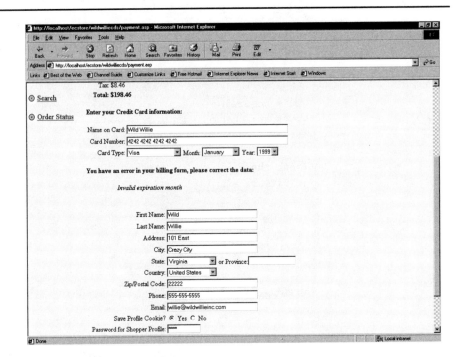

Now that the shopper can enter in their payment data, and we have seen it validated, let's explore the payment validation phase of the checkout process.

Validate Payment Page

The payment validation page is where it all comes together to complete the shopper's order. Certainly we need to validate the data and ensure everything is properly entered, but it is also where we will handle placing the order.

The first thing we do in the validation page is retrieve the data entered in by the user. A series of variables are set by calling the request function against the appropriate fields. Listing 8.46 shows the code for the ValidatePayment.asp page.

LISTING 8.46 ValidatePayment.asp

```
<%@ Language=VBScript %>
<%

'  Retrieve the credit card data
chrCCName = request("chrCCName")
chrCCNumber = request("chrCCNumber")
chrCCType = request("chrCCType")
chrCCExpMonth = request("chrCCExpMonth")
chrCCExpYear = request("chrCCExpYear")

'  Retrieve the billing data
chrBillFirstName = request("chrBillFirstName")
chrBillLastName = request("chrBillLastName")
chrBillAddress = request("chrBillAddress")
chrBillCity = request("chrBillCity")
chrBillState = request("chrBillState")
chrBillProvince = request("chrBillProvince")
chrBillCountry = request("chrBillCountry")
chrBillZipCode = request("chrBillZipCode")
chrBillPhone = request("chrBillPhone")
chrBillEmail = request("chrBillEmail")
chrPassword = request("chrPassword")
intCookie = request("intCookie")
```

We then start the error validation phase of the project. The first section check is against the payment data. The name on the credit card is checked to ensure something is entered.

LISTING 8.47 ValidatePayment.asp Continued

```
'  Check to see if a credit card name was entered
if chrCCName = "" then

    '  Build the error.
    strError = strError & "Invalid name on credit card<BR>"

end if
```

Next we will validate the credit card number. Typically the shopper enters in a credit card number as all one number, with dashes between the breaks in the number or with spaces in the breaks. In either case we want to be able to validate that it is an actual number.

The first thing we do is replace any dash characters or space characters with nothing, to convert the entered number into one long number. Then we can validate the number by ensuring it isn't blank and that it is a valid number.

LISTING 8.48   **ValidatePayment.asp Continued**

```
'   Replace any - characters or spaces to make it a
'   pure number
chrCCNumber = replace(chrCCNumber, "-", "")
chrCCNumber = replace(chrCCNumber, " ", "")

'   Check to ensure the credit card number is not blank and
'   is a number.
if (chrCCNumber = "") or (isNumeric(chrCCNumber) = False) then

    strError = strError & "Invalid credit card number<BR>"

end if
```

Next we validate the expiration date entered for the credit card. We have to ensure that the date entered is not earlier than the current date. First a check is done to see if the entered year is equal to the current year. If so, then we need to check and ensure that the month entered is not earlier than the current month. Then a check is done to ensure that the year entered isn't earlier than the current year.

LISTING 8.49   **ValidatePayment.asp Continued**

```
'   Check to see the year is equal to this year
if cint(chrCCExpYear) = year(date) then

    '   If it is the current year then we need to ensure the
    '   month is not earlier than the current month.
    if cint(chrCCExpMonth) < month(date) then

        strError = strError & "Invalid expiration month<BR>"

    end if
```

```
end if

'   Check to ensure the year is not less than the current year
if chrCCExpYear < year(date) then

    strError = strError & "Invalid expiration date<BR>"

end if
```

Credit Card Validation

Ensuring that proper credit card data has been retrieved is critical to ensuring we receive payment properly. There are a number of additional validation steps we can take to ensure the data is correct. The first is to utilize checksum calculations to ensure the credit card number meets the proper validation set forth by the credit card companies.

We can also use tools such as Cybercash to do live validation and clearing at the point the data is entered. There are even tools on the market that keep lists of fraudulent cards that can be checked against your customers' cards to ensure valid payment is being received.

Next we will move to the basic validation of the billing address data. The standard fields are validated to ensure that at least something has been entered into the fields.

LISTING 8.50   ValidatePayment.asp Continued

```
'   Ensure there is a first name
if chrBillFirstName = "" then

    strError = strError & "Invalid first name<BR>"

end if

'   Ensure there is a last name
if chrBillLastName = "" then

    strError = strError & "Invalid last name<BR>"

end if
```

```
'  Ensure a billing address was entered
if chrBillAddress = "" then

    strError = strError & "Invalid address<BR>"

end if

'  Ensure a billing city was entered.
if chrBillCity = "" then

    strError = strError & "Invalid city<BR>"

end if
```

As on the shipping page, we will need to validate the shipping country and shipping state. Again, we need to ensure that a U.S. state is selected when the United States has been selected as the country. If the country is not the United States, then we need to ensure a province is entered along with an international country.

LISTING 8.51   ValidatePayment.asp Continued

```
'  Check to see if an international country or
'  US was entered.
if chrBillCountry = "US" then

    '  Ensure a bill to state was entered
    if chrBillState = "" then

        strError = strError & "Invalid state<BR>"

    end if

else

    '  If it is an international country then
    '  ensure a province was entered
    if chrBillProvince = "" then

        strError = strError & "Invalid province<BR>"
```

```
        end if

    end if

    '  Ensure a bill to country was entered
    if chrBillCountry = "" then

        strError = strError & "Invalid country<BR>"

    end if
```

The rest of the fields are validated per the standard fashion. The e-mail address is again validated to ensure both an @ sign and a dot are entered.

LISTING 8.52   ValidatePayment.asp Continued

```
    '  Ensure a bill to zip code was entered
    if chrBillZipCode = "" then

        strError = strError & "Invalid zip code<BR>"

    end if

    '  Ensure a bill to phone was entered
    if chrBillPhone = "" then

        strError = strError & "Invalid phone number<BR>"

    end if

    '  Validate the email address to ensure it has an '@' sign
    '  and a '.'
    if (instr(1, chrBillEmail, "@") = 0) or _
       (instr(1, chrBillEmail, ".") = 0) then

        strError = strError & "Invalid email address<BR>"

    end if
```

As before we also check to ensure that a province *or* a state has been entered (not *both*).

LISTING 8.53   ValidatePayment.asp Continued

```
' Ensure that the user didn't enter in both a state and province.
if (chrBillState <> "") and (chrBillProvince <> "") then

    strError = strError & "You can not fill in both " & _
                          "the state and province " & _
                          "fields<BR>"


end if
```

Finally, we check to see if an error has been set. If it has been set, then we copy the data entered by the shopper into session variables. These session variables will be retrieved in the payment.asp page to default the form back to the data entered in by the shopper.

The Error session variable is set. Then the shopper is redirected back to the payment.asp page to update the data they entered.

LISTING 8.54   ValidatePayment.asp Continued

```
' Check to see if there was an error.
if strError <> "" then

    ' Retrieve all of the billing data and store it in session
    ' variables
    session("chrCCName") = request("chrCCName")
    session("chrCCNumber") = request("chrCCNumber")
    session("chrCCType") = request("chrCCType")
    session("chrCCExpMonth") = request("chrCCExpMonth")
    session("chrCCExpYear") = request("chrCCExpYear")
    session("chrBillFirstName") = _
            request("chrBillFirstName")
    session("chrBillLastName") = request("chrBillLastName")
    session("chrBillAddress") = request("chrBillAddress")
    session("chrBillCity") = request("chrBillCity")
    session("chrBillState") = request("chrBillState")
    session("chrBillProvince") = request("chrBillProvince")
```

```
        session("chrBillCountry") = request("chrBillCountry")
        session("chrBillZipCode") = request("chrBillZipCode")
        session("chrBillPhone") = request("chrBillPhone")
        session("chrBillEmail") = request("chrBillEmail")
        session("chrPassword") = request("chrPassword")

        '  Store the error in a session variable
        session("Error") = strError

        '  Send the user back to the payment page
        Response.Redirect "payment.asp"

    else
```

If the order is valid, we then start the process of completing the order. This is going to happen in several steps, as outlined in Table 8.4.

TABLE 8.4: Order Completion Steps

Order Completion Step	Description
Clean the data	We will need to ensure the shipping data is ready to be inserted into the SQL database.
Retrieve the data	The data entered into the form is retrieved again and set in session variables.
Insert the order data	The order data is inserted into the database.
Insert the payment data	The payment data is inserted into the database.
Initialize order status	The order status tracking for this order is initialized.
Update basket	The basket data is updated.
Update profile	The profile is updated.
Send e-mail receipt	An e-mail receipt is sent to the shopper.
Write out cookie	A cookie with the profile ID is set.

Now let's take a look at the code behind each of these steps. First we will clean the shipping data. We need to ensure that any single quotes (or apostrophes) that may be entered in the shipping data (like O'Malley) are doubled up for our insert into the database.

LISTING 8.55   **ValidatePayment.asp Continued**

```
' We are ready to store and finish the order.  This
' happens in many steps.


'****************************************************
'**** 1.  Clean the data.
'****************************************************


' Ensure that the shipping data is validated for SQL
' inserts.  We will check for single quotes and double
' them up
session("chrShipFirstName") = _
replace(session("chrShipFirstName"), "'", "''")
session("chrShipLastName") = session("chrShipLastName")
session("chrShipAddress") = session("chrShipAddress")
session("chrShipCity") = session("chrShipCity")
session("chrShipProvince") = session("chrShipProvince")
```

Next we are ready to retrieve the billing data to prepare for insertion into the database. We check the fields for an appropriate replacement of single quotes for insertion into the database.

LISTING 8.56   **ValidatePayment.asp Continued**

```
'****************************************************
'**** 2.  Retrieve the data
'****************************************************


' Retrieve all of the payemnt data and ensure that it
' is ready for a SQL insert.
session("chrCCName") = _
      replace(request("chrCCName"), "'", "''")
session("chrCCNumber") = request("chrCCNumber")
session("chrCCType") = request("chrCCType")
```

```
session("chrCCExpMonth") = request("chrCCExpMonth")
session("chrCCExpYear") = request("chrCCExpYear")
session("chrBillFirstName") = _
        replace(request("chrBillFirstName"), "'", "''")
session("chrBillLastName") = _
    replace(request("chrBillLastName"), "'", "''")
session("chrBillAddress") = _
    replace(request("chrBillAddress"), "'", "''")
session("chrBillCity") = _
        replace(request("chrBillCity"), "'", "''")
session("chrBillState") = request("chrBillState")
session("chrBillProvince") = _
        replace(request("chrBillProvince"), "'", "''")
session("chrBillCountry") = request("chrBillCountry")
session("chrBillZipCode") = request("chrBillZipCode")
session("chrBillPhone") = request("chrBillPhone")
session("chrBillEmail") = request("chrBillEmail")
session("chrPassword") = request("chrPassword")
session("intCookie") = request("intCookie")
```

Now that all of the data is finalized, we are ready to execute an insert into the database. An ADO database connection is opened up to handle the database connectivity.

Then we start building a long SQL insert statement. The stored procedure to be utilized is the sp_InsertOrderData. All of the billing and shipping fields are inserted into the database. This particular stored procedure returns an ID of the order so that we can give the order number to the shopper. This is stored in a session variable for use on the confirmation.asp page.

LISTING 8.57   ValidatePayment.asp Continued

```
'**************************************************
'**** 3.  Insert the order information into
'****     the database
'**************************************************

'  Create an ADO database connection
set dbOrderData = _
        server.createobject("adodb.connection")
set rsOrderData = _
```

```
          server.CreateObject("adodb.recordset")

     '  Open the connection using our ODBC file DSN
     dbOrderData.open("filedsn=WildWillieCDs")

     '  SQL insert statement to insert the the order
     '  data into the OrderData table.
     sql = "execute sp_InsertOrderData " & _
          session("idShopper") & ", '" & _
          session("chrShipFirstName") & "', '" & _
          session("chrShipLastName") & "', '" & _
          session("chrShipAddress") & "', '" & _
          session("chrShipCity") & "', '" & _
          session("chrShipState") & "', '" & _
          session("chrShipProvince") & "', '" & _
          session("chrShipCountry") & "', '" & _
          session("chrShipZipCode") & "', '" & _
          session("chrShipPhone") & "', '" & _
          session("chrShipEmail") & "', '" & _
          session("chrBillFirstName") & "', '" & _
          session("chrBillLastName") & "', '" & _
          session("chrBillAddress") & "', '" & _
          session("chrBillCity") & "', '" & _
          session("chrBillState") & "', '" & _
          session("chrBillProvince") & "', '" & _
          session("chrBillCountry") & "', '" & _
          session("chrBillZipCode") & "', '" & _
          session("chrBillPhone") & "', '" & _
          session("chrBillEmail") & "', " & _
          session("idBasket")

     '  Execute the SQL statement
     set rsOrderData = dbOrderData.execute(sql)
     session("idOrder") = rsOrderData("idOrder")
```

Remember that we are storing the payment data separately from the order data. This is to allow easy management of credit card data, which we likely will not store for the long term. The sp_InsertPaymentData stored procedure is called. The credit card data along with the ID of the order are stored.

LISTING 8.58   ValidatePayment.asp Continued

```
'****************************************************
'**** 4.  Insert the payment information into
'****        the database
'****************************************************


'  Build a SQL statement to insert the
'  payment data into the paymentdata table
sql = "execute sp_InsertPaymentData " & _
      session("idOrder") & ", '" & _
      session("chrCCType") & "', '" & _
      session("chrCCNumber") & "', '" & _
      session("chrCCExpMonth") & "/" & _
      session("chrCCExpYear") & "', '" & _
      session("chrCCName") & "'"


'  Execute the SQL statement
set rsOrderData = dbOrderData.execute(sql)
```

Next we will need to initialize the order history for the order. The first status is that of the order being received. The `sp_InitializeOrderStatus` stored procedure is utilized. Note that the use of the stored procedure encapsulates the business rules behind order tracking. That way if the codes for initial status change, the programming in this page will not have to be changed.

LISTING 8.59   ValidatePayment.asp Continued

```
'****************************************************
'**** 5.  Initialize the order status tracking
'****        to indicate the order is received
'****************************************************


'  Build a SQL statement to insert the
'  payment data into the paymentdata table
sql = "execute sp_InitializeOrderStatus " & _
      session("idOrder")


'  Execute the SQL statement
set rsOrderData = dbOrderData.execute(sql)
```

The next step is to ensure the basket has the final data. Remember that the shopping basket stores the total quantity, subtotal, shipping fees, tax fees, and final total. Remember that business rules such as shipping and tax calculations can change over time. We want the basket to hold a snapshot of what the charges are at this point in time.

LISTING 8.60   ValidatePayment.asp Continued

```
'*************************************************
'**** 6.   Update the basket with the final
'****      order data.
'*************************************************

'  Finally we need to update the basket with the final
'  amounts for quantity, subtotal, shipping, tax and
'  total
sql = "execute sp_UpdateBasket " & _
        session("idBasket") & ", " & _
        session("Quantity") & ", " & _
        session("Subtotal") & ", " & _
        session("Shipping") & ", " & _
        session("Tax") & "," & _
        session("Total") & ", 1"

'  Execute the SQL statement
set rsOrderData = dbOrderData.execute(sql)
```

The next step is to update the profile of the shopper. Remember that if no previous profile can be retrieved, a new profile is created when the shopper begins browsing through the store.

The sp_UpdateShopper stored procedure handles updating the data. We are using the billing information and the long-term profile data. It is conceivable that we could also store the shipping data and have that retrieved at a later date.

Note that the cookie and password are both set as well. If the shopper does not enter in a password, then there is no way they can retrieve the profile for order history status retrieve. If they have the cookie set, the profile will be retrieved automatically upon the next visit.

LISTING 8.61   ValidatePayment.asp Continued

```
'*************************************************
'**** 7.  Update the profile based on the new
'****     billing information.
'*************************************************

'  Create an ADO database connection
set dbProfile = server.createobject("adodb.connection")

'  Open the connection using our ODBC file DSN
dbProfile.open("filedsn=WildWillieCDs")

'  SQL update statement to update the profile in the
'  database
sql = "execute sp_UpdateShopper  '" & _
      session("chrBillFirstName") & "', '" & _
      session("chrBillLastName") & "', '" & _
      session("chrBillAddress") & "', '" & _
      session("chrBillCity") & "', '" & _
      session("chrBillState") & "', '" & _
      session("chrBillProvince") & "', '" & _
      session("chrBillCountry") & "', '" & _
      session("chrBillZipCode") & "', '" & _
      session("chrBillPhone") & "', '" & _
      session("chrBillFax") & "', '" & _
      session("chrBillEmail") & "', '" & _
      session("chrPassword") & "', " & _
      session("intCookie") & ", " & _
      session("idShopper")

      '  Execute the SQL statement
      dbProfile.execute(sql)
```

It has become almost mandatory that an e-mail confirmation receipt go out when an order is completed. We can accomplish this fairly easily with the Collaboration Data Objects for Windows NT (CDONTS). The NewMail object supports easily sending e-mail from an NT server using an SMTP server. Table 8.5 outlines the key properties and methods of the NewMail object.

TABLE 8.5 The NewMail Object's key properties and methods

Property/Method	Description
Bcc	Blind copy e-mail addresses.
Body	The text of the e-mail message.
BodyFormat	Sets the text format of the messages. Options include HTML or Text.
Cc	The copy e-mail addresses.
ContentBase	Sets the base for all URLs relating to the message body.
ContentLocation	Indicates the location of any data URLs in the message body.
From	The e-mail address of who the message is from.
Importance	Sets the importance associated with the e-mail address.
MailFormat	Sets the encoding of the NewMail object. Options include Mime and Text.
Subject	Sets the subject of the message.
To	Sets the e-mail address the mail is being sent to.
Value	Sets the value and contents of an additional header for the NewMail object.
Version	Indicates the CDONTS version.
AttachFile	Adds an attachment to the message by reading a file.
AttachUrl	Adds an attachment to the message and associates a Uniform Resource Locator (URL) with the attachment.
Send	Sends the NewMail object to the specified recipients.
SetLocalIds	Sets identifiers that define a messaging user's locale.

TIP

Understanding how to utilize the SMTP server provided with Windows NT is beyond the scope of this book. The Microsoft Developer Network (MSDN) provides good information on utilizing the tool. You are not limited to just using the Microsoft SMTP server; the option stands for using any SMTP compatible mail server along with other objects available besides CDONTS for sending e-mail.

We start out by creating an instance of the `NewMail` object using the `Server` `.CreateObject` method. We then set the appropriate properties of the object. The *To* property is the e-mail address of the billing recipient. The *Subject* is set to indicate this is a receipt.

Then we build the body of the e-mail. In this case we are going to send an order ID and the final totals on the basket. If we wanted, we could loop through the basket items and provide a complete summary order detail. But the shopper can always retrieve that by visiting the site.

We set the *Body* property to the *strBody* variable. Then we are ready to send the message using the *Send* method of the `NewMail` object.

LISTING 8.62   **ValidatePayment.asp Continued**

```
'**************************************************
'**** 8.  Send an email receipt to the shopper
'**************************************************

set Mailer = Server.CreateObject("CDONTS.NewMail")
Mailer.From = "support@wildwillieinc.com"
Mailer.To = session("chrBillEmail")
Mailer.Subject = "Wild Willie CD Receipt"

strBody = "Thank You for your Order!" & _
          vbCrLf & vbCrLf

strBody = strBody & "Order Id = " & _
          session("idOrder") & vbCrLf

strBody = strBody & "Subtotal = " & _
        formatcurrency(session("Subtotal")/100, 2) & _
        vbCrLf

strBody = strBody & "Subtotal = " & _
        formatcurrency(session("Shipping")/100, 2) & _
        vbCrLf

strBody = strBody & "Subtotal = " & _
        formatcurrency(session("Tax")/100, 1) & vbCrLf

strBody = strBody & "Subtotal = " & _
```

```
          formatcurrency(session("Total")/100, 2) & _
          vbCrLf & vbCrLf

strBody = strBody & "Please call 1-800-555-Wild " & _
          "with any questions.    "

strBody = strBody & "Be sure and check back to " & _
          "retrieve your order status."

Mailer.Body = strBody

Mailer.Send
```

The last step in the process is to see if the user wants a cookie set to make retrieving their profile easier. To do this we will use the Cookies collection of the Request object. The name of our cookie is *WWCD* (for Wild Willie's CDs). All we need to store in the cookie is the ID of the shopper.

We also need to set an expiration date to make the cookie stay "permanently" on the machine. That is done with the *Expires* property of the cookies collection. When that is completed, we are ready to send the shopper on to the confirmation page.

LISTING 8.63   **ValidatePayment.asp Continued**

```
'**************************************************
'**** 9.  Write out a cookie if the user
'****       requested it to be written
'**************************************************

'  Write out the cookie if they selected the 'Yes'
'  radio button.
if request("intCookie") = 1 then

    Response.Cookies("WWCD") = session("idShopper")

    Response.Cookies("WWCD").Expires = _
            "December 31, 2001"

end if

'  Send the user to the confirmation page
```

```
        Response.Redirect "Confirmed.asp"

end if

%>
```

Multiple stored procedures are utilized on this page to handle the checkout process. The first is the `sp_IntializeOrderStatus` stored procedure. In this case we pass in the ID of the order. A new row is then inserted into the OrderStatus table. Note that the `idStage` field in the database is defaulted to *0* when the initial insert is done.

LISTING 8.64   sp_InitializeOrderStatus Stored Procedure

```
/*  Initialize the order status table for
    a new order */
CREATE PROCEDURE sp_InitializeOrderStatus

/*  Pass in the ID of the order */
@idOrder int

AS

/*  Insert the new order status and set the ID of
    the order */
insert into OrderStatus(idOrder) values(@idOrder)
```

The next stored procedure is `sp_InsertOrderData`. This stored procedure takes in all of the key shipping and billing data. It then executes an insert statement to create the new order data. Note that this data is independent of the profile data for the shopper. Again, that can change over time.

LISTING 8.65   sp_InsertOrderData Stored Procedure Continued

```
/*  Stored procedure to insert the order data
    into the database.
*/
CREATE PROCEDURE sp_InsertOrderData

/*  All key values are inserted into the
```

```
      database.
*/
@idShopper int,
@chrShipFirstName varchar(150),
@chrShipLastName varchar(150),
@chrShipAddress varchar(150),
@chrShipCity varchar(150),
@chrShipState varchar(25),
@chrShipProvince varchar(150),
@chrShipCountry varchar(150),
@chrShipZipCode varchar(150),
@chrShipPhone varchar(150),
@chrShipEmail varchar(150),
@chrBillFirstName varchar(150),
@chrBillLastName varchar(150),
@chrBillAddress varchar(150),
@chrBillCity varchar(150),
@chrBillState varchar(25),
@chrBillProvince varchar(150),
@chrBillCountry varchar(150),
@chrBillZipCode varchar(150),
@chrBillPhone varchar(150),
@chrBillEmail varchar(150),
@idBasket int

AS

/*  Insert the data */
insert into orderdata(idShopper, chrShipFirstName,
                  chrShipLastName, chrShipAddress,
                  chrShipCity, chrShipState,
                  chrShipProvince, chrShipCountry,
                  chrShipZipCode, chrShipPhone,
                  chrShipEmail, chrBillFirstName,
                  chrBillLastName, chrBillAddress,
                  chrBillCity, chrBillState,
                  chrBillProvince, chrBillCountry,
                  chrBillZipCode, chrBillPhone,
                  chrBillEmail, idBasket)

        values(@idShopper, @chrShipFirstName,
                  @chrShipLastName, @chrShipAddress,
```

```
                              @chrShipCity, @chrShipState,
                              @chrShipProvince, @chrShipCountry,
                              @chrShipZipCode, @chrShipPhone,
                              @chrShipEmail, @chrBillFirstName,
                              @chrBillLastName, @chrBillAddress,
                              @chrBillCity, @chrBillState,
                              @chrBillProvince, @chrBillCountry,
                              @chrBillZipCode, @chrBillPhone,
                              @chrBillEmail, @idBasket)

 select idOrder = @@identity
```

The last statement in the SQL stored procedure is to select the value of the *@@identity* variable into the *idOrder* return value. This *@@identity* is set to the last value of an identity column insert for the specified table. In this case, the idOrder column of the OrderData table is returned.

The next stored procedure handles inserting the payment data into the database. The stored procedure takes in the ID of the order, the card type, the card number, the expiration date, and the name on the card. Note that the expiration date is the combination of the expiration month and expiration year from our form. The stored procedure then inserts the data into the paymentdata table.

LISTING 8.66   sp_InsertPaymentData Stored Procedure

```
/*  Stored Procedure used to insert payment
    from an order.
*/
CREATE PROCEDURE sp_InsertPaymentData

/*  Pass in the order id, credit card type, credit
    card number, credit card expiration date and name
    of the customer on the card.
*/
@idOrder int,
@chrCardType varchar(100),
@chrCardNumber varchar(50),
@chrExpDate varchar(25),
@chrCardName varchar(150)

AS
```

```
/*  Insert the data into the paymentdata table */
insert into paymentdata(idOrder, chrCardType,
          chrCardNumber, chrExpDate,
          chrCardName)

     values(@idOrder, @chrCardType,
          @chrCardNumber, @chrExpDate,
          @chrCardName)
```

That does it for payment data validation. At then end of this code, the shopper has successfully completed an order and updated their profile. Now they are ready to get their order number and move on.

Confirmation Page

The confirmation page is fairly straightforward. The primary purpose is to provide an initial indicator the order is completed. The shopper will be thanked for their order and receive their order number for tracking.

The first thing we do in the page is check to ensure an order ID is set for the page. If not, then the shopper should not be accessing this page. The shopper is sent back to the basket page where they can continue shopping.

LISTING 8.67   **Confirmed.asp**

```
<%@ Language=VBScript %>
<!--
    Confirmed.asp - Displays the order number and thanks the user
-->
<%
    ' Ensure an order id was returned
    if session("idOrder") = "" then Response.Redirect "basket.asp"
%>
```

The page then starts out with the usual header. We show a thank-you message as well. Then the order ID is shown by accessing the session variable.

The last thing we want to do is ensure that all session data is cleared in case the shopper decides to continue shopping. This is done using the Abandon method of the session object.

LISTING 8.68 **Confirmed.asp Continued**

```
<HTML>

<!-- #include file="include/header.asp" -->

Thank you for your order!  Have fun grooving to the cool
music you have ordered! <BR><BR>

<!-- Show the order ID returned from the database. -->
Your order number is <B><%=session("idOrder")%></b> for your refer-
ence.<BR>

<%

' Clear the session so all data is lost.  This way
' we ensure that the old basket is not retrieved, etc.
session.Abandon

%>

<!-- #include file="include/footer.asp" -->

</BODY>
</HTML>
```

Figure 8.12 shows the confirmation page upon completing our order. And, if you try and click on the shopping basket, your contents will be cleared and a new shopping session will be started.

FIGURE 8.12:

The confirmation page

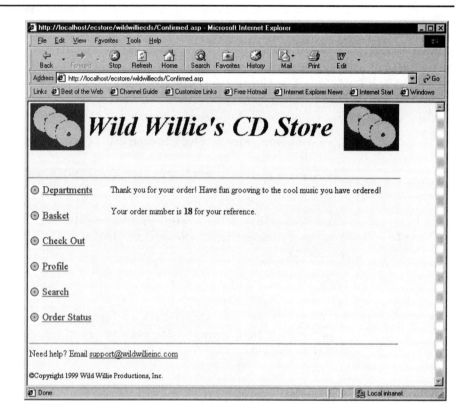

Summary

The shopper has finally made it to completing an order. Our sample shopping system provides all of the key processes for browsing, managing a basket, and checking out. As noted throughout this chapter, there are many different options on how the checkout process is managed. But the bottom line goal is to quickly allow the shopper to check out and ensure we collect as valid data as possible.

The goal in the next chapter will be to manage the shopper's interaction the next time they visit the site. This will include profile management and order history retrieval.

CHAPTER

NINE

9

Order Status and Profile Management

- Order History Management

- Profile Interface

- Order History Interface

We are on the last leg of building the shopper experience. In this section, we are going to work on the profile interface for the shopper and managing the order history interface. These are the post-purchasing touches that help facilitate the customer service aspects of the online store.

Order History Management

We hope we have built a store that will drive shoppers to purchase many times over and over. We want to be able to let the shopper retrieve their order history right up to the status of the last order. Table 9.1 outlines the order status options that will be tracked on each order.

T A B L E 9 . 1 : Order Status Settings

Order Status Setting	Description
0	The order has been retrieved from the system.
1	The order has been fulfilled and is ready for shipment.
2	The order has been shipped. A corresponding shipping number may be provided.

The initial order status when an order is placed is set to 0. In the next section, we will be working on building management tools for updating the order status.

The process for retrieving the order history is fairly straightforward. Figure 9.1 shows the basic process.

FIGURE 9.1:

The Order History process

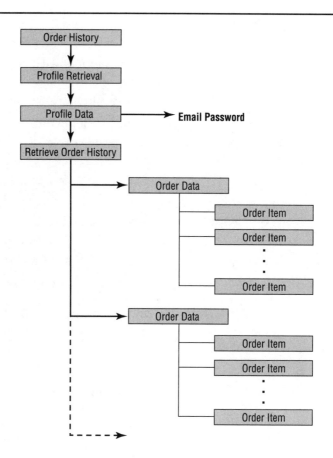

First the shopper will go to the Order History page. They will be presented with a login page. If they cannot remember their username and password, they have the option to have the password e-mailed to the profile's e-mail address.

If they do remember their username and password, then they are granted access to a listing of their orders and the status. They can then select an order and get a complete order recap.

Before we jump into the order history process, let's review the profile interface tools. This is the interface for accessing an existing profile and being able to update it.

Profile Interface

On the navigation menu for the shopper we have had an option to work with the profile, but haven't explored it yet. When the shopper clicks on the link, she is presented with an option to check in with an e-mail address and password.

The profile.asp page provides the login form. The page starts with the include structure per the standard on the rest of the site. Then some appropriate customer service text is presented next.

Figure 9.2 shows the other possibility for accessing a profile in the checkout process. If that shopper has purchased before and has moved to a new machine, she can still retrieve her profile.

FIGURE 9.2:

Empty shipping form

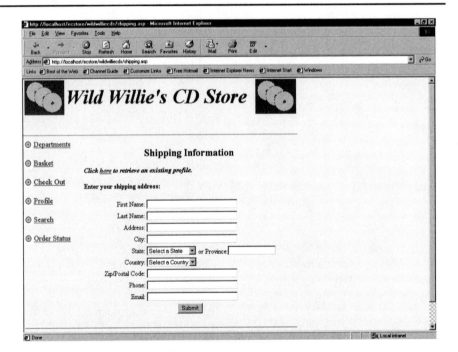

LISTING 9.1   Profile.asp

```
<%@ Language=VBScript %>
<HTML>
<!--
    Profile.asp - Display a login in to the profile.
```

```
-->

<!-- #include file="include/header.asp" -->

To retrieve your profile, please enter in
your email address and password.
<BR><BR>

<b><i>Note:</b></i> If you do NOT have a username or
password, upon your first purchase you will have the
option to create one.

<BR><BR>
```

The form is built and will be posted to the ProfileDisplay.asp page. The form has two fields, e-mail and password. Then the form is ended along with the page.

LISTING 9.2   **Profile.asp Continued**

```
<!-- Form to post the request -->
<form method="post" action="ProfileDisplay.asp">

<!-- Table that allows the user to enter in an email
     address and password.
-->
<table>
<tr>
  <td align="right">
    email:
  </td>
  <td>
    <input type="text" name="email" value="">
  </td>
</tr>
<tr>
  <td align="right">
    Password:
  </td>
  <td>
    <input type="password" name="password" value="">
  </td>
</tr>
<tr>
```

```
          <td colspan="2" align="center">
             <input type="submit" value="Submit" name="submit">
          </td>
       </tr>
    </table>

    </form>

    <!-- #include file="include/footer.asp" -->

    </BODY>
    </HTML>
```

Figure 9.3 shows the profile login page. Enter in an invalid e-mail name and password.

FIGURE 9.3:

Profile login page

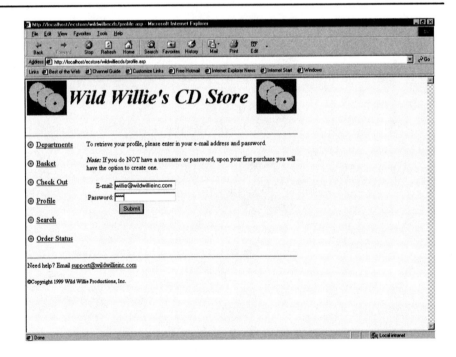

Figure 9.4 shows the page that is presented if the shopper was unable to log in properly. We want to be able to provide a way for the shopper to retrieve their password.

FIGURE 9.4:

Error page when logging in

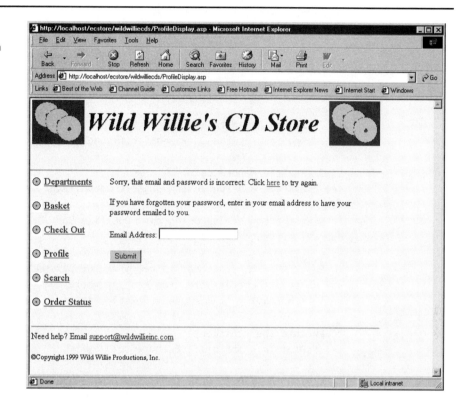

The e-mail password page will also use CDONTS to e-mail the password to the shopper. The idea on the security is that we will only e-mail a password to a corresponding e-mail address. That way, only the e-mail address owner can receive his own password. So, if someone is trying to breach security and get into someone's profile or order history, she will first have to get into the e-mail of the targeted shopper.

The first thing we do in the page is open up a database connection. We then retrieve the profile based on the e-mail address entered in by shopper using a standard inline SQL statement.

LISTING 9.3   EmailPassword.asp

```
<%@ Language=VBScript %>
<HTML>
<!--
    EmailPassword.asp - Sends the password to the
```

```
      address specified by the user.
-->

<!-- #include file="include/header.asp" -->

<%

'  Create an ADO database connection
set dbProfile = server.createobject("adodb.connection")

'  Create the record set
set rsProfile = server.CreateObject("adodb.recordset")

'  Open the connection using our ODBC file DSN
dbProfile.open("filedsn=WildWillieCDs")

'  Build the SQL statement to retrieve the password
sql = "select chrPassword from shopper where " & _
      "chrEmail = '" & request("email") & "'"

'  Execute the statement
set rsProfile = dbProfile.Execute(sql)

'  Create the CDONTS mail object
Set objNewMail = server.CreateObject("CDONTS.NewMail")
```

We first check to see if a profile was returned at all. If so then we will use a different format for calling the Send method than we saw in the last chapter. In this case will build all of the address, subject, and body data right in the call to the Send statement. Following the sending of the e-mail, we indicate that e-mail address has been sent and close out the page.

LISTING 9.4 **EmailPassword.asp Continued**

```
'  Check to ensure that a profile exists with
'  that email address
If not rsProfile.eof Then

'  Execute the mail object to send the email
'  We pass in the from address, the to address,
'  the subject and the body with the password.
objNewMail.Send "support@wildwillieinc.com", _
```

```
                    request("email"), _
                    "Wild Willie's CD Store", _
"Here is your password:  " & _
                    rsProfile("chrPassword")


End If

%>

<B>Your password has been sent to your email address.</b>

<!-- #include file="include/footer.asp" -->

</BODY>
</HTML>
```

If you enter in a valid e-mail address into the request, then it will be sent to your e-mail address just as soon as your e-mail server can send it out. Note that, either way, we indicate it was sent; for security purposes, we don't want to give any clues about whether a password does or does not exist.

Next we are ready to handle the display of the profile. The page starts out in the standard format. The database connection is opened and ready to retrieve data.

LISTING 9.5   **ProfileDisplay.asp**

```
<%@ Language=VBScript %>
<HTML>
<!--
   ProfileDisplay.asp - Displays the shoppers
   profile.
-->

<!-- #include file="include/header.asp" -->

<%

'  Create an ADO database connection
set dbProfile = server.createobject("adodb.connection")

'  Create the record set
```

```
set rsProfile = server.CreateObject("adodb.recordset")

'  Open the connection using our ODBC file DSN
dbProfile.open("filedsn=WildWillieCDs")
```

We have to account for several different entry points into this page. The first is when the shopper logs in for the first time. In that case we will read the e-mail and password from the request variables of the posted form.

In the second case the page is being entered because there was an error in the profile update submitted by the shopper. In that case the e-mail address and password are stored in session variables for our retrieval.

LISTING 9.6	**ProfileDisplay.asp Continued**

```
'  Check to see if we have a parameter on the URL.
'  Parameters will be on the URL if we are sending
'  the shopper back because of errors in the profile.
'  If so, then the username and password will be
'  retrieved from session variables.
if request("check") = "1" then

    '  Retrieve the values
    email = session("email")
    password = session("password")

else

    '  Otherwise we retrieve the values from
    '  the profile form.
    email = request("email")
    password = request("password")

end if
```

When we have the e-mail address and password, we are ready to execute the sp_RetrieveProfile stored procedure. This will return the specific profile based on that combination.

LISTING 9.7   ProfileDisplay.asp Continued

```
' Build the SQL stored procedure to retrieve the profile
' based on the email and password
sql = "execute sp_RetrieveProfile '" & email & _
    "', '" & password & "'"

' Execute the statement
set rsProfile = dbProfile.Execute(sql)
```

The next check is to see if a profile was returned. If not, then we build the text that allows the shopper to enter in their e-mail address and have the password sent to them.

LISTING 9.8   ProfileDisplay.asp Continued

```
' Check to see if a profile was returned
if rsProfile.EOF then

%>

<!-- If nothing is returned then we notify the user -->
Sorry, that email and password is incorrect.
Click <a href="profile.asp">here</a> to try again.<BR><BR>

If you have forgotten your password, enter in your email
address to have your password emailed to you.<BR><BR>

<!-- Display a form that will email the password
     to the user if it has been forgotten
-->
<form method="post" action="emailpassword.asp">

email Address:  <input type="text" value="" name="email"><BR><BR>

<input type="submit" value="Submit" name="submit">

</form>

<%

else
```

The first thing we do when the profile is retrieved, is to set our global shopper ID. Remember in the shipping.asp page, we do a number of checks to see if we should retrieve the shopper's profile. In this case we want to indicate that there is a profile, but that the final retrieval of default data for the address fields should still be done.

LISTING 9.9   ProfileDisplay.asp Continued

```
'  Set the shopper value so the profile can
'  be later retrieved.
session("idShopper") = rsProfile("idShopper")

'  Set the profile retrieve to 0.
session("ProfileRetrieve") = "0"


%>
```

Next we are going to display the profile data in a form. The form will post to the UpdateProfile.asp page, which will handle the error validation and updating of the profile.

LISTING 9.10   ProfileDisplay.asp Continued

```
<!-- Display the profile. -->
<B>Edit your profile below:</b><BR><BR>

<!-- Form to post the changes -->
<form method="post" action="UpdateProfile.asp">
```

As we have seen with the previous shipping and billing forms, the text boxes are built for entering in the data. Each of the values will be defaulted to the existing data in the profile.

LISTING 9.11   ProfileDisplay.asp Continued

```
<!-- Table to display the profile data -->
<table>
<!-- First Name -->
<tr>
  <td align="right">First Name:</td>
  <td>
```

```
        <input type="text" value="<%=rsProfile("chrFirstName")%>"
               name="chrFirstName">
     </td>
  </tr>
  <!--  Last Name -->
  <tr>
     <td align="right">Last Name:</td>
     <td>
        <input type="text" value="<%=rsProfile("chrLastName")%>"
               name="chrLastName">
     </td>
  </tr>
  <!--  Address -->
  <tr>
     <td align="right">Address:</td>
     <td>
        <input type="text" value="<%=rsProfile("chrAddress")%>"
               name="chrAddress">
     </td>
  </tr>
  <!--  City -->
  <tr>
     <td align="right">City:</td>
     <td>
        <input type="text" value="<%=rsProfile("chrCity")%>"
               name="chrCity">
     </td>
  </tr>
```

Again we are going to want to default the state to the previously selected state.
We will check the current value in the database and set an appropriate variable to
have the *Selected* text default for the right select option.

LISTING 9.12   ProfileDisplay.asp Continued

```
  <!--  State -->
  <tr>
     <td align="right">State:</td>
     <td>

     <%

     '  Check to see which state was selected previously
```

```
'  if there was an error.
if rsProfile("chrState") = "AL" then
   SelAL = "Selected"
end if

if rsProfile("chrState") = "AK" then
   SelAK = "Selected"
end if

if rsProfile("chrState") = "AZ" then
   SelAZ = "Selected"
end if

if rsProfile("chrState") = "AR" then
   SelAR = "Selected"
end if

if rsProfile("chrState") = "CA" then
   SelCA = "Selected"
end if

if rsProfile("chrState") = "CT" then
   SelCT = "Selected"
end if

if rsProfile("chrState") = "CO" then
   SelCO = "Selected"
end if

if rsProfile("chrState") = "DC" then
   SelDC = "Selected"
end if

if rsProfile("chrState") = "DE" then
   SelDE = "Selected"
end if

if rsProfile("chrState") = "FL" then
   SelFL = "Selected"
end if

if rsProfile("chrState") = "GA" then
   SelGA = "Selected"
```

```
end if

if rsProfile("chrState") = "HI" then
    SelHI = "Selected"
end if

if rsProfile("chrState") = "ID" then
    SelID = "Selected"
end if

if rsProfile("chrState") = "IL" then
    SelIL = "Selected"
end if

if rsProfile("chrState") = "IN" then
    SelIN = "Selected"
end if

if rsProfile("chrState") = "IA" then
    SelIA = "Selected"
end if

if rsProfile("chrState") = "KS" then
    SelKS = "Selected"
end if

if rsProfile("chrState") = "KY" then
    SelKY = "Selected"
end if

if rsProfile("chrState") = "LA" then
    SelLA = "Selected"
end if

if rsProfile("chrState") = "ME" then
    SelME = "Selected"
end if

if rsProfile("chrState") = "MA" then
    SelMA = "Selected"
end if

if rsProfile("chrState") = "MD" then
```

```
        SelMD = "Selected"
    end if

    if rsProfile("chrState") = "MI" then
        SelMI = "Selected"
    end if

    if rsProfile("chrState") = "MN" then
        SelMN = "Selected"
    end if

    if rsProfile("chrState") = "MS" then
        SelMS = "Selected"
    end if

    if rsProfile("chrState") = "MO" then
        SelMO = "Selected"
    end if

    if rsProfile("chrState") = "MT" then
        SelMT = "Selected"
    end if

    if rsProfile("chrState") = "NE" then
        SelNE = "Selected"
    end if

    if rsProfile("chrState") = "NV" then
        SelNV = "Selected"
    end if

    if rsProfile("chrState") = "NH" then
        SelNH = "Selected"
    end if

    if rsProfile("chrState") = "NJ" then
        SelNJ = "Selected"
    end if

    if rsProfile("chrState") = "NM" then
        SelNM = "Selected"
    end if
```

```
if rsProfile("chrState") = "NY" then
    SelNY = "Selected"
end if

if rsProfile("chrState") = "NC" then
    SelNC = "Selected"
end if

if rsProfile("chrState") = "ND" then
    SelND = "Selected"
end if

if rsProfile("chrState") = "OH" then
    SelOH = "Selected"
end if

if rsProfile("chrState") = "OK" then
    SelOK = "Selected"
end if

if rsProfile("chrState") = "OR" then
    SelOR = "Selected"
end if

if rsProfile("chrState") = "PA" then
    SelPA = "Selected"
end if

if rsProfile("chrState") = "RI" then
    SelRI = "Selected"
end if

if rsProfile("chrState") = "SC" then
    SelSC = "Selected"
end if

if rsProfile("chrState") = "SD" then
    SelSD = "Selected"
end if

if rsProfile("chrState") = "TN" then
    SelTN = "Selected"
end if
```

```
if rsProfile("chrState") = "TX" then
      SelTX = "Selected"
end if

if rsProfile("chrState") = "UT" then
      SelUT = "Selected"
end if

if rsProfile("chrState") = "VT" then
      SelVT = "Selected"
end if

if rsProfile("chrState") = "VA" then
      SelVA = "Selected"
end if

if rsProfile("chrState") = "WY" then
      SelWY = "Selected"
end if

if rsProfile("chrState") = "WI" then
      SelWI = "Selected"
end if

if rsProfile("chrState") = "WV" then
      SelWV = "Selected"
end if

if rsProfile("chrState") = "WA" then
      SelWA = "Selected"
end if

%>
```

Next we build the select box for the states. In each case we will insert the value of the corresponding state variable. The one that was in the database will then have the *Selected* text.

LISTING 9.13   ProfileDisplay.asp Continued

```
<!-- State select box. -->
<select name="chrState">
        <option value="">Select a State
        <option value="AL" <%=SelAL%>>Alabama
        <option value="AK" <%=SelAK%>>Alaska
        <option value="AZ" <%=SelAZ%>>Arizona
        <option value="AR" <%=SelAR%>>Arkansas
        <option value="CA" <%=SelCA%>>California
        <option value="CT" <%=SelCT%>>Connecticut
        <option value="CO" <%=SelCO%>>Colorado
        <option value="DC" <%=SelDC%>>D.C.
        <option value="DE" <%=SelDE%>>Delaware
        <option value="FL" <%=SelFL%>>Florida
        <option value="GA" <%=SelGA%>>Georgia
        <option value="HI" <%=SelHI%>>Hawaii
        <option value="ID" <%=SelID%>>Idaho
        <option value="IL" <%=SelIL%>>Illinois
        <option value="IN" <%=SelIN%>>Indiana
        <option value="IA" <%=SelIA%>>Iowa
        <option value="KS" <%=SelKS%>>Kansas
        <option value="KY" <%=SelKY%>>Kentucky
        <option value="LA" <%=SelLA%>>Louisiana
        <option value="ME" <%=SelME%>>Maine
        <option value="MA" <%=SelMA%>>Massachusetts
        <option value="MD" <%=SelMD%>>Maryland
        <option value="MI" <%=SelMI%>>Michigan
        <option value="MN" <%=SelMN%>>Minnesota
        <option value="MS" <%=SelMS%>>Mississippi
        <option value="MO" <%=SelMO%>>Missouri
        <option value="MT" <%=SelMT%>>Montana
        <option value="NE" <%=SelNE%>>Nebraska
        <option value="NV" <%=SelNV%>>Nevada
        <option value="NH" <%=SelNH%>>New Hampshire
        <option value="NJ" <%=SelNJ%>>New Jersey
        <option value="NM" <%=SelNM%>>New Mexico
        <option value="NY" <%=SelNY%>>New York
        <option value="NC" <%=SelNC%>>North Carolina
        <option value="ND" <%=SelND%>>North Dakota
        <option value="OH" <%=SelOH%>>Ohio
```

```
            <option value="OK" <%=SelOK%>>Oklahoma
            <option value="OR" <%=SelOR%>>Oregon
            <option value="PA" <%=SelPA%>>Pennsylvania
            <option value="RI" <%=SelRI%>>Rhode Island
            <option value="SC" <%=SelSC%>>South Carolina
            <option value="SD" <%=SelSD%>>South Dakota
            <option value="TN" <%=SelTN%>>Tennessee
            <option value="TX" <%=SelTX%>>Texas
            <option value="UT" <%=SelUT%>>Utah
            <option value="VT" <%=SelVT%>>Vermont
            <option value="VA" <%=SelVA%>>Virginia
            <option value="WA" <%=SelWA%>>Washington
            <option value="WY" <%=SelWY%>>Wyoming
            <option value="WI" <%=SelWI%>>Wisconsin
            <option value="WV" <%=SelWV%>>West Virginia
        </select>
```

As on the shipping and billing forms, we also want the shopper to be able to store her province if she is located internationally. And, on the country select option, we need to also default it to the previously selected country.

LISTING 9.14   **ProfileDisplay.asp Continued**

```
        <!-- Province input -->
        or Province:<input type="text"
        value="<%=rsProfile("chrProvince")%>"
        name="chrProvince" size="15">

        </td>
    </tr>

    <!-- Country -->
    <tr>
        <td align="right">Country:</td>
        <td>

        <%

        ' Check to see which country was selected previously
        ' if there was an error.
        if rsProfile("chrCountry") = "US" then
            SelUS = "Selected"
        end if
```

```
        if rsProfile("chrCountry") = "CA" then
             SelCA = "Selected"
        end if

        if rsProfile("chrCountry") = "MX" then
             SelMX = "Selected"
        end if

%>
<!-- Country select box -->
<select name="chrCountry">
        <option value="">Select a Country
        <option value="US" <%=SelUS%>>United States
        <option value="CA" <%=SelCA%>>Canada
        <option value="MX" <%=SelMX%>>Mexico
</select>

        </td>
</tr>
```

The form finishes out with the standard fields for the address.

LISTING 9.15   **ProfileDisplay.asp Continued**

```
<!-- Zip Code -->
<tr>
        <td align="right">Zip/Postal Code:</td>
        <td>
        <input type="text" value="<%=rsProfile("chrZipCode")%>"
             name="chrZipCode">
        </td>
</tr>
<!-- Phone -->
<tr>
        <td align="right">Phone:</td>
        <td>
        <input type="text" value="<%=rsProfile("chrPhone")%>"
             name="chrPhone">
        </td>
</tr>
<!-- Fax -->
<tr>
        <td align="right">Fax:</td>
```

```
         <td>
         <input type="text" value="<%=rsProfile("chrFax")%>"
         name="chrFax">
         </td>
</tr>
<!-- email -->
<tr>
         <td align="right">email:</td>
         <td>
         <input type="text" value="<%=rsProfile("chrEmail")%>"
         name="chrEmail">
         </td>
</tr>
```

The password and cookie fields are also provided. The cookie will be defaulted to the previously selected value. Note that the password field is set to an HTML password element type.

LISTING 9.16   **ProfileDisplay.asp Continued**

```
<!-- Password -->
<tr>
         <td align="right">Password:</td>
         <td>
         <input type="password" value="<%=rsProfile("chrPassword")%>"
               name="chrPassword")>
         </td>
</tr>
<!-- Option to save the profile as a cookie -->
<tr>
         <td align="right">Save Profile Cookie?:</td>
         <td>

         <%
         '  Default the cookie based on the previous selection.
         if rsProfile("intCookie") = 1 then

               YesChecked = "CHECKED"

         else

               NoChecked = "CHECKED"
```

```
        end if
        %>

        <!--  Radio button input for defaulting a cookie
                with the shopper ID   -->
        <input type="radio" value="1" name="intCookie" <%=YesChecked%>>
        Yes
        <input type="radio" value="0" name="intCookie" <%=NoChecked%>> No
        </td>
    </tr>
```

Finally, the page finishes out with the Submit button. Note that we store the ID of the shopper in a hidden variable as well to ensure we can identify the profile to be updated. Then the page is closed out as usual.

LISTING 9.17   ProfileDisplay.asp Continued

```
    <!--  Submit Button -->
    <tr>
        <td colspan="2" align="center">
            <input type="hidden" name="idShopper"
                value="<%=rsProfile("idShopper")%>">
            <input type="submit" value="Submit" name="Submit">
        </td>
    </tr>

    </table>

    </form>

    <%

    end if

    %>

    <!-- #include file="include/footer.asp" -->

    </BODY>
    </HTML>
```

The sp_RetrieveProfile stored procedure finds the profile in the database where the e-mail and password match the passed-in entries. The data is pulled from the Shopper table.

LISTING 9.18   sp_RetrieveProfile

```
/*  Retrieve the profile based on email
    and password */
CREATE PROCEDURE sp_RetrieveProfile

/*  The email address and password
    are passed in */
@email varchar(255),
@password varchar(25)

AS

/*  Select the shopper data */
select * from shopper
where chremail = @email and
      chrPassword = @Password
```

Figure 9.5 shows the displayed profile. Note that all of the default fields are set properly. Now we are ready to make changes and perform the update.

The UpdateProfile.asp page acts in much the same way as the ValidateShipping .asp and ValidateBilling.asp pages. We will need to validate the entered profile data and then determine the next step.

The first step is to retrieve all of the data in the profile. In this case we are storing it into local variables.

FIGURE 9.5:

Profile display

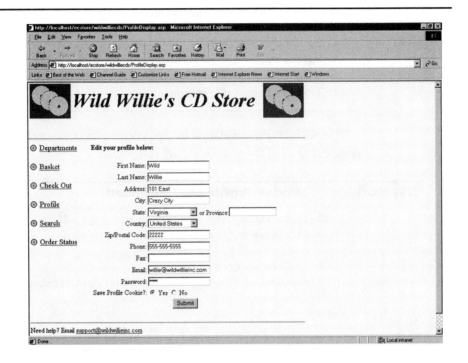

LISTING 9.19   UpdateProfile.asp

```
<%@ Language=VBScript %>
<%
'    ********************************************************
'    UpdateProfile.asp - This page updates the profile
'    based on the entries by the user.
'    ********************************************************

'    Retrieve all of the data that the user entered
'    by using the request object.
chrFirstName = request("chrFirstName")
chrLastName = Request("chrLastName")
chrAddress = Request("chrAddress")
chrCity = Request("chrCity")
chrState = Request("chrState")
chrProvince = Request("chrProvince")
chrCountry = Request("chrCountry")
```

```
chrZipCode = Request("chrZipCode")
chrPhone = Request("chrPhone")
chrFax = Request("chrFax")
chrEmail = Request("chrEmail")
chrPassword = Request("chrPassword")
intCookie = request("intCookie")
```

Next we start the validation of the profile data. Essentially we are checking to ensure that all of the data fields are not blank.

LISTING 9.20   UpdateProfile.asp Continued

```
'  Check to see if the first name was entered.
if chrFirstName = "" then

    '  Give an error if not.
    strError = "You did not enter in your first name.<BR>"

end if


'  Check to see if a last name was entered.
if chrLastName = "" then

    strError = strError & "You did not enter in your last name.<BR>"

end if


'  Check to see if an address was entered
if chrAddress = "" then

    strError = strError & "You did not enter in your address.<BR>"

end if


'  Check to see if a city was entered.
if chrCity = "" then

    strError = strError & "You did not enter in your city.<BR>"

end if
```

We have to validate the country and state/province combination. We want to ensure that a state is selected when the country is U.S. Likewise we want to ensure that a province is entered if the country is not U.S.

LISTING 9.21   UpdateProfile.asp Continued

```
' Check to see if the selected country is US
if chrCountry = "US" then

        ' Check to see if a state was entered.
        if chrState = "" then

                ' Build the error.
                strError = strError & "Invalid state<BR>"

        end if

    else

        ' If a International country then check the
        ' province field.
        if chrProvince = "" then

                ' Build the error.
                strError = strError & "Invalid province<BR>"

        end if

    end if
```

We also need to check and ensure a country was selected as well. Then the validation continues with the rest of the fields.

LISTING 9.22   UpdateProfile.asp Continued

```
' Ensure a country was entered.
if chrCountry = "" then

        ' Build an error string.
        strError = strError & "Invalid country<BR>"
```

```
       end if

    '  Check to see if a zip code was entered.
    if chrZipCode = "" then

          '  Build an error string.
          strError = strError & "You did not enter in your zip code.<BR>"

    end if

    '  Check to see if a zip code was entered.
    if chrPhone = "" then

          strError = strError & "You did not enter in your phone " & _
          "number.<BR>"

    end if

    '  Check to see if a zip code was entered.
    if chrEmail = "" then

          strError = strError & "You did not enter in your email " & _
          "address.<BR>"

    end if

    '  Check to see if a zip code was entered.
    if chrPassword = "" then

          strError = strError & "You did not enter in your password.<BR>"

    end if
```

Next we check to see if there is an error. If so, then we will display the error on this page. For some variation from the checkout pages, we will not jump back to the profile page to display the error.

Note how all of the page tags are built within that section of displaying the error. The e-mail address and password data are stored in session variables and the shopper is given a link back to the profile page.

LISTING 9.23   **UpdateProfile.asp Continued**

```
'   Now we check to see if there are any errors.
if strError <> "" then

%>

<HTML>

<!-- #include file="include/header.asp" -->

    <!-- Note the error -->
    <B><font color="red">
        There is an error in your profile:<BR><BR>
    </b></font>

<%

    '   Write out the error messages
    Response.Write strError

    '   Save the email and password in session
    '   variables for reference on the profile
    '   form.
    session("email") = chremail
    session("password") = chrPassword

%>

<!-- Link back to the profile page. The check
     parameter indicates the email and password
     should be retrieved from session variables.
-->
<BR>
Click <a href="profiledisplay.asp?Check=1">here</a> to update.

<%

else
```

If there was no error, then we are ready to open a database connection and update the profile data in the database. As in our previous updates of data, we have to ensure that any single quotes are doubled for insert into the SQL database.

LISTING 9.24   **UpdateProfile.asp Continued**

```
'  Create an ADO database connection
set dbProfile = server.createobject("adodb.connection")

'  Open the connection using our ODBC file DSN
dbProfile.open("filedsn=WildWillieCDs")

'  If any of our names have a single quote, we will
'  need to double it to insert it into the database
chrFirstName = replace(chrFirstName, "'", "''")
chrLastName = replace(chrLastName, "'", "''")
chrAddress = replace(chrAddress, "'", "''")
chrCardName = replace(chrCardName, "'", "''")
chrCity = replace(chrCity, "'", "''")
```

The stored procedure sp_UpdateShopper is called with all of the values passed in. The SQL statement is then executed.

LISTING 9.25   **UpdateProfile.asp Continued**

```
'  SQL statement to update the profile in the
'  database
sql = "execute sp_UpdateShopper  '" & _
request("chrFirstName") & "', '" & _
request("chrLastName") & "', '" & _
request("chrAddress") & "', '" & _
request("chrCity") & "', '" & _
        request("chrState") & "', '" & _
        request("chrProvince") & "', '" & _
        request("chrCountry") & "', '" & _
        request("chrZipCode") & "', '" & _
        request("chrPhone") & "', '" & _
        request("chrFax") & "', '" & _
        request("chremail") & "', '" & _
        request("chrPassword") & "', " & _
        request("intCookie") & ", " & _
        request("idShopper")
```

```
'   Execute the SQL statement
dbProfile.execute(sql)
```

We next check to see if the shopper wants to have a cookie set for her profile to be easily retrieved at a later date. If so, then the Cookies collection of the Request object is utilized to set the cookie. The value stored in the cookie will be *WWCD*. And, it is important that we set a expiration date to ensure the cookie is available for a good while.

LISTING 9.26   UpdateProfile.asp Continued

```
'   Write out the cookie
if request("intCookie") = 1 then

        '   Store the shopper ID
        Response.Cookies("WWCD") = request("idShopper")

        '   Expire the cookie down the road.
        Response.Cookies("WWCD").Expires = "December 31, 2001"

    else

    Response.Cookies("WWCD") = ""

    end if

%>
```

Again, we build a full page with in this option to indicate that the profile has been updated successfully. And, the page is then finally finished out in the usual fashion.

LISTING 9.27   UpdateProfile.asp Continued

```
<HTML>

<!-- #include file="include/header.asp" -->

    <!-- Indicate the profile has been updated. -->
    <b>Your profile has been updated!</b>
```

```
<%

end if

%>

<!-- #include file="include/footer.asp" -->

</BODY>
</HTML>
```

We utilize the sp_UpdateShopper stored procedure to make changes if we have a successful profile update. All of the key values are entered into the stored procedure up front. Then the Update statement is executed where the ID of the shopper matches the passed-in value.

LISTING 9.28   sp_UpdateShopper

```
/*  Stored procedure to update the shopper
    data */
CREATE PROCEDURE sp_UpdateShopper

/*  Pass in the key shopper data */
@chrFirstName varchar(150),
@chrLastName varchar(150),
@chrAddress varchar(150),
@chrCity varchar(150),
@chrState varchar(150),
@chrProvince varchar(150),
@chrCountry varchar(100),
@chrZipCode varchar(50),
@chrPhone varchar(25),
@chrFax varchar(25),
@chremail varchar(100),
@chrPassword varchar(25),
@intCookie int,
@idShopper int

AS

/*  Update the shopper data for the given
```

```
      shopper ID */
 update shopper  set
    chrFirstName = @chrFirstName,
    chrLastname = @chrLastName,
    chrAddress = @chrAddress,
    chrCity = @chrCity,
    chrState = @chrState,
    chrProvince = @chrProvince,
    chrCountry = @chrCountry,
    chrZipCode = @chrZipCode,
    chrPhone = @chrPhone,
    chrFax = @chrFax,
    chremail = @chremail,
    chrPassword = @chrPassword,
    intCookie = @intCookie
 where idShopper = @idShopper
```

Now let's make some updates to the shopper profile. To test the error handling, Figure 9.6 shows the error when an invalid country is entered into the profile.

FIGURE 9.6:

Profile error

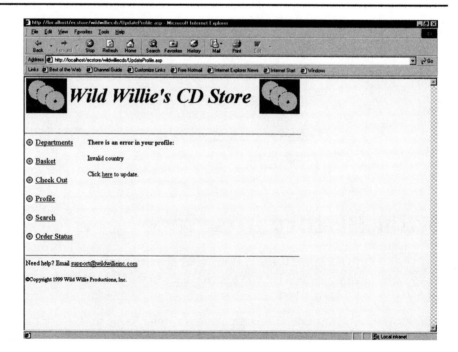

When a correct profile is entered, the profile is updated. The appropriate message is shown in Figure 9.7.

That is it for our profile management. Don't forget about the different interactions with the profile throughout the shopping process as outlined in Chapter 8.

FIGURE 9.7:

Profile update

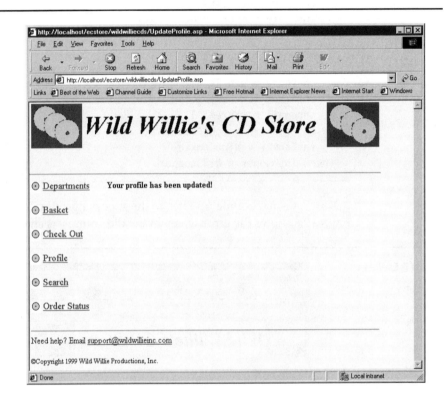

Order History Interface

Next up on the list is the Order History interface. This is the feature where the shopper will be able to come back to the Web site and see what the status of their order is. The first task is to have the shopper login to retrieve their list of orders.

The OrderStatus.asp page is similar to the profile.asp page. We are going to require the site visitor to enter in a username and password to retrieve their order history.

The page starts out in the standard fashion. We then build a form with a place to enter in the e-mail address and password.

LISTING 9.29   OrderStatus.asp

```
<%@ Language=VBScript %>
<HTML>
<!--
     OrderStatus.asp - Login page to retrieve order status.
-->

<!-- #include file="include/header.asp" -->

To retrieve your order history, please enter in
your email address and password.
<BR><BR>


<!--  Form to post the request -->
<form method="post" action="OrderHistoryDisplay.asp" id=form1
name=form1>

<!--  Table that allows the user to enter in an email
      address and password.
-->
<table>
<tr>
     <td align="right">
          email:
     </td>
     <td>
       <input type="text" name="email" value="">
     </td>
</tr>
```

Note that the password field uses the HTML password element type. That way the actual password is not displayed on-screen. The form is finished out with a submit button and then the page is closed out.

LISTING 9.30   OrderStatus.asp Continued

```
<tr>
    <td align="right">
        Password:
    </td>
    <td>
        <input type="password" name="password" value="">
    </td>
</tr>
<tr>
    <td colspan="2" align="center">
        <input type="submit" value="Submit" name="submit">
    </td>
</tr>
</table>

</form>

<!-- #include file="include/footer.asp" -->

</BODY>
</HTML>
```

Figure 9.8 shows an order status login page. As mentioned, it is a simple login page for users to identify themselves.

The goal of this page is to provide a list of all orders placed by the shopper and show their status. The first thing we do in the page is open up an ADO connection so we can validate the e-mail address and password entered.

FIGURE 9.8:

Order status login page

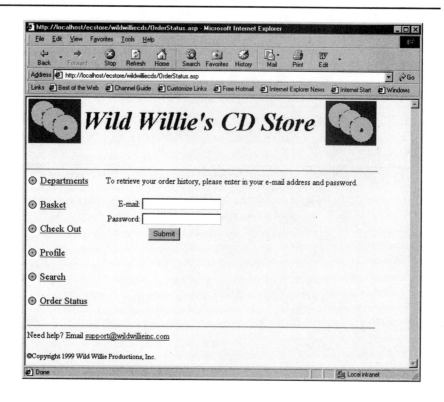

LISTING 9.31	**OrderHistoryDisplay.asp**

```
<%@ Language=VBScript %>
<%
'    ********************************************************
'    OrderHistoryDisplay.asp - This page displays the
'    order history for the shopper.
'    ********************************************************

'    Create an ADO database connection
set dbProfile = server.createobject("adodb.connection")

'    Create the record set
set rsProfile = server.CreateObject("adodb.recordset")

'    Open the connection using our ODBC file DSN
```

```
dbProfile.open("filedsn=WildWillieCDs")

'  Retrieve the values from the login form.
email = request("email")
password = request("password")
```

We execute the sp_RetrieveProfile stored procedure to get the profile based on the e-mail address and password. Then we start the page building.

LISTING 9.32   OrderHistoryDisplay.asp Continued

```
'  Build the SQL stored procedure to retrieve the profile
'  based on the email and password
sql = "execute sp_RetrieveProfile '" & email & _
"', '" & password & "'"

'  Retrieve the record set.
set rsProfile = dbProfile.Execute(sql)
%>

<HTML>

<!-- #include file="include/header.asp" -->
```

If there is a profile returned, then we are ready to list out the orders. A database connection is opened and we will execute the sp_RetrieveOrders stored procedure. This stored procedure will retrieve all orders that the shopper has placed.

LISTING 9.33   OrderHistoryDisplay.asp Continued

```
<%

'  Check to see if something was returned.
if rsProfile.EOF = false then

%>

<B>Here is a list of your orders:</b><BR><BR>

<%

'  Create an ADO database connection
set dbOrders = server.createobject("adodb.connection")
```

```
'  Create the record set
set rsOrders = server.CreateObject("adodb.recordset")

'  Open the connection using our ODBC file DSN
dbOrders.open("filedsn=WildWillieCDs")

'  Build the SQL stored procedure to retrieve the
'  shopper orders based on the ID of the shopper.
sql = "execute sp_RetrieveOrders " & rsProfile("idShopper")

'  Retrieve the record set.
set rsOrders = dbOrders.Execute(sql)
```

We still need to do a check to ensure that orders are returned. There is always the chance that the shopper has never completely finished an order even though they have a profile or they have orders that have been cleared out of the system.

A table is built that simply displays the order number, the date the order was placed, the total order amount, and the status.

LISTING 9.34   **OrderHistoryDisplay.asp Continued**

```
'  Ensure data is returned.
if not rsOrders.EOF then

%>

<!--  This table displays the list of orders  -->
<Table border=1 Cellpadding=3 Cellspacing=3>
<!--  Show the order number and total  -->
<tr>
    <th>Order #</th><th>Date Ordered</th>
    <th>Order Total</th><th>Status</th>
</tr>
```

Next we start the loop through the order data. The first thing we do is check the order status. Note that a number signifies the status. The select case statement checks the number and then sets the appropriate text message. If for some reason the status does not match any of the settings, then we will indicate customer service should be called.

LISTING 9.35   OrderHistoryDisplay.asp Continued

```
<%
'  Loop through the orders
do until rsOrders.EOF

'  Check the status of the order.
select case rsOrders("idStage")

      '  Case 0 is that the order has been retrieved.
      case 0
            status = "Order Received and to be Processed"

      '  Case 1 is that the order is fulfilled and ready
      '  for shipping.
      case 1
            status = "Order Fulfilled and Ready to be Shipped"

      '  Case 2 indicates the order has been shipped and we
      '  display the shipping number.
      case 2
            status = "Order Shipped - Confirmation#: " & _
            rsOrders("chrShippingNum")

      '  If none of these are set then we indicate that
      '  customer service should be called.
      case else
            status = "Call Customer Service for Assistance."

end select
```

Next we pull the order ID, the date ordered, and the total of the order. Then the row is build with all of the appropriate data. A link is built on the order ID so we can click on it to get the full receipt of the order.

LISTING 9.36   OrderHistoryDisplay.asp Continued

```
'  Get the ID of the order, the date of the order
'  and the total of the order.
idOrder = rsOrders("idOrder")
dtOrdered = rsOrders("dtOrdered")
intTotal = formatcurrency(rsOrders("intTotal")/100, 2)
```

```
%>

<!-- Row to display the order data. -->
<tr>
    <!-- Build a link to the order receipt -->
    <td align="center">
        <a href="OrderReceipt.asp? ↵
        idOrder=<%=idOrder%>&idShopper= ↵
          <%=rsProfile("idShopper")%>">
        <%=idOrder%></a>
    </td>
    <!-- Show the date of the order, the total of the order
         and the status.
    -->
    <td align="center"><%=dtOrdered%></td>
    <td align="center"><%=intTotal%></td>
    <td align="center"><%=status%></td>
</tr>
```

Then we move to the next row and loop back to display all of the orders. The table is then ended.

LISTING 9.37   **OrderHistoryDisplay.asp Continued**

```
<%

'  Move to the next row
rsOrders.MoveNext

'  Loop back
Loop

%>

</table>

<%

'  Else indicate no order history.
else

%>
```

If there is no order data, we indicate that there is no order history for the shopper. If the shopper profile could not be retrieved, we are going to display a message that the shopper should call customer service.

We do have some options on how we handle this case. We could indicate to the shopper that they could have their password e-mailed to them. We also could give the customer an option of trying again. But, it is most likely the case that they were really trying to get their order history and need assistance. Following that, the page finishes out in the usual fashion.

LISTING 9.38   **OrderHistoryDisplay.asp Continued**

```
You have no order history.

<%

end if

'   Indicate no order status could be retrieved and
'   customer service should be called.
else

%>

<BR><B>Sorry, we could not retrieve your order status.
Please call 1-800-555-wild for help.<BR></b>

<%

end if

%>

<!-- #include file="include/footer.asp" -->

</BODY>
</HTML>
```

We use a couple of stored procedures for handling the order data. The first is sp_RetrieveOrders. The ID of the shopper is passed in. Then we have to join together the OrderData, OrderStatus, and Basket tables to get all of the appropriate data.

LISTING 9.39   sp_RetrieveOrders

```
/*  Retrieve orders for the shopper */
CREATE PROCEDURE sp_RetrieveOrders

/*  Pass in the ID of the shopper */
@idShopper int

AS

/*  Select the order data for the shopper. To return
    all of the core order data we have to join the
    OrderData, OrderStatus and Basket tables.
*/
select * from OrderData, OrderStatus, basket
where @idShopper = @idShopper and
      OrderData.idOrder = OrderStatus.idOrder and
      basket.idBasket = OrderData.idBasket
```

Once again we will use the sp_RetrieveProfile stored procedure to get the profile data. The e-mail address and password are passed in to be used in the WHERE clause.

LISTING 9.40   sp_RetrieveProfile

```
/*  Retrieve the profile based on email
    and password */
CREATE PROCEDURE sp_RetrieveProfile

/*  The email address and password
    are passed in */
@email varchar(255),
@password varchar(25)

AS

/*  Select the shopper data */
select * from shopper
where chrEmail = @email and
      chrPassword = @Password
```

Figure 9.9 shows a sample order history display. Note that the order ID is linked so we can get the full receipt. And, the status is indicated for each order. Note that we have not yet built a tool to update the order status settings.

FIGURE 9.9:

Order status history

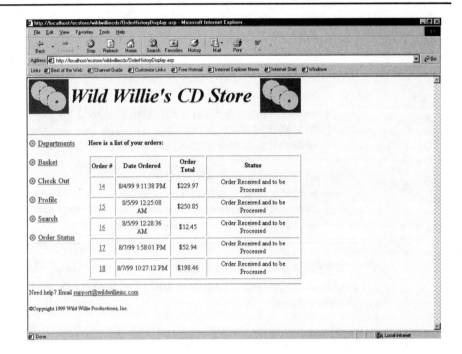

The last piece of the puzzle is for the shopper to print out a complete receipt. This page is linked to from the order history display. It starts out in the usual fashion.

LISTING 9.41   OrderReceipt.asp

```
<%@ Language=VBScript %>
<HTML>
<!--
     OrderReceipt.asp - Displays the items in the shoppers receipt.
-->


<!-- #include file="include/header.asp" -->
```

The first thing to do is to retrieve the receipt header. That will consist of the address data, order ID, date placed, etc. The `sp_RetrieveReceiptHeader` stored procedure is utilized with the ID of the shopper and the ID of the order passed in.

LISTING 9.42   **OrderReceipt.asp Continued**

```asp
<%

'  Create an ADO database connection
set dbOrderReceiptHeader = _
    server.createobject("adodb.connection")
set rsOrderReceiptHeader = _
    server.CreateObject("adodb.recordset")

'  Open the connection using our ODBC file DSN
dbOrderReceiptHeader.open("filedsn=WildWillieCDs")

'  Call the stored procedure to retrieve the
'  receipt header.
sql = "execute sp_RetrieveReceiptHeader " & _
        Request("idShopper") & ", " & _
        Request("idOrder")

'  Execute the SQL statement
set rsOrderReceiptHeader = _
    dbOrderReceiptHeader.execute(sql)

%>
```

We start building a table for displaying the receipt header. There will be two columns of data. The first is the billing information and the second is the shipping information. Right above each is displayed the order number and the date the order was placed.

LISTING 9.43   **OrderReceipt.asp Continued**

```asp
<!--  Build the table for the header -->
<table>
<!--  Row to display the order id abd
      the date ordered.
-->
<tr>
```

```
      <td><B>Order # <%=rsOrderReceiptHeader("idOrder")%></b></td>
      <td width="75"></td>
      <td><b>Order Date:
<%=rsOrderReceiptHeader("dtOrdered")%></b></td>
<tr>
<!-- Blank column -->
<tr>
      <td colspan="3"> </td>
</tr>
<!-- Bill to and Ship to header -->
<tr>
      <td><b>Bill To:</b></td>
      <td width="75"></td>
      <td><b>Ship To:</b></td>
<tr>
<!-- Shipping and Billing information -->
<tr>
      <td><%Response.Write _
   rsOrderReceiptHeader("chrBillFirstName") & _
         " " & _
   rsOrderReceiptHeader("chrBillLastName")%></td>

      <td width="75"></td>
      <td><%Response.write _
   rsOrderReceiptHeader("chrShipFirstName") & _
         " " & _
   rsOrderReceiptHeader("chrShipLastName")%></td>

<tr>
<!-- Billing and shipping address. -->
<tr>
      <td><%=rsOrderReceiptHeader("chrBillAddress")%></td>
      <td width="75"></td>
      <td><%=rsOrderReceiptHeader("chrShipAddress")%></td>
<tr>
<!-- Billing and shipping address.  -->
<tr>
      <td><%Response.write _
        rsOrderReceiptHeader("chrBillCity") & _
          ", " & rsOrderReceiptHeader("chrBillState") & _
          " " & rsOrderReceiptHeader("chrBillZipCode")%></td>
      <td width="75"></td>
      <td><%Response.write _
```

```
                rsOrderReceiptHeader("chrShipCity") & ", " & _
                    rsOrderReceiptHeader("chrShipState") & " " & _
                    rsOrderReceiptHeader("chrShipZipCode")%></td>
    <tr>
    <!-- Billing and shipping phone. -->
    <tr>
        <td><%=rsOrderReceiptHeader("chrBillPhone")%></td>
        <td width="75"></td>
        <td><%=rsOrderReceiptHeader("chrShipPhone")%></td>
    <tr>
    <!-- Billing and shipping email. -->
    <tr>
        <td><%=rsOrderReceiptHeader("chrBillemail")%></td>
        <td width="75"></td>
        <td><%=rsOrderReceiptHeader("chrShipemail")%></td>
    <tr>

    </table>
```

Next we move to the items purchased. We want to process and display this section in much the same way as the shopping basket is handled.

The sp_RetrieveReceiptItems stored procedure is utilized to retrieve the items from the BasketItems table. The ID of the shopper and the ID of the order are passed in.

LISTING 9.44   OrderReceipt.asp Continued

```
<%

'  Create an ADO database connection
set dbOrderReceiptItems = _
    server.createobject("adodb.connection")
set rsOrderReceiptItems = _
    server.CreateObject("adodb.recordset")

'  Open the connection using our ODBC file DSN
dbOrderReceiptItems.open("filedsn=WildWillieCDs")

'  SQL statement to retrieve the items orders.
sql = "execute sp_RetrieveReceiptItems " & _
        Request("idShopper") & ", " & _
        Request("idOrder")
```

```
'  Execute the SQL statement
set rsOrderReceiptItems = dbOrderReceiptItems.execute(sql)


%>
```

The table is started to display the receipt items. The item code, name, attributes, quantity, price, and total will be displayed.

LISTING 9.45   **OrderReceipt.asp Continued**

```
<!-- Build the receipt table -->
<table border="0" cellpadding="3" cellspacing="2" width="500">

<tr><td colspan="6"><HR></td></tr>

<!-- Build the header row -->
<tr>
      <th>Item Code</th>
      <th>Name</th>
      <th>Attributes</th>
      <th>Quantity</th>
      <th>Price</th>
      <th>Total</th>
</tr>
```

The items returned are looped through. With each iteration, the item data is displayed. Note that we do some checking to ensure an attribute is displayed if set.

LISTING 9.46   **OrderReceipt.asp Continued**

```
<%

'  Loop through the items.
do until rsOrderReceiptItems.EOF

%>

<!-- Show the row -->
<tr>
      <!-- Show the product id -->
```

```
    <td align="center">
     <%=rsOrderReceiptItems("idProduct")%></td>
    <!-- Show the product name -->
    <td><%=rsOrderReceiptItems("chrName")%></td>

    <!-- Show the product attributes -->
    <td>
        <% if rsOrderReceiptItems("chrColor") <> " " then %>
        <%=rsOrderReceiptItems("chrSize")%>,
        <%=rsOrderReceiptItems("chrColor")%>
        <% end if %>
    </td>

    <!-- Show the product quantity -->
    <td align="center">
    <%=rsOrderReceiptItems("intQuantity")%></td>

    <!-- Show the product price -->
    <td>
 <%=formatcurrency(rsOrderReceiptItems("intPrice")/100,↵
                2)%></td>

    <!-- Show the product total cost -->
    <td align="right">
  <%Response.write ↵
  formatcurrency(rsOrderReceiptItems("intPrice")/100 * ↵
  rsOrderReceiptItems("intQuantity"), 2)%></td>
</tr>

<%

'  Move to the next row
rsOrderReceiptItems.MoveNext

loop

%>
```

We then build the bottom half of the receipt. We want to display the subtotal, shipping, tax, and order total. These will be pulled directly from the basket table.

Each is displayed in the appropriate column in the receipt. Then the page is finished out as appropriate.

LISTING 9.47   **OrderReceipt.asp Continued**

```
<!-- Build a break -->
<tr>
    <td colspan="6"><HR></td>
</tr>

<!-- Show the sub total of the basket -->
<tr>
    <td colspan="5" align="right"><b>Subtotal:</b></td>
    <td align="right"><%Response.Write ↵
    formatcurrency(rsOrderReceiptHeader("intSubtotal")/↵
    100, 2) %></td>
</tr>
<!-- Show the shipping total of the basket -->
<tr>
    <td colspan="5" align="right"><b>Shipping:</b></td>
    <td align="right"><%Response.Write ↵_
    formatcurrency(rsOrderReceiptHeader("intShipping")/↵
    100, 2) %></td>
</tr>
<!-- Show the tax total of the basket -->
<tr>
    <td colspan="5" align="right"><b>Tax:</b></td>
    <td align="right"><%Response.Write ↵
    formatcurrency(rsOrderReceiptHeader("intTax")/↵
    100, 2) %></td>
</tr>
<!-- Show the total of the basket -->
<tr>
    <td colspan="5" align="right"><b>Total:</b></td>
    <td align="right"><%Response.Write ↵
    formatcurrency(rsOrderReceiptHeader("intTotal")/↵
    100, 2) %></td>
</tr>

</table>

<!-- #include file="include/footer.asp" -->
```

```
</BODY>
</HTML>
```

We utilize a couple of stored procedures for retrieving the order data. The sp_RetrieveReceiptHeader stored procedure will get the basic customer order data. The OrderData and Basket tables are joined to retrieve the proper data.

LISTING 9.48   **sp_RetrieveReceiptHeader**

```
/*  Retrieve the receipt header by shopper ID
    and Order ID */
CREATE PROCEDURE sp_RetrieveReceiptHeader

/*  Pass in the ID of the shopper and
    the ID of the Order */
@idShopper int,
@idOrder int

AS

/*  Select the receipt header which requires
    joining the orderdata and basket tables
*/
select * from OrderData, Basket
where Orderdata.idOrder = @idOrder and
      OrderData.idShopper = @idShopper and
      OrderData.idBasket = Basket.idBasket
```

The sp_RetrieveReceiptItems stored procedure gets the items in the basket for the completed order. In order to get all of the right data, the BasketItem, basket, and OrderData tables need to be joined together. The ID of the order and the shopper ID are passed in.

LISTING 9.49   **sp_RetrieveReceiptItems**

```
/*  Stored Procedure to retrieve the
    receipt items.
*/
CREATE PROCEDURE sp_RetrieveReceiptItems

/*  Pass in the ID of the shopper and the
    Id of the order */
```

```
@idShopper int,
@idOrder int

AS

/*  Select the contents of the basketitem,
    basket and orderdata tables.
*/
select * from basketitem, basket, orderdata
where orderdata.idshopper = @idShopper and
      orderdata.idOrder = @idOrder and
      basket.idBasket = orderdata.idbasket and
      basketitem.idbasket = basket.idbasket
```

Figure 9.10 shows the order receipt. This is something that should be printable, easily readable by the shopper, and contain all of the appropriate data if there are any questions on the order.

FIGURE 9.10:

Order receipt

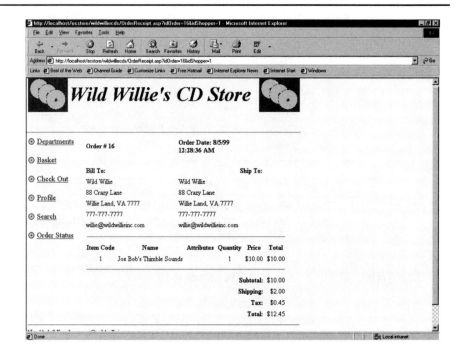

Summary

That does it for Part II of the book. By now you should have a good understanding of the ins and outs of building a functioning e-commerce store from the shopper's perspective.

But that is only half the picture. In Parts III and IV we will explore the management tools need for the store upkeep. And, we will explore the marketing tools that will hopefully entice the shoppers to explore and spend more.

PART III

Managing the Solution

In the last part we built out the foundation of the shopping experience. We presumed all of the data was already loaded and ready to go. Now we need to work on the foundation interface for store management. This can be a vast topic and has the potential to be exceedingly complex depending on the business needs.

What we will tackle in this part are the basics of product, department, tax, shipping, and order management. These are key tools that will be useful in any store. Even if the data is ultimately being populated from a back end system, on the fly changes to the live store will most likely be necessary.

CHAPTER
TEN

10

Product Management

- Designing the Store Manager

- Managing Security

- Managing Products

- Managing Departments

To get started with our store manager, we are going to work on the security infrastructure, product, and department management. We want to provide the ability to add, update, and delete products and departments. This will include managing department assignments, attributes, images, and generally all aspects of store data management.

We also need to define the interface for our store manager, in much the same way we did for the shopping side of the store. And, we will need in this case a security system to ensure not just anybody can get into the manager.

Designing the Store Manager

The store manager is a complex application for working with the database behind our online store. There is a series of functionality we will build in this chapter that will provide the fundamental tools for product and department management. Figure 10.1 lays out the key functional items to be created.

FIGURE 10.1:

Store manager functionality

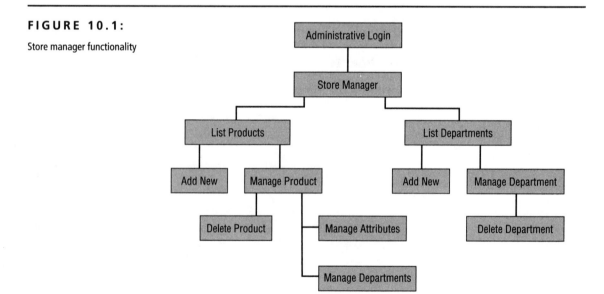

At the top level, the user must log in to the store manager. Then the user will have initial options—product listing, department listing, tax, shipping, and order reporting. From there the functional tree expands into management actions for each area. Table 10.1 outlines the core functionality developed in this chapter.

T A B L E 1 0 . 1 : Store Manager Core Functionality for Products and Departments

Functionality	Description
Administrative Login	Provides login security for the store manager.
Add new product	Adds a new product into the store.
Product listing	Lists products in the database.
Product search	Searches for products in the database.
Product deletion	Deletes a product from the database.
Product update	Updates the product data.
Product attribute management	Adds, updates, and deletes product attributes.
Department listing	Lists departments in the database.
Department update	Updates the department data.
Add new department	Adds a new department to the database.
Department update	Updates the department data.

One key element we will need in the Web site is a straightforward navigation to the different product management features. Figure 10.2 shows the navigation style.

FIGURE 10.2:

Manager navigation

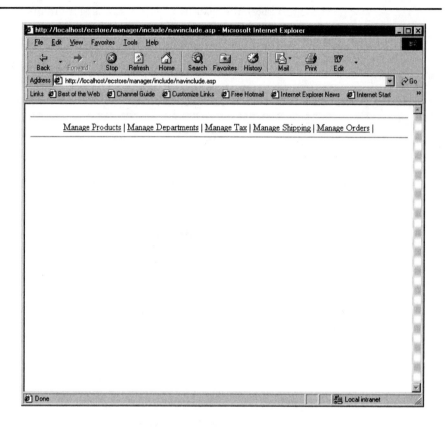

We will follow a method similar to the shopper side of the store for construct-
ing the navigation bar throughout all of the pages in the site. Listing 10.1 shows
navigation bar include code:

LISTING 10.1   NavInclude.asp

```
<!--    NavInclude.asp - Top navigation include for the    site man-
ager.-->
<hr>

<center>

<!-- Link to the listing of products  -->
<a href="ListProducts.asp">
```

```
Manage Products<a> |

<!-- Link to the listing of departments  -->
<a href="ListDepts.asp">
Manage Departments</a> |

<!-- Link to the management of the tax settings -->
<a href="ManageTax.asp">
Manage Tax</a> |

<!-- Link to the management of the shipping settings. -->
<a href="ManageShipping.asp">
Manage Shipping</a> |

<!-- Link to the management of the orders.  -->
<a href="ManageOrders.asp">
Manage Orders</a> |

</center>

<hr>
```

The navigation bar is basically a series of links to each of the core pages for the management features of the store. We will want this to be included at the top of each page as an ASP include. That way we can easily update the navigation as new features are added.

Managing Security

We are also going to need to have security for our store manager. We don't want just anybody getting into the management functions. The first item we will need is the login page. Figure 10.3 shows the login page.

FIGURE 10.3:

Login page

The login page is a simple form with fields for input of the username and password. The page is posted to the store manager page. Listing 10.2 shows the login page code.

LISTING 10.2   Login.asp

```
<%@ Language=VBScript %>
<HTML>
<!--
    Login.asp - Login in page for the site
    administrator.
-->

<HEAD>
<META NAME="GENERATOR" Content="Microsoft Visual Studio 6.0">
</HEAD>
```

```
<BODY>

<B>Please login:</b><BR><BR>

<!--  Start the form for the user to enter in
      their username and password.  -->
<form method="post" action="ManagerMenu.asp">

<table>
<tr>
    <td align="right">Username:</td>
    <td>
        <!--  The input text box for the username.  -->
        <input type="text" value="" name="username">
    </td>
</tr>

<tr>
    <td align="right">Password:</td>
    <td>
        <!--  The input text box for the password.  -->
        <input type="password" value="" name="password">
    </td>
<tr>

<tr>
    <td colspan="2">
        <!--  The submit button for the form.  -->
        <input type="Submit" value="Submit" name="Submit">
    </td>
</tr>

</table>

</form>

</BODY>
</HTML>
```

When the user fills out the form, the code is passed to the ManagerMenu.asp page. There, a check will be done to see if the proper username and password have been entered. Listing 10.3 shows the security check portion of the page.

LISTING 10.3   **ManagerMenu.asp**

```
<%@ Language=VBScript %>
<%
'   *******************************************************
'   ManagerMenu.asp - Provides a menu listing of options
'   for the store.
'   *******************************************************

'   Check the login in to ensure it meets the administrative
'   requirements.
if request("username") <> "Admin" and _
   request("password") <> "Password" then

    '   Redirect to the login.asp page.
    Response.Redirect "login.asp"

else

    '   Indicate the shopper has been validated
    Session("Validated") = true

end if

%>
```

In this section of code (see Listing 10.4), we check the posted values to see if they match the Admin and Password values. If not, then the user is sent back to the login page. If they are correct, then we set a session variable to indicate that the user has successfully logged in. That will be checked throughout the rest of the site to ensure validation.

LISTING 10.4   **ManagerMenu.asp Continued**

```
<HTML>
<HEAD>
<META NAME="GENERATOR" Content="Microsoft Visual Studio 6.0">
</HEAD>
<BODY>

<!-- Welcome the user -->
```

```
<center>
<BR><BR><b>
Welcome to Wild Willie's CD Store Order Manager.
Select a function below
</b><br></br>

<!-- Build a table to show the management opitons. -->
<table border="1" cellpadding="3" cellspacing="3">
<tr>
    <th>Function</th>
</tr>
<tr>
    <!-- Manage products -->
    <td><a href="ListProducts.asp">
        Manage Products<a></td>
</tr>
<tr>
    <!-- Manage departments. -->
    <td><a href="ListDepts.asp">
        Manage Departments</a></td>
</tr>
<tr>
    <!-- Manage tax -->
    <td><a href="ManageTax.asp">
        Manage Tax</a></td>
</tr>
<tr>
    <!-- Manage shipping -->
    <td><a href="ManageShipping.asp">
        Manage Shipping</a></td>
</tr>
<tr>
    <!-- Manage orders -->
    <td><a href="ManageOrders.asp">
        Manage Orders</a></td>
</tr>
</table>
</center>

</BODY>
</HTML>
```

The rest of the store manager page simply lists a quick menu to the different functions of the store manager. This is listed in lieu of the top navigation bar. Figure 10.4 shows the page.

Store manager page

The last piece of code we need is a simple security check include that will also go at the top of each page. Listing 10.5 shows the code.

LISTING 10.5   ValidateCheck.asp

```
<%
'*****************************************************
' ValidateCheck.asp - Ensures that the manager has
' been validated.
'*****************************************************
```

```
'  Check our session variable to see if the user has
'  been validated.  This will help to ensure that
'  none of the admin pages are accessed with out
'  authorization.
if    Session("Validated") <> true  then

    '  Redirect back to the login page.
    Response.Redirect("login.asp")

end if

%>
```

All we do in this page is check to see if our session variable is set. If not, then the user is sent back to the login page.

If the user's session times out, then the session variable will be cleared and the user will have to log in again. The default session timeout is 20 minutes, but this can be adjusted from within the IIS management tools or by setting the session timeout in ASP code.

Login Security

In our example, we use a very simple security model for validating the user and protecting the pages. But there are many more options for implementing security. For example, we may want only certain users to manage products and departments while other users may need to access only order management. Thus we would need different levels of access. This could be implemented with a database of usernames and references.

We also might want to go to extended lengths to tighten down the security. For example, we could place the store manager pages on a different server under a different domain name. And we could also place directory level security on the store manager directory. In that case, the user would log in with NT Authentication.

Managing Products

Now we are ready to begin working on the product management. The first step is to provide a solid navigation for listing out the products. And we will need to provide a way to search for products.

Because we potentially may have many products in the database, we will need to provide a way for the user to browse through the products easily.

Listing 10.6 shows the listproducts.asp page. This page handles showing a set number of products on the page. The code starts out with the usual entry items on the page. The first item is the ValidateCheck.asp to perform the security check. Following that the navigation include is at the top of the page.

LISTING 10.6   **ListProducts.asp**

```
<%@ Language=VBScript %>
<!-- #Include file="include/validatecheck.asp" -->
<HTML>
<!--
    ListProducts.asp - Lists the products in the
    store.
-->

<HEAD>
<META NAME="GENERATOR" Content="Microsoft Visual Studio 6.0">
</HEAD>
<BODY>

<!-- #include file="include/navinclude.asp" -->
```

In Listing 10.7, we start the database interaction by creating the appropriate database connections. We then perform a check to ensure that the *ProdInc* session variable is set. This variable indicates how many products are shown on each page in the product listing.

LISTING 10.7   **ListProducts.asp Continued**

```
<%

' Create an ADO database connection
set dbProducts = server.createobject("adodb.connection")
```

```
'  Create the record set
set rsProducts = server.CreateObject("adodb.recordset")

'  Open the connection using our ODBC file DSN
dbProducts.open("filedsn=WildWillieCDs")

'  The products will not all be displayed at once.  We
'  want to set the Product Increment in a session variable.
'  If the product increment is not set, then we will set
'  it.  In this case, we are defaulting it to 4.
if session("ProdInc") = "" then

    '  Default it to 4
    session("ProdInc") = "4"

end if
```

Next, as shown in Listing 10.8, we read the *StartProd* variable off of the URL. This will indicate where the product listing should start. This is set at the end of the page based on the products shown. We also check to ensure that the *StartProd* variable is set and that it is not less than 1.

LISTING 10.8   ListProducts.asp Continued

```
'  Get the starting point where this list should begin.
StartProd = request("StartProd")

'  If there is no starting point, then we will
'  default it to 1.
if StartProd = "" then
    StartProd = 1
end if

'  If the user tries to decrement past the first product,
'  we default back to 1 for the first product.
if StartProd < 1 then

    StartProd = 1

end if
```

Next we execute our stored procedure that will return the number of products specified, starting at the product item indicated. Following that we execute the stored procedure (see Listing 10.9).

If the result set returns nothing, then we will move the start product back to 1 to ensure products are returned.

LISTING 10.9   **ListProducts.asp Continued**

```
'   Build the stored procedure to retrieve the list of
'   products starting at the specified beginning product
'   and for the specified increment.
sql = "execute sp_ManagerRetrieveProducts " & _
        StartProd & ", " & session("ProdInc")


'   Execute the statement
set rsProducts = dbProducts.Execute(sql)


'   Ensure some products are returned.
if rsProducts.EOF then

    '   If none were, then lets return to the
    '   beginning of the list.
    StartProd = 1

    '   Build the stored procedure
    sql = "execute sp_ManagerRetrieveProducts " & _
            StartProd & ", " & session("ProdInc")

    '   Execute the statement
    set rsProducts = dbProducts.Execute(sql)

end if


%>
```

Now we are ready to begin building the page (see Listing 10.10). The first link on the page is the option to add a new product into the database. Then the listing of the products starts in a listing table.

LISTING 10.10   ListProducts.asp Continued

```
<!-- Build a link to the new product page.  -->
<BR><b>Click <a href="NewProduct.asp">here</a>
to add a new product.</b>

<!-- Start the display of the product listing.  -->
<BR><BR>
<b>To edit a product, select from the list below:</b>
<BR><BR>

<table cellpadding="3" cellspacing="3">
<tr>
    <th>Product ID</th>
    <th>Name</th>
    <th>Price</th>
</tr>
```

The loop through the product listing starts, as shown in Listing 10.11. With each product we build a link to the ManageProduct.asp so the particular product can be worked on. The name of the product is also linked. Then the price is also displayed.

LISTING 10.11   ListProducts.asp Continued

```
<%

'  Loop through the returned products.
do until rsProducts.EOF

%>

<!-- Build a row to display the list of products. -->
<tr>
    <!-- A link is built to the ManageProduct.asp page.
         The id of the product is passed on the URL and
         the ID of the product is displayed.
    -->
    <td>
    <a href="ManageProduct.asp ⏎
        ?idProduct=<%=rsProducts("idProduct")%>"> ⏎
        <%=rsProducts("idProduct")%></a>
```

```
          </td>

          <!--  A link is built to the ManageProduct.asp page.
                The id of the product is passed on the URL and
                the name of the product is displayed.
          -->
          <td>
          <a href="ManageProduct.asp ↵
                ?idProduct=<%=rsProducts("idProduct")%>"> ↵
                <%=rsProducts("chrProductName")%></a>
          </td>

          <!--  Display the product price.  NOte that the price is
                stored as an integer.  -->
          <td>
          <%=formatcurrency(rsProducts("intPrice")/100, 2)%>
          </td>
    </tr>

    <%

    '   Move to the next row
    rsProducts.MoveNext

    '   Loop back
    Loop

    %>

    </table>
```

At the end of the page, we build the *first*, *previous*, and *next* links on the navigation bar. The *first* product link sets the *StartProd* variable to 1. For the *previous* link it will move the product listing back by the product listing display. Finally, the *next* link increments the *start product* session variable by the product listing display. (See Listing 10.12.)

LISTING 10.12   ListProducts.asp Continued

```
<BR>
<!-- This navigation is built to allow the shopper to move
     back and forth between the product listings.  Note
     that each link has the starting product number on the
     URL.  The StartProd variable is set appropriately
     Corresponding to the Procuct Increment session
     variable. -->

<a href="ListProducts.asp?StartProd=1">First Product</a> |

<a href="ListProducts.asp?StartProd=
<%=StartProd - cint(Session("ProdInc"))%>">
Previous</a> |

<a href="ListProducts.asp?StartProd=  ↵
<%=StartProd + cint(Session("ProdInc"))%>">
Next</a>

<BR><BR>
```

The last item on the page is the search feature. A text element is provided for entering the key word searches. The form posts to the SearchProducts.asp page. (See Listing 10.13.)

LISTING 10.13   ListProducts.asp Continued

```
<!-- Build a form to allow the user to search for
     a specific product.  THe link is built to the
     SearchProducts.asp page.  -->
<form method="post" action="SearchProducts.asp">

<!-- The table is created to display the search
     option -->
<table>
<tr>
    <td align="right">Search Text:</td>
    <!-- The input text box for the search text.  -->
    <td><input type="text" value="" name="SearchText"></td>
```

```
</tr>
<tr>
    <td colspan="2">
    <!--  The submit button for the form.  -->
    <input type="submit" value="Submit" name="Submit">
    </td>
</tr>
</table>

</form>

</BODY>
</HTML>
```

One stored procedure, sp_ManageRetrieveProducts, is utilized in the page. The rowcount is set to return only the number of products set in the product increment. Then the listing starts at the specified start product. (See Listing 10.14.)

LISTING 10.14   sp_ManageRetrieveProducts Stored Procedure

```
CREATE PROCEDURE sp_ManagerRetrieveProducts

@intStartProdID int,
@intRowCount int

AS

set rowcount @intRowCount

select idProduct, chrProductName, intPrice
from products where idProduct >= @intStartProdID
GO
```

That does it for providing the key features of the product listing. This serves as the gateway to product management. Figure 10.5 shows the product listing page as it starts out.

FIGURE 10.5:

Product listing

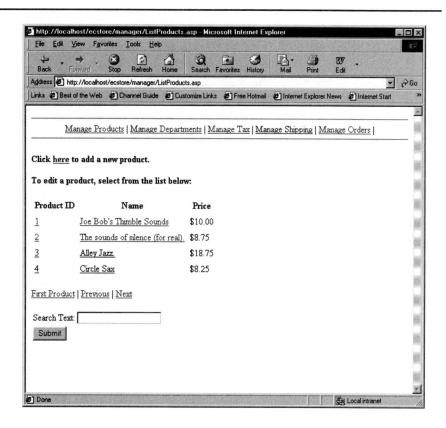

Click on the *next* link and move the listing to the next set of products. Figure 10.6 shows the listing.

FIGURE 10.6:

Second page in product listing

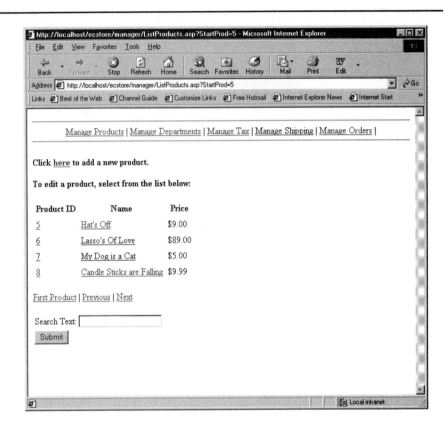

The search page works in much the same way as the product listing page. But in this case we are narrowing down the list products that contain the searched-for keywords.

Listing 10.15 shows the SearchProducts.asp page. The page starts in the usual fashion with the appropriate includes.

LISTING 10.15   **SearchProducts.asp**

```
<%@ Language=VBScript %>
<!-- #Include file="include/validatecheck.asp" -->
<HTML>
<!--
    SearchProducts.asp - Provides a feature to search
    for products from the list.
-->
```

```
<HEAD>
<META NAME="GENERATOR" Content="Microsoft Visual Studio 6.0">
</HEAD>
<BODY>

<!-- #include file="include/navinclude.asp" -->
```

The beginning of the coding starts in the same way with creating a new database connection and checking the product increment variables. The search text is also retrieved from the posted query. If a query is not posted, then it is read from the session variable which is set after the first posting. (See Listing 10.16.)

LISTING 10.16   SearchProducts.asp Continued

```
<%

'  Create an ADO database connection
set dbProducts = server.createobject("adodb.connection")

'  Create the record set
set rsProducts = server.CreateObject("adodb.recordset")

'  Open the connection using our ODBC file DSN
dbProducts.open("filedsn=WildWillieCDs")

'  Check to see if there is any search text.
if request("SearchText") <> "" then

    '  Retrieve the search text
    session("SearchText") = request("SearchText")

end if
```

The *ProdInc* and *StartProd* variables are checked as in the product listing page (see Listing 10.17). They are defaulted as appropriate if not set.

LISTING 10.17   SearchProducts.asp Continued

```
'  Check for the product increment setting for the
'  number of items to be displayed at once.
```

```
if session("ProdInc") = "" then

    '   Set the increment to 4 products.
    session("ProdInc") = "4"

end if

'   Get the starting product number
StartProd = request("StartProd")

'   Check to see if it is set.
if StartProd = "" then

    '   If not then start at the first product
    StartProd = 1

end if

'   Check to see if the user has moved before
'   the first product
if StartProd < 1 then

    '   Go to the first product
    StartProd = 1

end if
```

Next, in Listing 10.18, we execute the sp_ManagerRetrieveProdSearch stored procedure. Unlike the sp_ManageRetrieveProducts stored procedure, this one includes a search parameter to return only products that meet the criteria. Note that unlike the listing of products, we don't need to check if a blank record set was returned since that is a possibility on the search.

LISTING 10.18   SearchProducts.asp Continued

```
'   Execute the sp_ManageRetrieveProdSearch stored procedure
'   to get products that match the search criteria.
sql = "execute sp_ManagerRetrieveProdSearch " & _
    StartProd & ", " & session("ProdInc") & ", '" & _
    Session("SearchText") & "'"

'   Execute the statement
```

```
set rsProducts = dbProducts.Execute(sql)

%>
```

Now the listing begins (see Listing 10.19). There is a link to create a new product. There is also a link back to the full product listing in case the user wants to end the search. Next the products list out with links to the product manager page.

LISTING 10.19   SearchProducts.asp Continued

```
<!-- Build a link to the NewProduct.asp page in case the
     user wants to add a new product.  -->
<BR><b>Click <a href="NewProduct.asp">here</a>
to add a new product.</b>

<!-- Build a link to list the full product selection  -->
<BR><BR><b>Click <a href="ListProducts.asp">here</a>
 to see the full listing.</b>

<!-- Start the display of the search list.  -->
<BR><BR><b>To edit a product, select from the
list below:</b><BR><BR>

<table cellpadding="3" cellspacing="3">
<tr>
    <th>Product ID</th>
    <th>Name</th>
    <th>Price</th>
</tr>

<%

' Loop through the products.
do until rsProducts.EOF

%>

<tr>
    <td>
    <!-- Display the product id.  And, build a link to the
         ManageProduct.asp with the product id  -->
    <a href="ManageProduct.asp?idProduct=<%=rsProducts("idProduct")%>">
```

```
<%=rsProducts("idProduct")%></a></td>

<td>
<!-- Display the product name.  And, build a link to
    the ManageProduct.asp with the product id  -->
<a href="ManageProduct.asp ↵
?idProduct=<%=rsProducts("idProduct")%>">
  <%=rsProducts("chrProductName")%></a>
</td>

<!-- Show the product price.  Note it is stored as an
      integer.  -->
<td>
<%=formatcurrency(rsProducts("intPrice")/100, 2)%>
</td>
</tr>

<%

'  Move to the next row
rsProducts.MoveNext

'  Loop back
Loop

%>

</table>
```

Finally, as shown in Listing 10.20, the page ends with the same navigation features as the list products. But in this case we are posting back to this page so the search can be re-executed and the next list of products shown.

LISTING 10.20   SearchProducts.asp Continued

```
<BR>
<!-- Build the navigation to move backwards and forwards
      between the product screens.  -->
<a href="SearchProducts.asp
        ?StartProd=1">First Product</a> |
<a href="SearchProducts.asp?StartProd= ↵
  <%=StartProd - cint (Session("ProdInc"))%>
```

```
        Previous</a> |
<a href="SearchProducts.asp?StartProd= ↵
   <%=StartProd + cint(Session("ProdInc"))%>">
   Next</a>

<BR><BR>

<!-- Build the form to execute a new search. -->
<form method="post" action="SearchProducts.asp">

<!-- Build the table -->
<table>
```

A search option is also provided in case the user wants to search again for another product (see Listing 10.21).

LISTING 10.21 **SearchProducts.asp Continued**

```
<!-- Build the input HTML element for the search text. -->
<tr>
    <td align="right">Search Text:</td>
    <td><input type="text" value="" name="SearchText"></td>
</tr>

<!-- Build a submit button for the search. -->
<tr>
    <td colspan="2">
        <input type="submit" value="Submit" name="Submit">
    </td>
</tr>
</table>

</form>

</BODY>
</HTML>
```

One stored procedure is utilized on the page, sp_ManageRetrieveProdSearch. In this case, a search is done on the product name for the keyword entered by the user (see Listing 10.22).

LISTING 10.22   **sp_ManagerRetrieveProdSearch Stored Procedure**

```
CREATE PROCEDURE sp_ManagerRetrieveProdSearch

@intStartProdID int,
@intRowCount int,
@chrSearchText varchar(100)

AS

set rowcount @intRowCount

select idProduct, chrProductName, intPrice
from products
where idProduct >= @intStartProdID and
      chrProductName like '%' + @chrSearchText+ '%'
```

Now we can execute a product search from the product listing page. Type in the keyword "Dog." Figure 10.7 shows the search results.

FIGURE 10.7:

Product search on "Dog"

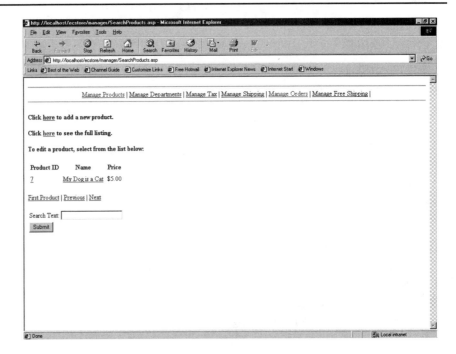

Next we can move to the adding of a new product to the database. We can click on the *Add New Product* link on the product listing or the listing search page.

Listing 10.23 builds the page for entering in a new product into the database. This page is basically a data entry form with no direct VBScript code. The page starts out with the standard validation check and the navigation bar include at the top of the page.

LISTING 10.23   NewProduct.asp

```
<%@ Language=VBScript %>
<!-- #Include file="include/validatecheck.asp" -->
<html>
<!--
    NewProduct.asp - Handles adding in a new product
    into the store.
-->

<head>
<meta NAME="GENERATOR" Content="Microsoft Visual Studio 6.0">
</head>
<body>

<!-- #Include file="include/navinclude.asp" -->
```

The form will post to the AddNewProduct.asp page (see Listing 10.24). Then a series of HTML elements is created for entering in the product name, description, image, and active status. Note that the attributes and department assignments are not defined in this page, but will be managed in the ManageProduct.asp page.

LISTING 10.24   NewProduct.asp Continued

```
<!-- Form to post the new product to the database  -->
<form method="post" action="AddNewProduct.asp">

<!-- Table build the form for adding the new product  -->
<table cellpadding="3" cellspacing="3">

<!-- Product Name Input  -->
<tr>
    <td align="right"><b>Product Name:</b></td>
```

```
            <td>
              <input type="text" value=""
              name="chrProductName" size="60">
            </td>
        </tr>

        <!--  Product Description Input  -->
        <tr>
            <td align="right"><b>Product Description:</b></td>
            <td>
        <textarea cols="50" rows="10" name="txtDescription">
        </textarea>
            </td>
        </tr>

        <!--  Product Image Input  -->
        <tr>
            <td align="right"><b>Product Image:</b></td>
            <td><input type="text" value=""
                name="chrProductImage">
            </td>
        </tr>

        <!--  Product Price Input  -->
        <tr>
            <td align="right"><b>Product Price:</b></td>
            <td>
            <input type="text" value="" name="intPrice">
            </td>
        </tr>

        <!--  Check box to indicate the product is active  -->
        <tr>
            <td align="right"><b>Active:</b></td>
            <td>
                <input type="checkbox" value="1" name="intActive">
            </td>
        </tr>

        <!--  Submit button to add the product  -->
        <tr>
            <td colspan="2" align="center">
```

```
                <input type="submit" value="Add Product"
                        name="Submit">
        </td>
    </tr>

    <!-- Close out the page.  -->
    </table>
    </form>

    </body>
    </html>
```

Listing 10.25 shows the code to add the new product data into the database. The different values are retrieved from the database. Note that the price is multiplied by 100 to store the value as a whole integer.

The sp_InsertProduct stored procedure is called to then insert the data. Once the product is inserted, the ID of the new product is returned and the user is sent to the ManagepProduct.asp page to edit the data.

LISTING 10.25   AddNewProduct.asp

```
<%@ Language=VBScript %>
<%
'   ********************************************************
'   AddNewProduct.asp - Handles adding a new product to
'   the store.
'   ********************************************************

'   Retrieve the product name and ensure that any
'   single quotes are doubled.
chrProductName = replace(request("chrProductName"), "'", _
    "''")

'   Retrieve the product description and ensure that
'   any single quotes are doubled.
txtDescription = replace(request("txtDescription"), "'", _
    "''")

'   Retrieve the product image.
chrProductImage = request("chrProductImage")
```

```
'  Retrieve the price.  Ensure that we multiply
'  times 100 to store as a whole integer.
intPrice = request("intPrice") * 100


'  Retrieve the active setting.
intActive = request("intActive")


'  We have to check and see if any setting is made.
'  It will not be set if the box is not checked.
if intActive = "" then

    '  Set the flag to 0 so it is not active.
    intActive = 0

else

    '  Set the flag to 0 so it is active.
    intActive = 1

end if



'  Create an ADO database connection
set dbProduct = server.createobject("adodb.connection")

'  Create the record set
set rsProduct = server.CreateObject("adodb.recordset")

'  Open the connection using our ODBC file DSN
dbProduct.open("filedsn=WildWillieCDs")

'  Execute the sp_InsertProduct stored procedure
'  to add the product into the database.
sql = "execute sp_InsertProduct '" & _
    chrProductName & "', '" & _
    txtDescription & "', '" & _
    chrProductImage & "', " & _
    intPrice & ", " & _
    intActive

'  Execute the statement
```

```
set rsProduct = dbProduct.Execute(sql)

'  Send the user to the ManageProduct.asp page to allow
'  the user to edit the new product.
Response.Redirect "ManageProduct.asp?idProduct=" & _
                     rsProduct("idProduct")

%>
```

The sp_InsertProduct stored procedure handles adding the new product into the database (see Listing 10.26). The appropriate data is passed in as variables and inserted into the database. Note that the new product ID is returned.

LISTING 10.26   sp_InsertProduct Stored Procedure

```
CREATE PROCEDURE sp_InsertProduct
@chrProductName varchar(255),
@txtDescription text,
@chrProductImage varchar(255),
@intPrice int,
@intActive int

AS

insert into Products(chrProductName, txtDescription, chrProductImage,
intPrice, intActive)
values(@chrProductName, @txtDescription, @chrProductImage, @intPrice,
@intActive)

select idProduct = @@identity
```

Figure 10.8 shows the *add new product* page. Simply fill out the form and the data is entered into the database. Then the edit mode will come up on the product management page.

FIGURE 10.8:

Add a new product

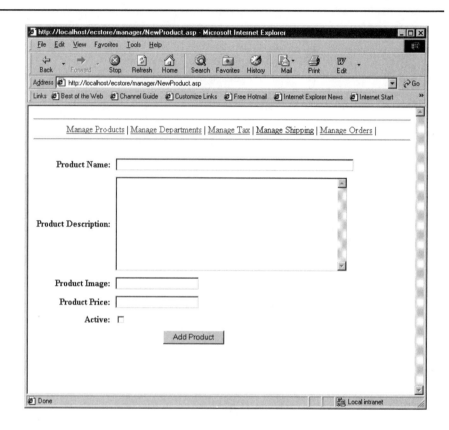

Next, as shown in Listing 10.27, we start with our complex product management page. This is going to provide in one view all of the settings for the product data. The page starts out in the usual format with the header of the page being set with the security validation and the navigation bar.

LISTING 10.27   ManageProduct.asp

```
<%@ Language=VBScript %>
<!-- #Include file="include/validatecheck.asp" -->
<html>
<!--
    ManageProduct.asp - Provides the tools to manage
    the product data.
-->
```

```
<head>
<meta NAME="GENERATOR"
      Content="Microsoft Visual Studio 6.0">
</head>
<body>

<!-- #Include file="include/navinclude.asp" -->
```

The first step is to retrieve the product data. The ID of the product is passed on the URL to the page. This is read and the sp_RetrieveProduct stored procedure is executed to return the product data. (See Listing 10.28.)

LISTING 10.28   ManageProduct.asp Continued

```
<%

'  Create an ADO database connection
set dbProduct = server.createobject("adodb.connection")

'  Create the record set
set rsProduct = server.CreateObject("adodb.recordset")

'  Open the connection using our ODBC file DSN
dbProduct.open("filedsn=WildWillieCDs")

'  The sp_RetrieveProduct stored procedure is utilized to
'  get the data for the specified product.
sql = "execute sp_RetrieveProduct " & request("idProduct")

'  Execute the statement
set rsProduct = dbProduct.Execute(sql)

%>
```

The display is started with a form where the core product information will be posted to the UpdateProduct.asp page, shown in Listing 10.29. A table is then built for displaying the product information. Note that a preview link is built to see the product displayed in the real store. This can be helpful in seeing how the product looks before setting the *active* flag.

LISTING 10.29   ManageProduct.asp Continued

```
<!-- Start the form to update the product data.  -->
<form method="post" action="UpdateProduct.asp">

<!-- Start the table to display the product data.  -->
<table cellpadding="3" cellspacing="3">

<tr>
    <td align="right"><b>Preview Product:</b></td>
    <!-- To preview the product a link is built to
         the product.asp page in the live store.
         The Id of the product is passed on the URL.  -->
    <td>
     <a href="/ecstore/wildwilliecds/product.asp↵
     ?idProduct=<%=request("idProduct")%>">Preview</a>
    </td>
</tr>

<tr>
    <td align="right"><b>Delete Product:</b></td>
    <!-- A link to the deleteproduct.asp page is
         created to remove the product from the
         database.  The ID of the product is
         passed.  -->
    <td>
     <a href="../Manager/DeleteProduct.asp ↵
     ?idProduct=<%=request("idProduct")%>">Delete</a>
    </td>
</tr>

<tr>
    <td colspan="2"><hr></td>
</tr>
<tr>
    <!-- The product ID is displayed.  To ensure the ID
         can be retrieved for the update a hidden
         HTML element is created.  -->
    <td align="right"><b>Product ID:</b></td>
    <td><%=rsProduct("idProduct")%>
        <input type="hidden"
        value="<%=request("idProduct")%>"
      name="idProduct">
```

```
            </td>
        </tr>
        <tr>
            <td align="right"><b>Product Name:</b></td>
            <!--  Display the product name.   -->
            <td><input type="text"
                value="<%=rsProduct("chrProductName")%>"
                name="chrProductName" size="60">
            </td>
        </tr>
        <tr>
            <td align="right"><b>Product Description:</b></td>
            <!--  Display the product description.   -->
            <td>
                <textarea cols="50" rows="10"
                name="txtDescription"> ↵
<%=rsProduct("txtDescription")%></textarea></td>
        </tr>
```

The product image file is displayed in an HTML input element. We also display the image on the page (see Listing 10.30).

LISTING 10.30   ManageProduct.asp Continued

```
        <tr>
            <td align="right"><b>Product Image:</b></td>
            <!--  Display the product image file name and display
                  the image as well.   -->
            <td>
            <input type="text"
            value="<%=rsProduct("chrProductImage")%>"
                name="chrProductImage">     

            <img src="../wildwilliecds/images/products/sm_ ↵
            <%=rsProduct("chrProductImage")%>"
                align="center">
            </td>
        </tr>
        <tr>
            <td align="right"><b>Product Price:</b></td>
            <!--  The product price is displayed.   -->
            <td><input type="text"
```

```
            value="<%=rsProduct("intPrice")/100%>"
              name="intPrice"></td>
    </tr>
    <tr>
       <td align="right"><b>Active:</b></td>
       <td>
```

Note that the Active check box will be defaulted to the previous setting. We check the setting and then build the right HTML code to have it checked or not (see Listing 10.31).

LISTING 10.31   **ManageProduct.asp Continued**

```
        <%

        '  Check to see if the product is active.
        if rsProduct("intActive") = 1 then

        %>

        <!--  Display the check box checked if the
              product is active.  -->
        <input type="checkbox" value="1" CHECKED
        name="intActive">

        <%
        else
        %>

        <!--  Display the check box with out the check.  -->
        <input type="checkbox" value="1" name="intActive">

        <% end if %>

      </td>
    </tr>

    <tr>
       <td colspan="2" align="center">
         <!--  Submit button for the form update -->
         <input type="submit" value="Update Product"
```

```
        name="Submit">
     </td>
  </tr>

  </table>
  </form>

  <hr>
```

The next section of the page will handle the management of the department assignments for the products. Remember that a product can be assigned to many different departments. The sp_RetrieveDeptByProd stored procedure is executed to retrieve all current department assignments. (See Listing 10.32.)

LISTING 10.32   ManageProduct.asp Continued

```
<%

'  Create an ADO database connection
set dbDeptProd = server.createobject("adodb.connection")

'  Create the record set
set rsDeptProd = server.CreateObject("adodb.recordset")

'  Open the connection using our ODBC file DSN
dbDeptProd.open("filedsn=WildWillieCDs")

'  Execute the sp_RetrieveDeptByProd to retrieve
'  the departments for the product being edited.
sql = "execute sp_RetrieveDeptByProd " & _
      request("idProduct")

'  Execute the statement
set rsDeptProd = dbDeptProd.Execute(sql)

%>
```

The departments are then listed in a table. Each option on the table allows for a corresponding deletion of the department assignment. The ID of the product is added on to the URL to the RemoveProdDept.asp page. (See Listing 10.33.)

LISTING 10.33   ManageProduct.asp Continued

```
<!-- Start the table to display the
     department list. -->
<table cellpadding="3" cellspacing="3" border="1">
<tr>
    <th>Department</th>
    <th>Delete</th>
<tr>
<%
'  Loop through the departments.
do until rsDeptProd.eof
%>

<tr>
    <!-- Display the department name. -->
    <td><%=rsDeptProd("chrDeptName")%></td>
    <!-- Build a link to the RemoveProdDept.asp page
         to remove the department from the list. -->
    <td>
     <a href="RemoveProdDept.asp ↵
?idProduct=<%=request("idProduct")%> ↵
&idDepartmentProduct= ↵
<%=rsDeptProd("idDepartmentProduct")%>"> ↵
Delete</a>
    </td>
</tr>

</tr>

<%
'  Move to the next department product
rsDeptProd.movenext
Loop
%>

</table>
```

Following the list of current department assignments, we now add in a list of
existing departments so we can make new assignments. Note that this is a new
form that will post to ProdAddDept.asp.

NOTE

> **NOTE** Note that in this case we simply list all available departments. But it may make more sense to list only departments that are currently not assigned. Or, we may wish to do some error checking when the new department is posted to be added.

The sp_RetrieveDepts stored procedure will retrieve all current departments. Then a Do Loop is executed to build the select option box. Note that the ID of the product is added as a hidden variable on the form. That way when the department is to be added, it can be easily determined which product to make the assignment to. (See Listing 10.34.)

LISTING 10.34   ManageProduct.asp Continued

```
<br>

<!--  Start a new form to add an addition
      department for the product.  -->
<form method="post" action="ProdAddDept.asp">
<b>Add a department:</b>

<%

'  Create an ADO database connection
set dbDepts = server.createobject("adodb.connection")

'  Create the record set
set rsDepts = server.CreateObject("adodb.recordset")

'  Open the connection using our ODBC file DSN
dbDepts.open("filedsn=WildWillieCDs")

'  Retrieve all of the departments in the database
sql = "execute sp_RetrieveDepts"

'  Execute the statement
set rsDepts = dbDepts.Execute(sql)

%>

<!--  Start the select box for the list of
      departments.  -->
<select name="idDepartment">
```

```
<%
'  Loop through the departments
do until rsDepts.eof
%>

    <!--  Build the option list for each
          department.  -->
    <option value="<%=rsDepts("idDepartment")%>">
                  <%=rsDepts("chrDeptName")%>

<%
'  Move to the next row
rsDepts.movenext
loop
%>

</select>

<!--  Build a hidden variable in this form so
      we know what product to assign this
      department to.  -->
<input type="hidden" name="idProduct"
value="<%=request("idProduct")%>">

<!--  Submit button from the form.  -->
<input type="submit" value="Submit" name="Submit">

</form>

<hr>
```

Following the departments, we are ready to manage the attributes (see Listing 10.35). In this case we will build the logic to specifically work with the Color and Size attributes.

The first section is for the *color* attribute. The sp_Attributes stored procedure is utilized to retrieve all of the current attributes assigned to the product.

LISTING 10.35   ManageProduct.asp Continued

```
<%

'  Create an ADO database connection
```

```
set dbAttributes = server.createobject("adodb.connection")

'  Create a record set
set rsAttributes = server.CreateObject("adodb.recordset")

'  Open the connection using our ODBC file DSN
dbAttributes.open("filedsn=WildWillieCDs")

'  Execute the stored procedure to retrieve the attributes
'  for the products.
sql = "execute sp_Attributes " & request("idProduct")

'  Execute the SQL statement
set rsAttributes = dbProduct.Execute(sql)

%>
```

A table is built to list the attributes (see Listing 10.36). As with the departments, we will build a delete option next to each attribute so it can be deleted from the product settings.

LISTING 10.36   ManageProduct.asp Continued

```
<!--  Start the table to build list of color and
      size attributes.  -->
<table>

<tr>
    <td>
        <b>COLOR:</b>

        <!--  Build a list of current color assignments.  -->
        <table cellpadding="3" cellspacing="3" border="1">

            <%

            '  Loop through the attributes.
            do until rsAttributes.EOF

            '  Check to see if we have moved beyond the
            '  color attribute in the list..
            if rsAttributes("chrCategoryName") <> _
```

```asp
                    "Color" then

                        '  Exit the do loop
                        exit do

                end if

                %>

                <tr>
                <td>
                <!-- Display the attribute name.  -->
                <%=rsAttributes("chrAttributeName")%>
                </td>
                <td>
                    <!--  Build a link to the
                            DeleteAttribute.asp page
                            to remove the attribute for the
                            product.  -->
                    <a href="DeleteAttribute.asp ↵
                ?idProduct=<%=request("idProduct")%> ↵
                &idProductAttribute= ↵
                <%=rsAttributes("idProductAttribute")%>">
                    Delete</a>
                </td>
                </tr>
                <%

                '  Move to the next row
                rsAttributes.MoveNext

                '  Loop back
                loop

                %>

        </table>
    </td>
</tr>
<!--  Build a buffer between the listings.  -->
<tr><td> </td></tr>
```

Next, as shown in Listing 10.37, the current size attributes are displayed as well. As with the color attribute, the table is built with the names of the size attributes. And, there is a *delete* link put next to each size attribute with the ID of the attribute on the URL.

LISTING 10.37   ManageProduct.asp Continued

```
<tr>
    <!-- Start the size listings -->
    <td>
        <b>SIZE: </b>

        <!-- Start the size listing table.  -->
        <table cellpadding="3" cellspacing="3" border="1">

            <%

            ' Loop through the size attributes
            do until rsAttributes.EOF

            %>

            <tr>
            <td>
            <!-- Display the name of the size
                 attribute -->
            <%=rsAttributes("chrAttributeName")%>
            </td>
            <td>
                <!-- Build a link to the
                     DeleteAttribute.asp page to remove
                     the size setting for the product.
                  -->
                <a href="DeleteAttribute.asp ⏎
?idProduct=<%=request("idProduct")%> ⏎
&idProductAttribute= ⏎
<%=rsAttributes("idProductAttribute")%>">
Delete</a>
            </td>
            </tr>
```

```
<%

'  Move to the next row
rsAttributes.MoveNext

'  Loop back
loop

%>

</table>

</td>

</tr>

</table>
```

Next we will need to show the attribute list so the shopper can pick from the available list of size and color attributes for the product. To help break out the code a bit we will call a subroutine, ShowAttributeList, to build this section of the page (see Listing 10.38). Then the page ends appropriately.

LISTING 10.38   ManageProduct.asp Continued

```
<!-- Call the ShowAttributeList subroutine -->
<% ShowAttributeList %>

<!-- Close out the page -->
</body>
</html>
```

The ShowAttributeList subroutine follows much of the same logic as the listing of the current size and color attributes. In this case the sp_RetrieveAttributes stored procedure is called to retrieve all of the attributes in the database (see Listing 10.39).

LISTING 10.39   ManageProduct.asp Continued

```
<!-- Start the ShowAttributeList subroutine. -->

<%
```

```
'  Start the subroutine.
Sub ShowAttributeList()

'  Create an ADO database connection
set dbAttributes = server.createobject("adodb.connection")

'  Create a record set
set rsAttributes = server.CreateObject("adodb.recordset")

'  Open the connection using our ODBC file DSN
dbAttributes.open("filedsn=WildWillieCDs")

'  Execute the stored procedure to retrieve the attributes
'  in the database.
sql = "execute sp_RetrieveAttributes"

'  Execute the SQL statement
set rsAttributes = dbProduct.Execute(sql)

%>

<br>

<!-- Start the option to build the list of
     attributes in the database.  -->
<b>Select an Attribute to Add:</b>
```

In Listing 10.40, a table is created to hold the select boxes. Each set of attributes is listed as an option to be added to the attribute list for the product. Note that a form is created for each select box. The form posts to the AddAttribute.asp page. Note that a hidden variable in the form is created to indicate which product the attribute should be added to.

LISTING 10.40   ManageProduct.asp Continued

```
<table>

<tr>
    <!-- Color column -->
    <td>
        <!-- Build a form to post the adding of the
```

```
            attribute.  -->
<form method="post" action="AddAttribute.asp">
Color:

<!-- Select box for display of the color options -->
<select name="idAttribute">

    <%

    ' Loop through the attributes.
    do until rsAttributes.EOF

    ' Check to see if we have moved beyond the
    ' color attribute in the list..
    if rsAttributes("chrCategoryName") <> _
      "Color" then

        ' Exit the do loop
        exit do

    end if

    %>

    <!-- Build the option value for the color.  The
         value will be the ID of the color -->
    <option value="
          <%=rsAttributes("idAttribute")%>">
          <%=rsAttributes("chrAttributeName")%>
    <%

    ' Move to the next row
    rsAttributes.MoveNext

    ' Loop back
    loop

    %>

</select>

<!--  Build a hidden variable to store the id
      of the product so we know what product to
```

```
                add the attribute to.  -->
            <input type="hidden"
            value="<%=rsProduct("idProduct")%>"
            name="idProduct">

            <!--  Submit button to add the attribute to the list.
            -->
            <input type="Submit" value="Add" name="Submit">
            </form>
        </td>
    </tr>
```

After the Color select box, the Size select box is created in the same manner (see Listing 10.41).

NOTE   Again, we may not want to list current size and color attributes that have already been assigned to the product.

LISTING 10.41   ManageProduct.asp Continued

```
    <tr>
        <!--  Build the size attributes select box.  -->
        <td>
            <form method="post" action="AddAttribute.asp">
            Size:

            <!--  Start the size select box -->
            <select name="idAttribute">

                <%

                '  Loop through the size attributes
                do until rsAttributes.EOF

                %>

                <!--  Display the options -->
                <option value="
                <%=rsAttributes("idAttribute")%>">
                <%=rsAttributes("chrAttributeName")%>
```

```
<%

    '   Move to the next row
    rsAttributes.MoveNext

    '   Loop back
    loop

%>

</select>

<!--  Build the hidden HTML element to store the
      product id.  -->
<input type="hidden"
value="<%=rsProduct("idProduct")%>"
name="idProduct">

<!--  Build the submit button for the form.  -->
<input type="Submit" value="Add" name="Submit">
</form>
        </td>

    </tr>

    </table>

    <%
    End Sub
    %>
```

That does it for the management of the product. We have three primary sections of the page that provide our product management. The first is the management of the core product data. The second is the department management and the third section is the attribute assignment.

We utilize several stored procedures in this page. The first, sp_Retrieve-Product, handles pulling back the core product data based on the product ID passed into the stored procedure. (See Listing 10.42.)

LISTING 10.42   **sp_RetrieveProduct Stored Procedure**

```
/*  Retrieve the product data */
CREATE PROCEDURE sp_RetrieveProduct

/*  Pass in the ID of the product */
@idProduct int

AS

/*  Select the product data */
select * from products
where idProduct = @idProduct
```

Next, in Listing 10.43, we have a stored procedure that will retrieve the department details for any given product. The ID of the product is passed into the stored procedure.

LISTING 10.43   **sp_RetrieveDeptByProd Stored Procedure**

```
CREATE PROCEDURE sp_RetrieveDeptByProd

@idProduct int

AS

select * from department, departmentproducts
where departmentproducts.idProduct = @idProduct and
department.iddepartment = departmentproducts.iddepartment
```

We also need to be able to retrieve all current departments from the database. The sp_RetrieveDepts stored procedure will do this for us (see Listing 10.44).

LISTING 10.44   **sp_RetrieveDepts Stored Procedure**

```
/*  Stored procedure to retrieve all of
    the departments in the database */
CREATE PROCEDURE sp_RetrieveDepts AS

/*  Select all of the departments data */
select * from department
```

The next stored procedure handles retrieving attribute assignments for the current product (see Listing 10.45). The ID of the product is passed into the stored procedure. In this case we have to combine the products, productattribute, attribute, and attributecategory tables; we do this using a SQL join.

LISTING 10.45   sp_Attributes Stored Procedure

```
/*  Returns the attributes in the database for the
    specified product.
*/
CREATE PROCEDURE sp_Attributes

/*  Pass in the ID of the product */
@idProduct int

AS

/*  select statement to return attributes for the product. */
select products.idproduct,
       attribute.idattribute,
       attribute.chrattributename,
       attributecategory.chrcategoryname,
       productattribute.idproductattribute

from products, productattribute, attribute, attributecategory

where

products.idproduct = @idProduct and
productattribute.idproduct = @idProduct and
productattribute.idattribute = attribute.idattribute and
attribute.idattributecategory = attributecategory.idattributecategory

order by chrcategoryname
```

Finally, in Listing 10.46, we build a stored procedure to return all of the attributes in the current database.

LISTING 10.46   sp_RetrieveAttributes Stored Procedure

```
CREATE PROCEDURE sp_RetrieveAttributes AS

select * from attribute, attributecategory
where
  attribute.idattributecategory =
  attributecategory.idAttributeCategory

order by attributecategory.chrCategoryName
```

Figure 10.9 shows the product being edited. All of the current data is retrieved from the database and populated into the form. Note that there are no department or attribute assignments on the page.

FIGURE 10.9:

Product editing

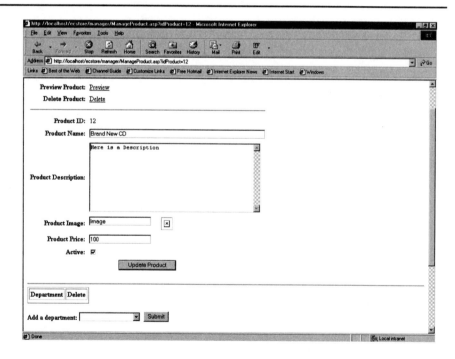

Now let's add a new department to the product. Select "Cool Backstreet Jazz" department and click Submit. Figure 10.10 shows the new department assignment for the product.

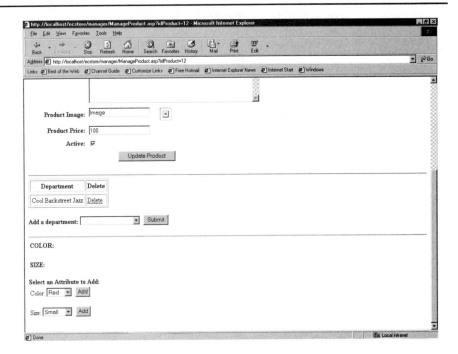

Next let's add a second department to the product. Select the "Punked Out" department and add it to the list. Figure 10.11 shows the department added.

FIGURE 10.11:

Adding a second
department

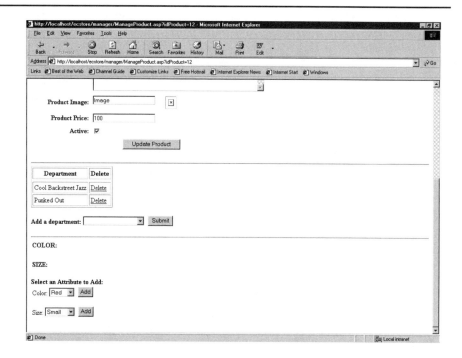

Now we can choose an option to remove a department that we have just
assigned. Figure 10.12 shows the "Cool Backstreet Jazz" department being
removed from the product assignment.

FIGURE 10.12:

Removing a department

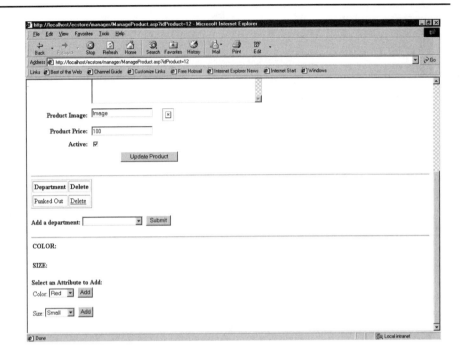

Next we can move on to the attribute assignments for the product. Select from the select boxes the *red* and *small* attributes and add them to the product. Figure 10.13 shows the settings. You can also experiment with deleting attributes.

Now that we have our new product set up, you can preview the product in the store by clicking on the *preview* link.

Next let's look at the maintenance pages behind the functionality. First, in Listing 10.47, we have the code to delete the product from the database, DeleteProduct .asp. This is a code-only page that will return to the listing of the products.

FIGURE 10.13:

Adding color and size attributes

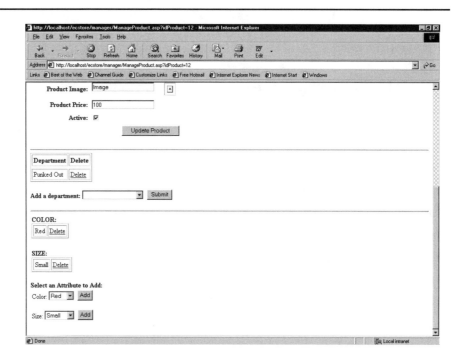

LISTING 10.47   DeleteProduct.asp

```
<%@ Language=VBScript %>
<%
'    ******************************************************
'    DeleteProduct.asp - Deletes the produce from the
'    store.
'    ******************************************************

'    Create an ADO database connection
set dbProduct = server.createobject("adodb.connection")

'    Create the record set
set rsProduct = server.CreateObject("adodb.recordset")

'    Open the connection using our ODBC file DSN
dbProduct.open("filedsn=WildWillieCDs")
```

The sp_DeleteProduct stored procedure is called with the ID of the product passed into it (see Listing 10.48). The product is deleted and the user is sent back to the listing of the products.

LISTING 10.48   **DeleteProduct.asp Continued**

```
'   Call the sp_DeleteProduct stored procedure to
'   remove the product from the database.
sql = "execute sp_DeleteProduct " & request("idProduct")

'   Execute the statement
set rsProduct = dbProduct.Execute(sql)

'   Send the user back to the list of producs.
Response.Redirect "ListProducts.asp"

%>
```

Listing 10.49 shows the code for the stored procedure. It contains a delete SQL statement that removes the product data.

TIP   We are not actually deleting all corresponding department and attribute assignments for the product as well. To ensure strong referential integrity this could be done in the stored procedure as well as by using triggers in the database.

LISTING 10.49   **sp_DeleteProduct Stored Procedure**

```
CREATE PROCEDURE sp_DeleteProduct

@idProduct int

AS

delete from products where idProduct = @idProduct
```

Next, in Listing 10.50, we have the UpdateProduct.asp page that handles updating the data entered by the user. The first thing that is done is to retrieve the core data entered by the shopper. We have to ensure that any single quotes are doubled for insertion into the database.

LISTING 10.50   UpdateProduct.asp

```
<%@ Language=VBScript %>
<%
'    ********************************************************
'    UpdateProduct.asp - Handles updating the product
'    data.
'    ********************************************************


'    Retrieve the product id
idProduct = request("idProduct")

'    Retrieve the product name and ensure any single
'    quotes are doubled.
chrProductName = replace(request("chrProductName"), _
    "'", "''")


'    Retrieve the product description and ensure any single
'    quotes are doubled.
txtDescription = replace(request("txtDescription"), _
    "'", "''")


'    Retrieve the product image
chrProductImage = request("chrProductImage")


'    Retrieve the product price and multiply by 100 to
'    ensure it is stored as an integer.
intPrice = request("intPrice") * 100


'    Retrieve the active status.
intActive = request("intActive")
```

A check is done on the active setting to see what the value is (see Listing 10.51). If it is not set, then we need to insert 0 into the database.

LISTING 10.51   UpdateProduct.asp Continued

```
'    Check to see if the active check box was set.
if intActive = "" then

    '    If not then make the product inactive
    intActive = 0
```

```
else

    '  If it is then set it to be active
    intActive = 1

end if
```

Once we have the data from the posted form, we are ready to create our database connection and post the changes to the database (shown in Listing 10.52). The sp_UpdateProduct stored procedure is called to execute the SQL statement. Finally the shopper is sent back to the ManageProduct.asp page to continue editing the product.

LISTING 10.52   **UpdateProduct.asp Continued**

```
'  Create an ADO database connection
set dbProduct = server.createobject("adodb.connection")

'  Create the record set
set rsProduct = server.CreateObject("adodb.recordset")

'  Open the connection using our ODBC file DSN
dbProduct.open("filedsn=WildWillieCDs")

'  Execute the SQL stored procedure to update the
'  product data
sql = "execute sp_UpdateProduct " & _
      request("idProduct") & ", '" & _
      chrProductName & "', '" & _
      txtDescription & "', '" & _
      chrProductImage & "', " & _
      intPrice & ", " & _
      intActive

'  Execute the statement
set rsProduct = dbProduct.Execute(sql)

'  Send the user back to the product manager page and
'  pass back the product i.
Response.Redirect "ManageProduct.asp?idProduct=" & _
                  request("idProduct")

%>
```

The sp_UpdateProduct stored procedure handles updating the product data based on the values passed into the stored procedure (see Listing 10.53).

LISTING 10.53   sp_UpdateProduct Stored Procedure

```
CREATE PROCEDURE sp_UpdateProduct

@idProduct int,
@chrProductName varchar(255),
@txtDescription text,
@chrProductImage varchar(100),
@intPrice int,
@intActive int

AS

update products set
    chrProductName = @chrProductName,
    txtDescription = @txtDescription,
    chrProductImage = @chrProductImage,
    intPrice = @intPrice,
    intActive = @intActive
where
    idProduct = @idProduct
```

The remove product department page will handle removing the assignment of a department to a product (see Listing 10.54). The ID of the department product assignment is passed into the page. This is retrieved and the sp_DeleteProdDept stored procedure is called. The user is then passed back to the product management page.

LISTING 10.54   RemoveProdDept.asp

```
<%@ Language=VBScript %>
<%
'    ****************************************************
'    RemoveProdDept.asp - Removes the product from a
'    specific department.
'    ****************************************************

'    Create an ADO database connection
set dbProdDept = server.createobject("adodb.connection")
```

```
'  Create the record set
set rsProdDept = server.CreateObject("adodb.recordset")

'  Open the connection using our ODBC file DSN
dbProdDept.open("filedsn=WildWillieCDs")

'  Execute the sp_DeleteProdDept stored procedure to remove
'  the department assignment for the product.
sql = "execute sp_DeleteProdDept " & request("idDepartmentProduct")

'  Execute the statement
set rsProdDept = dbProdDept.Execute(sql)

'  Send the user back to the product management page
Response.Redirect "ManageProduct.asp?idProduct=" & _
                     request("idProduct")

%>
```

The sp_DeleteProdDept stored procedure removes the product and department relationship in the departmentproducts table (see Listing 10.55). The ID of the relationship is passed into the stored procedure.

LISTING 10.55   **sp_DeleteProdDept Stored Procedure**

```
CREATE PROCEDURE sp_DeleteProdDept

@idDepartmentProduct int

AS

delete from departmentproducts
where idDepartmentProduct = @idDepartmentProduct
```

Our next utility function is the ProdAddDept.asp page (see Listing 10.56). This handles building the assignment of a product to a department. The ID of the product and the ID of the department are passed into the stored procedure. Once the relationship is set up, the user is sent back to the product management page for continued editing.

LISTING 10.56   ProdAddDept.asp

```
<%@ Language=VBScript %>
<%
'    ********************************************************
'    ProdAddDept.asp - Adds a new product into a
'    department.
'    ********************************************************

'    Create an ADO database connection
set dbProdDept = server.createobject("adodb.connection")

'    Create the record set
set rsProdDept = server.CreateObject("adodb.recordset")

'    Open the connection using our ODBC file DSN
dbProdDept.open("filedsn=WildWillieCDs")

'    Execute the sp_AddProdDept stored procedure to
'    tie together the product and the department
sql = "execute sp_AddProdDept " & _
      request("idProduct") & ", " & _
      request("idDepartment")

'    Execute the statement
set rsProdDept = dbProdDept.Execute(sql)

'    Send the user back to the manageproduct.asp page
Response.Redirect "ManageProduct.asp?idProduct=" & _
                  request("idProduct")

%>
```

The sp_AddProdDept stored procedure inserts a new row into the Department-Products table (see Listing 10.57). The relationship is built by passing in the ID of the product and the ID of the department.

LISTING 10.57   sp_AddProdDept Stored Procedure

```
CREATE PROCEDURE sp_AddProdDept
```

```
@idProduct int,
@idDepartment int

AS

insert into DepartmentProducts(idProduct, idDepartment)
values(@idProduct, @idDepartment)
```

Next we move to the attribute management (see Listing 10.58). The first page handles deleting an attribute assignment for the product. In this case the sp_DeleteProductAttribute is utilized. The ID of the product attribute assignment is passed into the page. Once the attribute is deleted, the user is sent to the ManageProduct.asp page.

LISTING 10.58   DeleteAttribute.asp

```
<%@ Language=VBScript %>
<%
'   ********************************************************
'   DeleteAttribute.asp - Deletes an attribute assigned
'   to a product.
'   ********************************************************

'   Create an ADO database connection
set dbProductAttribute = server.createobject("adodb.connection")

'   Create the record set
set rsProductAttribute = server.CreateObject("adodb.recordset")

'   Open the connection using our ODBC file DSN
dbProductAttribute.open("filedsn=WildWillieCDs")

'   The SQL statement removes the product
'   attribute setting for the specified product.
sql = "sp_DeleteProductAttribute " & request("idProductAttribute")

'   Execute the statement
set rsProductAttribute = dbProductAttribute.Execute(sql)

'   Send the user to the ManageProduct.asp page
'   to allow the user to continue editing the
'   product.
```

```
Response.Redirect "ManageProduct.asp?idProduct=" & _
request("idProduct")

%>
```

The ID of the relationship row in the productattribute table is passed into the stored procedure (see Listing 10.59). The row is deleted from the table.

LISTING 10.59   sp_DeleteProductAttribute Stored Procedure

```
CREATE PROCEDURE sp_DeleteProductAttribute

@idProductAttribute int

AS

delete from productattribute
where idProductAttribute = @idProductAttribute
```

Our last page handles adding an attribute assignment for the product (see Listing 10.60). The sp_AddProductAttribute stored procedure makes the relationship combination. The ID of the attribute and the ID of the product are passed into it.

LISTING 10.60   AddAttribute.asp

```
<%@ Language=VBScript %>
<%
'    ********************************************************
'    AddAttribute.asp - Adds the attribute setting for
'    the specified product.
'    ********************************************************

'    Create an ADO database connection
set dbProdAttr = server.createobject("adodb.connection")

'    Create the record set
set rsProdAttr = server.CreateObject("adodb.recordset")

'    Open the connection using our ODBC file DSN
dbProdAttr.open("filedsn=WildWillieCDs")
```

```
'  Execute the sp_AddProductAttribute stored procedure to
'  indicate the attribute is to be assigned to the product.
sql = "execute sp_AddProductAttribute " & _
      request("idAttribute") & ", " & _
      request("idProduct")

'  Execute the statement
set rsProdAttr = dbProdAttr.Execute(sql)

'  Send the user back to the product management page.
Response.Redirect "ManageProduct.asp?idProduct=" & _
                  request("idProduct")

%>
```

The stored procedure builds the insert statement into the productattribute table (see Listing 10.61).

LISTING 10.61   **sp_AddProductAttribute Stored Procedure**

```
CREATE PROCEDURE sp_AddProductAttribute

@idAttribute int,
@idProduct int

AS

insert into ProductAttribute(idAttribute, idProduct)
values(@idAttribute, @idProduct)
```

That does it for the product management. We went from listing and searching of products to adding and editing products. There are a few additional issues we need to address.

Many stores have pre-assigned SKUs by which products are tracked. Typically these SKUs are built of a combination of an internal system product ID combined with the product attributes.

For example, if product 1234 is purchased in yellow and large the SKU might be 1234YL. In our system, we are allowing the product database to generate the SKU. And, we are not allowing the user to edit the SKU. For your system, you may need to provide an additional functionality for SKU management and generation.

There is another note to consider on SKUs regarding prices. For example, some retailers will charge more for XXL sizes or special versions of products, etc. Our store presumes one price per product. If prices were to change by product attribute, we would need to restructure the databases to store prices by attribute.

With regard to images, we are assuming the user will have direct network access to the location where the product images will be placed. If the user is managing the products over the Internet, then we may need to provide additional methods for accessing the location where the images go. We could provide FTP access to the images directory or we could provide an HTML file upload feature.

Next we will move on to the management of the departments.

Managing Departments

We want to be able to add, update, and delete departments in the same fashion as we managed the products. Of course, the department data is much simpler than the product data.

Listing 10.62 begins the listing of the departments. The list is created in a similar fashion to the list of the products. But, a presumption is made that the departments can easily be listed on one page and the previous/next functionality is not needed. And, given the smaller number of listings, the search feature is not needed.

The page starts out in the standard fashion with the security and navigation include on each page. Then an ADO connection is opened to the database to retrieve the current listing of departments.

LISTING 10.62   **ListDepts.asp**

```
<%@ Language=VBScript %>
<!-- #Include file="include/validatecheck.asp" -->
<HTML>
<!--
    ListDepts.asp - Lists the departments in the
    store.
-->

<HEAD>
<META NAME="GENERATOR" Content="Microsoft Visual Studio 6.0">
```

```
</HEAD>
<BODY>

<!-- #include file="include/navinclude.asp" -->

<%

'  Create an ADO database connection
set dbDepts = server.createobject("adodb.connection")

'  Create the record set
set rsDepts = server.CreateObject("adodb.recordset")

'  Open the connection using our ODBC file DSN
dbDepts.open("filedsn=WildWillieCDs")

'  Call the sp_RetrieveDepts stored procedure to
'  return the departments in the database.
sql = "execute sp_RetrieveDepts"

'  Execute the statement
set rsDepts = dbDepts.Execute(sql)

%>
```

The first item on the page is a link to create a new department (see Listing 10.63). That is followed by the setup to list out the departments in a table on the page. The ID of the department and the name are displayed.

LISTING 10.63   ListDepts.asp Continued

```
<!--  Build a link the new department page
      if the user wants to add a department. -->
<BR><b>Click <a href="NewDept.asp">here</a> to add
a new department.</b>

<!--  Start out the structure to show the list
      of departments.
-->
<BR><BR>
<b>To edit a department, select from the list below:</b>
<BR><BR>
```

```
<table cellpadding="3" cellspacing="3">
<tr>
    <th>Department ID</th>
    <th>Name</th>
</tr>
```

Next a loop is built to list out each department (see Listing 10.64). A link to the ManageDept.asp page is created with the ID of the department passed on the link. The link is placed on the ID and the name.

LISTING 10.64   ListDepts.asp Continued

```
<%

'  Loop through the list of departments.
do until rsDepts.EOF

%>

<!--  Create a link to the ManageDept.asp to work
      with the department. -->
<tr>
    <td>
    <!--  The link to the department needs to include the
          id of the department.  Following that the id
          of the deparment is displayed.  -->
    <a href="ManageDept.asp?idDepartment=<%=rsDepts("idDepartment")%>">
<%=rsDepts("idDepartment")%></a></td>

    <!--  The link to the department needs to include the
          id of the department.  Following that the name
          of the deparment is displayed.  -->
    <td>
    <a href="ManageDept.asp?idDepartment=<%=rsDepts("idDepartment")%>">
<%=rsDepts("chrDeptName")%></a></td>

</tr>

<%

'  Move to the next row
```

```
rsDepts.MoveNext

'  Loop back
Loop

%>

</table>

</BODY>
</HTML>
```

One stored procedure, sp_RetrieveDepts, is utilized on the page (see Listing 10.65). It simply performs a select statement to retrieve all department data.

LISTING 10.65   sp_RetrieveDepts Stored Procedure

```
/*  Stored procedure to retrieve all of
    the departments in the database */
CREATE PROCEDURE sp_RetrieveDepts AS

/*  Select all of the departments data */
select * from department
```

Once the list is created, we are ready to begin working on either new or existing departments. Let's first take a look at the code to create a new department. Listing 10.66 shows the NewDept.asp code.

This page will simply build a table of the our key data fields for the department. The page starts out with the usual constructs.

LISTING 10.66   NewDept.asp

```
<%@ Language=VBScript %>
<!-- #Include file="include/validatecheck.asp" -->
<HTML>
<!--
    NewDept.asp - Handles adding in a new department
    into the store.
-->
```

```
<HEAD>
<META NAME="GENERATOR" Content="Microsoft Visual Studio 6.0">
</HEAD>
<BODY>
<!-- #Include file="include/navinclude.asp" -->
```

A form is created that will handle the posting of the new department data to the AddNewDept.asp page. The form will allow input for the department name, description, and image file name. (See Listing 10.67.)

LISTING 10.67   NewDept.asp Continued

```
<!--  Start the form to add the new dept -->
<form method="post" action="AddNewDepartment.asp">

<!--  Start the table to display the input form  -->
<table cellpadding="3" cellspacing="3">

<!--  Department Name Input  -->
<tr>
    <td>Department Name</td>
    <td><input type="text" value="" name="chrDeptName"</td>
</tr>

<!--  Department Description Input  -->
<tr>
    <td>Department Description</td>
    <td><textarea name="txtDeptDesc" cols="40"
    rows="5"></textarea></td>
</tr>

<!--  Department Image Input  -->
<tr>
    <td>Department Image</td>
    <td><input type="text" value="" name="chrDeptImage"></td>
</tr>
```

The page is finished off with a Submit button to post the form and the closing tags for the form, table, and page (see Listing 10.68).

LISTING 10.68 **NewDept.asp Continued**

```
<!-- Submit button to add the new department.  -->
<tr>
    <td colspan="2">
        <input type="Submit" value="Add Department"
        name="Submit"></td>
</tr>

<!-- Close out the page  -->
</table>

</form>

</BODY>
</HTML>
```

Listing 10.69 shows the AddNewDept.asp code that the NewDept.asp page posts to. This page takes in the values posted in the adding new department page and handles inserting them into the database.

The first thing that is done in the page is to retrieve the department name, description, and image file.

LISTING 10.69 **AddNewDept.asp**

```
<%@ Language=VBScript %>
<%
'    *****************************************************
'    AddNewDept.asp - Handles adding a new
'    department to the store.
'    *****************************************************


'    Retrieve the department name and ensure any single
'    quotes are doubled.
chrDeptName = replace(request("chrDeptName"), "'", "''")

'    Retrieve the department description and ensure any
'    single quotes are doubled.
txtDeptDesc = replace(request("txtDeptDesc"), "'", "''")

'    Retrieve the department image file name.
chrDeptImage = request("chrDeptImage")
```

Next our database connection is created (see Listing 10.70). The sp_InsertDept stored procedure is utilized to insert the department into the database. Once the department has been inserted, the user is sent back to the ManageDept.asp page where the new department should be listed.

LISTING 10.70   AddNewDept.asp Continued

```
' Create an ADO database connection
set dbDept = server.createobject("adodb.connection")

' Create the record set
set rsDept = server.CreateObject("adodb.recordset")

' Open the connection using our ODBC file DSN
dbDept.open("filedsn=WildWillieCDs")

' Execute the sp_InsertDept stored procedure to add
' the new department into the database.
sql = "execute sp_InsertDept '" & _
      chrDeptName & "', '" & _
      txtDeptDesc & "', '" & _
      chrDeptImage & "'"

' Execute the statement
set rsDept = dbDept.Execute(sql)

' Redirect the user to the ManageDept.asp page to do some
' any editing on the product.  Note that the ID of the
' new department is returned from the stored procedure.
Response.Redirect "ManageDept.asp?idDepartment=" & _
                    rsDept("idDepartment")

%>
```

One stored procedure is utilized on the page (see Listing 10.71). The sp_Insert-Dept stored procedure takes in our three values as parameters. It then creates a SQL insert statement to place the data in the table. Finally, the ID of the new department is returned.

LISTING 10.71   sp_InsertDept Stored Procedure

```
CREATE PROCEDURE sp_InsertDept
```

```
@chrDeptName varchar(255),
@txtDeptDesc text,
@chrDeptImage varchar(100)

AS

insert into department(chrDeptName, txtDeptDesc,
                       chrDeptImage)
values(@chrDeptName, @txtDeptDesc, @chrDeptImage)

select idDepartment = @@identity
```

Now we are ready to begin working on managing the department data. In this case we are going to build a page that will allow us to both edit and delete existing department data.

Listing 10.72 shows the ManageDept.asp page. The page starts out with the security check code and the navigation include. Note that the ID of the department is passed into the page.

LISTING 10.72   ManageDept.asp

```
<%@ Language=VBScript %>
<!-- #Include file="include/validatecheck.asp" -->
<HTML>
<!--
    ManageDept.asp - Handles the management of the the
    department and allows the shopper to update the
    data.
-->

<HEAD>
<META NAME="GENERATOR" Content="Microsoft Visual Studio 6.0">
</HEAD>
<BODY>

<!-- #Include file="include/navinclude.asp" -->
```

An ADO record set is created to retrieve the product data. The `sp_RetrieveDept` stored procedure is utilized with the ID of the department passed into it. (See Listing 10.73.)

LISTING 10.73   ManageDept.asp Continued

```asp
<%

'  Create an ADO database connection
set dbDept = server.createobject("adodb.connection")

'  Create the record set
set rsDept = server.CreateObject("adodb.recordset")

'  Open the connection using our ODBC file DSN
dbDept.open("filedsn=WildWillieCDs")

'  The retrieve sp_RetrieveDept stored procedure to
'  retrieve the data on the specified departments.
sql = "execute sp_RetrieveDept " & request("idDepartment")

'  Execute the statement
set rsDept = dbDept.Execute(sql)

%>
```

In Listing 10.74, a form is created to post the updated department data to the database. The form is posted to the UpdateDept.asp page.

Just like in the product management, we want to be able to preview a department while we are editing it. A link is built to the products.asp page to preview the department listing.

Following the preview option is a link to delete the department from the database. The ID of the department is passed on the URL.

LISTING 10.74   ManageDept.asp Continued

```asp
<!-- The form is created to post the changes -->
<form method="post" action="UpdateDept.asp">

<!-- Start the table to display the product data -->
<table cellpadding="3" cellspacing="3">
<tr>
    <td>Preview Department:</td>
    <td>
    <!-- Build a link to the products.asp page
         in the live store.  The id of the department
```

```
                        is passed into the page.  This will provide a
                        quick preview of the department.  -->
                <a href="/ecstore/wildwilliecds/products.asp ↵
                    ?idDept=<%=request("idDepartment")%>">Preview</a>
            </td>
        </tr>
        <tr>
            <td>Delete Department:</td>
            <!--  A link is built to the DeleteDept.asp page.
                The id of the department is sent into the page.
            -->
            <td><a href="DeleteDept.asp ↵
        ?idDepartment=<%=request("idDepartment")%>"> ↵
        Delete</a></td>
        </tr>
        <!--  Build a buffer between this setion and the next -->
        <tr>
            <td colspan="2"><hr></td>
        </tr>
```

Next, as shown in Listing 10.75, we are ready to display the current department data in the form. The ID of the department is displayed first. Along with the display of the department data we are building a hidden variable to post with the form. It will hold the ID of the department we are editing so we know which department to update on the post page.

LISTING 10.75   ManageDept.asp Continued

```
        <tr>
            <td>Department ID</td>
            <!--  The ID of the department is displayed.  It is not
                allowed to be edited since it is set.  -->
            <td><%=rsDept("idDepartment")%>
                <input type="hidden"
                value="<%=rsDept("idDepartment")%>"
            name="idDepartment">
            </td>
        </tr>
        <!--  Edit department name.  -->
        <tr>
            <td>Department Name</td>
```

```
    <td><input type="text"
        value="<%=rsDept("chrDeptName")%>" name="chrDeptName"></td>
</tr>

<!-- Edit department description in a text box. -->
<tr>
    <td>Department Description</td>
    <td><textarea name="txtDeptDesc" cols="40" rows="5"> ↵
<%=rsDept("txtDeptDesc")%></textarea></td>
</tr>
```

Note that the department image file name is displayed along with the department image itself, shown in Listing 10.76. As with the product images, it is presumed that the department file will be uploaded to the system through an appropriate method.

LISTING 10.76   ManageDept.asp Continued

```
<!-- Edit department image.  Note the image is displayed
     next to the image file name.  -->
<tr>
    <td>Department Image</td>
    <td>
      <input type="text" value="
         <%=rsDept("chrDeptImage")%>"
          name="chrDeptImage">

        

      <img src="../wildwilliecds/images/
          <%=rsDept("chrDeptImage")%>"
           align="center">
    </td>
</tr>
<!-- Submit button for the form. -->
<tr>
    <td colspan="2">
        <input type="Submit"
         value="Update Department" name="Submit">
    </td>
</tr>
```

```
</table>
</form>

</BODY>
</HTML>
```

The sp_RetrieveDept stored procedure is utilized on the page. The ID of the department is passed into it and then a select statement is performed to retrieve the specified department data (see Listing 10.77).

LISTING 10.77   sp_RetrieveDept Continued

```
/*  Retrieve the department data */
CREATE PROCEDURE sp_RetrieveDept

/*  Pass in the ID of the department */
@idDepartment int

AS

/*  Select all of the data on the
    department */
select * from department
where idDepartment = @idDepartment
```

Now we are ready to look at the update and delete functions specified on the ManageDept.asp page. Let's first look at the updating of the department, UpdateDept.asp.

In this page the form values posted to the page are retrieved, including the ID of the department, name, description, and department image (see Listing 10.78).

LISTING 10.78   UpdateDept.asp

```
<%@ Language=VBScript %>
<%
'    **********************************************************
'    UpdateDept.asp - Handles updating the department
'    department data.
'    **********************************************************
```

```
'  Retrieve the id of the department
idDepartment = request("idDepartment")

'  Retrieve the department name and ensure that any
'  single quotes are doubled.
chrDeptName = replace(request("chrDeptName"), "'", "''")

'  Retrieve the department description and ensrue that
'  any single quotes are doubled.
txtDeptDesc = replace(request("txtDeptDesc"), "'", "''")

'  Retrieve the department image
chrDeptImage = request("chrDeptImage")
```

Once the values are retrieved, we are ready to perform the update query, as shown in Listing 10.79. An ADO connection is opened to the database. The sp_UpdateDepartment stored procedure is utilized to perform the update. The appropriate department values are passed into the query. Once the query is executed, the user is sent back to the department manager page.

LISTING 10.79   UpdateDept.asp Continued

```
'  Create an ADO database connection
set dbDept = server.createobject("adodb.connection")

'  Create the record set
set rsDept = server.CreateObject("adodb.recordset")

'  Open the connection using our ODBC file DSN
dbDept.open("filedsn=WildWillieCDs")

'  Execute the sp_UpdateDepartment stored procedure to
'  update the department data.
sql = "execute sp_UpdateDepartment " & _
      request("idDepartment") & ", '" & _
      chrDeptName & "', '" & _
      txtDeptDesc & "', '" & _
      chrDeptImage & "'"

'  Execute the statement
set rsDept = dbDept.Execute(sql)
```

```
'   Send the user back to department manager and pass back
'   the department id.
Response.Redirect "ManageDept.asp?idDepartment=" & _
                  request("idDepartment")


%>
```

Listing 10.80 shows the code for the sp_UpdateDepartment stored procedure. The key values are passed in as parameters and a SQL update statement is created to update the specified department.

LISTING 10.80   **sp_UpdateDepartment Stored Procedure**

```
CREATE PROCEDURE sp_UpdateDepartment

@idDepartment int,
@chrDeptName varchar(255),
@txtDeptDesc text,
@chrDeptImage varchar(100)

AS

update department set
    chrDeptName = @chrDeptName,
    txtDeptDesc = @txtDeptDesc,
    chrDeptImage = @chrDeptImage
where idDepartment = @idDepartment
```

That handles the updating of the department. Next, let's look at the deleting of a department. Listing 10.81 shows the DeleteDept.asp code.

In this page the ID of the department is passed into the page. An ADO connection is created to execute the sp_DeleteDept query. Once the delete is performed, the user is sent back to the listing of departments.

LISTING 10.81   **DeleteDept.asp**

```
<%@ Language=VBScript %>
<%
```

```
'    ****************************************************
'    DeleteDept.asp - Deletes the department from the
'    store.
'    ****************************************************

'    Create an ADO database connection
set dbDept = server.createobject("adodb.connection")

'    Create the record set
set rsDept = server.CreateObject("adodb.recordset")

'    Open the connection using our ODBC file DSN
dbDept.open("filedsn=WildWillieCDs")

'    The sp_DeleteDept stored procedure removes the
'    department from the database.
sql = "execute sp_DeleteDept " & request("idDepartment")

'    Execute the statement
set rsDept = dbDept.Execute(sql)

'    Send the user back to the list of departments.
Response.Redirect "ListDepts.asp"

%>
```

Listing 10.82 is the code for the sp_DeleteDept stored procedure. The ID of the department is passed into it and then a SQL delete query is executed to remove the data from the table.

LISTING 10.82   sp_DeleteDept Stored Procedure

```
CREATE PROCEDURE sp_DeleteDept

@idDepartment int

AS

delete from department
where idDepartment = @idDepartment
```

To get started with demonstrating our new department management functions, Figure 10.14 shows the listing of departments in the store. Note the option to add a new department as well.

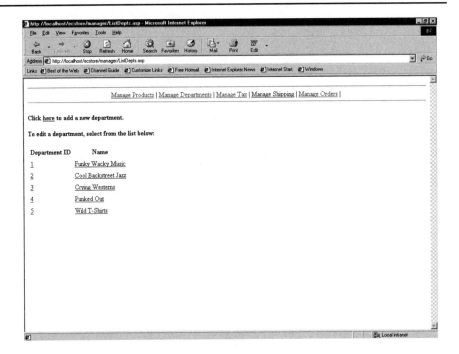

Let's next work on adding a new department. Click on the *new department* link in the department listing. Figure 10.15 shows the page to add the new department. Fill out the data appropriately and submit the form.

FIGURE 10.15:

Adding a new department

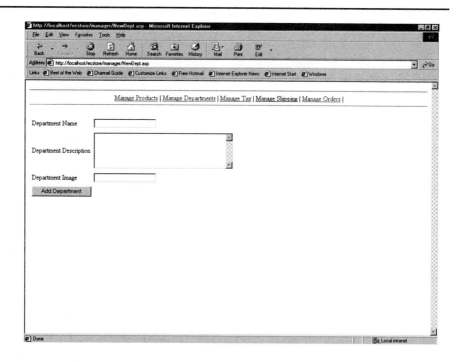

Once you have added the new department to the database, you are ready to edit it. Select the new department from the listing and you will be taken to the edit page. Figure 10.16 shows the department data ready for edit.

FIGURE 10.16:

Editing a department

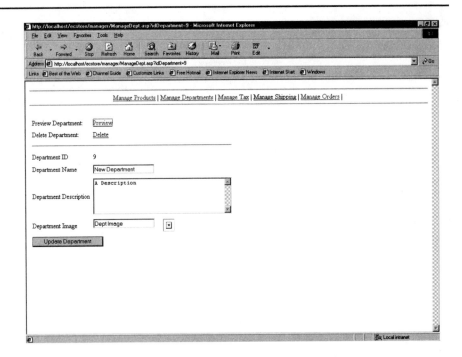

You now have the option to update the department data, remove the department, or preview it. Figure 10.17 shows the department in preview mode. Note that we have not uploaded a new image for the department so a broken graphic is showing up on the preview of the department.

> **TIP**
>
> In our product and department management, we did not build in data checking or user validation. Adding these would provide additional functionality. For example, when the user clicks on the option to delete a product or department, we might want to have them verify the request before performing the actual deletion. Likewise, when a new product or department is added or an update is performed, we might want to validate the data to ensure key fields are not left blank.

FIGURE 10.17:

Previewing the department

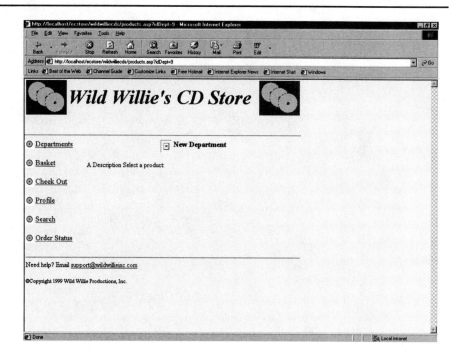

Summary

In this chapter we handled the key functions of managing product and department data. In the next chapter we will explore methods for administering the tax and shipping settings in the store. And, in the final chapter of this section, we will explore the management of order data.

CHAPTER

ELEVEN

11

Managing Tax and Shipping

- Managing Tax

- Managing Shipping

Tax and shipping are two key areas of business rule management for which we need a convenient management interface. In Chapter 10, "Product Management," we built a Visual Basic COM object for utilizing the values in the database to calculate shipping and tax. In this chapter we are going to build an ASP interface to manage the values in the database.

It is important to note that the ASP pages will be built to manage the data based on the current set of business rules. If your store requires support for one-day and two-day shipping and/or tax calculations at various local levels, then you will need to modify these pages along with the Visual Basic COM object.

Managing Tax

The first action is to work on the management of the tax data. Our store will calculate tax at the state level. We will need to be able to update the tax rates for each state. In our sample store, tax was only being calculated in Virginia and Texas.

The ManageTax.asp page handles building an input form that easily allows all state tax data to be updated in one screen and submitted to the database. The page starts out with the usual tags and includes (see Listing 11.1).

LISTING 11.1   **ManageTax.asp**

```
<%@ Language=VBScript %>
<!-- #Include file="include/validatecheck.asp" -->
<HTML>
<!--
    ManageTax.asp - Supports managing the tax table
    settings for the store.
-->

<HEAD>
<META NAME="GENERATOR" Content="Microsoft Visual Studio 6.0">
</HEAD>
<BODY>
<!-- #include file="include/navinclude.asp" -->

<!-- Start the update display -->
<BR><B>Update the tax tables below:</b><BR>
```

To retrieve the current tax settings, the sp_RetrieveTaxRates stored procedure is executed, as shown in Listing 11.2. That will retrieve the current settings for all of the states.

LISTING 11.2   **ManageTax.asp Continued**

```
<%

' Create an ADO database connection
set dbTax = server.createobject("adodb.connection")

' Create the record set
set rsTax = server.CreateObject("adodb.recordset")

' Open the connection using our ODBC file DSN
dbTax.open("filedsn=WildWillieCDs")

' Execute the Retrieve Tax Rates stored
' procedure to retrieve all of the current
' tax rates.
sql = "execute sp_RetrieveTaxRates"

' Execute the statement
set rsTax = dbTax.Execute(sql)
```

Next we loop through the tax settings and simply retrieve each value by using a select case statement (see Listing 11.3). Each value is stored in a variable for later display.

LISTING 11.3   **ManageTax.asp Continued**

```
' Loop through the tax rates.
do until rsTax.EOF

    ' We will retrieve the tax rate for each state
    ' and store it in a variable.
    select case ucase(rsTax("chrState"))
        case "AL"
            fltAL = rsTax("fltTaxRate")
        case "AK"
            fltAK = rsTax("fltTaxRate")
        case "AZ"
```

```
               fltAZ = rsTax("fltTaxRate")

         case "PA"
               fltPA = rsTax("fltTaxRate")
         case "RI"
               fltRI = rsTax("fltTaxRate")
         case "SC"
               fltSC = rsTax("fltTaxRate")
         case "SD"
               fltSD = rsTax("fltTaxRate")
         case "TN"
               fltTN = rsTax("fltTaxRate")
         case "TX"
               fltTX = rsTax("fltTaxRate")
         case "UT"
               fltUT = rsTax("fltTaxRate")
         case "VT"
               fltVT = rsTax("fltTaxRate")
         case "VA"
               fltVA = rsTax("fltTaxRate")
         case "WA"
               fltWA = rsTax("fltTaxRate")
         case "WY"
               fltWY = rsTax("fltTaxRate")
         case "WI"
               fltWI = rsTax("fltTaxRate")
         case "WV"
               fltWV = rsTax("fltTaxRate")
      end select

      rsTax.movenext

   Loop
```

NOTE   Only a subset of the states is shown here. The full set can be found on the CD.

Next, as shown in Listing 11.4, we create a form that will list out all of the states. The form will post to the UpdateTaxes.asp page. Each will have an input element for updating the tax rate. The form starts out with an appropriate header.

LISTING 11.4   ManageTax.asp Continued

```
%>

<!--  The form is created to post the changes -->
<form method="post" action="UpdateTaxes.asp">

<!--  Start the table to dispay the tax rates  -->
<table cellpadding="3" cellspacing="3" border="1">
<!--  Show the header row  -->
<tr>
    <th>State</th><th>Rate</th>
    <th>State</th><th>Rate</th>
    <th>State</th><th>Rate</th>
    <th>State</th><th>Rate</th>
</tr>
```

A series of rows is created for entering the values of each state. The name of the state is displayed along with an input field for the tax rate. Note that the input field is defaulted to the current value (see Listing 11.5).

LISTING 11.5   ManageTax.asp Continued

```
<!-- Build the first row of four tax rates. -->
<tr>
    <!--  Display the Alabama symbol and the Alabama tax rate -->
    <td>Alabama</td><td><input type="text" name="AL" value="<%=fltAL%>"
    size="5"></td>
    <td>Alaska</td><td><input type="text" name="AK" value="<%=fltAK%>"
    size="5"></td>
    <td>Arizona</td><td><input type="text" name="AZ" value="<%=fltAZ%>"
    size="5"></td>
    <td>Arkansas</td><td><input type="text" name="AR"
    value="<%=fltAR%>" size="5"></td>
</tr>
<tr>
    <td>California</td><td><input type="text" name="CA"
    value="<%=fltCA%>" size="5"></td>
    <td>Connecticut</td><td><input type="text" name="CT"
    value="<%=fltCT%>" size="5"></td>
    <td>Colorado</td><td><input type="text" name="CO"
    value="<%=fltCO%>" size="5"></td>
```

```
        <td>District of Columbia</td><td><input type="text" name="DC"
value="<%=fltDC%>" size="5"></td>
    </tr>

    <tr>
        <td>Utah</td><td><input type="text" name="UT" value="<%=fltUT%>"
        size="5"></td>
        <td>Vermont</td><td><input type="text" name="VT" value="<%=fltVT%>"
        size="5"></td>
        <td>Virginia</td><td><input type="text" name="VA"
value="<%=fltVA%>" size="5"></td>
        <td>Washington</td><td><input type="text" name="WA"
value="<%=fltWA%>" size="5"></td>
    </tr>
    <tr>
        <td>Wyoming</td><td><input type="text" name="WY" value="<%=fltWY%>"
        size="5"></td>
        <td>Wisconsin</td><td><input type="text" name="WI"
value="<%=fltWI%>" size="5"></td>
        <td>West Virgnia</td><td><input type="text" name="WV"
value="<%=fltWV%>" size="5"></td>
        <td></td><td></td>
    </tr>
```

NOTE   Only a subset of the states is shown here. The full set can be found on the CD.

Finally, the form is closed out with an appropriate Submit button and closing tags for the page (see Listing 11.6).

LISTING 11.6   ManageTax.asp Continued

```
    <tr>
        <td colspan="8" align="center">
            <input type="submit" value="Update Tax Table" name="Submit">
        </td>
    </tr>
    </table>

    </form>

    </BODY>
    </HTML>
```

Updating Taxes

In this example, we use a rather lengthy method of building out a field for each separate state value. We could use a couple of alternative methods for handling this data update. The first would be a simple Select box of state values and an Input box for setting the rate; the user would then select a state in the Select box and set the rate. A second alternative would be to simply build the input fields in the loop above, and not build each out separately. However, the method we've illustrated in this chapter does a couple of things that the two alternatives do not do. It shows all of the fields together, for easier management. And it shows full state names, rather than state abbreviations.

Listing 11.7 shows one stored procedure utilized on the page, sp_Retrieve-TaxRates. This simply returns all data in the tax table.

LISTING 11.7   sp_RetrieveTaxRates

```
CREATE PROCEDURE sp_RetrieveTaxRates AS

select * from tax
```

Now we are ready to review the tax update code. Again, this is fairly straight-forward. The first thing we do is retrieve the current list of states in the database using the same stored procedure (see Listing 11.8).

LISTING 11.8   UpdateTaxes.asp

```
<%@ Language=VBScript %>
<%
' *****************************************************
' UpdateTaxes.asp - Handles the updates of the tax
' tables.
' *****************************************************

' Create an ADO database connection
set dbTaxUpd = server.createobject("adodb.connection")

' Create the record set
set rsTaxUpd = server.CreateObject("adodb.recordset")

' Open the connection using our ODBC file DSN
```

```
dbTaxUpd.open("filedsn=WildWillieCDs")

'   Create an ADO database connection
set dbTax = server.createobject("adodb.connection")

'   Create the record set
set rsTax = server.CreateObject("adodb.recordset")

'   Open the connection using our ODBC file DSN
dbTax.open("filedsn=WildWillieCDs")

'   Exeute the stored procedure to retrieve the
'   current tax rate settings.
sql = "execute sp_RetrieveTaxRates"

'   Execute the statement
set rsTax = dbTax.Execute(sql)
```

We next loop through the states in the database and retrieve the corresponding value from the input form (see Listing 11.9). A *select case* statement is utilized to retrieve the current value for the state. It then executes the `sp_UpdateTaxRate` stored procedure to update the tax rate for the state.

LISTING 11.9   **UpdateTaxes.asp Continued**

```
'   Loop through the tax rate settings.
do until rsTax.EOF

    '   Do a select case to check which state we are
    '   going to update.
    select case ucase(rsTax("chrState"))

    '   Check for Alabama
    case "AL"
        '   Execute the sp_UpdateTaxRate stored procedure
        '   to change the tax rate setting for Alabama
        dbTaxUpd.execute "execute sp_UpdateTaxRate " & _
            request("AL") & ", " & rsTax("idState")

    case "AK"
        dbTaxUpd.execute "execute sp_UpdateTaxRate " & _
            request("AK") & ", " & rsTax("idState")
```

```
case "PA"
    dbTaxUpd.execute "execute sp_UpdateTaxRate " & _
        request("PA") & ", " & rsTax("idState")

case "RI"
    dbTaxUpd.execute "execute sp_UpdateTaxRate " & _
        request("RI") & ", " & rsTax("idState")

case "SC"
    dbTaxUpd.execute "execute sp_UpdateTaxRate " & _
        request("SC") & ", " & rsTax("idState")

case "SD"
    dbTaxUpd.execute "execute sp_UpdateTaxRate " & _
        request("SD") & ", " & rsTax("idState")

case "TN"
    dbTaxUpd.execute "execute sp_UpdateTaxRate " & _
        request("TN") & ", " & rsTax("idState")

case "TX"
    dbTaxUpd.execute "execute sp_UpdateTaxRate " & _
        request("TX") & ", " & rsTax("idState")

case "UT"
    dbTaxUpd.execute "execute sp_UpdateTaxRate " & _
        request("UT") & ", " & rsTax("idState")

case "VT"
    dbTaxUpd.execute "execute sp_UpdateTaxRate " & _
        request("VT") & ", " & rsTax("idState")

case "VA"
    dbTaxUpd.execute "execute sp_UpdateTaxRate " & _
        request("VA") & ", " & rsTax("idState")

case "WA"
    dbTaxUpd.execute "execute sp_UpdateTaxRate " & _
        request("WA") & ", " & rsTax("idState")

case "WY"
    dbTaxUpd.execute "execute sp_UpdateTaxRate " & _
```

```
                    request("WY") & ", " & rsTax("idState")

            case "WI"
               dbTaxUpd.execute "execute sp_UpdateTaxRate " &  _
                  request("WI") & ", " & rsTax("idState")

            case "WV"
               dbTaxUpd.execute "execute sp_UpdateTaxRate " &  _
                  request("WV") & ", " & rsTax("idState")

         end select

         '  Move to the next state.
         rsTax.movenext

      Loop
```

NOTE   Only a subset of the states is shown here. The full set can be found on the CD.

Once the state rate updates are completed, we send the user back to the ManageTax.asp page so they can review the changes (see Listing 11.10).

LISTING 11.10   UpdateTaxes.asp Continued

```
'  Send the user back to the tax manager
'  for a final check on the tax rate
'  settings.
Response.Redirect "managetax.asp"

%>
```

The sp_UpdateTaxRate stored procedure will update the fltTaxRate field of the tax table for the specified state (see Listing 11.11). The tax rate and the ID of the state are passed in.

LISTING 11.11   sp_UpdateTaxRate Stored Procedure

```
CREATE PROCEDURE sp_UpdateTaxRate

@fltTaxRate float,
```

```
@idState int

AS

update tax set fltTaxRate = @fltTaxRate
where idState = @idState
```

Let's now use the interface we have built for tax management. Figure 11.1 shows the page with each of the state listings. Note that Virginia and Texas are already set. Let's put in new values for Alabama and Alaska and submit the form for processing.

FIGURE 11.1:

Tax listing

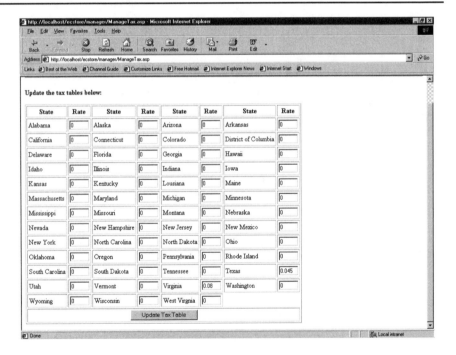

Update the tax tables below:

State	Rate	State	Rate	State	Rate	State	Rate
Alabama	0	Alaska	0	Arizona	0	Arkansas	0
California	0	Connecticut	0	Colorado	0	District of Columbia	0
Delaware	0	Florida	0	Georgia	0	Hawaii	0
Idaho	0	Illinois	0	Indiana	0	Iowa	0
Kansas	0	Kentucky	0	Lousiana	0	Maine	0
Massachusetts	0	Maryland	0	Michigan	0	Minnesota	0
Mississippi	0	Missouri	0	Montana	0	Nebraska	0
Nevada	0	New Hampshire	0	New Jersey	0	New Mexico	0
New York	0	North Carolina	0	North Dakota	0	Ohio	0
Oklahoma	0	Oregon	0	Pennsylvania	0	Rhode Island	0
South Carolina	0	South Dakota	0	Tennessee	0	Texas	0.045
Utah	0	Vermont	0	Virginia	0.08	Washington	0
Wyoming	0	Wisconsin	0	West Virginia	0		

Update Tax Table

Figure 11.2 shows the updated taxing rates with Virginia and Texas still set. But now Alabama and Alaska are set to the values we specified. Let's reset those values back to 0.

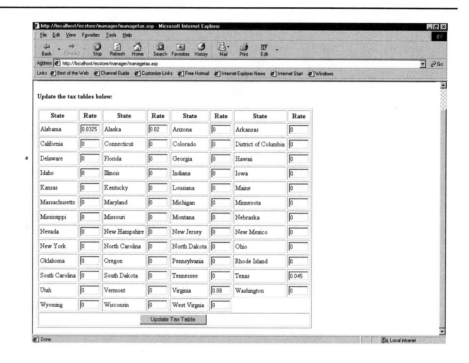

Figure 11.3 shows the Alaska and Alabama values now set back to 0. Through
this interface we can easily manage tax at the state level.

FIGURE 11.3:

Clearing Alabama and Alaska

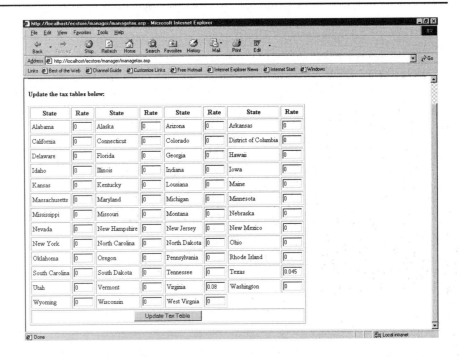

Managing Shipping

Next we are ready to begin working on management of the shipping calculations for the store, as shown in Listing 11.12. The first page we will begin working with is the ManageShipping.asp page.

The page starts out with the appropriate security and navigation bar include. Then an ADO connection is opened to the database.

LISTING 11.12   ManageShipping.asp

```
<%@ Language=VBScript %>
<!-- #Include file="include/validatecheck.asp" -->
<HTML>
<!--
    ManageShipping.asp - Handles the listing of the
```

```
                    shipping rates. And, it provides functions for
                    deleting shipping rates and adding new ones.
              -->

              <HEAD>
              <META NAME="GENERATOR" Content="Microsoft Visual Studio 6.0">
              </HEAD>
              <BODY>
              <!-- #include file="include/navinclude.asp" -->

              <%

              '  Create an ADO database connection
              set dbShipping = server.createobject("adodb.connection")

              '  Create the record set
              set rsShipping = server.CreateObject("adodb.recordset")

              '  Open the connection using our ODBC file DSN
              dbShipping.open("filedsn=WildWillieCDs")
```

The sp_GetShippingRate stored procedure is utilized to return the current shipping rate settings in the database (see Listing 11.13).

LISTING 11.13   ManageShipping.asp Continued

```
              '  Execute the Retrieve Shipping Rates stored
              '  procedure to retrieve all of the current
              '  shipping rates.
              sql = "execute sp_GetShippingRate"

              '  Execute the statement
              set rsShipping = dbShipping.Execute(sql)

              %>
```

In Listing 11.14 a form is started that will display the different shipping rate changes. The form will post to the UpdateShipping.asp page.

A table is created that will show the ID of the range, the low quantity, high quantity, and the fee. We will also provide an option to delete the corresponding shipping rate.

LISTING 11.14   ManageShipping.asp Continued

```
<!-- Start the form for updating the shipping -->
<form method="post" action="UpdateShipping.asp">

<!-- Start the table to display the shipping
     rates. -->
<table border="1" cellpadding="3" cellspacing="3">
<tr>
    <th>ID</th>
    <th>Low<BR>Quantity</th>
    <th>High<BR>Quantity</th>
    <th>Fee</th>
    <th>Delete</th>
</tr>
```

In Listing 11.15 we loop through the different shipping rates. With each iteration, the appropriate values are displayed and each is put into an input text element so it can be updated.

For the field names, we are combining the name of the field with the ID of the quantity range. That way we can easily retrieve each value when the form is updated.

LISTING 11.15   ManageShipping.asp Continued

```
<%

'  Loop through the shipping rates.
do until rsShipping.EOF

%>

<!-- Loop through the shipping rate ranges -->
<tr>
    <!-- Show the quantity range id -->
    <td><%=rsShipping("idQuantityRange")%></td>
    <td>
        <!-- Built input for the low quantity. Note that
             the field name is built to include the id
             of the quantity range. -->
        <input type="text"
```

```
         name="intLow<%=rsShipping("idQuantityRange")%>"
           value="<%=rsShipping("intLowQuantity")%>"
         size="6">
     </td>
     <td>
         <!--  Built input for the high quantity. Note that
               the field name is built to include the id
               of the quantity range. -->
         <input type="text"
         name="intHigh<%=rsShipping("idQuantityRange")%>"
           value="<%=rsShipping("intHighQuantity")%>"
         size="6">
     </td>
     <td>
         <!--  Built input for the fee. Note that the field
             name is built to include the id of the quantity
             range. -->
         <input type="text"
         name="intFee<%=rsShipping("idQuantityRange")%>"
           value="<%=rsShipping("intFee")%>"
         size="6">
     </td>
```

For the *delete* function, we link to the DeleteShipping.asp page and pass on the ID of the quantity range (see Listing 11.16). Then the record set is moved forward and we loop back to create the next row.

LISTING 11.16   ManageShipping.asp Continued

```
     <td>
         <!--  Build a delete link with the id of the
               quantity range. -->
         <a href="deleteshipping.asp?idQuantityRange=
         <%=rsShipping("idQuantityRange")%>">Delete</a>
     </td>
   </tr>

<%

'  Move to the next row.
rsShipping.MoveNext
```

```
'  Loop back
Loop

%>
```

The form is then completed and the table is finished off (see Listing 11.17). A horizontal line is shown to divide the next section.

LISTING 11.17   ManageShipping.asp Continued

```html
<!--  Build the submit button -->
<tr>
    <td colspan="5" align="center">
        <input type="submit" value="Submit" name="Submit">
    </td>
</tr>

</table>
</form>

<BR><hr><BR>
```

Next, in Listing 11.18, we create a new form that will manage the adding of new shipping ranges. The form posts to the AddShipping.asp page. A table is created similar to the last table but with no *delete* option.

LISTING 11.18   ManageShipping.asp Continued

```html
<!--  Start the form for adding new quantity ranges  -->
<form method="post" action="AddShipping.asp">

<!--  Start the table  -->
<table border="1" cellpadding="3" cellspacing="3">

<!--  Build the header  -->
<tr>
    <th>Low<BR>Quantity</th>
    <th>High<BR>Quantity</th>
    <th>Fee</th>
</tr>
```

In Listing 11.19, we create three rows for adding new shipping ranges. Each row has appropriate input fields. In this case we simply number the fields for each reference.

LISTING 11.19   **ManageShipping.asp Continued**

```
<!-- Build the first new quantity option -->
<tr>
    <td>
        <input type="text" name="intLow1" value="" size="6">
    </td>
    <td>
        <input type="text" name="intHigh1" value="" size="6">
    </td>
    <td>
        <input type="text" name="intFee1" value="" size="6">
    </td>
</tr>
<!-- Build the second new quantity option -->
<tr>
    <td>
        <input type="text" name="intLow2" value="" size="6">
    </td>
    <td>
        <input type="text" name="intHigh2" value="" size="6">
    </td>
    <td>
        <input type="text" name="intFee2" value="" size="6">
    </td>
</tr>
<!-- Build the third new quantity option -->
<tr>
    <td>
        <input type="text" name="intLow3" value="" size="6">
    </td>
    <td>
        <input type="text" name="intHigh3" value="" size="6">
    </td>
    <td>
        <input type="text" name="intFee3" value="" size="6">
    </td>
</tr>
```

A Submit button is created for posting the new entries. Then the form, table, and page are completed (see Listing 11.20).

LISTING 11.20   ManageShipping.asp Continued

```
<!-- Build the submit button  -->
<tr>
<td colspan="3" align="center"><input type="submit" value="Submit"
name="Submit"></td>
</tr>
</table>
</form>

</BODY>
</HTML>
```

We utilize one stored procedure, sp_GetShippingRate, on this page (see Listing 11.21). It simply returns all of the shipping rate settings currently in the database.

LISTING 11.21   sp_GetShippingRate Stored Procedure

```
/*  Retrieve the shipping rates for the store */
CREATE PROCEDURE sp_GetShippingRate

AS

/*  Return all of the shipping values */
select * from shipping
```

Next, we can review the update of the current shipping settings. Listing 11.22 shows the UpdateShipping.asp code which will handle this.

The first part of the page creates an ADO connection to the database. The sp_GetShippingRate stored procedure handles retrieving the current settings so we can loop through them and update each.

LISTING 11.22   UpdateShipping.asp

```
<%@ Language=VBScript %>
<%
```

```
' ******************************************************
' UpdateShipping.asp - Handles updating the existing
' shipping rates.
' ******************************************************

' Create an ADO database connection
set dbShipUpdate = server.createobject("adodb.connection")

' Open the connection using our ODBC file DSN
dbShipUpdate.open("filedsn=WildWillieCDs")

' Create an ADO database connection
set dbShipping = server.createobject("adodb.connection")

' Create the record set
set rsShipping = server.CreateObject("adodb.recordset")

' Open the connection using our ODBC file DSN
dbShipping.open("filedsn=WildWillieCDs")

' Execute the sp_GetShippingRate to retrieve
' the shipping rates.
sql = "execute sp_GetShippingRate"

' Execute the statement
set rsShipping = dbShipping.Execute(sql)
```

Next, in Listing 11.23, we loop through current rate ranges. We will retrieve the new settings by combining the field name with the ID of the quantity range.

LISTING 11.23   **UpdateShipping.asp Continued**

```
' Loop through the shipping rates.
do until rsShipping.EOF

    ' Retrieve the low and high shipping quantities
    ' along with the shipping rate. On the
    ' ManageShipping.asp page, the field names are
    ' built with the id of the quantity range tacked
    ' onto the field name. We build the same naming
    ' here to retrieve the values.
    intLow = request("intLow" & _
```

```
          rsShipping("idQuantityRange"))

     intHigh = request("intHigh" & _
          rsShipping("idQuantityRange"))

     intFee = request("intFee" & _
          rsShipping("idQuantityRange"))
```

Once we have all of the values retrieved, the sp_UpdateShippingRate stored procedure handles updating the values (see Listing 11.24). Then the record set is moved forward and the next row is processed. Once the update is done, the user is sent back to the ManageShipping.asp page.

LISTING 11.24   UpdateShipping.asp Continued

```
     '  Execute the update stored procedure to change
     '  the range.
     dbShipUpdate.Execute _
       "execute sp_UpdateShippingRate " & _
          rsShipping("idQuantityRange") & ", " & _
          intLow & ", " & _
          intHigh & ", " & _
          intFee

     '  Move to the next row
     rsShipping.MoveNext

'  Loop back
loop

'  Send the user back to the shipping manager
'  range.
Response.Redirect "ManageShipping.asp"

%>
```

The sp_UpdateShippingRate stored procedure takes in all of the shipping rate range settings and the ID of the quantity range (see Listing 11.25). Then a SQL update statement is created to update the values for the specified range.

LISTING 11.25   **sp_UpdateShippingRate Stored Procedure**

```
CREATE PROCEDURE sp_UpdateShippingRate

@idQuantityRange int,
@intLowQuantity int,
@intHighQuantity int,
@intFee int

AS

update shipping set
   intLowQuantity = @intLowQuantity,
   intHighQuantity = @intHighQuantity,
   intFee = @intFee
where
   idQuantityRange = @idQuantityRange
```

Now that we have updated the current values, let's review the code to delete a shipping range (see Listing 11.26). The page creates an ADO record set and then executes the sp_DeleteShippingRate stored procedure. That will remove the entire row for that quantity rate range based on the ID of the quantity range. Then the user is sent back to the ManageShipping.asp page.

LISTING 11.26   **DeleteShipping.asp**

```
<%@ Language=VBScript %>
<%
'    ********************************************************
'    DeleteShipping.asp - Handles deleting the specific
'    shipping range.
'    ********************************************************

'    Create an ADO database connection
set dbShipping = server.createobject("adodb.connection")

'    Create the record set
set rsShipping = server.CreateObject("adodb.recordset")

'    Open the connection using our ODBC file DSN
dbShipping.open("filedsn=WildWillieCDs")
```

```
'  Execute the stored procedure to delete the
'  specified shipping rate.
sql = "execute sp_DeleteShippingRate " & _
      request("idQuantityRange")

'  Execute the statement
set rsShipping = dbShipping.Execute(sql)

'  Send the user back to the shipping manager
Response.Redirect "ManageShipping.asp"

%>
```

The delete shipping rate stored procedure removes the specified row from the shipping table (see Listing 11.27).

LISTING 11.27   sp_DeleteShippingRate Stored Procedure

```
CREATE PROCEDURE sp_DeleteShippingRate

@idQuantityRange int

AS

delete from shipping
where idQuantityRange = @idQuantityRange
```

Finally, we are ready to process any additions to the shipping range table. This is done in the AddShipping.asp page, as shown in Listing 11.28. This will read in the three entry rows to see what additions have been submitted. In the first part of the page, an ADO connection is opened to the database.

LISTING 11.28   AddShipping.asp

```
<%@ Language=VBScript %>
<%

'  Create an ADO database connection
set dbShipping = server.createobject("adodb.connection")
```

```
'  Create the record set
set rsShipping = server.CreateObject("adodb.recordset")

'  Open the connection using our ODBC file DSN
dbShipping.open("filedsn=WildWillieCDs")
```

The values for each row are read into local variables. Then a check is done to see if a fee was entered by the user. If so, then the `sp_InsertShippingRate` stored procedure is executed to add the shipping range into the table. Once the additions are done, the user is sent back to the shipping manager. (See Listing 11.29.)

LISTING 11.29   **AddShipping.asp Continued**

```
intLow1 = request("intLow1")
intHigh1 = request("intHigh1")
intFee1 = request("intFee1")

if intFee1 <> "" then

    dbShipping.Execute "execute sp_InsertShippingRate " & _
                        intLow1 & ", " & _
                        intHigh1 & ", " & _
                        intFee1

end if

intLow2 = request("intLow2")
intHigh2 = request("intHigh2")
intFee2 = request("intFee2")

if intFee2 <> "" then

    dbShipping.Execute "execute sp_InsertShippingRate " & _
                        intLow2 & ", " & _
                        intHigh2 & ", " & _
                        intFee2

end if

intLow3 = request("intLow3")
intHigh3 = request("intHigh3")
```

```
intFee3 = request("intFee3")

if intFee3 <> "" then

    dbShipping.Execute "execute sp_InsertShippingRate " & _
                        intLow3 & ", " & _
                        intHigh3 & ", " & _
                        intFee3

end if

Response.Redirect "ManageShipping.asp"

%>
```

The sp_InsertShippingRate stored procedure will insert a new row into the shipping table that will contain the low-quantity range, the high-quantity range, and the shipping fee (see Listing 11.30).

LISTING 11.30   sp_InsertShippingRate Stored Procedure

```
CREATE PROCEDURE sp_InsertShippingRate

@intLowQuantity int,
@intHighQuantity int,
@intFee int

AS

insert into shipping(intLowQuantity, intHighQuantity,
                     intFee)
values(@intLowQuantity, @intHighQuantity, @intFee)
```

Now we are ready to test the shipping manager interface. Figure 11.4 shows the shipping manager with current settings in the database. Note the options to change the existing values and to delete any range. And, at the bottom of the page are our options to add in new shipping ranges and fees.

FIGURE 11.4:

Shipping manager

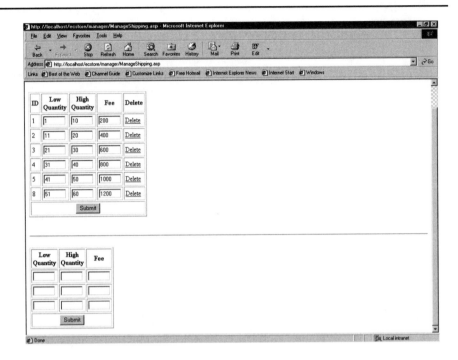

Now let's utilize the option to delete a current shipping range. Figure 11.5 shows the shipping manager after the last range is removed.

FIGURE 11.5:

Removing a shipping range

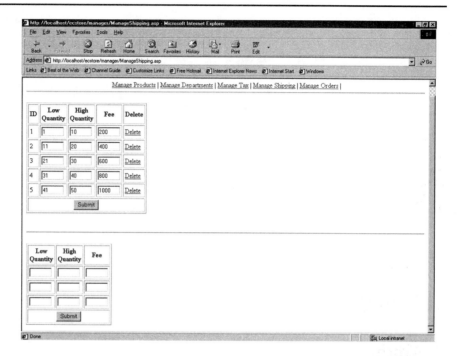

Now let's utilize the option to add a shipping range. Figure 11.6 shows two shipping ranges being added to the list. Note that there is no checking being done to ensure the ranges do not overlap or don't already exist. The presumption is that the user will be smart enough to ensure that each range is valid and there are no gaps or overlap.

FIGURE 11.6:

Adding shipping ranges

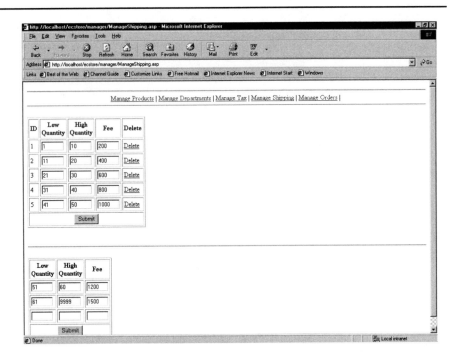

Figure 11.7 shows the updated shipping ranges after the new values are added.

FIGURE 11.7:

Final shipping ranges

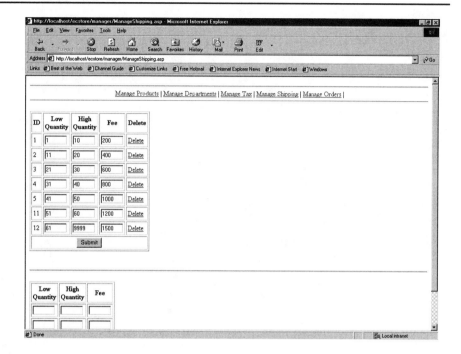

Summary

Through these pages, we can update the tax and shipping business rules of our store. If the rules for how we calculate sales tax or shipping change, these functions will also have to change.

Note that the underlying tax and shipping COM object used to calculate tax and shipping in the store relies on these same business rules. If we wanted to, we could use those COM objects to administer the database too. That would allow us to update just one set of code instead of both the COM object and this set of manager pages. That could make maintenance easier and not require the store code to be touched directly. But, in either case, both have to be updated if the rules change.

In Chapter 12, "Managing Orders," we will build tools for administrative order management.

CHAPTER
TWELVE

12

Managing Orders

- ■ Searching for Orders

- ■ Deleting an Order and Managing Order Status

- ■ Reviewing and Updating an Order

The last set of management features we will build is for order management. It is important for the business managers of the store to be able to easily and quickly sift through orders for processing, customer service support, setting shipping status, etc.

A search interface is built for quickly finding orders in the system that match the specified criteria. Then a listing of orders matching the criteria is provided. From there we will be able to manage order status and the details of an order.

Searching for Orders

Hopefully our new online store will be selling products left and right. And that means sifting through orders for simple order management. The first page will provide a series of search options for different data fields of the order. This will provide the fastest and easiest way to retrieve orders that meet certain criteria.

Listing 12.1 builds the data entry page. The page includes the standard security and navigation includes.

LISTING 12.1   **ManageOrders.asp**

```asp
<%@ Language=VBScript %>
<!-- #Include file="include/validatecheck.asp" -->
<!--
    ManageOrders.asp - Provides search option to find
    the specific orders that will be reviewed.
-->

<HTML>
<HEAD>
<META NAME="GENERATOR" Content="Microsoft Visual Studio 6.0">
</HEAD>
<BODY>

<!-- #include file="include/navinclude.asp" -->

<!-- Start the page out. A form is created for
     posting the search requirements. -->
```

```
<BR><BR>
<b>Enter in your search criteria:</b>
<BR><BR>
```

A form is started that will post to the OrderSearch.asp page. The table is then started with the input fields. The first field provides for input to search for a specific e-mail address.

The next set of fields provides for searching for an order date range. That is followed by fields to search for an order amount range. (See Listing 12.2.)

LISTING 12.2   ManageOrders.asp Continued

```
<form method="post" action="OrderSearch.asp">

<!-- Start the table to display the search fields. -->
<table>

<!-- Shopper name input field. -->
<tr>
    <td align="right">Search by Shopper Name:</td>
    <td><input type="text" name="srchShopperName" value=""></td>
</tr>

<!-- Shopper email address input field. -->
<tr>
    <td align="right">Search by Shopper Email Address:</td>
    <td>
    <input type="text" name="srchShopperEmail"
    value="">
    </td>
</tr>

<!-- Fields are created to enter in a starting
    date and end date. -->
<tr>
    <td align="right">Search by Order Date Range:</td>
    <td>
        <input type="text" name="srchStartDate" value="">
        <input type="text" name="srchEndDate" value="">
    </td>
</tr>
```

```
<!-- Fields are created to enter in a starting
     amount and end amount. -->
<tr>
   <td align="right">Search by Order Total Amount:</td>
   <td>
      <input type="text" name="srchStartAmount" value="">
      <input type="text" name="srchEndAmount" value="">
   </td>
</tr>
```

We also may want to search on products placed in orders. In that case there is an input field for the product name. That is followed by a Submit button for the form and the closing tags for the page (see Listing 12.3).

LISTING 12.3   ManageOrders.asp Continued

```
<!-- An option is built to search for orders with
     a specific product name. -->
<tr>
   <td align="right">Search by Product Name:</td>
   <td>
   <input type="text" name="srchProductName"
    value="">
   </td>
</tr>

<!-- Submit button for the form. -->
<tr>
   <td colspan="2" align="Center">
      <input type="Submit" value="Submit" name="Submit">
   </td>
</tr>

</table>

</form>

</BODY>
</HTML>
```

Once the user has filled out his search criteria, the data is posted to the Order-Search.asp page, as shown in Listing 12.4. This page will create a listing of orders based on the criteria.

The first section of the page creates the query that will be executed. In this case the query is directly created in VBScript instead of directly in a SQL stored procedure. The query will be created on the fly.

LISTING 12.4   OrderSearch.asp

```
<%@ Language=VBScript %>
<!-- #Include file="include/validatecheck.asp" -->

<!--
    OrderSearch.asp - Provides input fields for performing
    the order search against the order data and the basket.
-->


<HTML>
<BODY>
<!-- #include file="include/navinclude.asp" -->
```

The first thing we do, as shown in Listing 12.5, is retrieve the values entered in the search form. A check is done on the search *amount* fields to multiply them by 100 to match the integer storage of the amounts. Note that the product name and the shopper name are checked to ensure any single quotes are doubled for query in the database.

LISTING 12.5   OrderSearch.asp Continued

```
<%

'   The key fields are retrieved from the order
'   search page.
srchShopperName = replace(request("srchShopperName"), _
                    "'", "''")
srchShopperEmail = request("srchShopperEmail")
srchStartDate = request("srchStartDate")
srchEndDate = request("srchEndDate")
srchStartAmount = request("srchStartAmount")
```

```
srchEndAmount = request("srchEndAmount")

'  Now we begin the building of the SQL statement.
'  In this case instead of calling a stored procedure
'  we are going to create a SQL statement based upon
'  the input parameters on the search form.

'  Retrieve the starting search amount
if srchStartAmount <> "" then

    '  Remember to mulitply the search amount
    '  by one hundred to make it an integer.
    srchStartAmount = srchStartAmount * 100

end if

'  Retrieve the ending search amount
if srchEndAmount <> "" then

    '  Remember to mulitply the search amount
    '  by one hundred to make it an integer.
    srchEndAmount = srchEndAmount * 100

end if

'  Retrieve the product name to search by.
srchProductName = replace(request("srchProductName"), _
                    "'", "''")
```

The next phase is to begin building the SQL query, as shown in Listing 12.6. The tables that come into play include OrderData, Basket, BasketItem, and OrderStatus. We will join this data together to perform the search.

LISTING 12.6   OrderSearch.asp Continued

```
'  The first part of the SQL statement is built
'  automatically. Each of the fields to be returned
'  are defined in the query and the Distinct statement
'  is used so just individual rows for order are
'  returned (since we are querying each basket item
'  as well). The key tables are joined to return all
```

```
'   of the appropriate data.
sql = "select distinct orderdata.idOrder, OrderData.idShopper, " &_
      "dtOrdered, " & _
      "chrShipLastName, chrBillLastName, chrShipEmail, " & _
      "chrBillEmail, intTotal, idStage, chrShippingNum " & _
      "from OrderData, Basket, basketitem, orderstatus " & _
      "where OrderData.idBasket = Basket.idBasket and " & _
      "BasketItem.idBasket = Basket.idBasket and " & _
      "OrderStatus.idorder = orderdata.idOrder "
```

The first check is against the e-mail address, as shown in Listing 12.7. If an address was entered, we are going to search for a similar match in the *ship* and *bill* e-mail addresses. The SQL statement that has been started is added on to with the appropriate SQL syntax.

In this case we will check the e-mail addresses to see if they contain a matching string. That way a search can be done for an address such as "@sybex.com" that will return all orders where the person's e-mail address contains the text.

LISTING 12.7   OrderSearch.asp Continued

```
'  Next we check to see if an email address
'  was to be searched on.
if srchShopperEmail <> "" then

    '   The SQL statement is built to query the
    '   the entered text against the shipping
    '   and billing email address. Note that the
    '   LIKE syntax is used for the query.
    sql = sql & " and (" & _
    "chrShipEmail like '%" & srchShopperEmail & "%' or " & _
    "chrBillEmail like '%" & srchShopperEmail & "%') "

end if
```

Next we search on the shopper name. Again, we want to search multiple fields to see if the searched string text is found. In this case we will match the first and last names of the billing and shipping addresses. The *Like* SQL statement is utilized to perform the string search. Note we *OR* the string search together so that a result is returned if any one match is made. (See Listing 12.8.)

LISTING 12.8   **OrderSearch.asp Continued**

```
'  The shopper name is checked next. If
'  search text was entered, then the LIKE
'  statement is utilized again to see if the
'  text is found in any of the shipping and
'  billing first and last name fields.
if srchShopperName <> "" then

sql = sql & "and ( " & _
"chrShipFirstName like '%" & srchShopperName & "%' or " & _
"chrShipLastName like '%" & srchShopperName & "%' or " & _
"chrBillFirstName like '%" & srchShopperName & "%' or " & _
"chrBillLastName like '%" &  srchShopperName & "%') "

end if
```

Next, in Listing 12.9, we search on the starting and ending date ranges. A check is done on each field to see if something was entered. If so, then we add on the SQL query matching the dtOrdered field against the date(s) entered.

LISTING 12.9   **OrderSearch.asp Continued**

```
'  The searching start date is checked next.
'  A check is done to ensure the starting date
'  ordered is entered. Then the SQL query is
'  updated to have the start date.'
if srchStartDate <> "" then

    sql = sql & " and dtOrdered >= '" & srchStartDate & "' "

end if

'  Next we check the ending date for the search. If it
'  is set then the SQL query is updated.
if srchEndDate <> "" then

    sql = sql & " and dtOrdered <= '" & srchEndDate & "' "

end if
```

A SQL check is done on the search amounts to build similar SQL statements to check against a total order amount range. The SQL statements are added on to the existing one we are building (see Listing 12.10).

LISTING 12.10   OrderSearch.asp Continued

```
'  The next check is the starting amount
'  entered by the user. If it is set,
'  then the query is updated.
if srchStartAmount <> "" then

    sql = sql & " and intTotal >= " & srchStartAmount

end if


'  The ending amount is next checked.
'  If it is set, then the query is updated.
if srchEndAmount <> "" then

    sql = sql & " and intTotal <= " & srchEndAmount

end if
```

Finally, in Listing 12.11, we will check the product name. The SQL *Like* statement is again used to see if the search text matches any sub-string in the product names.

LISTING 12.11   OrderSearch.asp Continued

```
'  Finally we check the product name to ensure
'  it has been entered. If so then the query
'  is updated to include the search.
if srchProductName <> "" then

    sql = sql & "and chrName like '%" & _
        srchProductName & "%'"

end if
```

Now we are ready to execute our SQL statement (see Listing 12.12). An ADO connection is opened to the database. Then the SQL statement is executed. Next we will be ready to list out any orders retrieved.

LISTING 12.12   **OrderSearch.asp Continued**

```
'  Create an ADO database connection
set dbOrderSearch = server.createobject("adodb.connection")

'  Create the record set
set rsOrderSearch = server.CreateObject("adodb.recordset")

'  Open the connection using our ODBC file DSN
dbOrderSearch.open("filedsn=WildWillieCDs")

'  Execute our built on the fly query.
set rsOrderSearch = dbOrderSearch.Execute(sql)

%>

<!--  Next we work on the display of the search
      results. A table is started to display
      the data. -->
<BR><BR>
```

We next begin building a table for displaying the order data (see Listing 12.13). All of the key values will be displayed, including the order status and the ability to easily change it.

LISTING 12.13   **OrderSearch.asp Continued**

```
<table border="1" cellpadding="3" cellspacing="3">

<!--  Build the header. -->
<tr>
    <th>Order ID</th>
    <th>Date Ordered</th>
    <th>Order Total</th>
    <th>Ship to<BR>Last Name</th>
    <th>Ship to<BR>Email Address</th>
    <th>Bill to<BR>Last Name</th>
    <th>Bill to<BR>Email Address</th>
    <th>Order Status</th>
```

```
        <th>Delete</th>
    </tr>
```

We are now ready to loop through the returned result set (see Listing 12.14). The first column shows the order ID, which is linked to retrieve the detail for the order.

LISTING 12.14   OrderSearch.asp Continued

```
<%

'   Loop through the returned results.
do until rsOrderSearch.EOF

%>

<!--  Start a results row. -->
<tr>
    <td align="center">
        <!--  A link is built on the order id to give
              the user a link to the order details. -->
        <a href="OrderDetail.asp?idOrder= ↵
<%=rsOrderSearch("idOrder")%>& ↵
idShopper=<%=rsOrderSearch("idShopper")%>">
<%=rsOrderSearch("idOrder")%>
        </a>
    </td>
```

Next, in Listing 12.15, the date ordered and the order total are displayed. Following that, the shipping last name is displayed along with the shipping e-mail address. Note that the e-mail address is hooked up with the mailto: function so it can be clicked and an e-mail sent. Likewise the billing e-mail address and last name are also displayed.

LISTING 12.15   OrderSearch.asp Continued

```
<!--  Next we display the date of the order, the order
      total and the shipping last name. -->
<td align="center"><%=rsOrderSearch("dtOrdered")%></td>
<td align="center">
```

```
    <%=formatcurrency(rsOrderSearch("intTotal")/100, ⤶
      2)%>
</td>
 <td align="center">
 <%=rsOrderSearch("chrShipLastName")%>
</td>

 <td align="center">
    <!-- Next the shipping email address is displayed
         and it built as a link so an email can be
         easily sent. -->
    <a href="mailto:<%=rsOrderSearch("chrShipEmail")%>">
    <%=rsOrderSearch("chrShipEmail")%></a>
</td>
 <!-- Show the billing last name. -->
 <td align="center">
  <%=rsOrderSearch("chrBillLastName")%>
</td>

 <td align="center">
    <!-- Next the billing email address is displayed
        and it built as a link so an email can be
        easily sent. -->
    <a href="mailto:<%=rsOrderSearch("chrBillEmail")%>">
    <%=rsOrderSearch("chrBillEmail")%></a>
</td>
```

Now we are ready to display the current status of the order (see Listing 12.16). There are four different status settings. We are going to build a *select* box that will show the current status. Around the select box will be a form that will allow us to change the status.

The first thing we do is retrieve the status and set a variable indicating the value that should be defaulted.

LISTING 12.16   **OrderSearch.asp Continued**

```
<td>
<%

'  Check the status of the order. A check is
'  done to build a defaulted selected variable
```

```
'  so the current shipping status is defaulted.
select case rsOrderSearch("idStage")

    '  Case 0 is that the order has been retrieved.
    case 0
        Stat0 = "Selected"

    '  Case 1 is that the order is fulfilled and ready
    '  for shipping.
    case 1
        Stat1 = "Selected"

    '  Case 2 indicates the order has been shipped and we
    '  display the shipping number.
    case 2
        Stat2 = "Selected"

    '  If none of these are set then we indicate that
    '  customer service should be called.
    case 3
        Stat3 = "Selected"

end select

%>
```

Next, in Listing 12.17, a form is created for submitting a status update to the UpdateStatus.asp page. A hidden variable is set on the form that will store the order ID so that we know what order status to update.

LISTING 12.17   OrderSearch.asp Continued

```
<!-- A form is built to update the
     order status. -->
<form method="post" action="UpdateStatus.asp">

<!-- In order to know what form will be updated, a
     hidden variable is stored with the order id. -->
<input type="hidden" name="intOrder"
value="<%=rsOrderSearch("idOrder")%>">
```

Next, in Listing 12.18, the select box is created. Each status is displayed. The corresponding variable is inserted into the option.

LISTING 12.18   **OrderSearch.asp Continued**

```
<!-- A select box is created with the different order
     status variables. Note the default selected
     variables are utilized in each option. And,
     the shipping number is shown if the status
     is shipped.-->
<select name="intStage">
    <option value="0" <%=Stat0%>>Order Received and
                                 to be Processed

    <option value="1" <%=Stat1%>>Order Fulfilled and
                                 Ready to be Shipped

    <option value="2" <%=Stat2%>>Order Shipped -
            <%=rsOrderSearch("chrShippingNum")%>

    <option value="3" <%=Stat3%>>Call Customer Service
                                 for Assistance
</select><BR>
```

We also want to be able to put in the shipping tracking number if we are indicating the order has been shipped. An input box is created for typing in the value. Following that, a Submit button is created and the form is ended.

LISTING 12.19   **OrderSearch.asp Continued**

```
<!-- An input element is created so the shipping
     number can be entered. -->
<input type="text"
value="<%=rsOrderSearch("chrShippingNum")%>"
name="chrShippingNum">

<!-- Submit button for the form. -->
<input type="Submit" value="Update"
       name="Submit">
</form>
</td>
```

Then, in Listing 12.20, we build a link to delete an order from the system. The link is made to the DeleteOrder.asp page and the ID of the order is passed on the URL. Finally, we move to the next record and continue to display orders. Then the page is completed.

LISTING 12.20   OrderSearch.asp Continued

```
        <td>
            <!-- Build a link to delete teh order from
                the database. -->
            <a href="DeleteOrder.asp? ↵
                idOrder=<%=rsOrderSearch("idOrder")%>">
    Delete</a>
        </td>
    </tr>
    <%

    ' Move to the next row.
    rsOrderSearch.MoveNext

    Loop

    %>

    </table>

    </body>

    </html>
```

Now we are ready to test out our new search interface. Figure 12.1 shows the order search page. The first test we will do is to simply search for all orders in the system (be sure you have some entered).

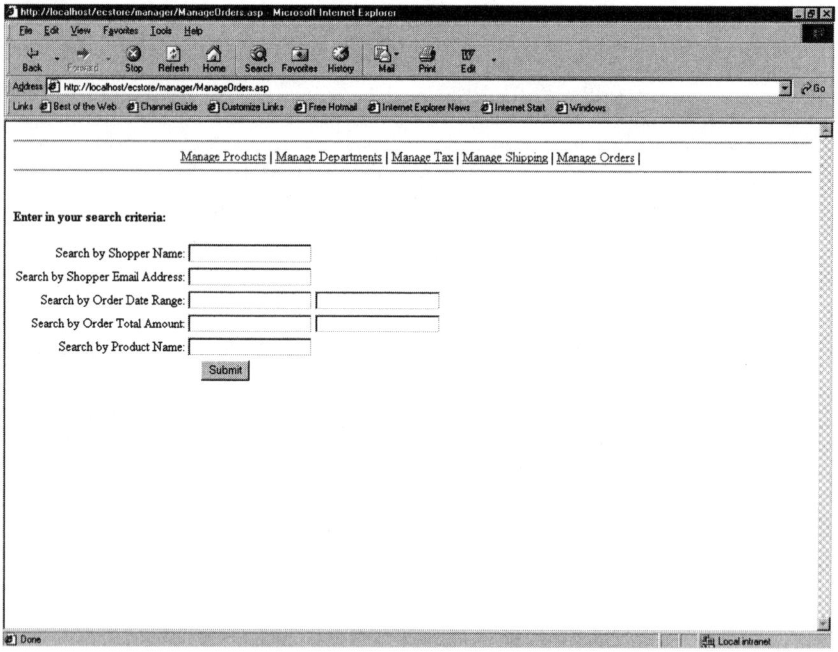

FIGURE 12.1:

Order search page

Figure 12.2 shows the listing of all orders returned. So, basically we do not have to enter any criteria at all to retrieve orders. Note all of the data returned for each order including the current order status. The ID of the order on the left is linked to retrieve further detail.

FIGURE 12.2:

All orders returned

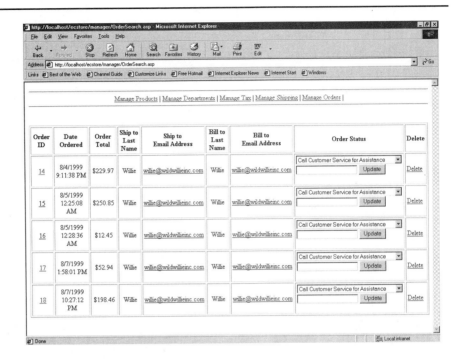

Next let's perform a very specific search. Enter a specific date range and a specific order amount range (being sure that at least one order meets both requirements). Figure 12.3 shows the search form with sample data.

FIGURE 12.3:

Searching by date range
and by amount

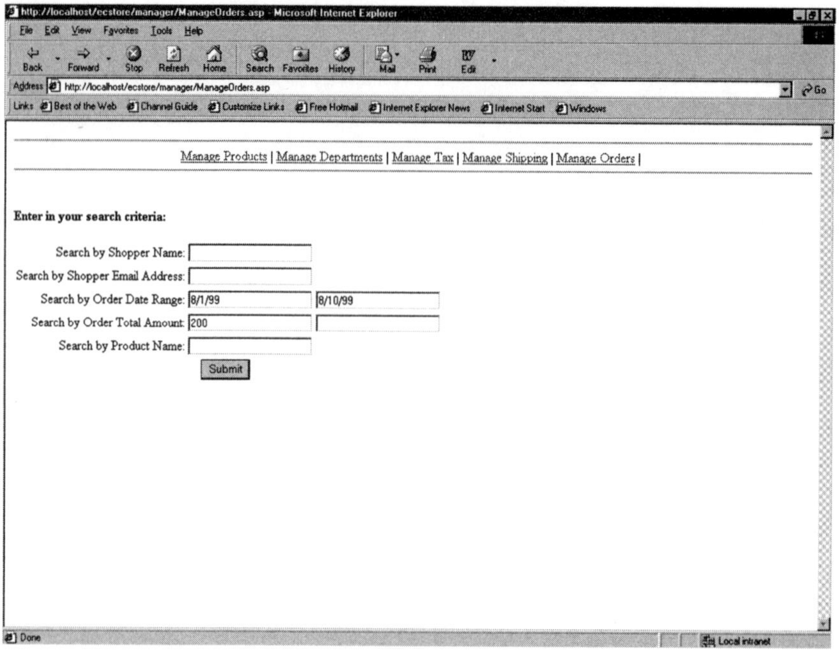

Figure 12.4 shows the search results. Note that all of the dates of the order and
the total dollar amounts of the order fall within the specified date range.

FIGURE 12.4:

Search results

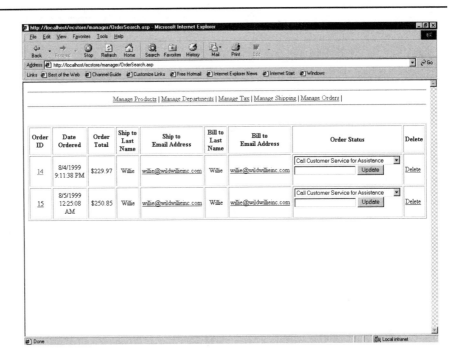

Deleting an Order and Managing Order Status

Now that we have been able to search and retrieve orders, let's work on two of the functions for managing those orders, *deleting* and *status updates*.

First we will take a look at deleting an order. Remember that the ID of the order is passed on the URL to the page. In Listing 12.21, an ADO database connection is opened. Then a SQL query is created to call the sp_DeleteOrder stored procedure. The ID of the order is passed to it. When the query has executed, the user is sent back to the order search page.

| TIP | You may want to send the user back to the search results page. But the order we just deleted would no longer be valid. One idea might be to store the SQL statement created for the order search in a session variable and then re-execute the query without re-creating it. |

LISTING 12.21   DeleteOrder.asp

```asp
<%@ Language=VBScript %>
<%
'    *******************************************************
'    DeleteOrder.asp - Handles deleting the order from
'    the database.
'    *******************************************************

'    Create an ADO database connection
set dbDeleteOrder = server.createobject("adodb.connection")

'    Create the record set
set rsDeleteOrder = server.CreateObject("adodb.recordset")

'    Open the connection using our ODBC file DSN
dbDeleteOrder.open("filedsn=WildWillieCDs")

'    Call the sp_DeleteOrder stored procedure to
'    delete the specified order from the database.
sql = "execute sp_DeleteOrder " & request("idOrder")

'    Execute the statement
set rsDeleteOrder = dbDeleteOrder.Execute(sql)

Response.Redirect "OrderSearch.asp"

%>
```

The sp_DeleteOrder stored procedure is utilized to remove the order from the database. Keep in mind that we not only need to remove the OrderData table information—we also want to delete the order data from the PaymentData table, the OrderStatusTable, the Basket table, and the BasketItem table.

The first thing done in the stored procedure is to retrieve the ID of the basket so we can make the relational link to the other tables. Then the appropriate delete SQL statements are executed. (See Listing 12.22.)

LISTING 12.22   sp_DeleteOrder Stored Procedure

```
CREATE PROCEDURE sp_DeleteOrder

@idOrder int

AS

declare @idBasket int

select @idBasket = idBasket from OrderData where
idOrder = @idOrder

delete from orderdata where idOrder = @idOrder
delete from paymentdata where idOrder = @idOrder
delete from OrderStatus where idOrder = @idOrder

delete from Basket where idBasket = @idBasket

delete from BasketItem where idBasket = @idBasket
```

Next we can work on updating the order status. To do this we need three data values. The first is the ID of the order, which is passed on a hidden variable. The second is the ID of the new status. And the third is a shipping tracking number (if there is one).

Then we create a SQL statement and utilize the sp_UpdateOrderStatus stored procedure and pass in our three data values. Once the order status has been updated, the user is sent back to the order search page. (See Listing 12.23.)

LISTING 12.23   UpdateStatus.asp

```
<%@ Language=VBScript %>
<%
'   *******************************************************
'   UpdateStatus.asp - Handles updating the order status
'   for the specified order.
'   *******************************************************

'   Create an ADO database connection
```

```
set dbUpdateStatus = _
    server.createobject("adodb.connection")

'  Create the record set
set rsUpdateStatus = server.CreateObject("adodb.recordset")

'  Open the connection using our ODBC file DSN
dbUpdateStatus.open("filedsn=WildWillieCDs")

'  Retrieve the order it, order stage
'  and shipping number
intOrder = request("intOrder")
intStage = request("intStage")
chrShippingNum = request("chrShippingNum")

'  Build the sql statement and call the
'  sp_UpdateOrderStatus stored procedure
sql = "execute sp_UpdateOrderStatus " & _
      intOrder & ", " & _
      intStage & ", '" & _
      chrShippingNum & "'"

'  Execute the statement
set rsUpdateStatus = dbUpdateStatus.Execute(sql)

'  Send the user back to the order search
Response.Redirect "OrderSearch.asp"

%>
```

The sp_UpdateOrderStatus stored procedure handles changing the order status of a current order (see Listing 12.24). The order ID, stage ID, and shipping number are passed in. Then an Update SQL statement is created for updating the current data. Remember that when an order is placed by the shopper, an initial order status row is inserted into the table.

LISTING 12.24   sp_UpdateOrderStatus Stored Procedure

```
CREATE PROCEDURE sp_UpdateOrderStatus

@idOrder int,
```

```
@intStage int,
@chrShippingNum varchar(100)

AS

update OrderStatus set
    idStage = @intStage,
    chrShippingNum = @chrShippingNum
where
    idOrder = @idOrder
```

Next we can test our update order status functionality. Figure 12.5 shows the current order status settings. Let's change the first to be "Call Customer Service for Assistance." Then hit the Update button.

FIGURE 12.5:

Current order status settings

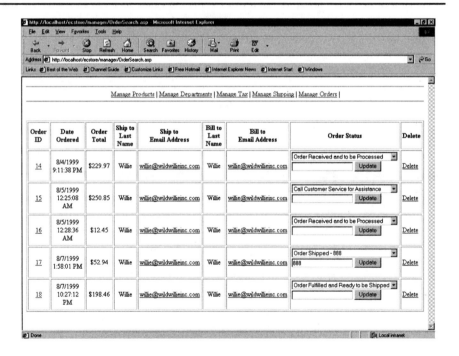

Figure 12.6 shows the order listing again, but note that the first item status has changed. This will also be reflected on the order status setting that the user can retrieve through their profile.

FIGURE 12.6:

Changing status of first
order

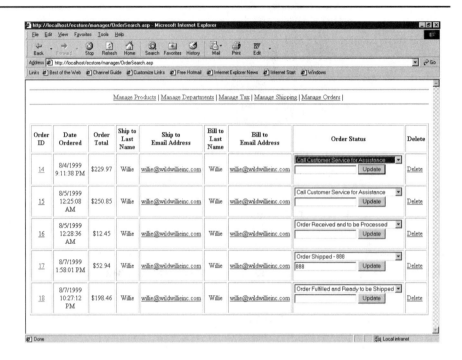

Reviewing and Updating an Order

Now we need to build an order detail that is similar to the receipt listing we created
for the shopper. But, in this case we want the store manager to be able to update the
order if something has changed. Listing 12.25 shows the code for the page.

As with our other pages, it begins with the appropriate security include and
navigation bar include.

LISTING 12.25   OrderDetail.asp

```
<%@ Language=VBScript %>
<!-- #Include file="include/validatecheck.asp" -->
<HTML>
<!--
    OrderDetail.asp - Displays the detail on the order
```

```
        and allows for the key fields to be updated.
-->

<body>
<!-- #include file="include/navinclude.asp" -->
```

Next we are ready to begin querying data for the order (see Listing 12.26). The first stored procedure we execute is sp_RetrieveReceiptHeader. This will get all of the address information for the order.

LISTING 12.26   OrderDetail.asp Continued

```
<%

'  Create an ADO database connection
set dbOrderReceiptHeader = _
    server.createobject("adodb.connection")
set rsOrderReceiptHeader = _
    server.CreateObject("adodb.recordset")

'  Open the connection using our ODBC file DSN
dbOrderReceiptHeader.open("filedsn=WildWillieCDs")

'  Call the stored procedure to retrieve the
'  receipt header.
sql = "execute sp_RetrieveReceiptHeader " & _
    Request("idShopper") & ", " & _
    Request("idOrder")

'  Execute the SQL statement
set rsOrderReceiptHeader = dbOrderReceiptHeader.execute(sql)

%>
```

Now we start a form that will post the updates to the UpdateOrder.asp page (see Listing 12.27). Then the table is started for displaying the basic order and address information.

LISTING 12.27   OrderDetail.asp Continued

```
<!-- Start the form to update the order data. -->
<form method="post" action="UpdateOrder.asp">

<!-- Build the table for the header -->
<table>
<!-- Row to display the order id abd
     the date ordered.
-->
```

The order ID is displayed; of course this will not be editable since it is unique to this order. We also create a series of hidden variables that will help identify which data in the database is to be updated. These include the order ID, the shopper ID, and the basket ID. Following that, the date of the order is displayed. This too is not editable. (See Listing 12.28.)

LISTING 12.28   OrderDetail.asp Continued

```
<tr>
    <td><B>
        Order # <%=rsOrderReceiptHeader("idOrder")%></b>

        <!-- Several hidden variables are built in so we
             can easily update by the key fields for each
             table. -->
        <input type="hidden" name="idOrder"
         value="<%=request("idOrder")%>">
        <input type="hidden" name="idShopper"
         value="<%=request("idShopper")%>">
        <input type="hidden" name="idBasket"
         value="<%=rsOrderReceiptHeader("idBasket")%>">
    </td>
    <td width="75"></td>
    <td><b>Order Date: <%=rsOrderReceiptHeader("dtOrdered")%></b></td>
<tr>

<!-- Blank column -->
<tr>
    <td colspan="3"> </td>
</tr>
```

Next we get into the display of the billing and shipping addresses (see Listing 12.29). In this case we are going to build input text elements for each field.
We want the user to be able to completely update this data.

LISTING 12.29   OrderDetail.asp Continued

```
<!--  Bill to and Ship to header -->
<tr>
    <td><b>Bill To:</b></td>
    <td width="75"></td>
    <td><b>Ship To:</b></td>
<tr>
<!--  Shipping and Billing information -->
<tr>
    <td>
        <input type="text" name="chrBillFirstName"
        value="<% = rsOrderReceiptHeader("chrBillFirstName")%>">

        <input type="text" name="chrBillLastName"
         value=" ↵
         <% = rsOrderReceiptHeader("chrBillLastName")%>">
    </td>

    <td width="75"></td>

    <td>

        <input type="text" name="chrShipFirstName"
         value=" ↵
         <% = rsOrderReceiptHeader("chrShipFirstName")%>">

        <input type="text" name="chrShipLastName"
         value=" ↵
         <% = rsOrderReceiptHeader("chrShipLastName")%>">

    </td>
<tr>
<!--  Billing and shipping address. -->
<tr>
    <td>
        <input type="text" name="chrBillAddress"
```

```
             value=↵
             "<% = rsOrderReceiptHeader("chrBillAddress")%>">
        </td>
        <td width="75"></td>
        <td>
            <input type="text" name="chrShipAddress"
             value=" ↵
             <%=rsOrderReceiptHeader("chrShipAddress")%>">
        </td>
    <tr>
    <!-- Billing and shipping address.  -->
    <tr>
        <td>
            <input type="text" name="chrBillCity"
             value="<% = rsOrderReceiptHeader("chrBillCity")%>">,
            <input type="text" name="chrBillState"
             value="<% = rsOrderReceiptHeader("chrBillState")%>"
          size="2">
            <input type="text" name="chrBillZipCode"
         value=" ↵
          <% = rsOrderReceiptHeader("chrBillZipCode")%>"
          size="10">
        </td>

        <td width="75"></td>

        <td>
            <input type="text" name="chrShipCity"
            value="<% = rsOrderReceiptHeader("chrShipCity")%>">,

            <input type="text" name="chrShipState"
            value="<% = rsOrderReceiptHeader("chrShipState")%>"
            size="2">

            <input type="text" name="chrShipZipCode"
            value="<% = rsOrderReceiptHeader("chrShipZipCode")%>"
            size="10">
        </td>
    <tr>
    <!-- Billing and shipping phone. -->
    <tr>
        <td>
            <input type="text" name="chrBillPhone"
            value="<% = rsOrderReceiptHeader("chrBillPhone")%>">
```

```
        </td>
        <td width="75"></td>
        <td>
            <input type="text" name="chrShipPhone"
            value="<% = rsOrderReceiptHeader("chrShipPhone")%>">
        </td>
    <tr>
    <!--  Billing and shipping email. -->
    <tr>
        <td>
            <input type="text" name="chrBillEmail"
          value="<% = rsOrderReceiptHeader("chrBillEmail")%>"
          size="35">
        </td>
        <td width="75"></td>
        <td>
            <input type="text" name="chrShipEmail"
             value="<% = rsOrderReceiptHeader("chrShipEmail")%>"
             size="35">
        </td>
    <tr>

    </table>
```

Now that we have displayed the address and order information, we will need to display the payment information (see Listing 12.30). Note that this is data that is not displayed on the user's receipt.

To retrieve the payment data, the sp_RetrievePaymentData stored procedure is utilized. The ID of the order is passed into it.

LISTING 12.30   OrderDetail.asp Continued

```
<!--  Display the payment data . -->
<BR><BR>
<b>Payment Data:</b>
<BR>

<%

'  Create an ADO database connection
set dbPaymentData = server.createobject("adodb.connection")
set rsPaymentData = server.CreateObject("adodb.recordset")
```

```
'  Open the connection using our ODBC file DSN
dbPaymentData.open("filedsn=WildWillieCDs")

'  Call the stored procedure to retrieve the
'  payment data on the order.
sql = "execute sp_RetrievePaymentData " & _
      Request("idOrder")

'  Execute the SQL statement
set rsPaymentData = dbPaymentData.execute(sql)

%>
```

A new table is created for displaying the payment data (see Listing 12.31). The name on the card, card number, card type, and expiration date are shown and are all set up to be editable.

LISTING 12.31   OrderDetail.asp Continued

```
<!-- A table is created to dispaly the payment
      data. -->
<table cellpadding="3" cellspacing="3">
<tr>
    <!-- Dispaly the card name -->
    <td align="right">Card Name:</td>
    <td>
        <input type="text" name="chrCardName"
        value="<%=rsPaymentData("chrCardName")%>">
    </td>
    <!-- Display the card number  -->
    <td align="right">Card Number:</td>
    <td>
        <input type="text" name="chrCardNumber"
        value="<%=rsPaymentData("chrCardNumber")%>">
    </td>
</tr>
<tr>
    <!-- Display the card type. -->
    <td align="right">Card Type:</td>
    <td>
```

```
        <input type="text" name="chrCardType" value=" ⤸
        <%=rsPaymentData("chrCardType")%>">
    </td>
    <!-- Display the card expiration date  -->
    <td align="right">Card Expiration Date:</td>
    <td>
        <input type="text" name="chrExpDate"
        value="<%=rsPaymentData("chrExpDate")%>">
    </td>
  </tr>
  </table>
```

Now we are ready to show the items ordered (see Listing 12.32). The sp_RetrieveReceiptItems stored procedure handles returning all of the items for the order. The ID of the shopper and the ID of the order are passed in.

LISTING 12.32   **OrderDetail.asp Continued**

```
<%

' Create an ADO database connection
set dbOrderReceiptItems = _
    server.createobject("adodb.connection")
set rsOrderReceiptItems = _
    server.CreateObject("adodb.recordset")

' Open the connection using our ODBC file DSN
dbOrderReceiptItems.open("filedsn=WildWillieCDs")

' SQL statement to retrieve the items orders.
sql = "execute sp_RetrieveReceiptItems " & _
    Request("idShopper") & ", " & _
    Request("idOrder")

' Execute the SQL statement
set rsOrderReceiptItems = dbOrderReceiptItems.execute(sql)
%>
```

A table is started to display the data (see Listing 12.33). The item code (product ID), name, attributes, quantity, price, and line item total are displayed. Each of these fields is editable by the user.

LISTING 12.33   **OrderDetail.asp Continued**

```
<!--  Build the basket table -->
<table border="0" cellpadding="3" cellspacing="2"
       width="750">

<tr><td colspan="6"><HR></td></tr>

<!--  Build the header row -->
<tr>
    <th>Item Code</th>
    <th>Name</th>
    <th>Attributes</th>
    <th>Quantity</th>
    <th>Price</th>
    <th>Total</th>
</tr>
```

In Listing 12.34, a loop is started to go through each item. For each field an input text element is created. The tricky task is to give a unique name to each input element.

What we do is combine the name of the field, like chrName, with the ID of the product we are working on. For example, a value could be chrName99 for the name field of product 99. That way on the update page we can retrieve each unique value and then update the database appropriately.

Note that for the product attributes, no input is allowed unless previous attributes have been entered. Also, we do not explicitly allow an item to be deleted, although we could set its quantity to 0, which would have the same effect.

LISTING 12.34   **OrderDetail.asp Continued**

```
<%

'  Loop through the basket items.
do until rsOrderReceiptItems.EOF

%>

<!--  Show the row -->
```

```
<tr>
    <!-- Show the product id -->
    <td align="center">
        <input type="hidden" name="idBasketItem
     <% = rsOrderReceiptItems("idProduct")%>"
        value="<% = rsOrderReceiptItems("idBasketItem")%>">

      <input type="text" name="
       <% = rsOrderReceiptItems("idProduct")%>"
         value="<% = rsOrderReceiptItems("idProduct")%>"
       size="3">
    </td>

    <!-- Show the product name -->
    <td>
        <input type="text" name="chrName
        <% = rsOrderReceiptItems("idProduct")%>"
         value="<% = rsOrderReceiptItems("chrName")%>">
    </td>

    <!-- Show the product attributes -->
    <td>
        <% if rsOrderReceiptItems("chrColor") <> " " then %>

        <input type="text" name="chrSize
        <% = rsOrderReceiptItems("idProduct")%>"
        value=" ↵
         <% = rsOrderReceiptItems("chrSize")%>"
         size="7">,

        <input type="text" name="chrColor
        <% = rsOrderReceiptItems("idProduct")%>"
          value="<% = rsOrderReceiptItems("chrColor")%>"
         size="7">

        <% end if %>
    </td>

    <!-- Show the product quantity -->
    <td align="center">
        <input type="text" name="intQuantity
        <% = rsOrderReceiptItems("idProduct")%>"
```

```
        value="<%=rsOrderReceiptItems("intQuantity")%>"
        size="4">
    </td>

    <!--  Show the product price -->
    <td>
    <input type="text" name="intPrice
    <% = rsOrderReceiptItems("idProduct")%>"
    value=" ↵
    <%=formatcurrency(rsOrderReceiptItems("intPrice")/100 ↵
    , 2)%>"
    size="7">
    </td>

    <!--  Show the product total cost -->
    <td align="right">
      <%Response.write _
    formatcurrency(rsOrderReceiptItems("intPrice")/100 * ↵
    rsOrderReceiptItems("intQuantity"), 2)%>
    </td>
</tr>

<%

'  Move to the next row
rsOrderReceiptItems.MoveNext

loop

%>
```

Following the display of the line items, we are going to display the order subtotal, tax, shipping, and total. These will not support direct changing by the user, but will be updated when the any changes are submitted.

LISTING 12.35   **OrderDetail.asp Continued**

```
<!--  Build a break -->
<tr>
    <td colspan="6"><HR></td>
</tr>

<!--  Show the sub total of the basket -->
```

```
<tr>
  <td colspan="5" align="right"><b>Subtotal:</b></td>
  <td align="right"><%Response.Write _
  formatcurrency(rsOrderReceiptHeader("intSubtotal")/100, ↵
   2) %>
  </td>
</tr>
<!--  Show the shipping total of the basket -->
<tr>
 <td colspan="5" align="right"><b>Shipping:</b></td>
 <td align="right"><%Response.Write _
    formatcurrency(rsOrderReceiptHeader("intShipping")/ ↵
    100, 2) %>
 </td>
</tr>
<!--  Show the tax total of the basket -->
<tr>
 <td colspan="5" align="right"><b>Tax:</b></td>
 <td align="right"><%Response.Write _
    formatcurrency(rsOrderReceiptHeader("intTax")/100, ↵
   2) %>
 </td>
</tr>
<!--  Show the total of the basket -->
<tr>
 <td colspan="5" align="right"><b>Total:</b></td>
 <td align="right"><%Response.Write _
    formatcurrency(rsOrderReceiptHeader("intTotal")/100, ↵
   2) %>
 </td>
</tr>
```

Finally, as shown in Listing 12.36, the page is closed out with a Submit button for the form and closing tags for the page.

LISTING 12.36   OrderDetail.asp Continued

```
<!--  Submit button to process the updates. -->
<tr>
    <td colspan="6">
        <input type="Submit" value="Submit Changes"
            name="Submit">
    </td>
```

```
<tr>

</table>

</form>
</BODY>
</HTML>
```

Several stored procedures are utilized on this page. The first is sp_Retrieve-ReceiptHeader. This will retrieve the data stored in the OrderData and Basket tables and will allow us to display basic order information. (See Listing 12.37.)

LISTING 12.37   sp_RetrieveReceiptHeader Stored Procedure

```
/*  Retrieve the receipt header by shopper ID
    and Order ID */
CREATE PROCEDURE sp_RetrieveReceiptHeader

/*  Pass in the ID of the shopper and
    the ID of the Order */
@idShopper int,
@idOrder int

AS

/*  Select the receipt header which requires
    joining the orderdata and basket tables
*/
select * from OrderData, Basket
where Orderdata.idOrder = @idOrder and
      OrderData.idShopper = @idShopper and
      OrderData.idBasket = Basket.idBasket
```

Next we utilize the stored procedure to retrieve payment data. That simply returns the payment data fields for the given order ID. (See Listing 12.38.)

LISTING 12.38   sp_RetrievePaymentData

```
CREATE PROCEDURE sp_RetrievePaymentData

@idOrder int
```

```
AS

select * from paymentdata
where idOrder = @idOrder
```

Finally, in Listing 12.39, the `sp_RetrieveReceiptItems` stored procedure gets the items the shopper ordered. This is keyed from the order ID and the shopper ID.

LISTING 12.39   sp_RetrieveReceiptItems

```
/*  Stored Procedure to retrieve the
    receipt items.
*/
CREATE PROCEDURE sp_RetrieveReceiptItems

/*  Pass in the ID of the shopper and the
    Id of the order */
@idShopper int,
@idOrder int

AS

/*  Select the contents of the basketitem,
    basket and orderdata tables.
*/
select * from basketitem, orderdata
where orderdata.idshopper = @idShopper and
      orderdata.idOrder = @idOrder and
      basketitem.idbasket = orderdata.idbasket
```

NOTE   The editing performed on the order detail page is very free-form. The user could type in anything for product name, product ID, etc. We might want to tighten this up and force the user to select from pre-populated lists.

Now that we can display our order, and have prepared it for changes, we are ready to process those changes. Listing 12.40 shows the UpdateOrder.asp page, which will process all of the fields on the order detail.

An initial ADO database connection is created. Then we begin retrieving the key values from the order detail page including the ID of the order, the ID of the shopper, and the ID of the basket.

LISTING 12.40   UpdateOrder.asp

```
<%@ Language=VBScript %>
<%
'    ********************************************************
'    UpdateOrder.asp - Handles updating the order data
'    posted from the order detail page.
'    ********************************************************

'    Create an ADO database connection
set dbOrderUpdate = server.createobject("adodb.connection")
set rsOrderUpdate = server.CreateObject("adodb.recordset")

'    Open the connection using our ODBC file DSN
dbOrderUpdate.open("filedsn=WildWillieCDs")

'    Retrieve our three key values, the id of the order
'    the id of the shopper and the id of the basket for
'    the order.
idOrder = request("idOrder")
idShopper = request("idShopper")
idBasket = request("idBasket")
```

Next the billing and shipping address information is retrieved. We must be careful to update the appropriate fields if there are any single quotes in the text. (See Listing 12.41.)

LISTING 12.41   UpdateOrder.asp Continued

```
'    Next we retrieve the core order data which
'    includes the billing address and shipping
'    address. Note that the key fields are updated
'    to ensure any single quotes are doubled.
chrBillFirstName = _
    replace(request("chrBillFirstName"), "'", "''")

chrBillLastname = _
    replace(request("chrBillLastName"), "'", "''")
```

```
chrShipFirstName = _
    replace(Request("chrShipFirstName"), "'", "''")

chrShipLastname = _
    replace(request("chrShipLastName"), "'", "''")

chrBillAddress = _
    replace(request("chrBillAddress"), "'", "''")

chrShipAddress = _
    replace(request("chrShipAddress"), "'", "''")

chrBillCity = replace(request("chrBillCity"), "'", "''")
chrBillState = request("chrBillState")
chrBillZipCode = request("chrBillZipCode")
chrShipCity = replace(request("chrShipCity"), "'", "''")
chrShipState = request("chrShipState")
chrShipZipCode = request("chrShipZipCode")
chrBillPhone = request("chrBillPhone")
chrShipPhone = request("chrShipPhone")
chrBillEmail = request("chrBillEmail")
chrShipEmail = request("chrShipEmail")
```

To update the core order data, the sp_UpdateOrderData stored procedure is utilized. It takes in all of the address data and then updates the OrderData table. (See Listing 12.42.)

LISTING 12.42   UpdateOrder.asp Continued

```
'  The order data is updated by calling
'  the sp_UpdateOrderData stored procedure
sql = "execute sp_UpdateOrderData " & _
        idOrder & ", '" & _
        chrBillFirstName & "', '" & _
        chrBillLastname & "', '" & _
        chrBillAddress & "', '" & _
        chrBillCity & "', '" & _
        chrBillState & "', '" & _
        chrBillZipCode & "', '" & _
        chrBillPhone & "', '" & _
        chrBillEmail & "', '" & _
```

```
                    chrShipFirstName & "', '" & _
                    chrShipLastname & "', '" & _
                    chrShipAddress & "', '" & _
                    chrShipCity & "', '" & _
                    chrShipState & "', '" & _
                    chrShipZipCode & "', '" & _
                    chrShipPhone & "', '" & _
                    chrShipEmail & "'"

    '   Execute the SQL statement
    set rsOrderUpdate = dbOrderUpdate.execute(sql)
```

Next we move on to the payment data (see Listing 12.43). The values are retrieved from the order detail page. Again, we check as appropriate for any single quotes. Then the sp_UpdatePayment data stored procedure is utilized to submit the changes.

LISTING 12.43   UpdateOrder.asp Continued

```
    '   Next we are going to update the
    '   payment data. Each of the payment
    '   data fields are retrieved. Note that
    '   we check for single quotes in key
    '   fields.
    chrCardName = replace(request("chrCardName"), "'", "''")
    chrCardNumber = request("chrCardNumber")
    chrCardType = request("chrCardType")
    chrExpDate = request("chrExpDate")

    '   Build the SQL statement to update the
    '   payement data.
    sql = "execute sp_UpdatePaymentData " & _
            idOrder & ", '" & _
            chrCardType & "', '" & _
            chrCardNumber & "', '" & _
            chrExpDate & "', '" & _
            chrCardName & "'"

    '   Now execute the SQL statement
    set rsOrderUpdate = dbOrderUpdate.execute(sql)
```

Next we are ready to make changes to the receipt items. Remember that when we built the field names we used a combination of the data type name and the product ID. To create those names again, we will need to get a list of current products assigned to the order. The sp_RetrieveReceiptItems stored procedure is utilized again to get the list. (See Listing 12.44.)

LISTING 12.44   **UpdateOrder.asp Continued**

```
'   Create an ADO database connection
set dbOrderReceiptItems = _
     server.createobject("adodb.connection")

set rsOrderReceiptItems = _
     server.CreateObject("adodb.recordset")

'   Open the connection using our ODBC file DSN
dbOrderReceiptItems.open("filedsn=WildWillieCDs")

'   SQL statement to retrieve the items orders.
sql = "execute sp_RetrieveReceiptItems " & _
        Request("idShopper") & ", " & _
        Request("idOrder")

'   Execute the SQL statement
set rsOrderReceiptItems = dbOrderReceiptItems.execute(sql)
```

Once we have the list of items, we are going to loop through them and create the appropriate field name and retrieve the value. This is done by combining the ID of the product with the appropriate field name. (See Listing 12.45.)

LISTING 12.45   **UpdateOrder.asp Continued**

```
'   To read the input fields for each basket item,
'   we are going to have to loop through the
'   basket items again. Then that item can
'   be updated.
do until rsOrderReceiptItems.EOF

    '   Retrieve the product id. That will be utilized
    '   to build the name of the HTML input fields
```

```
'  from the posting page.
idProduct = rsOrderReceiptItems("idProduct")

'  The name of each basket item field is built with
'  the id of the product tacked onto the end.
idBasketItem = request("idBasketItem" & idProduct)

chrName = _
   replace(request("chrName" & idProduct), "'", "''")

chrColor = request("chrColor" & idProduct)
chrSize = request("chrSize" & idProduct)
intQuantity = request("intQuantity" & idProduct)
intPrice = request("intPrice" & idProduct) * 100
```

With each iteration the subtotal is calculated along with the total quantity of items orders. Then the sp_UdpateBasketItem stored procedure is utilized to change the basket item values. (See Listing 12.46.)

LISTING 12.46   **UpdateOrder.asp Continued**

```
'  Calculate the new subtotal as we loop through
'  each basket item.
subtotal = subtotal + (intPrice * intQuantity)

'  Calculate the total quantity of items with
'  each iteration through the basket item.
TotalQuantity = TotalQuantity + intQuantity

'  Build a SQL statement to update the basket
'  item.
sql = "execute sp_UpdateBasketItem " & _
     idBasketItem & ", '" & _
     chrName & "', '" & _
     chrColor & "', '" & _
     chrSize & "', " & _
     intQuantity & ", " & _
     intPrice

'  Execute the sql statement
set rsOrderUpdate = dbOrderUpdate.execute(sql)
```

```
'  Move to the next row
rsOrderReceiptItems.MoveNext

'  Loop back
Loop
```

The last stage is to update the order totals, as shown in Listing 12.47. To do that we will need to recalculate the shipping and tax values. This will be done with the ECStoreBizLogic COM object we created in Chapter 8, "Checking Out." An instance of the object is created.

Then we call the Shopping and Tax functions to calculate our shipping and tax values. For the shipping function, the total quantity ordered is passed in. For the tax function, the subtotal is passed in.

LISTING 12.47   **UpdateOrder.asp Continued**

```
'  Create the Bussiness Logic component to
'  calculate the tax and shipping.
set BizLogic = _
server.CreateObject("ECStoreBizLogic.TaxShip")
'  Call the shipping function of our component. The
'  quantity is passed in and must be in a long data type format. The
'  Shipping fee is returned.
Shipping = BizLogic.Shipping(cLng(TotalQuantity))

'  Calculate the tax by calling the Tax function of
'  our component. We pass in the shipping state and the
'  order subtotal. The value is also stored in a session
'  variable.
Tax = BizLogic.tax(cstr(chrShipState), clng(subtotal))
```

Once we have the subtotal, the tax, and shipping, we can calculate the order total. Then the sp_UpdateBasket stored procedure is utilized to update the corresponding basket values. Once that is done, the user is redirected to the OrderDetail.asp page to review the changes. (See Listing 12.48.)

LISTING 12.48   UpdateOrder.asp Continued

```
'  Calculate the new total.
Total = subtotal + shipping + tax

'  Build a SQL statement to update the basket data
sql = "execute sp_UpdateBasket " & _
     idBasket & ", " & _
     TotalQuantity & ", " & _
     SubTotal & ", " & _
     Shipping & ", " & _
     Tax & ", " & _
     Total & ", 1"

'  Execute the SQL statement
set rsOrderUpdate = dbOrderUpdate.execute(sql)

'  Send the user back to the order detail
'  page
Response.Redirect "OrderDetail.asp?idOrder=" & idOrder & _
                  "&idShopper=" & idShopper

%>
```

Several stored procedures are utilized on this page for updating all of the order data. The sp_UpdateOrderData stored procedure updates all of the core shipping and billing information in the OrderData table. A series of values are passed into it and then the Update SQL statement is created. (See Listing 12.49.)

LISTING 12.49   sp_UpdateOrderData Stored Procedure

```
CREATE PROCEDURE sp_UpdateOrderData

@idOrder int,
@chrBillFirstName varchar(255),
@chrBillLastName varchar(255),
@chrBillAddress varchar(255),
@chrBillCity varchar(255),
@chrBillState varchar(25),
@chrBillZipCode varchar(25),
```

```
@chrBillPhone varchar(255),
@chrBillEmail varchar(255),
@chrShipFirstName varchar(255),
@chrShipLastname varchar(255),
@chrShipAddress varchar(255),
@chrShipCity varchar(255),
@chrShipState varchar(25),
@chrShipZipCode varchar(25),
@chrShipPhone varchar(255),
@chrShipEmail varchar(255)

AS

update orderdata set
    chrBillFirstName = @chrBillFirstName,
    chrBillLastname = @chrBillLastname,
    chrBillAddress = @chrBillAddress,
    chrBillCity = @chrBillCity,
    chrBillState = @chrBillState,
    chrBillZipCode = @chrBillZipCode,
    chrBillPhone = @chrBillPhone,
    chrBillEmail = @chrBillEmail,
    chrShipFirstName = @chrShipFirstName,
    chrShipLastname = @chrShipLastname,
    chrShipAddress = @chrShipAddress,
    chrShipCity = @chrShipCity,
    chrShipState = @chrShipState,
    chrShipZipCode = @chrShipZipCode,
    chrShipPhone = @chrShipPhone,
    chrShipEmail = @chrShipEmail
where    idOrder = @idOrder
```

Similarly, the sp_UpdatePaymentData stored procedure handles updating the payment data for the order (see Listing 12.50). A series of values is passed into it with the appropriate Update SQL statement being created.

LISTING 12.50   **sp_UpdatePaymentData Stored Procedure**

```
CREATE PROCEDURE sp_UpdatePaymentData

@idOrder int,
@chrCardType varchar(100),
```

```
@chrCardNumber varchar(50),
@chrExpDate varchar(25),
@chrCardName varchar(150)

AS

update PaymentData set
    chrCardType = @chrCardType,
    chrCardNumber = @chrCardNumber,
    chrExpDate = @chrExpDate,
    chrCardName = @chrCardName
where
    idOrder = @idOrder
```

The sp_UpdateBasketItem stored procedure takes in each of the key values for the basket item and then updates them appropriately (see Listing 12.51). The ID of the basket item is passed in to identify which item should be updated.

LISTING 12.51   **sp_UpdateBasketItem Stored Procedure**

```
CREATE PROCEDURE sp_UpdateBasketItem

@idBasketItem int,
@chrName varchar(255),
@chrColor varchar(50),
@chrSize varchar(50),
@intQuantity int,
@intPrice int

AS

update BasketItem set
    chrName = @chrName,
    chrColor = @chrColor,
    chrSize = @chrSize,
    intQuantity = @intQuantity,
    intPrice = intPrice
where idBasketItem = @idBasketItem
```

Finally, in Listing 12.52, the sp_UpdateBasket stored procedure will update the key basket fields for the specified basket.

LISTING 12.52   sp_UpdateBasket Stored Procedure

```
/*  Stored procedure to update the basket
    values */
CREATE PROCEDURE sp_UpdateBasket

/*  Pass in the ID of the basket, the total
    quantity, the order subtotal, the shipping
    value, the tax value, the order total and a
    flag indicating the order was placed. */
@idBasket int,
@intQuantity int,
@intSubTotal int,
@intShipping int,
@intTax int,
@intTotal int,
@intOrderPlaced int

AS

/*  Update the basket */
update basket set
    intQuantity = @intQuantity,
    intSubtotal = @intSubtotal,
    intShipping = @intShipping,
    intTax = @intTax,
    intTotal = @intTotal,
    intOrderPlaced = @intOrderPlaced
where    idBasket = @idBasket
```

Let's now take a look at updating our order data. Figure 12.7 shows a full displayed order detail. Note all of the key fields that are set up for editing.

To test our edit capability, let's change the order quantities. That will have a trickle-down effect and force an update of the line item totals, the tax value, shipping value, and final order total. Figure 12.8 shows a change in the quantities.

FIGURE 12.7:

Order detail

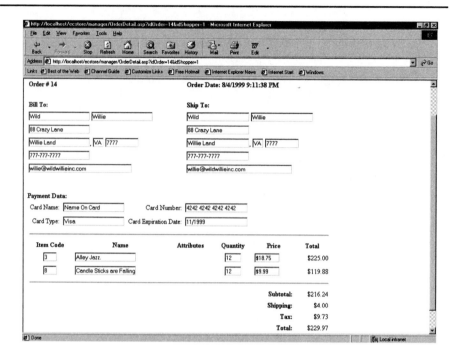

FIGURE 12.8:

Changing the order
quantities

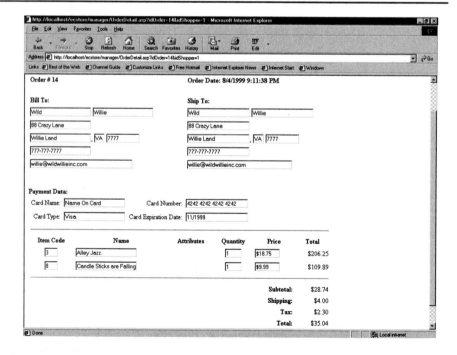

Figure 12.9 shows the updated order detail. Note that all of the calculation fields have been updated appropriately.

FIGURE 12.9:

Updated order

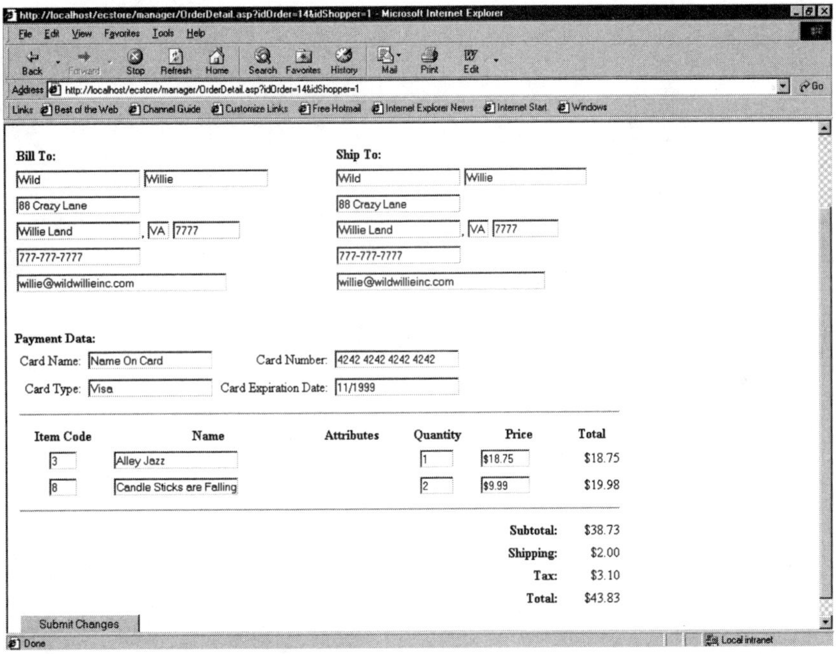

Summary

That ends our section on order management. Really, we have just touched the tip of the iceberg on what can be done on the manager side to provide complete store management.

In Part IV, "Promotions," we are going to take a look at developing code to provide different promotional tools on the Web site. This is a key component of the store that will provide valuable tools for engaging the consumer and enticing them to spend money in your store.

PART IV

Promotions

Now that we have our basic store and management functions in place, we are ready to look at some new promotional functions for the store. In the first chapter we will look at *up-sell* and *cross-sell* functions. This will push options at the shopper for buying related products in the store. And, in the shopping basket, the shopper will have options to buy product upgrades.

In Chapter 14, "Featured Products," we will look at options to feature certain products at different stages in the process. That will allow us to provide different options for pushing products that are new, on clearance, etc.

Finally, in Chapter 15, "On Sale," we will explore providing sale options in the store. We want to provide sale start and end dates, set prices, etc.

This section will just touch on a few of the many creative options available for providing marketing opportunities through the Web pages.

CHAPTER

THIRTEEN

13

Up-Sell and Cross-Sell

- Designing the Related Products

- Building the Relationships

- Managing Related Products

We need to provide ways for consumers to find similar or upgraded products. That will help to sell more product and assist the consumer in finding products that may be required/desired to be purchased in groups. In this chapter we will explore building these features in the user interface and adding on to our management interface to set up these relationships.

Designing the Related Products

Two types of relationships occur in our database. The first type, the *cross-sell*, relates complementary products. An example might be pants that would go with a shirt, or a monitor to go with a computer.

The second kind of relationship is an *up-sell* to a better or more full-featured product instead of the product they are currently viewing. An example of this may be a 21-inch monitor instead of a 15-inch monitor, or perhaps a bundled set of CDs instead of a single CD.

For our sample store, let's insert a couple of relationships we can work with to program the user interface. Listing 13.1 shows three SQL insert statements. The table consists of three columns. The first is ProductA, which is the first product in the relationship. The second is ProductB, which is the second product. The last column, idRelationType, defines the type of relationship. A *1* indicates a related cross-sell product. A *2* indicates an up-sell product. Of course we can combine these to offer both cross-sells and up-sells for the same product, and this can be accomplished easily by adding extra rows to our RelatedProducts table.

LISTING 13.1   **SQL Insert Code for Related Products**

```
insert into RelatedProducts(idProductA, idProductB,
            idRelationType)
        values(9, 10, 1)

insert into RelatedProducts(idProductA, idProductB,
                idRelationType)
        values(10, 9, 1)

insert into RelatedProducts(idProductA, idProductB,
                idRelationType)
        values(4, 3, 2)
```

Building the Relationships

We are going to build the interface for the relationships in two spots. The first will be on the product page. We will simply list cross-sell products on that page.

The second option will be shown in the shopping basket. When the user puts a product into their basket, and the product has an up-sell associated with it, the basket page will indicate to the user that there is another option. Figure 13.1 shows the process.

FIGURE 13.1:

Up-sell shopping process

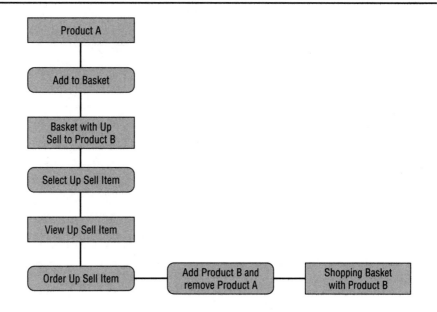

When a product that has an up-sell option is added to the shopping basket, a link is shown to the up-sell product. When that product link is clicked on, the product will be displayed. If the user decides to order that product, then it is inserted into the basket and the previous product is removed.

It will be important to ensure that the same quantity settings are made to replace the amount in the basket. Let's start by reviewing the code that handles showing the related cross-sell products.

Related Cross-Sell Products

We are going to need to modify the product.asp page to show the related product links. We will add these to the bottom of the page below the primary product data. To do this we will need to open a data connection.

We will utilize the stored procedure sp_RetrieveRelatedProducts and pass in the current product ID. If there is a resulting set of products, we will build links to each.

NOTE The code listing only shows the necessary script for the related products display. We presume the rest of the page code is in place.

LISTING 13.2   **Product.asp**

```
<%

'   Create an ADO database connection
set dbRetrieveRelatedProducts = _
    server.createobject("adodb.connection")

'   Create a record set
set rsRetrieveRelatedProducts = _
    server.CreateObject("adodb.recordset")

'   Open the connection using our ODBC file DSN
dbRetrieveRelatedProducts.open("filedsn=WildWillieCDs")

'   Call the appropriate stored procedure
sql = "execute sp_RetrieveRelatedProducts " & _
      request("idProduct")

'   Execute the stored procedure to retrieve
'   related products.
set rsRetrieveRelatedProducts = _
    dbRetrieveRelatedProducts.Execute(sql)

'   Check to see if there are any related products for
'   a cross sell.
if not rsRetrieveRelatedProducts.EOF then

%>
```

```
<B>Related Products:</B><BR><BR>

<%

end if
```

Once the record set is retrieved, we are ready to loop through each product. A hyperlink is built to the product.asp page with the ID of the product on the link. Following that, the rest of the page will continue with the existing product.asp code.

LISTING 13.3   Product.asp Continued

```
'   Loop through the related products
do until rsRetrieveRelatedProducts.EOF

%>

<!--  Build a link to the product -->
<a href="product.asp?idProduct= ↵
    <%=rsRetrieveRelatedProducts("idProduct")%>">
   <%=rsRetrieveRelatedProducts("chrProductName")%>
</a>

<%

'   Move to the next row.
rsRetrieveRelatedProducts.MoveNext

'   Loop back
loop

%>
```

The stored procedure we utilize takes in the ID of the product we are going to check for a relationship. This is what will be checked against the ProductA column. Note that the relation type, *1*, is set in the stored procedure.

LISTING 13.4   sp_RetrieveRelatedProducts Stored Procedure

```
/*  Stored procedure to retrieve related
    products to the specified product.
*/
CREATE PROCEDURE sp_RetrieveRelatedProducts
```

```
/*  Pass in the ID of the product */
@idProduct int

AS

/*  Select the related products.  Note
    that cross sell related products are
    defined by a setting of 1. */
select * from relatedproducts, products
where  relatedproducts.idProductb = products.idproduct and
       relatedproducts.idProducta = @idProduct and
       idRelationType = 1
```

Related Up-Sell Products

Next we will work on the up-sell logic. The first feature to work on is the listing of the up-sell in the basket.asp page. With each iteration of the items in the basket, we need to check to see if there is a related up-sell item. If so, we will insert a row in the basket right after the related product. Some text will be displayed that will indicate there is a product the shopper just might want to take a look at.

We need to insert code into the item-listing loop of basket.asp. Listing 13.5 starts the code to be inserted into the basket page. We first create a connection to the database to retrieve related up-sell products for the current item we are processing in the basket.

LISTING 13.5   **Basket.asp**

```
<!-- Check for an up sell -->
<%

'  Create an ADO database connection
set dbUpSell = server.createobject("adodb.connection")

'  Create a record set
set rsUpSell = server.CreateObject("adodb.recordset")

'  Open the connection using our ODBC file DSN
dbUpSell.open("filedsn=WildWillieCDs")
```

```
'  Execute the Retrieve Up Sell stored procedure
'  to find out if there is an up sell on this product.
sql = "execute sp_RetrieveUpSell " & _
        rsBasketItem("idProduct")

'  Execute the SQL statement
set rsUpSell = dbUpSell.Execute(sql)
```

A check is done to see if anything was returned. If so, then we create a row that will span all of the columns of each row in the basket. In this case, we insert some standard text indicating a cross-sell.

We then link it to the UpgradeProduct.asp page, which will handle providing the option to order the product. (See Listing 13.6.)

TIP   You might want to have the supporting text promoting the up-sell in the database for each relationship so it can be customized to the specific up-sell.

LISTING 13.6   Basket.asp Continued

```
'  Show the up sell option if one exists.
if rsUpSell.EOF <> true then

%>

<!--  Build a row to show the message -->
<tr>
    <td></td>
    <td colspan="6">
    <!-- Build a link ot the UpgradeProduct.asp page -->
    <b>Why not try buying
    <a href="UpgradeProduct.asp? ↵
        intQuantity=<%=rsBasketItem("intQuantity")%> ↵
        &idBasketItem=<%=rsBasketItem("idBasketItem")%> ↵
          &idProduct=<%=rsUpSell("idProduct")%>">
      <%=rsUpSell("chrProductName")%></a> instead?</b>
    </td>
</tr>

<%
```

```
end if

'   Move to the next row
rsBasketItem.MoveNext

'   Loop back
loop

%>
```

To retrieve the up-sell, we utilize the `sp_RetrieveUpSell` stored procedure. The ID of the product is passed in, and will be checked against the ProductA column. We then check for a relationship type of 2 for the up-sell. (See Listing 13.7.)

NOTE In this case we chose to hard code the *1* and *2* relationship types in two different stored procedures for retrieving the relationships types. The stored procedures are very similar. This gives us maximum flexibility for changing the relationship via the database down the road.

LISTING 13.7   **sp_RetrieveUpSell Stored Procedure**

```
/*  Stored procedure to retrieve up sell products */
CREATE PROCEDURE sp_RetrieveUpSell

/*  Pass in the ID of the product */
@idProduct int

AS

/*  Select the up sell products.  Note the
    relationship is defined by a setting of 2.
    A setting of 1 indicates an cross sell. */
select * from relatedproducts, products
where products.idproduct = relatedproducts.idproductb and
      relatedproducts.idProducta = @idProduct and
      idRelationType = 2
```

Next we move on to the UpgradeProduct.asp page, which handles showing the product to which the shopper can upgrade. This page is similar to the product page but does have some key differences. The page starts out with the standard include code.

We then open our database connection to retrieve the product data from the database. The `sp_RetrieveProduct` stored procedure pulls the data. (See Listing 13.8.)

LISTING 13.8   UpgradeProduct.asp

```
<%@ Language=VBScript %>
<HTML>
<!--
     UpgradeProduct.asp - This page allows the user to upgrade the
product they have purchased.  It is linked to from the shopping basket.
-->

<!-- #include file="include/header.asp" -->

<%

'  Create an ADO database connection
set dbProduct = server.createobject("adodb.connection")

'  Create a record set
set rsProduct = server.CreateObject("adodb.recordset")

'  Open the connection using our ODBC file DSN
dbProduct.open("filedsn=WildWillieCDs")

'  Call the Retrieve Product stored procedure to get
'  the product data.
sql = "execute sp_RetrieveProduct " & request("idProduct")

'  Execute the SQL statement
set rsProduct = dbProduct.Execute(sql)

'  Retrieve the description, product image and
'  product name.
txtDescription = rsProduct("txtDescription")
chrProductImage = rsProduct("chrProductImage")
chrProductName = rsProduct("chrProductName")
%>
```

Next we build the form for adding the product to the basket. Note that the form posts to the AddUpgradeItem.asp page instead of the AddItem.asp page like the standard product page.

The standard product data is displayed. Note that the quantity for the item in the basket is passed on the URL. This is retrieved and defaulted to the quantity setting for this product. Also note that the ID of the product in the basket is stored in a hidden variable so we can remove it from the basket if this product is ordered.

The rest of the page finishes off in the standard fashion to show product attributes, the footer, etc. (See Listing 13.9.)

LISTING 13.9   **UpgradeProduct.asp Continued**

```
<!-- Form to post the upgrade request -->
<form method="post" action="addupgradeitem.asp">

<!-- Table to display the product information -->
<table border="0" cellpadding="3" cellspacing="3">

<!-- Show the product image, name and description. -->
<TR>
    <td><img src="images/products/<%=chrProductImage%>"></td>
    <td valign="top">
            <CENTER><b><font size="5">
            <%=chrProductName%></font></b>
            </center><BR><BR>
            <%=txtDescription%><BR><BR>
    </td>
</TR>

<!-- Show the price -->
<TR>
    <TD align="center">
            <B>Price:
            <%=formatcurrency(rsProduct("intPrice")/100, 2)%></b>
    </td>

    <TD align="center">
            <!-- Show the quantity of items already selected for
            the other product.  -->
            <B>Quantity: <input type="text"
            value="<%=request("intQuantity")%>" name="quantity"
```

```
    size="2"></b>

        <!-- Hidden variables to keep the product
        information -->
        <input type="hidden"
        value="<%=request("idProduct")%>" name="idProduct">

        <input type="hidden"
        value="<%=rsProduct("chrProductName")%>"
        name="ProductName">

        <input type="hidden"
        value="<%=rsProduct("intPrice")%>"
        name="ProductPrice">

        <!-- Pass along the basket item to indicate which
             product is to be upgraded. -->
        <input type="hidden"
         value="<%=request("idBasketItem")%>"
                name="idBasketItem">

    </td>
</TR>

<%

'  Create an ADO database connection
set dbAttributes = server.createobject("adodb.connection")

'  Create a record set
set rsAttributes = server.CreateObject("adodb.recordset")

'  Open the connection using our ODBC file DSN
dbAttributes.open("filedsn=WildWillieCDs")

'  Call the stored procedure to retrieve the
'  product attributes.
sql = "execute sp_Attributes " & request("idProduct")

'  Execute the SQL statement
set rsAttributes = dbProduct.Execute(sql)

'  Check to see if attributes should be displayed
if not rsAttributes.EOF then
```

```
%>

<!-- Display the color and size attributes. -->
<TR>
   <TD>
      <!--  Display the color attributes -->
      Color:
      <SELECT name="color">

         <%

            '  Loop through the attributes
            do until rsAttributes.EOF

         %>

         <!--  Show the color options -->
         <option
         value="<%=rsAttributes("chrAttributeName")%>">
         <%=rsAttributes("chrAttributeName")%>

         <%

            '  Check to see if we have reached the end of
            '  the attributes category.
            if rsAttributes("chrCategoryName") <> "Color" then

              '  Exit the do loop
             exit do

            end if

            '  Move to the next row.
            rsAttributes.MoveNext

            loop

         %>

      </select>

   </TD>
   <TD>
```

```
<!-- Display the size attributes -->
Size:
<SELECT name="color">

    <%

    ' Loop through the attributes.
    do until rsAttributes.EOF

    %>

    <!-- Option to display the attribute. -->
    <option
    value="<%=rsAttributes("chrAttributeName")%>">
    <%=rsAttributes("chrAttributeName")%>

    <%

    ' Move to the next row.
    rsAttributes.MoveNext

    ' Loop back.
    loop

    %>

    </select>

  </TD>

</TR>

<%

end if

%>

<!-- Show the submit button -->
<TR>
   <td colspan="2" align="center">
      <input type="submit" value="Order" name="Submit">
   </td>
</tr>
```

```
    </table>

    </form>

    <!-- #include file="include/footer.asp" -->

    </BODY>
    </HTML>
```

Once the user selects the product to be added to the basket, the AddUpgradeItem.asp page is called. This is similar to the AddItem.asp page in that it adds the product to the basket. But, it also checks to ensure that the original product being upgraded is removed from the basket.

The page starts out by ensuring the quantity ordered is not 0. Then all of the values for the item to be added to the basket are retrieved. (See Listing 13.10.)

LISTING 13.10   AddUpgradeItem.asp

```
<%@ Language=VBScript %>
<%

'    ********************************************************
'    AddUpgradeItem.asp - This page will upgrade an item
'    in the basket to the up-sell item.
'    ********************************************************

'    Check to ensure a quantity was set.
if request("quantity") = "0" then

     '    Send the user back to the upgrade page.
     Response.Redirect("upgradeproduct.asp?idProduct=" & _
     request("idProduct"))

end if

'    Get the product values
intQuantity = request("quantity")
idProduct = request("idProduct")
chrName = replace(request("productname"), "'", "''")
intPrice = request("productprice")
```

```
chrSize = request("size")
chrColor = request("color")
```

The sp_InsertBasketItem stored procedure is utilized to insert this item into our basket. That completes that transaction. Following that, we are ready to remove the original item from the basket.

The sp_RemoveBasketItem stored procedure is utilized. The ID of the original basket item is passed in to it. Then the user is sent back to the shopping basket. (See Listing 13.11.)

LISTING 13.11   AddUpgradeItem.asp Continued

```
'  Create an ADO database connection
set dbBasketItem = server.createobject("adodb.connection")


'  Create a record set
set rsBasketItem = server.CreateObject("adodb.recordset")


'  Open the connection using our ODBC file DSN
dbBasketItem.open("filedsn=WildWillieCDs")


'  Call the appropriate stored procedure to insert
'  the new item.
sql = "execute sp_InsertBasketItem " & _
      session("idBasket") & ", " & _
      intQuantity & ", " & _
      intPrice & ", '" & _
      chrName & "', " & _
      idProduct & ", '" & _
      chrSize & "', '" & _
      chrColor & "'"


'  Execute the SQL statement
set rsBasketItem = dbBasketItem.Execute(sql)



'  Call the stored procedure to remove an item from the
'  basket.  Note the id of the basket item is utilzed
sql = "execute sp_RemoveBasketItem " & _
      session("idBasket") & ", " & _
      request("idBasketItem")
```

```
'  Execute the SQL statement
dbBasketItem.Execute(sql)

'  Send the user to the basket
Response.Redirect "basket.asp"


%>
```

That's it for the user side programming. Now let's take a look at it in action. Figure 13.2 shows the product page for the most excellent T-Shirt Rip product. On the bottom of the page are the related links for the product. In this case it shows the Undershirt product.

FIGURE 13.2:

Related products

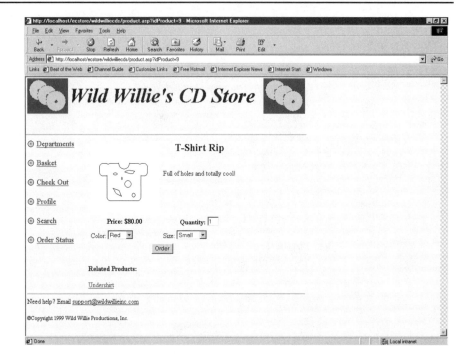

Figure 13.3 shows the basket with an up-sell message. To get this message, add the *Circle Sax* product to the basket. Next select the *Candle Sticks are Falling* product and add it to the basket.

Figure 13.4 shows the basket with the upgraded product. That makes a successful up-sell and more money for the store!

FIGURE 13.3:

Basket up-sell

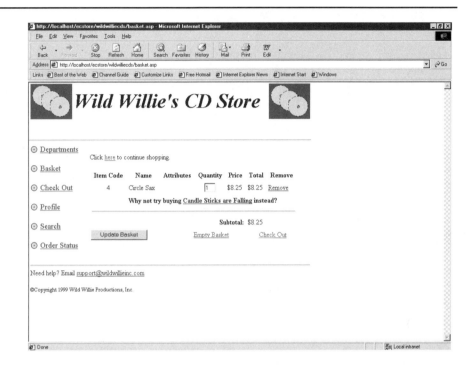

FIGURE 13.4:

Updated basket

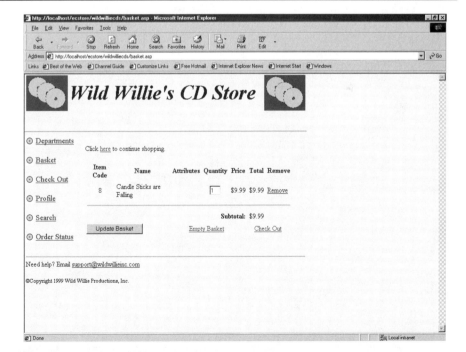

Managing Related Products

Now that we have the user side programmed, we need a way to manage the relationships. There are a couple of different approaches to take to accomplish this. We could provide a separate administration interface for selecting two products and setting the relationship. That would provide for each relationship management.

We could also provide relationship management at the product level and allow many different assignments per product. That is the approach we will take in this set of example code. Of course, there would be nothing wrong with taking both approaches.

To implement the management tools, we will need to modify the ManageProduct.asp page. One more section of the page will need to be added for handling adding, updating, and deleting relationships. This code will be inserted into the existing page.

The first thing we do is display the existing relationships. The ID of the relationship, the related product ID, name, and relationship type are shown. Following that, an ADO database connection is opened to retrieve the existing relationships. Then they are displayed. A column is added to delete an existing relationship. (See Listing 13.12.)

LISTING 13.12   ManageProduct.asp

```
<hr>

<table border="1" cellpadding="3" cellspacing="3">

<tr>
    <th>ID</th>
    <th>Related<BR>Product ID</th>
    <th>Related<BR>Product</th>
    <th>Relation<BR>Type</th>
    <th>Delete</th>
</tr>
<%

'   Create an ADO database connection
set dbRelated = server.createobject("adodb.connection")

'   Create a record set
set rsRelated = server.CreateObject("adodb.recordset")
```

```
'  Open the connection using our ODBC file DSN
dbRelated.open("filedsn=WildWillieCDs")

'  Execute the stored procedure to retrieve the
'  related products.
sql = "execute sp_RetrieveProductRelations " & _
      request("idProduct")

'  Execute the SQL statement
set rsRelated = dbRelated.Execute(sql)

'  Loop through the related products
do until rsRelated.EOF

%>

<!--  Build each row to display the related
      product information and an option to
      delete the product.  -->
<tr>
   <td><%=rsRelated("idRelatedProduct")%></td>
   <td><%=rsRelated("idProductB")%></td>
   <td><%=rsRelated("chrProductName")%></td>
   <td><%=rsRelated("idRelationType")%></td>
   <td><a href="DeleteRelated.asp? ↵
   idProduct=<%=request("idProduct")%> ↵
   &idRelatedProduct=<%=rsRelated("idRelatedProduct")%>">
Delete</a></td>
</tr>

<%

' Move to the next row
rsRelated.MoveNext

'  Loop back
Loop

%>

</table>

<BR><BR>
```

Next we will display a list of existing products so we can select one and add a relationship to it. All of the products are retrieved from the database and then built into a select box.

A form is created for posting the relationship to the AddRelation.asp page, which will insert the relationship into the database. We also have a set of radio buttons for indicating what type of relationship should be set up. (See Listing 13.13.)

LISTING 13.13   **ManageProduct.asp Continued**

```
<%

'  Create an ADO database connection
set dbProducts = server.createobject("adodb.connection")

'  Create a record set
set rsProducts = server.CreateObject("adodb.recordset")

'  Open the connection using our ODBC file DSN
dbProducts.open("filedsn=WildWillieCDs")

'  Execute the stored procedure to retrieve the
'  current list of products
sql = "execute sp_RetrieveProducts"

'  Execute the SQL statement
set rsProducts = dbProducts.Execute(sql)

%>

<!--  Build a form to post the new relation
      to the database.  The form will post to
      AddRelation.asp.   -->
<form method="post" action="AddRelation.asp">

<!--  Build a hidden variable so the posting page
      knows what product to relate this product to.
      -->
<input type="hidden" name="idProductA"
       value="<%=request("idProduct")%>">

<!--  Select box for the products to relate to
      this product.   -->
```

```
<select name="idProductB">

<%
'  Loop through the products
do until rsProducts.EOF
%>

<!--  Build the option value  -->
<option value="<%=rsProducts("idProduct")%>">
        <%=rsProducts("chrProductName")%>

<%

'  Move to the next row
rsProducts.MoveNext

'  Loop back
Loop

%>
</select>

<BR><BR>

<!--  Radio buttons to indicate the type of
      relationship.  -->
<input type="Radio" value="1"
       name="RelationType">1 - Related Products

<input type="Radio" value="2"
       name="RelationType">2 - Up Sell

<BR><BR>

<!--  Submit button for the form.  -->
<input type="Submit" name="Submit" value="Add Relation">

</form>
```

The sp_RetrieveProductRelations stored procedure handles retrieving all existing relationships for the specified product. (See Listing 13.14.)

LISTING 13.14   sp_RetrieveProductRelations Stored Procedure

```
CREATE PROCEDURE sp_RetrieveProductRelations

@idProduct int

AS

select * from relatedproducts, products
where idProductA = @idProduct and
      products.idProduct = relatedproducts.idProductb
```

To retrieve all of the products from the database, the sp_RetrieveProducts stored procedure makes a simple select SQL statement to return the data. (See Listing 13.15.)

LISTING 13.15   sp_RetrieveProducts Stored Procedure

```
CREATE PROCEDURE sp_RetrieveProducts AS
select * from products
```

Next we move the adding of relationships. This is handled in the AddRelation.asp page shown in Listing 13.16. The ID of the product we were managing, the ID of the product we want to add a relation to, and the type of relationship are retrieved from the posted form.

The sp_InsertProductRelation stored procedure is called to insert the relationship into the database. When the task is complete, the user is sent back to the ManageProduct.asp page to continue editing the product.

LISTING 13.16   AddRelation.asp

```
<%@ Language=VBScript %>
<%

'  Create an ADO database connection
set dbProdRelation = _
    server.createobject("adodb.connection")

'  Create a record set
```

```
set rsProdRelation = server.CreateObject("adodb.recordset")

'  Open the connection using our ODBC file DSN
dbProdRelation.open("filedsn=WildWillieCDs")

'  Execute the stored procedure to insert the relationship
'  into the RelatedProducts table.
sql = "execute sp_InsertProductRelation " & _
     request("idProductA") & ", " & _
     request("idProductB") & ", " & _
     request("RelationType")

'  Execute the SQL statement
set rsProdRelation = dbProdRelation.Execute(sql)

Response.Redirect "ManageProduct.asp?idProduct=" & _
                  request("idProductA")


%>
```

We have encapsulated the relationship SQL insert code reviewed at the beginning of the chapter into the sp_InsertProductRelation stored procedure. The two IDs of the products to be related and the type of relation are passed in. (See Listing 13.17.)

LISTING 13.17   sp_InsertProductRelation Stored Procedure

```
CREATE PROCEDURE sp_InsertProductRelation

@idProductA int,
@idProductB int,
@RelationType int

AS

insert into RelatedProducts(idProductA, idProductB, idRelationType)
values(@idProductA, @idProductB, @RelationType)
```

Next we are ready to look at the DeleteRelation.asp page in Listing 13.18. This shows the code for deleting an existing relationship. The ID of the relationship to be deleted is retrieved from the URL.

Then the sp_DeleteProductRelation stored procedure is utilized to remove the relationship. Once the deletion is done, the user is sent back to the Manage-Product.asp page to continue editing the product.

LISTING 13.18   DeleteRelated.asp

```
<%@ Language=VBScript %>
<%

'  Create an ADO database connection
set dbDelProdRelation = _
    server.createobject("adodb.connection")

'  Create a record set
set rsDelProdRelation = _
    server.CreateObject("adodb.recordset")

'  Open the connection using our ODBC file DSN
dbDelProdRelation.open("filedsn=WildWillieCDs")

'  Execute the stored procedure to delete the
'  relationship from the database.
sql = "execute sp_DeleteProductRelation " & _
      request("idRelatedProduct")

'  Execute the SQL statement
set rsDelProdRelation = dbDelProdRelation.Execute(sql)

'  Send the user back to the product
'  manager page
Response.Redirect "ManageProduct.asp?idProduct=" & _
                  request("idProduct")

%>
```

Finally our last bit of code for this chapter is in Listing 13.19. This stored procedure removes the specified product relationship.

LISTING 13.19   sp_DeleteProductRelation Stored Procedure

```
CREATE PROCEDURE sp_DeleteProductRelation

@idRelatedProduct int

AS

delete from RelatedProducts where
idRelatedProduct = @idRelatedProduct
```

Now let's test out our management interface. Figure 13.5 shows the related product listing for the *Circle Sax* product. Note the two existing relationships.

FIGURE 13.5:

Related product listing

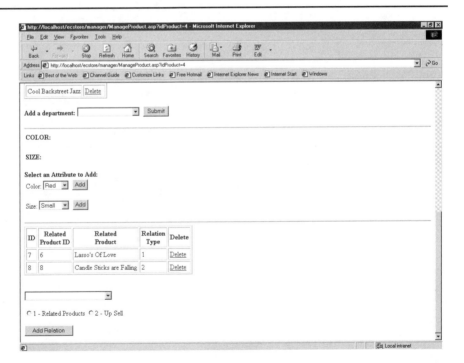

Figure 13.6 shows the list of relationships after the *Lassos of Love* product relationship is removed.

Figure 13.7 shows the listing after a new relationship to *Joe Bob's Thimble Sounds* is created.

FIGURE 13.6:

Relation deleted

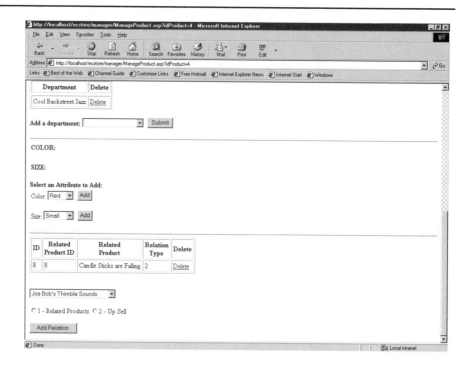

FIGURE 13.7:

Adding a new relation

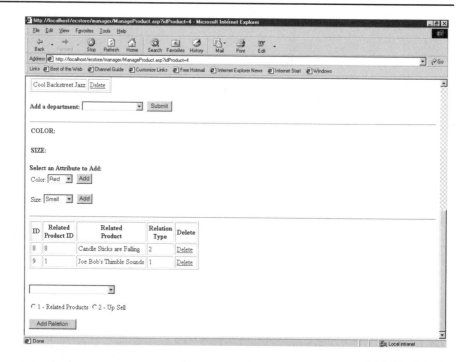

Summary

That completes the tools necessary to create two key marketing elements for showing consumers products they may be interested in. There are some different options for how to implement both the user interface and management tools, but this will provide the core for providing these functions.

In the next chapter we are going to explore how to display featured products in our store. This will provide additional features for showcasing selected products to the shopper.

CHAPTER

FOURTEEN

14

Featured Products

- Building and Designing the Featured Products

- Programming the User Interface

- Programming the Manager

In the last chapter we looked at ways to promote products by relating them to other products. In this chapter we will explore different ways to feature products as promotions. This would be similar to walking into your local retailer and having key products visible up front, on the end of aisles, etc.

Building and Designing the Featured Products

In our store we are going to promote featured products in three spots. The first will be on the default page. Right now, that page is a bit bland, with just a welcome message and navigation.

Also, we have some space available underneath our navigation bar where we could promote products as well. That would provide the opportunity to have those featured products purchased at any time.

Finally, we are going to also promote products in the shopping basket. In that case, we don't want to promote products that are already in the shopping basket, so we will need to add some logic to only list featured products that have not been purchased.

We will need to add three columns to the products table to track featured products. Table 14.1 shows the three columns with descriptions for each.

TABLE 14.1: Featured Product Table Columns

Field	Description
IntFeatured	Flags the product as featured or not featured
DtFeatureStart	Indicates the feature start date
DtFeatureEnd	Indicates the feature end date

Listing 14.1 shows several sample insert statements to set up a couple of featured products. Two products are updated with the start dates being today. The feature is set to end on the first day of 2000.

LISTING 14.1   **SQL Insert Code to Create Featured Products.**

```
update products set intFeatured = 1, dtFeatureStart = getdate(),
dtFeatureEnd = "1/1/2000" where idproduct = 1

update products set intFeatured = 1, dtFeatureStart = getdate(),
dtFeatureEnd = "1/1/2000" where idproduct = 2
```

Programming the User Interface

First we will work on the default page. We are going to show products right below the opening intro text on default.asp.

Listing 14.2 shows the code we are going to add to the page. First we show appropriate text indicating these are the featured products of the day. Following that we open up a data connection. The sp_RetrieveFeaturedProducts stored procedure is called to get a listing of current products.

LISTING 14.2   **Default.asp**

```
<!-- Show the featured products for today.  -->
<b>Here are our featured products for the day:</b><BR><BR>

<%

'  Create an ADO database connection
set dbFeaturedProd = server.createobject("adodb.connection")

'  Create a record set
set rsFeaturedProd = server.CreateObject("adodb.recordset")

'  Open the connection using our ODBC file DSN
dbFeaturedProd.open("filedsn=WildWillieCDs")

'  Retrieve all of the current featured products
sql = "execute sp_RetrieveFeaturedProducts"

'  Execute the SQL statement
set rsFeaturedProd = dbFeaturedProd.Execute(sql)
```

Next we are ready to loop through the products and display them (see Listing 14.3). With each iteration of the loop we retrieve the product name, product image, and the ID of the product.

We then use a flag that we flip back and forth to rotate the image from left to right. With each listing, the image and the product name are linked directly to the product.

LISTING 14.3   Default.asp Continued

```asp
'  Loop through the products
do until rsFeaturedProd.EOF

'  Retrieve the product information to be displayed.
chrProductName = rsFeaturedProd("chrProductName")
chrProductImage = rsFeaturedProd("chrProductImage")
idProduct = rsFeaturedProd("idProduct")

'  Check the display flag.  We will rotate the
'  product images from left to right.
If flag = 0 then

   '  Set the flag
   flag = 1

%>

      <!-- Build the link to the product information.   -->
      <a href="product.asp?idProduct=<%=idProduct%>">
         <img src="images/products/
               sm_<%=chrProductImage%>"
               align="middle" border="0">
         <%=chrProductName%></a><BR><BR>

   <% else %>

      <!-- Build the link to the product information.   -->
      <a href="product.asp?idProduct=<%=idProduct%>">
         <%=chrProductName%>
         <img src="images/products/
               sm_<%=chrProductImage%>"
               align="middle" border="0"></a>
      <BR><BR>
```

```
<%

    '  Reset the flag
    Flag = 0

    end if

'  Move to the next record
rsFeaturedProd.MoveNext

'  Loop back
Loop

%>
```

The sp_RetrieveFeaturedProducts stored procedure we utilize will retrieve all featured products that are currently active (see Listing 14.4). The starting and ending dates are checked against the current date.

LISTING 14.4   sp_RetrieveFeaturedProducts

```
CREATE PROCEDURE sp_RetrieveFeaturedProducts AS

select * from products where intFeatured = 1 and
getdate() >= dtFeatureStart and getdate() <= dtFeatureEnd

Go
```

That does it for the default page. Next we will take a look at the basket page (see Listing 14.5).

The page starts out with a database connection that calls the sp_RetrieveNon-PurchFeatureProd stored procedure. That will return all products that have not already been added into the shopping basket.

LISTING 14.5   Basket.asp

```
<%

    '  Create an ADO database connection
    set dbFeaturedProd = server.createobject("adodb.connection")
```

```
'  Create a record set
set rsFeaturedProd = server.CreateObject("adodb.recordset")

'  Open the connection using our ODBC file DSN
dbFeaturedProd.open("filedsn=WildWillieCDs")

'  Execute the sp_RetrieveNonPurchFeatureProd stored
'  procedure which will return any featured products not
'  currently in the basket.
sql = "execute sp_RetrieveNonPurchFeatureProd " & _
   session("idBasket")

'  Execute the SQL statement
set rsFeaturedProd = dbFeaturedProd.Execute(sql)
```

We next check to see if any products were returned (see Lising 14.6). If products are returned, then we display a message urging the customer to consider some of our featured products.

Next the returned products are looped through. In this case we will not clutter up the page with images. But we will list the product name and link to the product.

LISTING 14.6   Basket.asp Continued

```
if rsFeaturedProd.EOF <> false then
%>

<!-- Start the display of any featured products they
   didn't purchase.  -->
<b>Don't forget our featured products!</b><BR><BR>

<%

end if

'  Loop through the list
do until rsFeaturedProd.EOF

'  Retrieve the product information to be displayed.
chrProductName = rsFeaturedProd("chrProductName")
idProduct = rsFeaturedProd("idProduct")
```

```
%>

        <!-- Build the link to the product information.   -->
        <a href="product.asp?idProduct=<%=idProduct%>">
            <%=chrProductName%></a><BR><BR>

<%

'  Move to the next record
rsFeaturedProd.MoveNext

'  Loop back
Loop

%>
```

Our stored procedure to return featured products has to go through a number of different steps to pull back the right list of products. We need to return all featured products that are not in the list of basket item products.

The ID of the basket is passed into the stored procedure. In the WHERE clause we perform a SELECT statement to return the items in the basket. We then use the NOT IN operation to return featured products not in the basket item list.

The rest of the stored procedure does an appropriate check to ensure the current date falls into the featured product date range (see Listing 14.7).

LISTING 14.7   **sp_RetrieveNonPurchFeaturedProd Stored Procedure**

```
CREATE PROCEDURE sp_RetrieveNonPurchFeatureProd

@idBasket int

AS

select * from products
where
    intFeatured = 1 and
    getdate() >= dtFeatureStart and
    getdate() <= dtFeatureEnd and
```

```
products.idproduct Not In
(select idProduct from basketitem where
 basketitem.idbasket = @idBasket)
```

The last page we will work on is the header.asp include (see Listing 14.8). In this case we want to show a list of featured products below the navigation links.

The first thing we do is to ensure that we don't show the featured products on pages where they are already displayed. In this case we check to see if the current pages are either a default page or basket page. If so, then we will not display the featured products on the navigation bar.

Following that we display a horizontal bar to divide the navigation and the featured products. Then our text indicating which items are featured is displayed.

LISTING 14.8   Header.asp

```
<!-- Check to ensure we are not on the default or
     basket page.  -->
<%

if instr(1, lcase(Request.ServerVariables("URL")), _
            "default.asp") = 0 and _
   instr(1, lcase(Request.ServerVariables("URL")), _
            "basket.asp") = 0 then

%>
    <!-- Show a line and header text for our
             featured products of the day.  -->
    <hr>
    <font size="2" color="red">Featured
            Products:</font>
    <BR><BR>
```

The rest of the code on the page finishes out by opening a database connection and opening our sp_RetrieveFeaturedProducts stored procedure. Then we list out the products with no images.

LISTING 14.9   **Header.asp Continued**

```asp
<%

'  Create an ADO database connection
set dbFeaturedProd = _
     server.createobject("adodb.connection")

'  Create a record set
set rsFeaturedProd = _
     server.CreateObject("adodb.recordset")

'  Open the connection using our ODBC file DSN
dbFeaturedProd.open("filedsn=WildWillieCDs")

'  Retrieve the current featured products
sql = "execute sp_RetrieveFeaturedProducts"

'  Execute the SQL statement
set rsFeaturedProd = _
       dbFeaturedProd.Execute(sql)

'  Loop through the featured products
do until rsFeaturedProd.EOF

'  Retrieve the product information to be
'   displayed.
chrProductName = _
     rsFeaturedProd("chrProductName")
idProduct = rsFeaturedProd("idProduct")

%>

<font size="2">
<!-- Build the link to the product information.
    -->
<a href="product.asp?idProduct=<%=idProduct%>">
   <%=chrProductName%></a>
</font><BR><BR>

<%
```

```
'  Move to the next record set
rsFeaturedProd.MoveNext

'  Loop back
Loop

end if

%>
```

Now let's take a look at our pages in action. Figure 14.1 shows the new home page with our two featured products. Note that there are no featured products on the navigation bar since we are on the default page.

FIGURE 14.1:

Default page with featured products

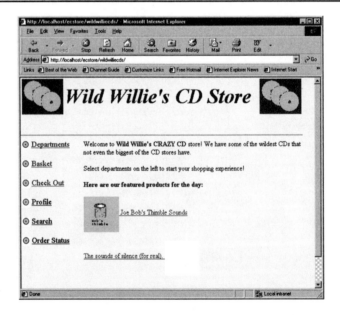

Figure 14.2 shows the department page. Note the list of featured products on the navigation bar. These will show up on any page except the default and basket pages.

Next, add a product other than one of the featured products into the shopping basket. Figure 14.3 shows the shopping basket with both featured products shown at the bottom of the page.

FIGURE 14.2:

Standard navigation page with featured products

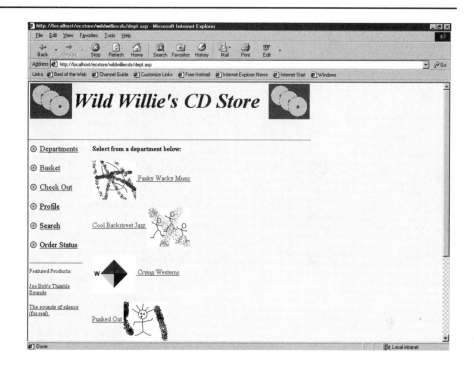

FIGURE 14.3:

Basket page with both featured products displayed

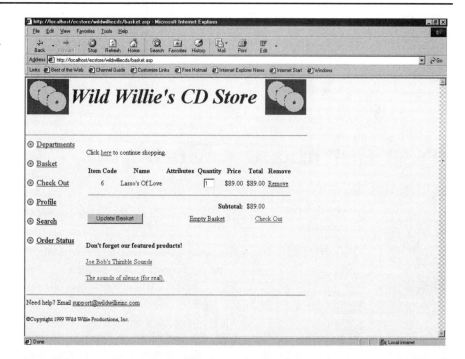

Now add one of the featured products to the basket. Figure 14.4 shows the shopping basket with *Joe Bob's Thimble Sounds* added to the basket. Now only the *Sounds of Silence (for real)* featured product is shown.

FIGURE 14.4:

Basket page with one featured product ordered

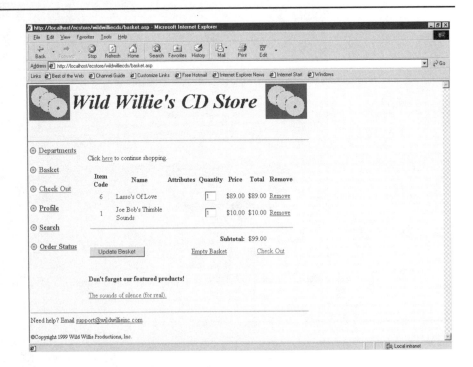

Next we will look at options for managing our featured products list in the store manager.

Programming the Manager

We will manage setting up our featured products on the ManageProduct.asp page. Options for setting the featured product, start date, and end date will need to be provided.

Listing 14.10 shows the code we will add to the ManageProduct.asp page. A check box will be provided for flagging and unflagging the product as a featured product. A check is done to see if the current product has been flagged or not. If it has, then the check box is set by default using the *checked* attribute.

LISTING 14.10   ManageProduct.asp

```
<tr>
  <td align="right"><b>Featured Product:</b></td>
  <td>

    <%

    '  Check to see if the product is featured.
    if rsProduct("intFeatured") = 1 then

    %>

    <!--  Display the check box checked if the
          product is featured.  -->
    <input type="checkbox" value="1" CHECKED
          name="intFeatured">

    <%
    else
    %>

    <!--  Display the check box without the check.  -->
    <input type="checkbox" value="1" name="intFeatured">

    <% end if %>
```

The page finishes out with two HTML input text boxes for the start date and end date (see Lisitng 14.11). Remember that the form posts to the UpdateProduct .asp page, where these values will be processed.

LISTING 14.11   ManageProduct.asp Continued

```
<!--  Show the start and end date for the product
      feature  -->
Start Date:
      <input type="text"
      value="<%=rsProduct("dtFeatureStart")%>"
```

```
            name="dtFeatureStart">
      End Date:
            <input type="text"
            value="<%=rsProduct("dtFeatureEnd")%>"
            name="dtFeatureEnd">

   </td>
  </tr>
```

Listing 14.12 shows the code we will add to the UpdateProduct.asp page. The first step is to retrieve the *intFeatured* value from the ManageProduct.asp form. A check is done to see if the check box has a value or not. If not, then we will set the value in the database to 0. Then the start and end dates for the featured product display are retrieved.

LISTING 14.12   **UpdateProduct.asp**

```
'  Retrieve the featured product.
intFeatured = request("intFeatured")

'  Check to see if the featured check box was set.
if intFeatured = "" then

   '  If not then set the product to be not featured
   intFeatured = 0

else

   '  If it is then set it to be featured
   intFeatured = 1

end if

dtFeatureStart = request("dtFeatureStart")
dtFeatureEnd = request("dtFeatureEnd")
```

Once these values are retrieved, we call the sp_UpdateProduct stored procedure to update the product data. Now we have to also pass in the featured product setting and the start and end dates (see Listing 14.13).

LISTING 14.13   UpdateProduct.asp Continued

```
'  Create an ADO database connection
set dbProduct = server.createobject("adodb.connection")

'  Create the record set
set rsProduct = server.CreateObject("adodb.recordset")

'  Open the connection using our ODBC file DSN
dbProduct.open("filedsn=WildWillieCDs")

'  Execute the SQL stored procedure to update the
'  product data
sql = "execute sp_UpdateProduct " & _
      request("idProduct") & ", '" & _
      chrProductName & "', '" & _
      txtDescription & "', '" & _
      chrProductImage & "', " & _
      intPrice & ", " & _
      intActive & ", " & _
      intFeatured & ", '" & _
      dtFeatureStart & "', '" & _
      dtFeatureEnd & "'"
```

Our original sp_UpdateProduct stored procedure is modified to accept the featured product values (see Listing 14.14). The featured product value along with the two date values are passed in. Then the update is performed to set the values accordingly.

LISTING 14.14   **sp_UpdateProduct Stored Procedure**

```
CREATE PROCEDURE sp_UpdateProduct

@idProduct int,
@chrProductName varchar(255),
@txtDescription text,
@chrProductImage varchar(100),
@intPrice int,
@intActive int,
@intFeatured int,
@dtFeatureStart datetime,
@dtFeatureEnd datetime

AS

update products set
    chrProductName = @chrProductName,
    txtDescription = @txtDescription,
    chrProductImage = @chrProductImage,
    intPrice = @intPrice,
    intActive = @intActive,
    intFeatured = @intFeatured,
    dtFeatureStart = @dtFeatureStart,
    dtFeatureEnd = @dtFeatureEnd
where
    idProduct = @idProduct
```

Now let's take a look the product manager in action. Figure 14.5 shows the product management page with the fields for the featured product. The check box and two input fields are shown.

FIGURE 14.5:

Product manager page

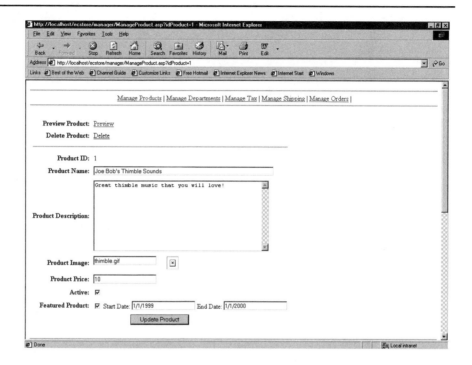

Let's take *Joe Bob's Thimble Sounds* off as a featured product. Clear out the check box and the date fields and update the data. Figure 14.6 shows the updated product page. Note that the date fields will default to beginning of the century dates in the database.

FIGURE 14.6:

Updated featured product

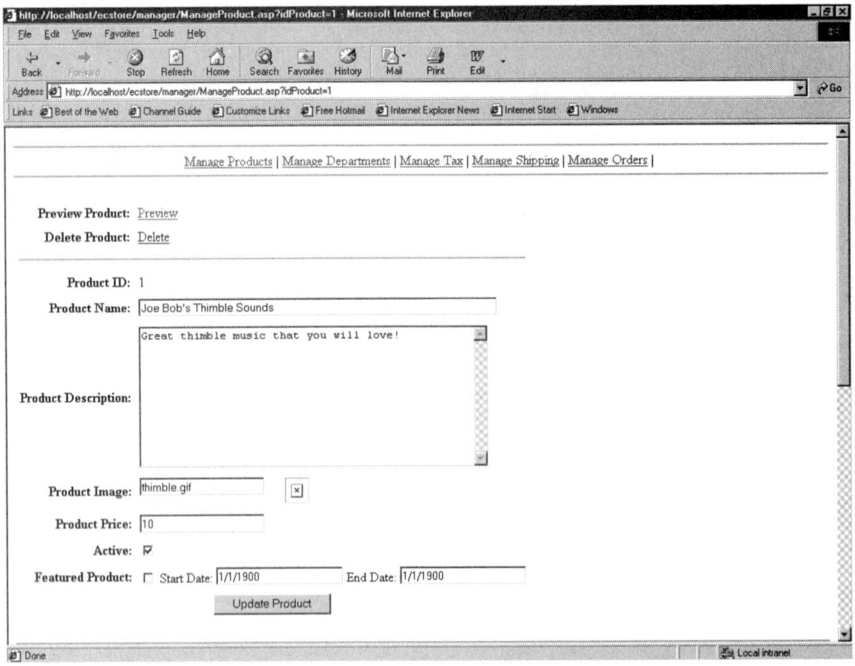

Figure 14.7 shows the default page for the store. Note that only one product is now featured.

TIP

You may also want to consider promoting products during the checkout process—kind of like having all kinds of stuff at the checkout aisle available for a last minute addition. This would require some logic to add the product to the shopping basket, update all of the totals, and continue the checkout process.

FIGURE 14.7:

New home page featured product listing

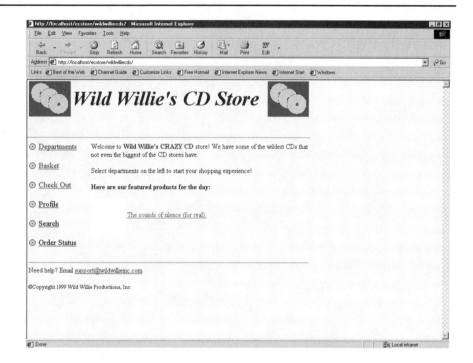

Summary

That is it for handling featured products in the store. Through the tools outlined in this chapter, the store manager can easily highlight new products in the store, fast selling products, products that need to move in inventory, etc. These are key tools the store manager can exploit to engage with the consumer.

In Chapter 15, "On Sale," we will work on that most popular of options in a store—sales. Our approach to sales will be similar to our handling of featured products, but definitely targeted at price reduction or lowering the overall cost of the purchase.

CHAPTER
FIFTEEN

15

On Sale

- Designing the Sale Features

- Building the Shopping Sale Features

- Building the Sale Management Features

It's a sale! In this chapter we explore how to provide sale prices for our products, and how to promote those sale products. But sales are not limited to reduced prices. They can also include promotional offers like free shipping, which is another option we will explore.

Designing the Sale Features

We already have fields in our Products table that will support setting sale prices and their effective date ranges. Listing 15.1 shows SQL code for setting up three initial items to be on sale in our store.

LISTING 15.1   Setting Sale Prices

```
update products set intSalePrice = 400, dtSaleStart = getdate(),
dtSaleEnd = "1/1/2000" where idproduct = 1

update products set intSalePrice = 500, dtSaleStart = getdate(),
dtSaleEnd = "1/1/2000" where idproduct = 2

update products set intSalePrice = 600, dtSaleStart = getdate(),
dtSaleEnd = "1/1/2000" where idproduct = 3
```

We will have many opportunities to query which products are on sale in our store. And, in the store manager, we will be able to manage the sale price settings for our products.

To handle the tracking of free shipping, we are going to need to add one field, intFreeShipping (integer), into our basket table. This will be used to track whether free shipping was applied to the order or not.

We are also going to add a new table to indicate whether or not we are currently running a free shipping campaign. Table 15.1 shows the table structure.

TABLE 15.1: FreeShip Table

Field	Description
IdFreeShip	Primary key for the table
dtStartDate	Start date of the shipping campaign
dtEndDate	End date of the shipping campaign

The SQL code in Listing 15.2 will update the database tables appropriately.

LISTING 15.2   Update Database Tables

```
ALTER TABLE dbo.Basket ADD
    intFreeShipping int NULL DEFAULT (0)

CREATE TABLE dbo.FreeShip (
    intFreeShip int IDENTITY (1, 1) NOT NULL ,
    dtStartDate datetime NULL
    CONSTRAINT DF_FreeShip_dtStartDate DEFAULT (getdate()),
    dtEndDate datetime NULL
    CONSTRAINT DF_FreeShip_dtEndDate DEFAULT (getdate()),
    CONSTRAINT PK_FreeShip PRIMARY KEY CLUSTERED
    (
        intFreeShip
    )
)
```

To get the user side of the free shipping working, we will need to insert some sample data. Listing 15.3 shows the SQL statement to insert values into the Free-Ship table.

LISTING 15.3   Setting Free Shipping

```
insert into FreeShip(dtStartDate, dtEndDate) values(getdate(),
'2/1/2000')
```

Now we are ready to begin building the user interface.

Building the Shopping Sale Features

Our code will be changed into two steps. The first step is for displaying sale items throughout the shopping process. The second step will be modifying the check-out process to support free shipping.

Implementing Sale Items

To get started, we will want to show a sale item along with the featured products on the home page of the store. We have to be careful though. We may have multiple sale products and we may not want to show all of them on the home page.

We will take the approach of selecting a sale product randomly and displaying it right before the featured products on the page. Listing 15.4 shows the code that should be inserted right before the featured product display code.

A database connection is opened and the sp_RetrieveSaleProducts stored procedure is called to return the sale products currently in the store.

LISTING 15.4   **Default.asp**

```
<!-- Show the sale products.  -->
<b>On sale Today!</b><BR><BR>

<%


'  Create an ADO database connection
set dbSaleProd = server.createobject("adodb.connection")

'  Create a recordset
set rsSaleProd = server.CreateObject("adodb.recordset")

'  Open the connection using our ODBC file DSN
dbSaleProd.open("filedsn=WildWillieCDs")

'  Retrieve all of the current sale products
sql = "execute sp_RetrieveSaleProducts"

'  Execute the SQL statement
set rsSaleProd = dbSaleProd.Execute(sql)
```

If products are returned, we will want to randomly select one to be displayed (see Listing 15.5). The stored procedure returns a column that is the total number of sale products. We can then use the VBScript RND function to randomly pick one of the items to be displayed.

Once the product is displayed, we then loop to the product in the record set returned. Once the product is found, then the product data is retrieved and displayed.

LISTING 15.5   Default.asp Continued

```
' Ensure something is returned so it can be displayed
if not rsSaleProd.EOF then

    ' Seed the random number generator
    randomize

    ' Pick a random sale product to display.  Note that the
    ' first column returned is the count of rows.
    Row = Int((rsSaleProd(0) - 1 + 1) * Rnd + 1)

    ' Loop to the row selected.
    for N = 1 to row - 1

        ' Move to the next row.
        rsSaleProd.MoveNext

    next

    ' Retrieve the product information to be displayed.
    chrProductName = rsSaleProd("chrProductName")
    chrProductImage = rsSaleProd("chrProductImage")
    dblSalePrice = rsSaleProd("intSalePrice")
    idProduct = rsSaleProd("idProduct")

%>

    <!-- Build the link to the product information.  -->
    <a href="product.asp?idProduct=<%=idProduct%>">
        <img src="images/products/sm_<%=chrProductImage%>"
          align="middle" border="0">
        <%=chrProductName%></a>
        <font color="red"><b>
        - Only <%=formatcurrency(dblSalePrice/100, 2)%>
```

```
        </b></font><BR><BR>

    <%
        '   Set the flag to that the next featured product shows the image
        '   on the right.
        Flag = 1

        end if

    %>
```

We utilize a key stored procedure to retrieve our list of sale products (see Listing 15.6). The first thing done in the stored procedure is to get a count of the products currently on sale. That is needed for our random selection for the home page. The count is stored in a variable for return in our next select statement.

Next a query is done to retrieve the data for those sale products. The first column will return the count with each row.

LISTING 15.6   sp_RetrieveSaleProducts

```
CREATE PROCEDURE sp_RetrieveSaleProducts AS

declare @cnt int

select @cnt = count(*) from products
where getdate() >= dtSaleStart and getdate() <= dtSaleEnd

select @cnt, *   from products
where getdate() >= dtSaleStart and getdate() <= dtSaleEnd
```

Next we will want to show a sale product on the navigation bar, along with our featured products. We will need to modify header.asp to include code to display a sale product.

Once again we will need to follow the same guideline to randomly select a sale item to be displayed on the navigation bar. Listing 15.7 shows the code changes for header.asp. This code goes right before the featured product listing.

As on the default page, we open our database connection and retrieve the list of sale products. We then randomly select one of the items and list it on the navigation bar. Note that the sale price will show on any page that is not the default or basket page, just like the featured products.

LISTING 15.7   Header.asp

```
<hr>
<font size="2" color="red">Sale Products:</font>
<br><br>

<%

'  Create an ADO database connection
set dbSaleProd = server.createobject("adodb.connection")

'  Create a record set
set rsSaleProd = server.CreateObject("adodb.recordset")

'  Open the connection using our ODBC file DSN
dbSaleProd.open("filedsn=WildWillieCDs")

'  Retrieve all of the current sale products
sql = "execute sp_RetrieveSaleProducts"

'  Execute the SQL statement
set rsSaleProd = dbSaleProd.Execute(sql)

'  Check to ensure a product was returned.
if not rsSaleProd.EOF then

    '  Seed the random number generator.
    randomize

    '  Randomly get the product to be displayed
    Row = Int((rsSaleProd(0) - 1 + 1) * Rnd + 1)

    '  Loop to that product.
    for N = 1 to row - 1

        '  Move to the next row.
        rsSaleProd.MoveNext

    next

'  Retrieve the product information to be displayed.
    chrProductName = rsSaleProd("chrProductName")
    chrProductImage = rsSaleProd("chrProductImage")
```

```
dblSalePrice = rsSaleProd("intSalePrice")
idProduct = rsSaleProd("idProduct")

%>

<!-- Build the link to the product information.   -->
<a href="product.asp?idProduct=<%=idProduct%>">
<%=chrProductName%></a>
<font color="red">
- <%=formatcurrency(dblSalePrice/100, 2)%>
</font><br><br>

<%

end if

%>
```

Now that we have our sale products showing up on the default page and the navigation page, we are ready to move to the product page. On the product page we need to show the sale price so the shopper knows. We also need to modify the logic so the sale price is added to the basket.

We need to add one section of code at the top of the product page that will check to see if the product is on sale. If so, then we will retrieve the sale price or default it to 0. Listing 15.8 shows the code to be added.

LISTING 15.8   Product.asp

```
'  Check to see if the product is currently on sale
if now >= cdate(rsProduct("dtSaleStart")) and _
   date <= cdate(rsProduct("dtSaleEnd")) then

   '  Set the sale price
   intSalePrice = rsProduct("intSalePrice")

else

   '  Default the sale price to 0.
   intSalePrice = 0

end if
```

Next we have to handle the display of the product price. In this case we want to show the original price as well as the sale price. In Listing 15.9, we modify the price listing under the image to include a check to see if it is on sale. If so, then we show text in red indicating the sale price.

LISTING 15.9   **Product.asp Continued**

```
<!-- Show the product price.  An input quantity box is
     created.  Also, several hidden variables will hold
     key data for adding the product to the database.  -->
<TR>
  <TD align="center"><B>Price:
    <%=formatcurrency(intPrice/100, 2)%></b>

    <!-- Check to see if the product is on sale.  -->
    <% if intSalePrice <> 0 then %>

      <!-- Show the sale price -->
      <font color="red"><b>
      <BR><BR> On Sale Now for
      <%=formatcurrency(intSalePrice/100, 2)%>!
      </font></b>

    <% end if %>

  </td>
```

The code shown in Listing 15.10 continues on to build the quantity and our hidden variables. Then we check to see if it is a sale product. If so, then the price we set in our hidden elements will be set to the sale price. When the item is added to the basket, it will have the sale price.

LISTING 15.10   **Product.asp Continued**

```
<TD align="center">
  <B>Quantity:
  <input type="text" value="1" name="quantity"
         size="2"></b>

  <input type="hidden" value="<%=idProduct%>"
         name="idProduct">

  <input type="hidden" value="<%=chrProductName%>"
```

```
                   name="ProductName">

          <%
          '  Check to see if the product is on sale.
          if intSalePrice = 0 then
          %>
          <!--  Set the hidden price to the standard
                price.  -->
            <input type="hidden" value="<%=intPrice%>"
                     name="ProductPrice">

          <%
          else
          %>
            <!--  Set the hidden price to the sale
                  price.  -->
            <input type="hidden" value="<%=intSalePrice%>"
                     name="ProductPrice">
          <%
          end if
          %>

        </td>
      </TR>
```

TIP
If you have limited inventory of sale products, you might want to develop product limits in your store. For example, we might allow a shopper to purchase only four items within a certain time period for any sale products. This could be tracked by the shopper profile.

That is it for the sale product management on the store interface. Let's take a look at it in action. Figure 15.1 shows the default page with our sale product listed before the featured products. Note how the images still flip-flop between left and right.

Figure 15.2 shows the navigation bar on the department page. The sale product is listed right above the featured products.

FIGURE 15.1:

Default.asp sale product

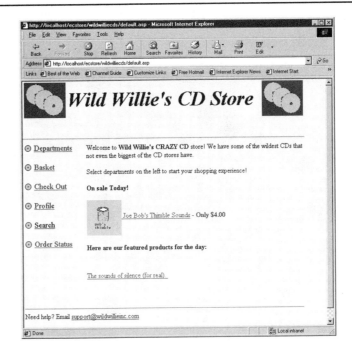

FIGURE 15.2:

Navigation bar sale

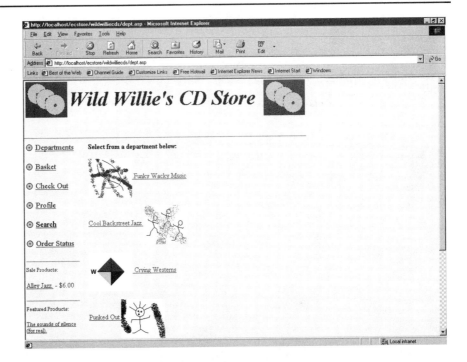

Next, in Figure 15.3, we have a product that is on sale. Note the sale price in bold red, right below the product price. Now let's add it to the shopping basket.

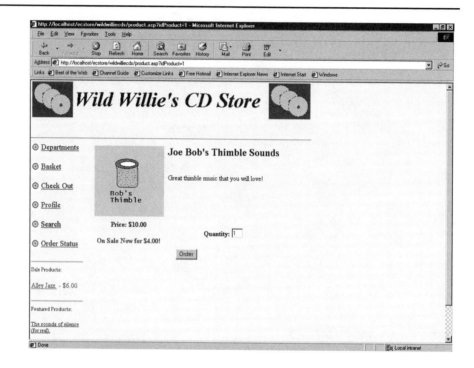

Figure 15.4 shows the shopping basket with our sale product added. Note that the price is the sale price. You can update the quantity, etc. and the price will stay constant all the way through to the post-purchase order detail.

FIGURE 15.4:

Basket sale prices

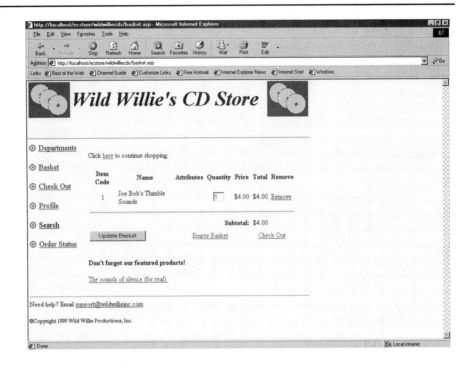

Implementing Free Shipping

Now we can implement free shipping. The idea is to have free shipping on certain days, based on the data in the FreeShip table.

The first page we need to work with is Payment.asp, as shown in Listing 15.11. We will need to rework the section where our tax and shipping component is called. Listing 15.11 shows the code changes from when we check to ensure the basket has a quantity greater than 0.

The first thing we do is open a database connection to query the FreeShip table. The sp_CheckFreeShip stored procedure is called to see if there is a current shipping promotion.

If a shipping promotion is on, then the shipping component is not called. If a shipping promotion is not on, then we call the component as usual. Note that a session variable, *FreeShipping*, is set so we can flag the database appropriately.

LISTING 15.11   **Payment.asp**

```
'  Check the quantity returned from the database
if rsBasket("quantity") > 0 then

    '  Create an ADO database connection
    set dbFreeShip = server.createobject("adodb.connection")

    '  Create the record set
    set rsFreeShip = server.CreateObject("adodb.recordset")

    '  Open the connection using our ODBC file DSN
    dbFreeShip.open("filedsn=WildWillieCDs")

    '  Check to see if free shipping is in effect.
    sql = "execute sp_CheckFreeShip"

    '  Execute the statement
    set rsFreeShip = dbBasket.Execute(sql)

    '  Check to see if a row was returned which indicates
    '  free shipping is currently in effect.
    if rsFreeShip.EOF then

        '  Call the shipping function of our component.  The
        '  quantity is passed in and must be in a long data
        '  type format.  The Shipping fee is returned.
        Shipping = _
          BizLogic.Shipping(clng(rsBasket("quantity")))

        '  Indicate free shipping is not in effect
        session("FreeShipping") = 0

    else

        '  Default the shipping to 0.
        Shipping = 0

        '  Indicate free shipping is in effect.
        session("FreeShipping") = 1
```

```
    end if

else

    '  Redirect to the basket page since the quantity is 0
    Response.Redirect("Basket.asp")

end if
```

The next set of the code continues with our tax and total amount calculations (see Listing 15.12). We next move into the display of the order totals. We will want to display to the shopper a message indicating free shipping is currently in promotion. The message displayed next to the shipping total is changed to red and bold to indicate free shipping. (Otherwise it would be displayed in the usual fashion.)

LISTING 15.12   Payment.asp Continued

```
'  Store the shipping value in a session variable
session("Shipping") = Shipping

'  Store the quantity in a session variable
session("Quantity") = rsBasket("quantity")

'  Calculate the tax by calling the Tax function of
'  our component.  We pass in the shipping state and the
'  order subtotal.  The value is also stored in a session
'  variable.
Tax = BizLogic.tax(session("chrShipState"), clng(subtotal))
session("Tax") = Tax

'  Calculate the total and store in a session variable.
Total = SubTotal + Shipping + Tax
session("Total") = Total

%>

<HTML>

<!-- #include file="include/header.asp" -->
```

```
<BR>

<center>
<font size="5"><b>Billing Information</b></font>
</center>

<BR>
<b>Order Recap:</b>
<BR><BR>

<!-- Build a table to display the order total -->
<table>

<!--  Display the Subtotal -->
<tr>
    <td align="right">Subtotal:</td>
    <td><%=formatcurrency(Subtotal/100, 2)%></td>
</tr>

<!--  Display the Shipping Value -->
<tr>
    <td align="right">

        <!--  Check to see if Free Shipping is in
              effect.  -->
        <% if session("FreeShipping") = 0 then %>
        <!--  Indicate standard shipping  -->
        Shipping:
        <% else %>
        <!--  Indicate free shipping -->
        <font color="red"><b>
        Free Shipping Today!
        </b></font>
        <% end if %>

    </td>
    <td><%=formatcurrency(Shipping/100, 2)%></td>
</tr>
```

The stored procedure we utilize checks to see if a free promotion is currently in place. The start and end dates are checked against the current system date using the GetDate function. (See Listing 15.13.)

LISTING 15.13   sp_CheckFreeShip

```
CREATE PROCEDURE sp_CheckFreeShip

AS

select * from FreeShip
where getdate() >= dtStartDate and getdate() <= dtEndDate
```

That takes care of the display and calculation of the free shipping. Now our session variables are all set and will be stored in the database. We are ready to ensure that free shipping is stored in our order.

Listing 15.14 show the code for the ValidatePayment.asp page. We are going to update the code to set the calculated amounts in the basket. The sp_UpdateBasket Stored Procedure is modified to accept the FreeShipping settings. Note that the Shipping session variable will be set to 0 when there is free shipping.

LISTING 15.14   ValidatePayment.asp

```
'**************************************************
'**** 6.  Update the basket with the final
'****     order data.
'**************************************************

'  Finally we need to update the basket with the final
'  amounts for quantity, subtotal, shipping, tax and
'  total
sql = "execute sp_UpdateBasket " & _
    session("idBasket") & ", " & _
    session("Quantity") & ", " & _
    session("Subtotal") & ", " & _
    session("Shipping") & ", " & _
    session("FreeShipping") & ", " & _
    session("Tax") & ", " & _
    session("Total") & ", 1"
```

As mentioned, we have to update the `sp_UpdateBasket` stored procedure to accept the free shipping settings (see Listing 15.15). A parameter is added to set the value of the free shipping and then the update statement sets the field value.

LISTING 15.15   **sp_UpdateBasket**

```
/*  Stored procedure to update the basket
    values */
ALTER PROCEDURE sp_UpdateBasket

/*  Pass in the ID of the basket, the total
    quantity, the order subtotal, the shipping
    value, the tax value, the order total and a
    flag indicating the order was placed. */
@idBasket int,
@intQuantity int,
@intSubTotal int,
@intShipping int,
@intFreeShipping int,
@intTax int,
@intTotal int,
@intOrderPlaced int

AS

/*  Update the basket */
update basket set
    intQuantity = @intQuantity,
    intSubtotal = @intSubtotal,
    intShipping = @intShipping,
    intFreeShipping = @intFreeShipping,
    intTax = @intTax,
    intTotal = @intTotal,
    intOrderPlaced = @intOrderPlaced
where    idBasket = @idBasket
```

Shipping Charges

There is more than one way to approach shipping charge reductions. We could provide logic that will give free shipping for orders over a certain amount. Or, we could provide free shipping on every third order. Each of these could be a key feature in providing incentive for the shopper to make that purchase.

Now let's test our free shipping logic. Be sure that the campaign data set in the FreeShip table is set to ensure the current date is within the campaign range.

Figure 15.5 shows the payment page indicating that the user will not be charged for shipping.

FIGURE 15.5:

Free shipping

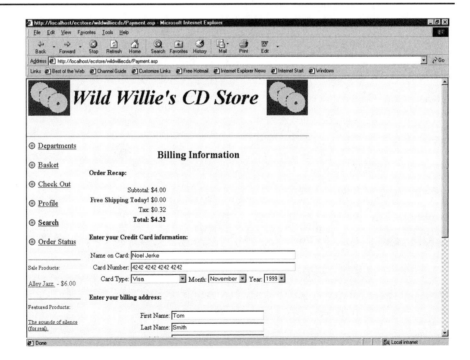

Go ahead and place the order. Check the order in the order status or order manager to ensure that the shipping values have been stored properly. Figure 15.6 shows our sample order detail.

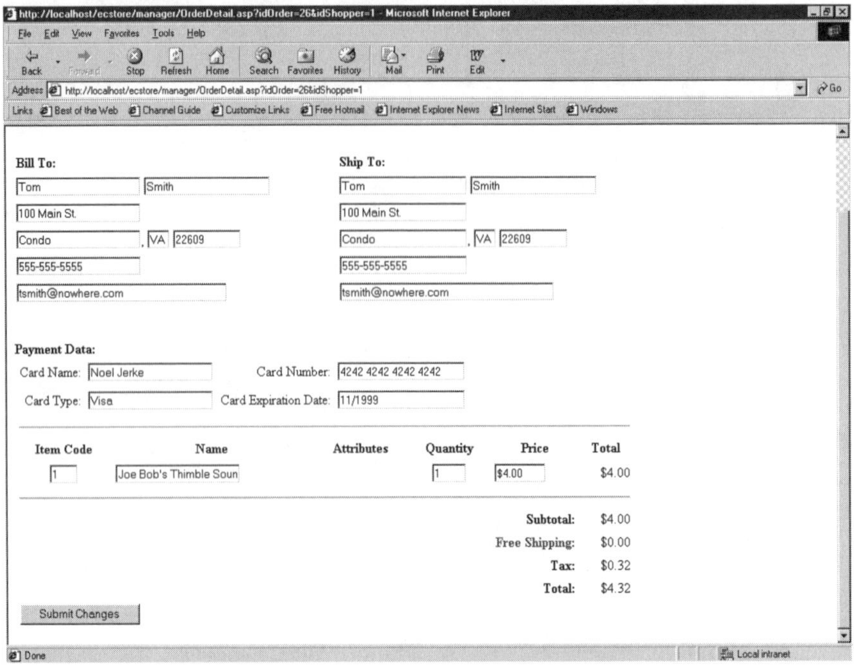

FIGURE 15.6:

Order detail with sale price and free shipping figure

Building the Sale Management Features

Now that we have seen the user interface in action, we are ready to tackle the management tools necessary to set our sale prices and manage the free shipping settings.

Managing Product Sales

Let's first tackle managing our sale settings. This will require an update to the ManageProduct.asp page, as shown in Listing 15.16.

Right below the featured product code that we added to the manager, we need to add similar code to manage the sale settings. We need to set the price and the start and end dates. A row with text input fields for the intSalePrice field, dtSaleStart field, and dtSaleEnd field is added to the page.

LISTING 15.16   **ManageProduct.asp**

```
<!-- Show the sale price settings.  -->
<tr>
  <td align="right"><b>Sale Price:</b></td>
  <td>

      <!-- Display an input box for the product
           sale price.  -->
      <input type="text"
            value="<%=rsProduct("intSalePrice")/100%>"
            name="intSalePrice" size="10">

      <!-- Show the start and end date for the sale price
           campaign.  -->
      Start Date:  <input type="text"
            value="<%=rsProduct("dtSaleStart")%>"
            size="10" name="dtSaleStart">

      End Date:  <input type="text"
              value="<%=rsProduct("dtSaleEnd")%>"
            size="10" name="dtSaleEnd">
  </td>
</tr>
```

Next we have to update the UpdateProduct.asp page to accept the new values and update the database. Listing 15.17 shows the code updates for the page. The values are retrieved from the form variables.

The stored procedure sp_UpdateProduct needs to accept the sale values. The values retrieved from the form are passed in.

LISTING 15.17   **UpdateProduct.asp**

```
'  Retrieve the sale price and start and end
'  date for the sale price campaign.
```

```
intSalePrice = request("intSalePrice") * 100
dtSaleStart = request("dtSaleStart")
dtSaleEnd = request("dtSaleEnd")

'  Create an ADO database connection
set dbProduct = server.createobject("adodb.connection")

'  Create the record set
set rsProduct = server.CreateObject("adodb.recordset")

'  Open the connection using our ODBC file DSN
dbProduct.open("filedsn=WildWillieCDs")

'  Execute the SQL stored procedure to update the
'  product data
sql = "execute sp_UpdateProduct " & _
      request("idProduct") & ", '" & _
      chrProductName & "', '" & _
      txtDescription & "', '" & _
      chrProductImage & "', " & _
      intPrice & ", " & _
      intActive & ", " & _
      intFeatured & ", '" & _
      dtFeatureStart & "', '" & _
      dtFeatureEnd & "', " & _
      intSalePrice & ", '" & _
      dtSaleStart & "', '" & _
      dtSaleEnd & "'"

'  Execute the statement
set rsProduct = dbProduct.Execute(sql)

'  Send the user back to the product manager page and
'  pass back the product ID.
Response.Redirect "ManageProduct.asp?idProduct=" & _
                  request("idProduct")
```

Listing 15.18 shows the updated sp_UpdateProduct stored procedure. The first change is adding the parameter values for each of the fields. Following that, the updated SQL statement is modified to set these values.

LISTING 15.18   sp_UpdateProduct

```
ALTER PROCEDURE sp_UpdateProduct

@idProduct int,
@chrProductName varchar(255),
@txtDescription text,
@chrProductImage varchar(100),
@intPrice int,
@intActive int,
@intFeatured int,
@dtFeatureStart datetime,
@dtFeatureEnd datetime,
@intSalePrice int,
@dtSaleStart datetime,
@dtSaleEnd datetime

AS

update products set
    chrProductName = @chrProductName,    txtDescription
    = @txtDescription,
    chrProductImage = @chrProductImage,
    intPrice = @intPrice,
    intActive = @intActive,
    intFeatured = @intFeatured,
    dtFeatureStart = @dtFeatureStart,
    dtFeatureEnd = @dtFeatureEnd,
    intSalePrice = @intSalePrice,
    dtSaleStart = @dtSaleStart,
    dtSaleEnd = @dtSaleEnd
where
    idProduct = @idProduct
```

The code changes to manage the sale prices are pretty simple. Figure 15.7 shows the product manager page with the sales fields displayed. These can be modified and the product data submitted.

FIGURE 15.7:

Product manager

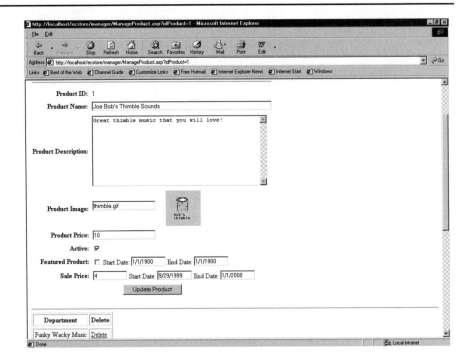

After making appropriate changes, submit the product data. Figure 15.8 shows the product data with the sale data updated.

That is it for managing sales prices. Next we can move to managing the free shipping campaign.

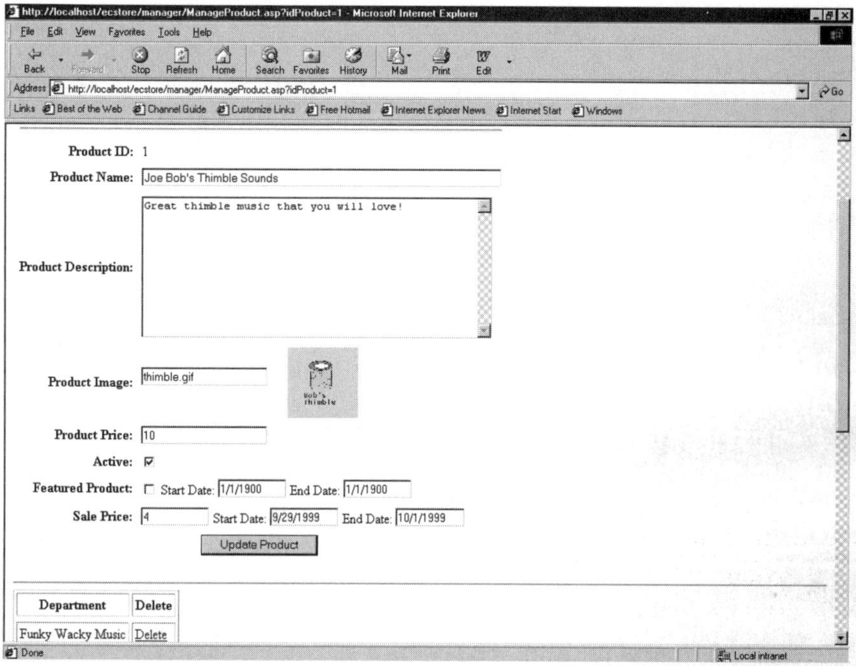

FIGURE 15.8:

Updated sale price

Free Shipping Campaign Management

We currently do not have any facility for managing free shipping. So we will have to add one more item to our manager menu and NavInclude pages. Listings 15.19 and 15.20 show the updates to the appropriate pages to add in the free shipping navigation.

In ManagerMenu.asp we add in one more row to the table that links to the ManageFreeShipping.asp page.

LISTING 15.19   **ManagerMenu.asp**

```
<tr>
    <!-- Manage free shipping -->
    <td><a href="ManageFreeShipping.asp">
        Manage Free Shipping</a></td>
</tr>
```

In Listing 15.20 the navigation bar has one more addition for linking to the *manage free shipping* option.

LISTING 15.20   NavInclude.asp

```
<!-- Link to the management of free shipping.  -->
<a href="ManageFreeShipping.asp">
Manage Free Shipping</a> |
```

Now we add one more page to our store manager to manage the free shipping campaign. Listing 15.21 shows the ManageFreeShipping.asp page. This page has the standard formatting with the appropriate includes for security and navigation.

LISTING 15.21   ManageFreeShipping.asp

```
<%@ Language=VBScript %>
<!-- #Include file="include/validatecheck.asp" -->
<HTML>
<!--
    ManageFreeShipping.asp - Provides options to set the
    next free shipping campaign date range.
-->

<HEAD>
<META NAME="GENERATOR" Content="Microsoft Visual Studio 6.0">
</HEAD>
<BODY>

<!-- #include file="include/navinclude.asp" -->

<BR><BR>
<B>Set free shipping campaign:
</b><BR><BR>
```

In Listing 15.22 we continue the page. The first thing we do is open a database connection to retrieve the current free shipping settings. The `sp_RetrieveFreeShip` stored procedure returns the data currently in the database.

LISTING 15.22   ManageFreeShipping.asp Continued

```
<%
'  Create an ADO database connection
set dbFreeShipping = server.createobject("adodb.connection")

'  Create the record set
set rsFreeShipping = server.CreateObject("adodb.recordset")

'  Open the connection using our ODBC file DSN
dbFreeShipping.open("filedsn=WildWillieCDs")

'  The sp_RetrieveFreeShip stored procedure returns the
'  last settings in the database.
sql = "execute sp_RetrieveFreeShip"

'  Execute the statement
set rsFreeShipping = dbFreeShipping.Execute(sql)
%>
```

Next a form is created for posting the start and end dates for the free shipping campaign. Then the form is completed with a submit form and the appropriate closing tags for the page. (See Listing 15.23.)

LISTING 15.23   ManageFreeShipping.asp Continued

```
<!-- The changes will be posted to the
     UpdateFreeShipping.asp page. -->
<form method="post" action="UpdateFreeShipping.asp">

<!-- Start a table to show the start and end date. -->
<table cellpadding="3" cellspacing"3">
<!-- Show the start date. -->
<tr>
   <td align="right">Start Date:</td>
   <td>
      <input type="text" name="dtStartDate"
      value="<%=rsFreeShipping("dtStartDate")%>">
   </td>
</tr>
```

```
<!--  Show the end date.  -->
<tr>
  <td align="right">End Date:</td>
  <td>
    <input type="text" name="dtEndDate"
    value="<%=rsFreeShipping("dtEndDate")%>">
  </td>
</tr>

<!--  Show a submit button for the form -->
<tr><td align="center" colspan="2">
  <input type="submit" value="Submit" name="Submit">
</td></tr>
</table>

</form>

</BODY>
</HTML>
```

WARNING   The date functions here assume the use of a U.S. system locale, where dates are stored as mm/dd/yy. When filling out this form, be sure to enter your dates in this format; otherwise you may get an unexpected error.

The sp_RetrieveFreeShip stored procedure simply returns all of the data in the table. In reality we are just working with the first row since we can have only one shipping campaign at a time. Note that we could provide management to set up multiple shipping campaigns and schedule them. (See Listing 15.24.)

LISTING 15.24   sp_RetrieveFreeShip

```
CREATE PROCEDURE sp_RetrieveFreeShip AS

select * from FreeShip
```

The UpdateFreeShipping.asp page handles updating the data in the FreeShip table. The first thing we do is open a database connection. Then the sp_Update-FreeShip stored procedure is called to make the changes to the database. (See Listing 15.25.)

LISTING 15.25   **UpdateFreeShipping.asp**

```
<%@ Language=VBScript %>
<%

'  ********************************************************
'  UpdateFreeShipping.asp - Handles updating the free
'  shipping campaign dates.
'  ********************************************************

'  Retrieve the start date
dtStartDate = request("dtStartDate")

'  Retrieve the end date
dtEndDate = request("dtEndDate")

'  Create an ADO database connection
set dbFreeShip = server.createobject("adodb.connection")

'  Create the record set
set rsFreeShip = server.CreateObject("adodb.recordset")

'  Open the connection using our ODBC file DSN
dbFreeShip.open("filedsn=WildWillieCDs")

'  Execute the sp_UpdateFreeShip stored procedure
'  to change the dates.
sql = "execute sp_UpdateFreeShip '" & _
     dtStartDate & "', '" & _
     dtEndDate & "'"

'  Execute the statement
set rsFreeShip = dbFreeShip.Execute(sql)

'  Send the user back to free shipping manager page.
Response.Redirect "ManageFreeShipping.asp"

%>
```

Listing 15.26 shows the update stored procedure. The start date and end date are passed into it. In this case we are updating all rows that exist in the table.

LISTING 15.26   **sp_UpdateFreeShip**

```
CREATE PROCEDURE sp_UpdateFreeShip

@dtStartDate datetime,
@dtEndDate datetime

AS

Update FreeShip set
    dtStartDate = @dtStartDate,
    dtEndDate = @dtEndDate
```

Order reporting must be updated also. We need to indicate that free shipping was in effect when the order was placed, and we cannot overwrite that if the order is updated for some reason.

Listing 15.27 shows code for the OrderDetail.asp pages. To display whether free shipping is in effect, a check is done on the intFreeShipping field in the database. If the value is set, then we show text indicating free shipping; if not, then we show standard text. Also, we have to be sure to post the free shipping value to the UpdateOrder.asp page so that we can make the appropriate update. Thus, in each case we set a hidden input element with the shipping value so it will be passed to the next page.

LISTING 15.27   **OrderDetail.asp**

```
<!-- Show the shipping total of the basket -->
<tr>
    <td colspan="5" align="right">
        <!-- Check to see if we have free shipping.  -->
        <% if rsOrderReceiptHeader("intFreeShipping") = 1 then %>
        <!-- Show that there is free shipping on this
             order.  -->
        <b><font color="red">
        Free Shipping:</b></font>
        <input type="hidden" value="1"
               name="intFreeShipping">
```

```
<% else %>
<!--  Show that there is standard shipping on this
      order.  -->
<b>Shipping:</b>
<input type="hidden" value="0"
       name="intFreeShipping">
<% end if %>
</td>
<td align="right">
<%Response.Write _
formatcurrency(rsOrderReceiptHeader("intShipping")/100,_
2) %></td>
</tr>
```

The UpdateOrder.asp page handles updating the order data with any changes we have made. That may include changing quantities of items in the order, which in turn would affect the order total and calculated fields.

The first thing we do is update the section where all header values are retrieved from the form. We have to add one more option to retrieve the intFreeShipping value. (See Listing 15.28.)

LISTING 15.28   **UpdateOrder.asp**

```
'  Next we retrieve the core order data which
'  includes the billing address and shipping
'  address.  Note that the key fields are updated
'  to ensure any single quotes are doubled.
chrBillFirstName = replace(request("chrBillFirstName"), _
                   "'", "''")

chrBillLastname = replace(request("chrBillLastName"), _
                  "'", "''")

chrShipFirstName = replace(Request("chrShipFirstName"), _
                   "'", "''")

chrShipLastname = replace(request("chrShipLastName"), _
                  "'", "''")

chrBillAddress = replace(request("chrBillAddress"), _
```

```
                                 "'",  "''")

chrShipAddress = replace(request("chrShipAddress"), _
                                 "'",  "''")

chrBillCity = replace(request("chrBillCity"), "'", "''")
chrBillState = request("chrBillState")
chrBillZipCode = request("chrBillZipCode")
chrShipCity = replace(request("chrShipCity"), "'", "''")
chrShipState = request("chrShipState")
chrShipZipCode = request("chrShipZipCode")
chrBillPhone = request("chrBillPhone")
chrShipPhone = request("chrShipPhone")
chrBillEmail = request("chrBillEmail")
chrShipEmail = request("chrShipEmail")

'   Get the free shipping setting for the order.
intFreeShipping = request("intFreeShipping")
```

In Listing 15.29 the UpdateOrder.asp code changes are continued. As with the payment.asp page, we need to check to see if free shipping is in effect. If it is, then we cannot calculate shipping for the order.

Once the shipping value is set, then we update the basket data with the new calculated values. If free shipping was in effect, then the shipping value will be set to 0. The **sp_UpdateBasket** stored procedure sets all of the values, including the intFreeShipping fields.

NOTE   Of course there are a number of ways in which we could increase the sophistication of this procedure. For example, we could give an option in the manager to turn off free shipping for the order. Alternatively, we might allow multiple sets of dates to be used for free shipping promotions. The code has been written in such a way as to make such modifications easy, and they have therefore been left as an exercise for the reader.

LISTING 15.29   **UpdateOrder.asp Continued**

```
'   Check to see if there is free shipping on the order.
if intFreeShipping = 0 then
```

```
'   Create the Business Logic component to
'   calculate the tax and shipping.
set BizLogic = _
server.CreateObject("ECStoreBizLogic.TaxShip")

'   Call the shipping function of our component.  The
'   quantity is passed in and must be in a long data type
'   format.  The Shipping fee is returned.
Shipping = BizLogic.Shipping(cLng(TotalQuantity))

else

'   Otherwise we default the shipping total to 0.
Shipping = 0

end if

'   Calculate the tax by calling the Tax function of
'   our component.  We pass in the shipping state and the
'   order subtotal.  The value is also stored in a session
'   variable.
Tax = BizLogic.tax(cstr(chrShipState), clng(subtotal))

'   Calculate the new total.
Total = subtotal + shipping + tax

'   Build a SQL statement to update the basket data
sql = "execute sp_UpdateBasket " & _
    idBasket & ", " & _
    TotalQuantity & ", " & _
    SubTotal & ", " & _
    Shipping & ", " & _
    intFreeShipping & ", " & _
    Tax & ", " & _
    Total & ", 1"

'   Execute the SQL statement
set rsOrderUpdate = dbOrderUpdate.execute(sql)

'   Send the user back to the order detail
'   page
```

```
Response.Redirect "OrderDetail.asp?idOrder=" & idOrder & _
              "&idShopper=" & idShopper

%>
```

Now let's take a look at our manager pages in action. Figure 15.9 shows the manager menu with the addition of the free shipping management. Now click that link.

FIGURE 15.9:

Manager menu

Figure 15.10 shows the free shipping management page. There are only two fields for setting the next campaign dates.

FIGURE 15.10:

Free shipping management

Figure 15.11 shows the campaign dates updated to reflect a new campaign period.

FIGURE 15.11:

Free shipping campaign update

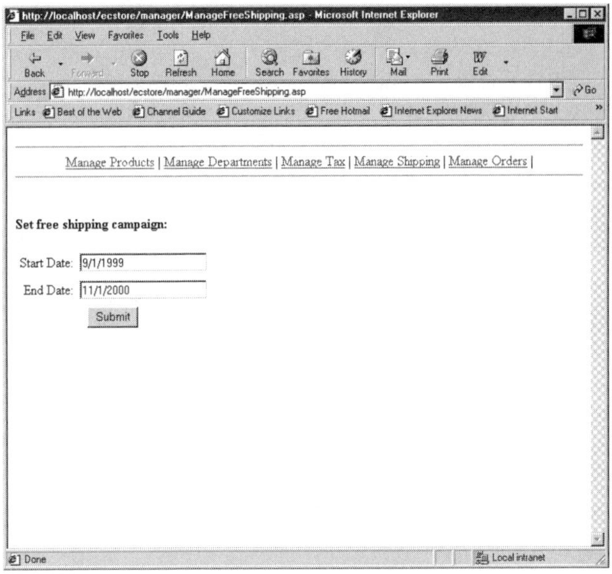

Summary

That does it for managing sales promotions in the store. We just scratched the service of what options we can build in for promoting special prices and promotions. There are many other ideas, including strategies such as providing a complete sale department with all items on sale, quantity discounts for purchases, and much more.

In Part V we will explore Microsoft's Site Server commerce tools. These tools provide many different options for building robust and feature-rich stores.

PART V

Advanced Topics

In the last part of our book we are going to explore several advanced topics. In Chapters 16 and 17 we'll take a look at Microsoft's Site Server 3, Commerce Edition, product. This tool is utilized to develop advanced e-commerce solutions.

In Chapter 18 we'll explore approaches to implementing the best practices and superscaling e-commerce sites.

CHAPTER
SIXTEEN

16

Introducing Site Server 3, Commerce Edition

- Core Site Server Components

- Commerce Tools Overview

- Installation

- Starter Stores Overview

In Parts II, III, and IV we explored building our own commerce store from scratch, using VBScript-based Active Server Pages together with Microsoft SQL Server. This served to show how to build the fundamentals of an e-commerce store.

The next level in development with Microsoft tools is based on the Microsoft Site Server platform. The first thing to understand about Site Server is that it is a complete platform for building community, content, and commerce-based sites. The core tool set is Microsoft Site Server. But the Commerce tools that are found in Site Server, Commerce Edition, are key components. These are two different products. For more information on each, visit `http://www.microsoft.com/siteserver`.

In Part V we are not going to go into great depth on all of the tools provided in Site Server. But what we *will* explore are the core Commerce components for building storefronts.

The good news is that all of the fundamentals we have seen in the last three parts apply to the code base we will see in the Commerce tool set. The stores built-in Site Server are based on the SQL Server, IIS/ASP platform.

> **NOTE**
> In this chapter we are going to provide a high-level overview of all the key features of the Commerce components. If it all seems a bit much, be patient. In the next chapter we will explore a Commerce Server starter store that will put all of the pieces into context.

Core Site Server Components

Site Server is a rich set of tools for building great Web sites on the Windows NT platform. The synergy is the combination of these tools to build sites that engage the consumer.

Requirements

The minimal server architecture requirements for installing Site Server are simply a Windows NT server with SQL Server running on it, with the minimum requirements for installing Windows NT and enough drive space for Site Server.

The realistic requirements for the server architecture in a production environment are a Windows NT server for Site Server only and SQL Server on a different Windows NT server. Table 16.1 shows the key requirements for installation.

TABLE 16.1:   Site Server 3, Commerce Edition, Minimum Installation Requirements

Requirement	Description
Microsoft Windows NT Server 4	The base operating system requirement. At least 128 megabytes of RAM should be dedicated to NT itself. An additional 128 MB of RAM as a minimum should be installed for Site Server.
Microsoft Windows NT Server Service Pack 3 or higher	All of the latest service packs should be installed.
Microsoft Windows NT Server 4 Option Pack	Provides the upgraded IIS services from the base services provided in the Windows NT 4.0 install.
1 GB required to install services	It is recommended that a minimum of 5 Gigabytes be available for installation, content files, etc.
Microsoft Internet Explorer 4.01	Provides key DLL updates for use on the system.
Microsoft SQL Server, or ODBC-compliant database	Note that for SQL Server, all of the latest service packs should be installed.

> **NOTE**   There are also a number of service packs available for Site Server 3 that fix various problems with Site Server (in particular, they allow the use of Microsoft SQL Server 7 as a back end database). It is highly recommended that they be installed as well.

For development, all of the same tools we have been utilizing throughout this book will be utilized for developing commerce stores. Visual Studio will be utilized for editing the store ASP pages. And, the SQL tools will still be utilized for managing the database. Of course, there are other tools provided with Site Server for development.

> **WARNING**   Windows 2000 requires a *minimum* of Site Server 3.0 Service Pack 3 to install and operate successfully. You should take care to read the instructions provided with Service Pack 3 before installing onto this platform.

Core Components

There are six core components in the Site Server base edition. These provide a rich development environment for developing the site that will *surround* your commerce site.

Table 16.2 overviews each of the components.

TABLE 16.2: Site Server 3 Core Components

Component	Description
Publishing	Used to manage the publishing process on your site and deploy content to local and remote servers. There are three key tools utilized to manage the publishing process. Content Management is an application used by content authors, editors, and site administrators to submit, tag, approve, and publish content on a single Web server. The second tool is the Tag Tool, which is a stand-alone application you can use to tag your HTML documents. The tags help you identify a document according to its author, title, submit date, or other information. The final tool is Content Deployment, which stages and deploys content such as Web pages, documents, Web server settings, file security information, and Java and COM applets, among directories and servers. Combined with these are powerful tools for managing and publishing content.
Search	Used to gather and index information and create keyword search capabilities on your site. With these keyword search capabilities, site visitors can use highly targeted search queries to find and retrieve the specific information they need. A key feature of Search is the ability to integrate it with the Tag Tool, Personalization & Membership, Push, and the Knowledge Manager. Note: This tool can be used in lieu of Index Server supplied with IIS and provides many more rich features.
Personalization & Membership	Used for any Internet or intranet site to build and manage customer relationships, manage memberships, direct personalized information to individual users, understand customer usage patterns, build community among members, and control access to application content and user information. Tools include direct mail, LDAP storage of membership information, personalization rules, site vocabulary for user and content attributes, and much more. P&M deserves a whole book in itself. Note that the Trey Research sample store provided with Site Server demonstrates how to integrate commerce with Personalization & Membership.

Continued on next page

TABLE 16.2 CONTINUED: Site Server 3 Core Components

Component	Description
Push	Used to automate the process of information delivery using channels. Provides users with channels, to which they can subscribe, that deliver specific content of interest. Updated information is then periodically *pushed* or delivered to the user's Web browser on their desktop. This concept was made very popular with PointCast several years ago but has since lost some of its buzz. For very specific content functions, this functionality can be powerful.
Knowledge Manager	Enables site visitors to create briefs or use shared briefs on topics of interest, and receive updates by e-mail or by channel, as well as browse or search the intranet and subscribe to channels. Knowledge Manager is based on four features of Site Server: Search, Personalization & Membership, Push, and the Tag Tool. It uses an Access 97 database to store briefs and sections of briefs.
Analysis	Used to analyze content and usage of your site. Analyzes the structure of your site, tracks its contents, manages its links, maintains local and remote sites, and monitors site usage. It is important to note that part of this tool set can be used to generate standard Web reports for visitors, top pages, browser types, etc. This is similar to other tools on the market, such as WebTrends.

These tools are vast and complex and can greatly enhance a Web site. They can also be utilized on the intranet/extranet side of the store for providing a rich management interface.

Commerce Edition Components

The Commerce Server edition adds key components to the mix for our site. One of these is the core component for store building. Table 16.3 overviews each.

TABLE 16.3: Site Server 3.0 Core Components

Component	Description
Advertising server	The advertising server provides banner ad management functions for your Web site. It has two core components, the Ad Manager and the Ad Server. The Ad Server handles all of the logic behind serving ads and handling ad campaigns. The Ad Manager is a series of ASP pages for managing the advertising campaigns.
Commerce server	Commerce Server consists of seven sets of different components for building and managing storefronts, including both business-to-business and business-to-consumer sites.

As you can see, Site Server is a rich set of tools for building complex intranet and Internet sites. It goes well beyond commerce functionality. The primary idea to keep in mind is that it is an integrated tool set that can be utilized to enhance and build all kinds of Web sites.

Commerce Tools Overview

Now let's dig further into the guts of the commerce tool set. As mentioned, there are seven core functions that make up the commerce functionality. Table 16.4 reviews each.

TABLE 16.4: Commerce Server Tools

Tools	Description
Site Builder Wizard	Provides a wizard interface with a step-by-step approach to creating a Commerce Server site. The wizard removes the complexity of database schema editing, scripting, and HTML coding and can dramatically reduce site development time. You can customize your site using code examples from the Commerce Server sample sites.
Site manager pages	Each Commerce Server site created by the Site Builder Wizard has a set of manager pages that make it easy to manage data in the store. This is similar to the manager pages created in Part III.
Commerce Server objects	These COM objects provide a broad range of functionality for the creation of online commerce sites, including shopper management, data validation, catalog display, and so on. These are core tools utilized in the development of a Commerce-Server-based site.
Order processing pipeline	The pipeline consists of a set of COM objects that process a customer's order by passing information from component to component in an organized way. The pipeline provides an easy plug-and-play framework for adding and modifying core functionality in the store, including sales, shipping, tax, etc.
Commerce Interchange	The Interchange consists of separate transmit and receive pipelines used for passing business objects (such as purchase orders, ship notices, receipts, and so on) from one application to another over a local area network (LAN), wide area network (WAN), Electronic Document Interchange (EDI), value-added network (VAN), or the Internet.

Continued on next page

TABLE 16.4 CONTINUED: Commerce Server Tools

Tools	Description
Microsoft Wallet	The Microsoft Wallet consists of client-side Payment and Address Selectors and protected storage. The Payment Selector provides for the entry, secure storage, and use of credit cards and other online payment methods. The Address Selector provides for the entry, storage, and use of address information.
Buy Now	A shopper can click an ad on any Web page and launch the Buy Now wizard, which facilitates impulse buying. The shopper can purchase the featured product from a Commerce Server site without leaving the current Web page. The idea is to buy a product (such as a subscription) quickly, from different locations that needn't be specifically in the store context.

WARNING   Using the Site Builder wizard can be good for building simple stores. It should be used only for sites that have simple functionality requirements and where there are no issues of scalability.

The components we are going to be most interested in are the commerce server objects, order processing pipeline, and to some extent the site manager pages. They provide the foundation that is utilized in the ASP page code and interfacing with the database. The Site Builder wizard, in effect, builds a store from a template. This store will have functionality similar to what we built in Parts II through IV. But don't be fooled, this is generated code that still will have to be modified to meet your store needs. And it doesn't necessarily follow best practices implementation.

Let's take a closer look at the core tools mentioned.

NOTE   Internet Information Server 4 includes Microsoft Transaction Server (MTS). MTS defines a programming model for COM components that run in the MTS environment, and Commerce Server sites are structured according to the MTS programming model. This structure enables Commerce Server sites to implement transactional order processing, in which an order that fails at some point in the pipeline can be rolled back without commitment of the data.

Commerce Server Objects

The commerce server objects provide an extensive set of tools for managing features in our site. This series of ActiveX COM objects extends the base objects provided in ASP. Many of these we will see in action when we review a sample site in Chapter 17, "Overview of a Site Server 3 Starter Store." Table 16.5 outlines each of these objects.

TABLE 16.5: Commerce Server Objects Overview

Object	Description
AdminFile	Provides access to server-side files.
Adminsite	Localizes information about a Commerce Server site, including data source names (DSNs), queries, and the path to the pipeline configuration file, within a single object. This makes changing the configuration of the location of these recourses easier for management of our store. It helps to abstract away the hardware layer from our store.
AdminWebServer	Provides access to read-only properties of the site.
ConfigurationCacheHelper	Caches a pipeline configuration in memory, helping to reduce the performance penalty associated with accessing a pipeline configuration (.pcf) on disk. That way, the pipeline is not read from disk every time we need to run it for our store.
DataFunctions	Supports a collection of functions that validate the format of data for database storage or for processing by the pipeline. These are very helpful in dealing with data such as money, dates, numbers, and conversions. Also useful for handling international formatting.
DBStorage	Supports mapping Dictionary and SimpleList objects to and from a database, primarily for the storage of receipt and order information. These tools can be useful in addition to working directly with Active Data Objects, but they do require more overhead and memory utilization to run the store.
Dictionary	Provides for the in-memory storage of name/value pairs. This is especially useful for tracking data like addresses, payment data, order items, etc.
FileDocument	Supports saving and restoring information contained in any persistable object to and from disk. This is similar to the file objects provided in ASP.
MessageManager	Stores error messages in multiple languages that the OPP components use to describe error conditions. This makes it easier to scale a site to multiple languages and contexts.

Continued on next page

TABLE 16.5 CONTINUED: Commerce Server Objects Overview

Object	Description
MicroPipe	Enables embedding and running a single pipeline component on an ASP page without requiring a pipeline and a .pcf file. For example, we might want to run a shipping pipe to estimate tax in the basket.
MtsPipeline	Loads and executes a pipeline configuration. This will do it in a transacted format to ensure all steps are successful. If they are not, they will be rolled back. This object is registered under MTS as "transactions not required."
MtsTxPipeline	Loads and executes a pipeline configuration. This object is registered under MTS as "transactions required."
OrderForm	Supports the in-memory storage of customer and purchase information for the current shopping session.
Page	Simplifies the layout of HTML pages and the interaction between these pages and the data sources used by the site. Used properly, this tool can help to manage page references and data retrieval.
Predictor	Enables intelligent cross-sell by suggesting other items that a customer might be interested in.
SimpleDBDS	Maps an Active Directory Service (ADS) to a standard database table, so that a Commerce Server site can maintain customer information using Personalization & Membership while retaining a pre-existing database.
SimpleList	Provides the ability to manage a general-purpose list of variants. A good example would be attributes of a product.
StandardSManager	Facilitates the creation, deletion, and retrieval of shopper IDs.

How much you choose to use these commerce objects is up to you. We saw in the first part of the book that they are not required to build a successful e-commerce solution. But these tools can be very helpful in speeding up site development and providing robust, well tested, and out-of-the-box functionality for your e-commerce store.

Tools such as the OrderForm, Predictor, MessageManager, DataFunctions, MTSPipeline, and MTSTxPipeLine would take considerable development to replace in Visual Basic or Visual C++. The rest of the objects can provide a framework for facilitating store development.

Let's next focus on use of the Dictionary Object. This plays a central role in the starter store provided with Site Server. Table 16.6 outlines the uses of the dictionary object. Note that many of these relate to the use of the pipeline, which is defined in the next section.

TABLE 16.6: Dictionary Object Use

Object	Utilization
PipeContext	Contains key values needed by pipeline components. These values are passed through to the pipeline.
QueryMap	Contains SQL query descriptions that may be used by various objects.
Site	Provides access to the Commerce Server site configuration stored in the Site.csc file. This contains basic configuration data about the store, such as the DSN for accessing the database, etc.

The dictionary easily tracks and references data that our store utilizes. This data can then be easily changed without changing the pipeline.

In the sample tax and shipping code we created earlier in the book, we had to set a DSN in our Visual Basic code. If that changed, we would have to recompile the code and deploy it. By abstracting key data in these dictionary objects, we can easily make changes to a file DSN name or other key values without changing the pipeline.

The OrderForm object, which constitutes the link between the Web site and the order processing pipeline, is designed to contain all the information necessary to process a purchase over the Web, including shopper, shipping, tax, and item price information.

We will see in the next chapter that the OrderForm object is utilized extensively throughout the shopping process. The OrderForm stores the central shopper data, and also holds the data about items (products) that have been added to the shopper's basket. Table 16.7 shows the methods for the OrderForm object.

TABLE 16.7:   OrderForm Object Methods

Method	Description
AddItem	Adds an item (product) to the OrderForm
ClearOrderForm	Empties the OrderForm
ClearItems	Clears the items collection from the OrderForm

These tools make it easy to add an item to the order form and manage the order form. We will see the OrderForm in action in the next chapter. Now let's take a look at the order processing pipeline.

Order Processing Pipeline

The order processing pipeline is the central component in the Commerce Server architecture. It provides a way to *componentize* the processing steps of shopping into discrete stages.

The developer can plug components into the pipeline and then request the pipeline to run with each of the components executing. As the pipeline runs through stages, the appropriate code execution will take place. Example stages would include tax calculations, shipping calculations, etc.

Each stage in a pipeline consists of zero or more components, and each of these components is run in sequence. A component is a Component Object Model (COM) object that is designed to perform some operation on the order form that is used in the shopping process. In many cases, the scope of this operation is quite small. For example, the DefaultShipping component, which is included in the shipping stage, makes sure that a default shipping cost of 0 is set on the order form. Each pipeline interacts with the data on the order form. Figure 16.1 shows the relationship between the pipelines and the order form.

FIGURE 16.1:

Pipeline and order form interaction

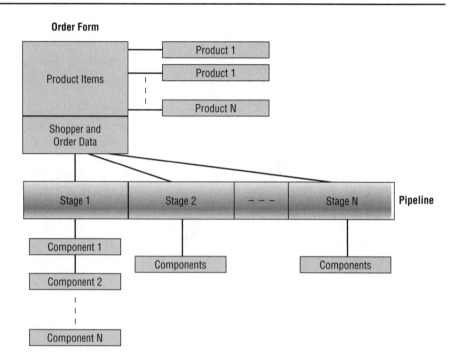

There are three primary pipelines used in the business-to-consumer shopping process. Each plays an integral role at various steps in the shopping process.

The first is the Product pipeline. The Product pipeline runs components that compute price and discount information on individual products. This pipeline is often used to compute information that is displayed on the Product.asp page. Table 16.8 reviews each of the stages in the Product pipeline.

TABLE 16.8: Product Pipeline Stages

Stage	Description
Product Info	The Product Info stage contains components that retrieve product information about the items in the site database.
Shopper Information	The Shopper Information stage adds information about the customer to the order form.

Continued on next page

TABLE 16.8 CONTINUED: Product Pipeline Stages

Stage	Description
Item Price	The Item Price stage contains components that set the standard or "regular" price for each item in the items list and that verify that this value has been set.
Item Adjust Price	The Item Adjust Price stage contains components that initialize the "current" price name/value pair. Typically the price is adjusted for sales or promotions.
Inventory	This stage verifies that every item ordered is in stock.

The Plan pipeline consists of 14 stages. These stages consist of components that verify the integrity of the order form for the specified shopper. For example, if the *items list* in an order form contains no items, then the RequiredProdInfo component in the Product Info stage fails. This pipeline ensures that everything up to the payment step is complete and in order. Table 16.9 outlines the 14 stages.

TABLE 16.9: Plan Pipeline Stages

Stage	Description
Product Info	Same as the product pipeline.
Merchant Information	The Merchant Information stage can retrieve static merchant data and write the data to the order form.
Shopper Information	The Shopper Information stage contains the DefaultShopperInfo component, which adds information about the customer to the order form.
Order Initialization	The Order Initialization stage sets initial order information on the order form and verifies that the order form contains an order ID.
Order Check	The Order Check stage verifies that the order can be processed. If necessary and possible, it alters the order so that it can be processed.
Item Price	Same as the Product Pipeline.
Item Adjust Price	Same as the Product Pipeline.
Order Adjust Price	The Order Adjust Price stage contains components that set the adjusted price of each item. This stage can use items other than those that are adjusted to update the order. This stage can use information used by the Item Price Adjust stage, as well as other information about the order.

Continued on next page

TABLE 16.9 CONTINUED: Plan Pipeline Stages

Stage	Description
Order Subtotal	The Order Subtotal stage calculates the subtotal for an order and stores the resulting value in the OrderForm.
Shipping	This stage calculates the total shipping charge for the order.
Handling	This stage calculates the total handling charge for the order.
Tax	This stage computes the sales tax for each item on the order, and the sum of tax for the entire order.
Order Total	This stage sums the subtotal (less any discount), tax, shipping, and handling values and writes the total to the order form.
Inventory	This stage verifies that every item ordered is in stock.

Our last pipeline is the Purchase pipeline, which consists of three stages. These stages use components that accept the final purchase of an order form, write an order to database storage, and, optionally, finalize a receipt and write the contents of the order form to the receipt database.

The Purchase pipeline can be run once you have run an order form successfully through the Plan pipeline, and have confirmed the customer's desire to finalize a purchase.

Because Purchase pipeline components write to a database, a Purchase pipeline is often a transacted pipeline using Microsoft Transaction Server. Table 16.10 reviews the stages of the Purchase pipeline.

TABLE 16.10:   Purchase Pipeline Stages

Stage	Description
Purchase Check	The Purchase Check stage is used to verify that the address and credit card information that the customer has provided meets certain validation criteria.
Payment	The Payment stage is used to approve credit card payments. This stage can be used with such third-party tools as CyberCash.
Accept	This stage handles the completed order, including initiating order tracking, generating purchase orders, and inventory.

There are also two business-to-business purchasing process pipelines. These include the Corporate Purchasing Plan and the Corporate Purchasing Submit pipelines.

As mentioned above, each stage can utilize a series of components. For example, in the shipping stage we might use the DefaultShipping component to set the shipping price to 0. The Site Server documentation provides a complete list of components and the stages in which they can be utilized.

There is one key component to be aware of though. And that is the Scriptor component. The Scriptor component makes it possible to insert code modules into your pipeline. These modules are written using either VBScript or JavaScript. From within a Scriptor component, you can access the order form, pipe context information, create other objects, and even execute other pipelines. In addition, because the Scriptor component supports configuration parameters, the Scriptor component provides perhaps the easiest way to write custom components for the order processing pipeline (OPP). You will find this to be an invaluable tool when building complex pipeline processes. A good example would be writing a script that does the shipping calculations in our Wild Willie's CD store.

To work with the pipeline, Site Server includes a pipeline editor tool. This tool provides a graphical interface for working with each of the stages in the pipeline. Figure 16.2 shows a plan pipeline opened up in the editor.

We can edit each stage by adding and deleting components that run in the stage. These components in many cases have properties that we can set directly in the pipeline editor interface. Figure 16.3 shows the Fixed Shipping component dialog box.

FIGURE 16.2:

Pipeline Editor

FIGURE 16.3:

Fixed Shipping component

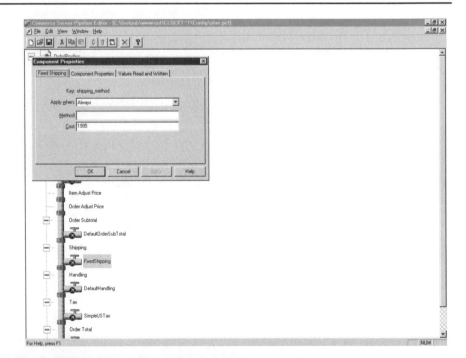

That does it for reviewing the core features of the Commerce tools. Now let's take a look at installing Site Server 3, Commerce Edition.

Installation

Installing Site Server, Commerce Edition, is a two-step process. First you must install the standard edition, then install the Commerce components. We are going to focus solely on installing the Commerce tools and not be concerned with the many other features of Site Server.

The first thing to be done is to complete all of the requisite installs to ensure our NT platform is ready for Site Server. The following items will need to be installed as a minimum:

1. Microsoft Windows NT Server version 4 and Service Pack 3. Windows NT Service Pack 3 is provided on the Windows NT 4.0 Option Pack compact disc.

2. Microsoft Internet Explorer version 4.01 or later. Internet Explorer is provided on the Windows NT 4.0 Option Pack compact disc.

3. Windows NT 4 Option Pack.

NOTE   When you install Microsoft Site Server 3 from its compact disc, the Setup program detects whether Windows NT Service Pack 3, Internet Explorer 4.01, and the Windows NT 4 Option Pack have been installed. If these applications are not present, Site Server Setup guides you through the process to install them.

For SQL Server, it is recommended that you install SQL Server 6.5 with Service Pack 4 or SQL Server 7. An evaluation copy of SQL Server is included on the Windows NT 4 Option Pack compact disc. SQL Server Service Pack 4 is included on the Site Server 3 compact disc.

You have many choices to make when installing Site Server. Figures 16.4 and 16.5 show two of the key opening screens for the install.

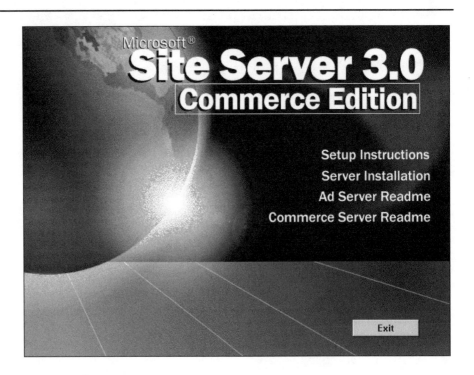

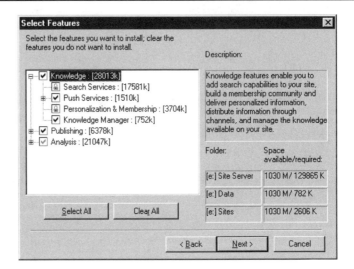

From the options, choose the features that you are interested in having installed. None are explicitly required to install the Commerce server tools, but you will have to ensure that at least some of the base edition is installed. Otherwise, the Commerce tools will not install.

Once you have the base edition installed, you are ready to install the Commerce Edition tools. Specifically, for the installation of the Commerce Server sample stores you will need to create a device (or more than one device) to hold the data. You can create one device for all with separate databases or multiple devices. And, you will need either system-level or file DSNs to point to each database for each sample store you are going to install.

As with the base edition, you will have options for what you install in the Commerce tools. Figure 16.6 shows the initial set of install options. Figure 16.7 shows the selection screen for *custom* install.

FIGURE 16.6:

Site Server, Commerce
Edition, install options

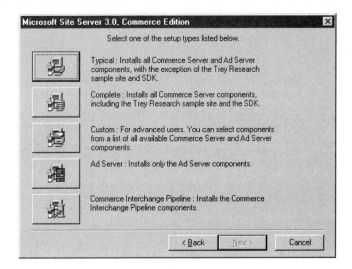

FIGURE 16.7:

Site Server, Commerce Edition, custom install options

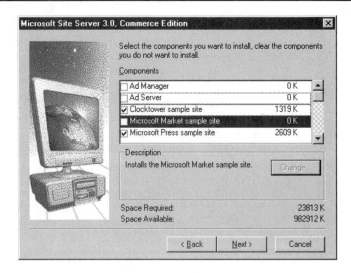

When you get to the database setup stage of the Commerce install, you will be asked to select DSN settings to connect the starter stores to your SQL Server database. Figure 16.8 shows the dialog box indicating the list of starter stores you have selected.

FIGURE 16.8:

Starter store database settings dialog box

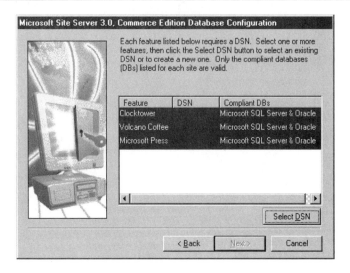

Select one of the stores and then click on the "Select DSN" button. Figure 16.9 shows the dialog box listing the current set of DSNs.

FIGURE 16.9:

DSN listing

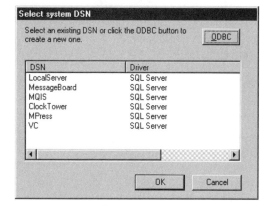

Select the appropriate DSN and you will then be prompted with one more dialog box to set the login ID and password. Figure 16.10 shows the dialog box.

FIGURE 16.10:

Setting the login ID and password

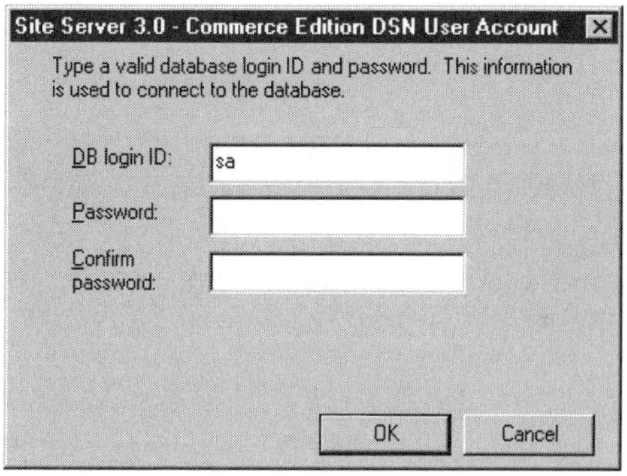

Complete the install and you are ready to begin browsing through the starter stores you selected. Each starter store represents a little different angle on utilizing the Commerce objects, OrderForm and pipeline. To access the starter stores and their settings, you will need to go to the Administration tools and launch the Site Server Administrator, which uses the Microsoft Management Console (MMC). Figure 16.11 shows the MMC with the Commerce Host Administration snap-in.

FIGURE 16.11:

Site Server Commerce Host
Administration

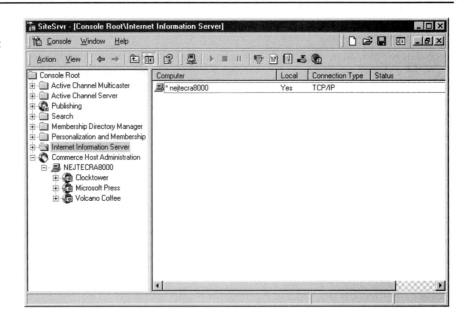

You can select one of the stores and in the panel on the right the link to the shopper and the manager will appear. Right click on either and select, then select Browse to begin working through each sample store.

The Site Server documentation provides detailed steps for installing features such as Ad Server, Personalization and Membership, Analysis, etc. These documents should be referred to in detail to have a successful install. Visit http://support.microsoft.com/support/siteserver for further detailed and updated information on service packs and installation issues.

Starter Stores Overview

There are five sample stores provided with Site Server. Each has its own unique characteristics and servers to demonstrate different techniques for utilizing Site Server.

In addition to these starter stores provided in the package, you can download several other customizable starter sites. See the Site Server documentation for information on where to get these sites. And, as we will review in Chapter 18, you can utilize the VC Turbo and VC Rocket sample sites to work on super-scaling your e-commerce stores.

Clock Tower

The Clock Tower site is a simple seller of clocks. It is also the most basic of the starter stores and provides a good demonstration of the base commerce functionality.

The database behind the site is very simple. There is one level for departments and each product is assigned to a department. The product data is very simple and does not contain any attributes (like size, color, etc.). The HTML utilization in the site will be compatible with almost any browser and any monitor resolution.

This store does require the use of cookies. The shopper's ID is generated by the StandardSManager component and stored as a cookie on the user's system. The shopper is not *remembered* between visits.

Volcano Coffee

This store provides an example of selling all kinds of coffee-related products. This site is unique in that it requires the customer to register before completing a purchase. Through this registration process the shopper is remembered.

> **WARNING** Requiring shoppers to register before they begin shopping can be a real turnoff for impulse shopping and purchasing. Standard industry practice seldom requires registration until after the initial purchase.

Volcano coffee is a good site to review for a number of key promotional features. It supports price promotions for sales and multiple product purchases, cross-sell promotions, and up-sell promotions.

There are also some interesting navigation features to allow the shopper to easily move from product to product as well as execute a product search. Other key features include support for product attributes and monogramming of certain products.

Two key Commerce Server features are also demonstrated in this store. To check out, you have the option of using the Microsoft Wallet. You can also use the Buy Now feature.

Microsoft Market

The Microsoft Market sample site is a business-to-business site demonstrating internal corporate purchasing, and is implemented using the Commerce Interchange Pipeline (CIP).

NOTE   This Commerce Server 3 sample site is based on the real Microsoft corporate purchasing site. Microsoft put 250,000 transactions, involving $1.6 billion of orders, through MS Market in its first year; they claim to have saved $35 million through implementing Site Server, Commerce Edition.

The application enables employees to order administrative goods and office supplies from multiple vendors in multiple countries. The employees order the supplies in a browser. The site saves employees time by providing direct links to preferred vendor catalogs, checking signature authority levels, validating account and cost center coding, and automatically supplying information in purchase order forms wherever possible.

The buyers are able to easily manage approvals, inventory, vendors, and the overall purchasing process. This saves time and money and provides faster response.

The Microsoft Market is an excellent demonstration of using the Commerce Interchange Pipeline (CIP) to receive and transmit pipelines, multi-language support, and much more. There is a lot to the Microsoft Market site that should be explored if you are going to do complex intranet transactions. Even if it is not a purchasing system, many of the demonstration features could be utilized in many different contexts.

Microsoft Press

The Microsoft Press site demonstrates the selling of books online. This site in particular demonstrates the use of the Predictor tool for providing intelligent cross-sell features.

Microsoft Press demonstrates some good techniques for caching frequently-read data so that we are not continually querying the database for common data. The interface to the store also provides some different techniques for browsing the catalog of products.

This site is particularly useful if you are developing catalog style sites that have a high level of transactions. Note that the site does require a member login.

Trey Research

Trey Research sells online content subscriptions. In particular, it is a good demonstration of how to integrate Personalization and Membership with a commerce store.

Once a new subscriber has been validated, they then have access to the content they have purchased. The user must log in through Membership and be validated. Then Personalization is utilized, based upon their member profile, to target the content they have purchased.

Trey Research presents an interesting and complex model for site security at the directory level with Membership and Personalization based on profile and the ability to purchase items. Note that the site utilizes Microsoft Access for some database base functionality and should be used only as a demonstration for larger scale sites.

Summary

Site Server provides a rich set of tools for building complex sites. The Commerce Server components provide extensive functionality for creating feature-rich stores with robust functionality. They can provide the next level of development for your e-commerce efforts.

In Chapter 17, "Overview of a Site Server 3 Starter Store," we are going to explore the Clock Tower sample site to get a feel for how the core features of the database, order form, and pipeline interact.

CHAPTER
SEVENTEEN

Overview of a Site Server 3 Starter Store

- Overview

- Key Pages

- SQL Database

- Use of Commerce Objects

- Pipeline Utilization

We are going to take a look at the Clock Tower sample store installed with Site Server, Commerce Edition. This store provides an excellent introductory sample of how a commerce store works.

Overview

The Clock Tower store sells clocks. The basic structure of the site is simple department and product links. Figure 17.1 shows the home page of the store.

FIGURE 17.1:

Clock Tower home page

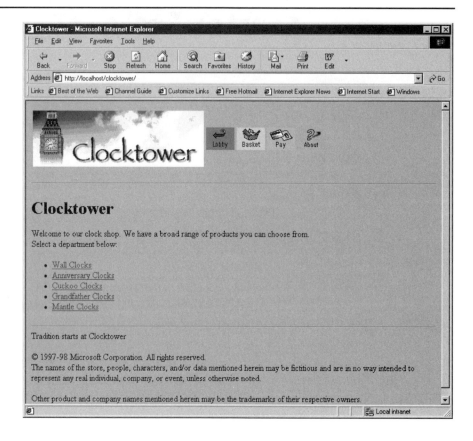

The navigation is done on the top right with simple button links. The bottom half of the page is used for the primary content. The checkout process requires a shipping and billing address form and a payment page.

The store also has a store manager. The manager provides functions for managing products and departments, editing the pipelines in a Web interface, closing the store, and reloading (or resetting) a store. Figure 17.2 shows the manager interface.

FIGURE 17.2:

Clock Tower manager home page

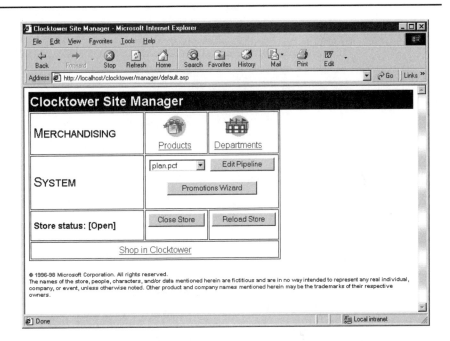

Navigating through both interfaces is quite easy. There are no frills, such as up-sell, cross-sell, sales, etc., in this particular store, although many such sophisticated facilities exist within the Site Server, Commerce Edition, architecture.

Key Pages

As with the sample store created earlier in the book, the primary code functionality is encapsulated on the various pages on the Web site. This will be your guide to finding appropriate capabilities within the store.

The code is separated into two sections between the store interface and the management interface. Let's first take a look at the shopping interface pages. Table 17.1 reviews each page.

TABLE 17.1: Shopping Interface

Page	Description
about.asp	Provides information about the store.
basket.asp	Displays the shopping basket contents.
confirmed.asp	Provides a confirmation page after a placed order.
default.asp	Home page for the store. Lists the departments.
dept.asp	Shows a listing of products in a department.
global.asa	Global application file. It sets up the query maps for interfacing with the database, opens the site configuration file, and creates objects for the shopper manager and the database functions.
orderform.asp	Provides a form for filling in the shipping and billing address information.
product.asp	Displays the product data.
purchase.asp	Provides a form for filling in the credit card data.
xt_orderform_additem.asp	Manages adding an item into the shopping basket and consequently onto the order form.
xt_orderform_clearitems.asp	Clears all items added to the order form.
xt_orderform_delitem.asp	Deletes an item from the order form.
xt_orderform_editquantities.asp	Updates quantities of items added to the order form.
xt_orderform_prepare.asp	Prepares an order for purchase by retrieving the shipping and billing address data.

Continued on next page

TABLE 17.1 CONTINUED: Shopping Interface

Page	Description
xt_orderform_purchase.asp	Completes the purchase of an order.
error.asp (include)	Writes out an error encountered in the shopping process.
footer.asp (include)	Closes out the page with copyright information and closing tags.
header.asp (include)	Sets up the navigation header for the store.
shop.asp (include)	Included on each page where shopping will take place. It checks to see if a shopper record has been created. And, it handles creating the appropriate commerce objects for the shopping process.
util.asp (include)	Provides utility functions for calling the pipelines and interfacing with the order form.

Key pages to review in terms of understanding how the core commerce components are utilized include shop.asp, util.asp, and all of the XT_ pages.

For the store manager, there are a number of pages that make up the department and product management pages. Note that there are no order management pages at all. Table 17.2 outlines each of the pages.

TABLE 17.2: Management Interface

Page	Description
default.asp	Manager menu page.
dept_delete.asp	Confirmation page for deleting a department from the database.
dept_edit.asp	Provides a form for editing a department.
dept_list.asp	Lists the departments in the database.
dept_new.asp	Provides a form for adding a new department.
product_delete.asp	Confirmation page for deleting a product from the database.
product_edit.asp	Provides a form for editing a product.
product_list.asp	Lists all products in the database.

Continued on next page

TABLE 17.2 CONTINUED: Management Interface

Page	Description
product_new.asp	Provides a form for adding a new product.
xt_data_add_update.asp	Provides an all-in-one script page for adding and updating product and department data.
xt_data_delete.asp	Performs a product or department delete from the database.
copyright.asp (include)	Copyright include for the manager.
error.asp (include)	Error handling page for the store manager.
list.asp (include)	Provides list management functionality for departments and products.
list_column.asp (include)	Provides the column headers based on the type of listing.
list_no_rows.asp (include)	Include when no rows are returned for a listing.
list_row.asp (include)	Shows the row data in a product or department listing.
manager.asp (include)	Include for default manager settings on each page. Database connections, dictionary objects, and constants are set on this page.
mgmt_footer.asp (include)	Footer for the management pages which includes navigation.
mgmt_header.asp (include)	Opening tags for the management pages.
siteutil.asp (include)	Utility functions for opening and closing the site, getting a list of pipelines for editing, and error handling.

The store manager is primarily straight ASP and SQL coding. There is very little use of the commerce tools for managing the products. A thorough review is not provided here since the concepts are laid out in Part III.

SQL Database

The database behind the Clock Tower store is fairly simple. There are only three tables that make up the database structure, and the SQL code is all contained in the ASP pages and not in stored procedures.

The first table is for storing the shopping basket. Table 17.3 outlines the fields in the table.

TABLE 17.3: clocktower_basket

Field	DataType	Description
shopper_id	varchar	Stores the shopper ID. It is a Globally Unique Identifier (GUID) generated by Site Server.
date_changed	datetime	Stores the date the last time the basket was changed.
marshalled_order	image	Stores the order form data in a binary format.

The only field to be aware of is `marshalled_order`. The `marshalled_order` contains the OrderForm data serialized into an encoded binary format. The DBStorage object is the component to utilize when reading and writing from this field.

The next table is for storing the department data. Table 17.4 outlines the fields.

TABLE 17.4: clocktower_dept

Field	DataType	Description
dept_id	int	Stores a unique identifier for the department
dept_name	varchar	Stores the department name
dept_description	varchar	Stores the department description

Unlike the sample database in Wild Willie's CDs, there is no pointer to an image for the department here. But, other than that, it is pretty similar.

The final table is for storing the product data. Table 17.5 outlines the fields in the table.

TABLE 17.5:   clocktower_product

Field	DataType	Description
sku	Varchar	Stores the product ID or SKU. Note they should all be unique.
name	Varchar	Stores the name of the product.
dept_id	int	Stores the department ID of the department the product is assigned to.
description	Text	Stores the product description.
manufacturer	Varchar	Stores the product manufacturer.
list_price	Int	Stores the product price.
image_file	Varchar	Name of the image file for the product.
image_width	Int	Width of the product image.
image_height	int	Height of the product image.

All of the fields are fairly standard. Note that the image width and height are stored in the database so that the width and height value in the Image tag can be set when the product page is built.

Use of Commerce Objects

Utilization of the commerce objects in Clock Tower is key to its functionality. We will look at snippets of code illustrating how to utilize these objects. The source code for Clock Tower is provided with the Site Server 3, Commerce Edition, CD.

Dictionary

The first object is the dictionary object. This is utilized for storing name value pairs of various data. In the global.asa file, the dictionary object is utilized to store product queries.

Listing 17.1 shows the use of the dictionary in the global.asa.

LISTING 17.1   **Dictionary Code**

```
' Create the Dictionary Object
Set MSCSQueryMap = _
    Server.CreateObject("Commerce.Dictionary")

' Create the Dictionary Object
Set MSCSQueryMap.products = _
    Server.CreateObject("Commerce.Dictionary")

' Create the query
MSCSQueryMap.products.SQLCommand = "select * " & _
    "from product where idProduct = ?"

' Create the Dictionary Object
Set MSCSQueryMap.departments = _
    Server.CreateObject("Commerce.Dictionary")

' Create the query
MSCSQueryMap.departments.SQLCommand = "select * " & _
    "from department where idDepartment = ?"
```

In this case we are creating a master MSCSQueryMap dictionary object. We then create a dictionary entry in MSCSQueryMap that actually points to a new dictionary, *products*. An entry is added into that dictionary that stores a query to retrieve product data by ID. That query can be read in the pipeline to retrieve product information. A second dictionary entry in MSCSQueryMap, *departments*, is created. Likewise, that dictionary will contain a series of queries for retrieving product data. Note that the ? in the queries will be replaced with parameter values.

MessageManager

Next we move to the message manager. Remember this is the object that stores all of the error messages for the site. Typically this is also set up and created in the global.asa file.

Listing 17.2 shows sample code for utilizing the message manager.

LISTING 17.2   Message Manager Component

```
' Create the Message Manager Object
Set  MSCSMessageManager = _
      Server.CreateObject("Commerce.MessageManager")

' Set the language and Hex Code for the language.
Call MSCSMessageManager.AddLanguage("usa", &H0409)

' Set the default.
MSCSMessageManager.defaultLanguage = "usa"

' Add a bad shipping message
Call MSCSMessageManager.AddMessage("no_shipping", _
      "No shipping value has been calculated.")

Call MSCSMessageManager.AddMessage("no_tax", _
      "No shipping value has been calculated.")

Call MSCSMessageManager.AddMessage("no_items", _
      "There are no items in the order.")

Call MSCSMessageManager.AddMessage("pur_badpayment", _
      "There was a problem authorizing your credit."
```

The first action is to create an instance of the message manager object. Then we begin calling the AddLanguage and the AddMessage methods of the message manager object. The default language is set to *USA*. Then a series of error messages are set with default *calling* names, like no_shipping and no_tax. These error messages will be displayed if there is an error in processing the order. These errors are utilized if anything fails in the ordering process. It is critical to note these are different than error messages put directly into the ASP code.

StandardSManager

The StandardSManager sets up the shopper ID and manages the shopper data. Typically the object is first created in the Global.asa in the Application_OnStart subroutine. This is an application-level variable. Listing 17.3 shows the code that creates an instance of the object.

LISTING 17.3   **StandardSManager Creation**

```
' Create the shopper manager
Set  MSCSShopperManager = _
    Server.CreateObject("Commerce.StandardSManager")
Call MSCSShopperManager.InitManager(SiteName, "cookie")
```

Once the object is created, the InitManager method is called, indicating the name of the site (a variable) and that the shopper data should be stored as a cookie (instead of tracked on the URL).

The shopper manager is then typically called on each page in the store to manage the shopper data. Listing 17.4 shows a sample of how it is utilized.

LISTING 17.4   **Shopper ID Management**

```
' Get the shopper id
mscsShopperID = mscsPage.GetShopperId

' Check to see if a shopper id was returned.
if IsNull(mscsShopperID) then

    ' If not then in this session, we have a new shopper
    ' and need to create an ID for the new site visitor.
    mscsShopperID = MSCSShopperManager.CreateShopperID()

    ' Store the shopper id for later use
    Call mscsPage.PutShopperId(mscsShopperID)
end if
```

A check is done to see if a Shopper ID (GUID) has been created. If it has not, then the CreateShopperID method is called to create the GUID. And then the PutShopperID method is called to store the shopper ID. The PutShopperID method stores the shopper ID generated by CreateShopperID as a cookie on the user's hard disk, or as a URL argument.

Data Functions

The data functions provide tools for managing data in an e-commerce context. Typically, the DataFunctions object is created in the global.asa when the application starts.

Listing 17.5 shows the creation code in the global.asa. Note that the Locale property is set for English (US). This will determine how money is formatted, how error messages are handled, etc.

LISTING 17.5   **Data Functions Creation**

```
' Create the data functions object
Set MSCSDataFunctions = _
    Server.CreateObject("Commerce.DataFunctions")

' Set the local to US
MSCSDataFunctions.Locale = &H0409
```

In Listing 17.6, a sample is shown for formatting the money. A product price is retrieved from the database and the Money method of the data function is called to format it properly with a $, etc.

LISTING 17.6   **Using the Data Functions to Format Money**

```
<%=MSCSDataFunctions.Money(rsProduct("price").Value)%>
```

Typically the data functions are used for formatting money, based on locale, as well as for string manipulation, conversions, and other data-manipulation-related functions.

Page

The Page object supports a group of methods that perform data type conversion and value checking to data retrieved from the client browser, either from a URL query string or form.

Performing these operations on user input ensures that values retrieved through a page can be inserted without error into the site's database storage or passed to the order processing pipeline in an OrderForm object without generating pipeline or page syntax errors.

The page object is typically created on each page in the site, as shown in Listing 17.7. How it is utilized depends on what is happening on the page itself.

LISTING 17.7   Creation of the Page Object

```
' Create the page object
Set mscsPage    = Server.CreateObject("Commerce.Page")
```

In Listing 17.8, we create sample code that generates a URL to the xt_OrderForm_AddItem.asp using the Page object. It automatically creates parameters on the URL based on the parameters passed into the function.

LISTING 17.8   Page Object Sample Call

```
<!--  Create a URL to to the xt_orderform_additem.asp
      page  -->
<A HREF="<% = mscsPage.URL("xt_orderform_additem.asp", _
     "idProduct", rsProduct("idProduct").Value) %>">
```

Note that this URL would contain the appropriate shopper ID that used URL tracking instead of cookie tracking.

In Listing 17.9, a redirection is done to basket.asp. The URLShopperArgs method generates a series of query string arguments in an appropriate form for passing in a URL, and includes in the arguments the shopper ID if the StandardSManager has been initialized to URL mode. The URLShopperArgs method appropriately URL encodes the values passed in.

LISTING 17.9   Page Object Sample Call

```
' Built a URL to redirect to the basket page
Response.Redirect "basket.asp?" & mscsPage.URLShopperArgs()
```

There are a number of options for using the Page object to build URL data and retrieve information entered by the user. Explore the different options and see how they can best facilitate the shopping process in your store.

Order Form

The order form object is central to storing data about the order. It contains lists of name value pairs of data that must be stored in the right field names for the pipeline to successfully do its operations.

Listing 17.10 shows how an OrderForm is created and set up.

LISTING 17.10   OrderForm Retrieval and Creation

```
<%
    '  Continue if there is an error.
    on error resume next

    '  Retrieve the order form.
    set orderForm = orderFormStorage.GetData(null,_
                        mscsShopperID)

    ' Continue
    on error goto 0

    ' Check to see if an orderform was retrieved
    if IsEmpty(orderForm) then

        '  Create the OrderForm object
        set orderForm = _
        Server.CreateObject("Commerce.OrderForm")

        '  Set the shopper id for the OrderForm
        orderForm.shopper_id = mscsShopperID

    end if
%>
```

Throughout the sample stores you will find code like Listing 17.10. At some point in the shopping process we have to be able to create an OrderForm to store the shopping data. If we try to retrieve the OrderForm and get an error, then we know we need to create one for this shopping session. That is what the error code handling does for us.

In Listing 17.11, sample code is created to manage the storage of the Order-Form. As the shopper goes between pages and leaves and returns from the site, the OrderForm data needs to be retrieved.

LISTING 17.11   OrderForm Storage Management

```
<%
'  Create the database store object
set orderFormStorage = _
    Server.CreateObject("Commerce.DBStorage")

'  The InitStorage method is called to create the storage
'  of the OrderForm data.  The first parameter indicates
'  the table the OrderForm should be stored in.  The second
'  defines the shopper id, the third is the field for
'  storing the BLOB data and the last is the last date the
'  OrderForm was changed.
call orderFormStorage.InitStorage(_
    MSCSSite.DefaultConnectionString, _
    "basket", "shopper_id", _
    "Commerce.OrderForm", "marshalled_order", _
    "date_changed")

%>
```

The DBStorage object will store the OrderForm in the database. The InitStorage method takes care of setting up the store parameters. In Listing 17.12, the code is set for storing.

LISTING 17.12   Saving the OrderForm

```
<%

'  Check to see if the OrderForm was created
if created = 0 then

    '  Commit/Save the data to the database
    call orderFormStorage.CommitData(NULL, orderForm)

else
```

```
'   Insert the data into the database for the first
'   time.
call orderFormStorage.InsertData(NULL, orderForm)

end if
%>
```

When the OrderForm changes, we will need to save it. The first time we need to save the data, we will need to use the *InsertData* method of the DBStorage object. And, once saved, the *CommitData* method updates the data.

The use of the OrderForm in the order pages is fairly straightforward. Listing 17.13 shows sample code for placing data on the OrderForm.

LISTING 17.13   Sample OrderForm Usage

```
'   Retrieve the ship to city and place it on the
'   OrderForm
orderForm.ship_to_city = _
mscsPage.RequestString("ship_to_city", null, 1, 100)

'   Retrieve the ship to country and place it on the
'   OrderForm
orderForm.ship_to_country = _
mscsPage.RequestString("ship_to_country", null, 1, 100)
```

The city and country data is retrieved using the Page object. The data is defaulted to NULL and will be truncated to be between 1 and 100 characters. Note that with a simple = statement we set the value to the *ship_to_country* name on the form. Note that we still must store the OrderForm data outlined in the previous listings.

The OrderForm is also utilized for the display of data. Listing 17.14 shows sample code to display a shopping basket based on the OrderForm data.

LISTING 17.14   Basket Display

```
<%
'   Get the product items on the OrderForm.
set orderFormItems = mscsOrderForm.items
%>
```

```
<table BORDER="0">
        <!--  Show the header for the table.  -->
        <tr>
            <th>Product ID</th>
            <th>Quantity</th>
            <th>Description</th>
            <th> Price</th>
            <th>Total Price</th>
            <th></th>
        </tr>

        <!--  Loop through the items in the basket.  -->
        <% for iLineItem = 0 to nOrderFormItems - 1
             ' Get the current item
            set lineItem = orderFormItems(iLineItem) %>
        <tr>
            <!--  Show the id of the product, quantity,
                  name, price and total price.  -->
            <td> <% = lineItem.idProduct %> </td>
            <td> <% = lineItem.quantity %>  </td>
            <td> <% = _
                    mscsPage.HTMLEncode(lineItem.name)
                %>
            </td>
            <td> <% = _
            MSCSDataFunctions.Money(lineItem.[price])
                %>
            </td>
            <td> <% = MSCSDataFunctions.Money(_
                    lineItem.[_oadjust_adjustedprice])
                %>
            </td>
        </tr>
        <% next %>

</table>
```

All of the products put into the shopping basket are stored in the *Items* collection of the OrderForm. This can be retrieved from the OrderForm object and then looped through to show the basket data. Note that several of the fields are accessed with [ ] characters. These fields are set by the pipeline. More information on the default fields handled in the OrderForm and Pipeline can be found in the Commerce Server documentation.

Pipeline Utilization

The last key section to review is the pipeline utilization. The pipeline itself will be edited with the pipleline editor tool. Let's first take a look at how the pipeline functions are called in the shopping ASP code.

Listing 17.15 shows the first step in pipeline management code. It sets up the pipe context to point to the message manager, data functions, query map, connection string map, site name, and default connection string. These will all be required for successful running of the pipeline. The language is also set.

LISTING 17.15   PipeLine Setup

```
<%

    ' Create the pipeContext dictionary object
    Set pipeContext = _
    Server.CreateObject("Commerce.Dictionary")

    ' Set up the message manager, data functions, query map
    ' and connection string map.
    Set pipeContext("MessageManager") = MSCSMessageManager
    Set pipeContext("DataFunctions") = MSCSDataFunctions
    Set pipeContext("QueryMap") = MSCSQueryMap
    Set pipeContext("ConnectionStringMap") = _
        MSCSSite.ConnectionStringMap

    ' Set the site name and default database connection
    ' string
    pipeContext("SiteName") = MSCSSite.DisplayName
    pipeContext("DefaultConnectionString") = _
            MSCSSite.DefaultConnectionString

    ' Set the language.
    pipeContext("Language") = "usa"

%>
```

Listing 17.16 shows how a pipeline is loaded and run. The example loads the Plan pipeline (plan.pcf) and executes it. Note that the pipeline requires the Order-Form to read the shopper data and the pipecontext (created in Listing 17.15) for running the pipeline. If any errors are created when running the pipeline, they are returned.

LISTING 17.16   Running the Pipeline

```
<%
    ' Create the pipeline object
    set pipeline = _
        Server.CreateObject("Commerce.MtsPipeline")

    ' Load the pipeline.  Note that the pipeline typically
    ' resides in the config directory under a store.
    call pipeline.LoadPipe(Request.ServerVariables(_
          "APPL_PHYSICAL_PATH") + "\config\" + "plan.pcf")

    ' Run the pipeline.  The first parameter is included
    ' for backwards compatibility.  The OrderForm and
    ' pipeContext dictionary are passed in.  The last
    ' parameter is not currently used.
    errorLevel = pipeline.Execute(1, orderForm, _
                    pipeContext, 0)

%>
```

As the pipeline runs, the OrderForm is operated on an updated-as-needed mode, based on the pipeline being run (for example, tax, shipping). Total prices, etc., are calculated and set in the OrderForm. If there are any failures, the messages in the message manager are utilized to return errors. The database is accessed through the data functions.

The actual pipelines for the Clock Tower store are fairly simple. Figure 17.3 is a screenshot of the plan pipeline.

FIGURE 17.3:

Clock Tower plan pipeline

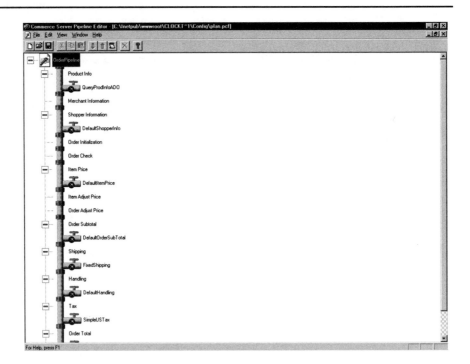

There are only three components of note in the plan pipeline. The first is the QueryProdInfoADO component. This is going to look in the query map setup in the global.asa for a query to retrieve product information. In this case the Query field is set to *productpl*, which is set up as a dictionary object of queries. The parameter passed is the SKU that will return the correct product data.

The second noteworthy event occurs in the shipping stage, which uses the FixedShipping component. This sets a fixed shipping cost per order regardless of any order quantity, weight, order amount, etc. In this case it is $19.95.

The third point to note is that the tax stage uses the SimpleUSTax component. This component sets the tax rate at the state level. In this case, eight percent tax is charged if the state is Pennsylvania.

The rest of the stages either have no components or use the default component to set the OrderForm value appropriately. For example, the Item Price stage uses the DefaultItemPrice component to default the price to the list price. In other words, there will be no adjustment for a sale or promotional price.

For the purchase pipeline, there are only three stages. Figure 17.4 shows the pipeline for the Clock Tower store.

FIGURE 17.4:

Clock Tower purchase pipeline

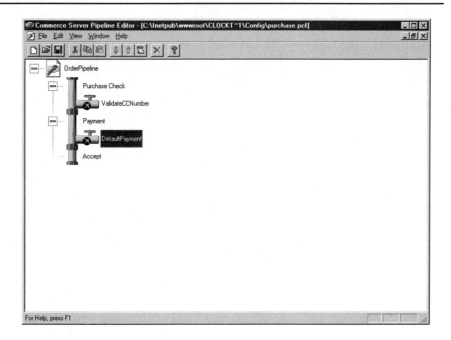

In this case, the store is using the ValidateCCNumber component in the Purchase Check stage. This component will do the appropriate checksum calculations depending on credit card type. The Payment and Accept stages perform no functions other than default as appropriate.

Summary

The code for the store is supplied on the CD with Site Server, Commerce Edition. A thorough review of the ASP pages will serve to show how the different commerce objects are utilized to make the store function. Clock Tower provides the simplest set of code to follow in terms of understanding the basics of the commerce tools' functionality.

Studying this store and the other stores that come with Site Server will provide good insight into how to build stores. For performance considerations, thoroughly review the VCTurbo and VCRocket stores.

CHAPTER

EIGHTEEN

18

Best Practices and Scalability

- Database Best Practices

- IIS Best Practices

- Programming

- Site Server, Commerce Edition

- Additional Resources

Throughout this book we have built a series of code examples to map out the building of an e-commerce store and we have reviewed sample Site Server code for building an e-commerce store. But it is important to understand that in a very dynamic Web environment with potential for incredible traffic peaks and difficult loading issues, use of best practices for scalability and performance is critical.

In this chapter we are going to explore all of the key elements that make up an e-commerce system. For each key, we will address plans for handling traffic load to ensure reliability and a solid user experience.

> **NOTE**   Note that the last section of the chapter will provide links to further resources regarding these topics.

System Architecture

In Chapter 4, "System Configuration," we covered the basics of planning for the system architecture. With respect to best practices and scalability, several key factors come into play.

System Hardware

The first critical piece is the underlying hardware. For Web servers, IIS is going to be more CPU bound than disk I/O or memory bound. So, planning for servers with single, dual, or quad processors will have a significant impact on performance.

With regard to reliability, a RAID 5 system will give the most redundancy and failover capability. But, on a database server with heavy write transactions, that architecture can have a significant overhead cost to write out the data to the different drives. RAID 1 can enhance database performance, but additional steps will need to be taken to ensure backup reliability.

Load Balancing

As also mentioned in Chapter 4, load balancing across multiple servers can be critical. If traffic exceeds what a single Web server can handle, then load will need to be spread across multiple servers. There are some critical items to consider in a load-balanced environment to make it successful.

Let's play out a scenario as follows:

1.   There are four Web servers sitting in front of a single database server.

2.   Each Web server can handle up to 500 concurrent users.

3.   Current traffic spikes have up to 450 concurrent users load-balanced to each server for a total of 1,800 users.

4.   One of the Web servers goes down.

When the Web server goes down we now have 600 users on each Web server. But, as specified, each Web server can handle only 500 users. That means our site is either down or giving very slow response.

Basically, our server farm of N (4) servers was able to handle the peak capacity. But we did not have $N + X$ capacity, where X would allow for reliability in the event some of the servers were not available.

Three Tier Architecture

In addition to load balancing, we can utilize other techniques to spread out the processing load. Specifically, we could model our architecture to use a third tier in addition to the Web server tier and the database tier.

The third tier is used to handle business code processing. We built a small example of this with our tax and shipping code in the sample e-commerce store. But, in reality, any of the code in an ASP application could be retargeted to be processed on another server. Figure 18.1 shows the architectural diagram for adding the third tier.

FIGURE 18.1:

Diagram of third tier
architecture

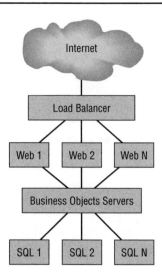

By adding the third tier, we accomplish several key scalability benefits, as outlined in Table 18.1.

TABLE 18.1:   Three Tier Architecture Benefits

Benefit	Description
Segmentation	By moving more of the code to secondary processing servers, we are segmenting more of the logic to multiple points instead of single points of failure.
Processor load spreading	The front end Web servers in this model are primarily involved in serving static content, calling our second tier objects, and retrieving responses.
Redundancy	We can have backups to our second tier architecture for specific redundancy.
Database abstraction	It will be easier to scale our databases by not directly affecting the front line Web servers. If one of the database servers is no longer available, our second tier objects should intelligently *know* what to do. The Web servers continue to process user requests regardless.
Code compilation	By moving code into a compiled environment instead of a scripted, interpreted environment, we will gain a significant performance increase.
Server optimization	By breaking out databases, Web servers, and business logic, we can tune each server to provide best performance for the specified functionality. And, we are loading less services and overhead onto each server.

By adding the second tier—make no mistake about it—there is more work and more planning to be done. Developing bulletproof compiled code takes more doing. Architecting the communication between the tiers takes more planning and staging. Also, the development and code publication environment becomes more complex. And, while adding this tier will give many more options for performance enhancement, estimating load and making decisions will become more complex.

Other Considerations

There are other considerations that have to be made concerning the scalability and reliability of the server farm.

Bandwidth will, of course, always be a key. A challenge in determining bandwidth is to know what the maximum spike traffic load will be. That is when maximum bandwidth will become most critical. A good hosting environment will provide a guaranteed average load of bandwidth and will provide a certain amount of peak loading beyond the average.

To save memory utilization in an NT system, make sure that any unneeded services are turned off. Especially in the case of a full Site Server install, if you are not using certain services, such as personalization and membership, be sure they are turned off.

Other factors, such as the basic network architecture for switches, hubs, backup software, etc., will all have an impact on performance and reliability. For example, in certain instances having a network card for each processor on a machine will make a difference in performance and processor utilization.

Database Best Practices

One of the biggest challenges in highly active sites with extensive database integration is managing database load. If there are database calls on nearly every page the user is requesting, the number of transactions can become significant.

Often these types of environments include Ad Server tracking, where multiple ads may show up on every page of a Web site. And, certainly, e-commerce sites tend to be heavily database driven with extensive shopper tracking, product data retrieval, etc.

Configuring and Utilizing SQL Server

In sites that have heavy database utilization, ensuring SQL Server is tuned appropriately is critical. Proper configuration settings for user connections, open connections, open databases, and other key values are critical. Additional information on making these changes and setting them appropriately can be found on Microsoft TechNet and Microsoft Developer Network (MSDN).

A second practice that is important to follow is the use of stored procedures (as was done throughout the book). Stored procedures are compiled code and can be executed very quickly on the Web server. And, any time that columns can be specified in a `select` query instead of * for all columns, the query will also return better results.

Finally, the careful use of Microsoft Transaction Server (and the COM+ Application Services in Windows 2000) can help you get the most out of the precious database resources that are available. MTS/COM+ allows for load balancing of components across multiple servers, with the least-heavily-loaded application server at any given time handling component-based services.

In addition, database connections can be pooled, allowing multiple threads of an application to use the database without each having to physically open and close a connection to that database.

Redundancy and Reliability

Another key practice for reliability is the use of some kind of failover for the SQL servers. If the database goes down for whatever reason, including maintenance, we need to ensure our Web site stays up.

As mentioned in Chapter 4, we can have a warm backup where we are performing backup through methods such as replication. A second method would be to utilize clustering. With clustering, a shared file storage system is utilized with two sets of servers. One is on real-time failover backup if the second server goes down. Technologies are available that will do a double commit on all database write transactions to servers on the same server farm or even to servers in different servers farms in different facilities.

In the sample code built in the book, we used the *sa* username with no password. In a live system, we would not want to use these settings. Instead, we would want to pick an appropriate login name and password and limit the rights of that account so that general SQL Server administration cannot be done. And, ideally, the password should change on a regular basis.

Database Design

There are many basic database design options available to improve performance. In the basic implementation we can strategically utilize indexes to speed up queries on heavily read-oriented databases.

Even with all of the techniques outlined in this chapter, on superscaled sites we may ultimately hit a point where one SQL server for a specified function (such as a commerce store) will not be able to independently handle all of the transactions. We will then have to look at splitting functions out to multiple servers for scalability.

In the case of the commerce store, a first step could be to split the product database from the basket and order database. That would make one of the servers heavily read-oriented and the other much more write-oriented. And, we will have successfully split the transactions across two servers.

If even that isn't enough, then we need to consider strategies for splitting the shoppers into different segments based on last name, having multiple cached reading servers, and reviewing the code architecture.

IIS Best Practices

Performance tuning IIS can be a little bit of an art form. It is not that there are so many options that can be tuned, but setting them depends on a large number of factors.

Two key factors in tuning IIS are queued requests and threads. Internet Information Server tunes the number of threads in its process dynamically. The dynamic values are usually optimal. In extreme cases of very active or underused processors, you might want to adjust the maximum number of threads in the Inetinfo process. If you do change the maximum number of threads, you should continue careful testing to make sure that the change has improved performance. The difference is usually quite subtle.

Tuning the IIS threads has to do with effective computer use. Allowing more threads generally encourages more CPU use. Fewer threads suggest low processor use. For example, if you have a busy site, the queue length never goes up, and the actual processor use is low, then you probably have more computer capacity than required. On the other hand, if the queue length goes up and down and the CPU use is still low, the threads should be increased because you have unused processor capacity.

Configuring the IIS queue is important because busy Web sites are defined by a high transaction volume. Ideally, each transaction has a very short life cycle. Under a high load, significant slowdowns (blocking) can occur when a component gets called at a greater rate than the number of transactions per second the component can satisfy. When this occurs, incoming requests are placed in a queue for later first in/first out processing. If the blocking only occurs for several seconds, the queue smoothes out and the request is handled in a timely fashion. However, when the blocking lasts for a longer period of time, an effect called *queue saturation* may occur. Queue saturation happens when the number of queued services exceeds the maximum number allowed (RequestQueueMax) and IIS returns a *Server Too Busy* message.

No matter what, there is a limit to what one Web server can handle in terms of the number of threads and items in the queue. Carefully monitoring the use of each will have a significant impact on the performance of the site and may allow you to squeeze out better and more performance.

Another option is to reduce logging on the Web server to an absolute minimum (if not completely). That will reduce the requirement to log every transaction request on the Web site. But this will have an effect on tracking Web statistics.

In general, with IIS you can improve performance and reduce the processor workload by substituting static Web pages for dynamic pages and eliminating large bitmapped images. For more information on these topics and the specifics of how to manage each, see the Microsoft IIS documentation.

Programming

As a developer, in many ways you have the most impact on how the Web site will perform and also have the most options available for improving performance and scalability (see Table 18.2).

Not only will the code handle how database connections are made, but it will also handle the kind of loading on the server that takes place. And that is what ultimately implements a three tier architecture.

TABLE 18.2:   Code Performance Techniques

Technique	Description
Caching	Any time commonly used data can be cached, so that it is not constantly being manipulated and potentially written or read from a database frequently, that will help performance. Also, it is possible to use techniques such as disconnected record sets and caching to manage database data on the Web server or business objects servers. These kinds of techniques are commonly used for data that is heavily read-oriented, such as a product database in a store, or heavily write-oriented, such as impressions and clicks of ads.
Database connections	Throughout the sample code in this book, most of the database connections were opened immediately before the data was utilized. That is important to keep that connection open for as short a time as possible. In high traffic sites, it is also good practice to immediately close the connection using the *close* connection.
Error handling	No matter how perfect the system is architected or how well the code is done, something will happen. Good error handling for gracefully recovering from high peak loads, database downtime, etc., can help to save ugly errors from showing up to the user and display something more user friendly.
Session variables	Adding on the overhead of managing session data for each user to a Web site can add significant overhead onto the server. Session variables can be replaced with URL parameters, but that requires significant work and tracking compared to session variables.
Option Explicit	By using Option Explicit at the start of each module or class in your code, you will ferret out any potentially unused variables that can be removed.
Application variables	Commonly used data that all users access will be far more efficient to store in an application-level variable instead of in many session variables.

Continued on next page

TABLE 18.2 CONTINUED: Code Performance Techniques

Technique	Description
Code compilation	As mentioned in the three tier discussion, moving script code into compiled Visual Basic or Visual C++ code will improve performance significantly. In addition, using the Site Server pipelines and commerce objects will help to immediately gain the benefit of scaled code.
Stored procedures	Always use stored procedures to store the SQL code in compiled fashion on the SQL server.
Static pages	If possible, make pages static. If data needs to be passed between pages, use the URL parameters.
Code blocking	When possible, place as much ASP code in the same block as possible. This will help to reduce context switching between HTML and Scripting.
Object tag	Instead of using Server.CreateObject, use the <OBJECT> tag. Server.CreateObject creates the object immediately. The <OBJECT> tag creates it only when needed.
Local versus global variables	Use local variables whenever possible. These are commonly created in subroutines and functions, but can be locally created by using the Set statement.

And of course, generally good programming practices will serve to build a better application. In the world of the Internet and superscaled sites, every little bit counts.

Site Server, Commerce Edition

All of the features and tools in Site Server, Commerce Edition, can be a blessing and a curse. From a development standpoint they are a blessing and can help speed development and add features. But they can also be a curse because they add overhead to the server and can hamper performance.

Microsoft has provided two demonstration stores for improving store performance—VCTurbo and VCRocket. They are based on the Volcano Coffee Company starter store, but they include significant enhancements. Table 18.3 outlines some of the structural changes that have been made.

TABLE 18.3: VCTurbo and VCRocket Performance Enhancements

Enhancement	Description
Eliminate the product information stage	The product queries can be highly optimized directly in ASP. And, we have opportunities to cache the products requests as well.
Eliminate DBStorage	The DBStorage object's functionality is powerful and useful, primarily because it enables a flexible database schema. However, this flexibility comes at a cost. The DBStorage object must be created on every page on which it is used, due to Microsoft Transaction Server (MTS) considerations. MTS transactional objects are destroyed after the transaction is committed. Additionally, the creation of this object requires that a query be executed to determine what columns exist in the database. Finally, because it works on the OrderForm as a whole, the OrderForm must be read in from the database, modified, and then written back to the database whenever changes are made. The DBStorage object is replaced with straight ADO/SQL code.
Remove the Marshalled_Order Field	Instead of storing the basket data in a binary format, which adds additional overhead to the read and write process, the basket is a traditional table (like the sample earlier in the book).
Writing receipts	In the original VC store, the orders were written out with the DBStorage object. In VCTurbo, the orders are written out directly in ADO from ASP.
Shopper management	Use ADO and ASP instead of the DBStorage object.
Eliminate query map	Instead of having queries run through the query map, they can be run directly in ASP with ADO.

These are just a few of the key changes made. If you really want to boil down the modifications between VCTurbo/VCRocket and the standard VC store, in the standard VC store everything but the core pipeline utilization is eliminated. In the VCRocket store we see the benefits of making more of the pages static, like the listing and product pages. That way, database calls are not being performed on those pages.

In some ways, the Wild Willie CD Store developed earlier in the book could be easily modified to add in pipeline functionality. In many ways, this would mirror the best practices outlined in the VCTurbo and VCRocket stores.

Additional Resources

There are many resources available for additional information on how to tune a Web server farm. Table 18.4 lists Web links to various resources you can turn to for additional information and support.

TABLE 18.4: Resource Links

Link	Description
TechNet	http://www.microsoft.com/technet/
MSDN	http://msdn.microsoft.com/default.asp
ASP Conventions	http://msdn.microsoft.com/workshop/server/asp/aspconv.asp
IIS 4.0 Tuning	http://msdn.microsoft.com/workshop/server/feature/tune.asp
Creating a highly available Web site	http://technet.microsoft.com/cdonline/default-f.asp?target=http ://technet.microsoft.com/cdonline/content/complete/windows/winnt/ winntas/technote/crhasite.htm
15 ASP programming tips	http://msdn.microsoft.com/workshop/server/asp/asptips.asp
VCRocket	http://www.microsoft.com/siteserver/commerce/DeployAdmin/ VolcanoCoffee.htm
Site Server	http://www.microsoft.com/siteserver
Commerce Server performance	http://www.microsoft.com/siteserver/commerce/DeployAdmin/ VolcanoCoffee.htm
SQL Server	http://www.microsoft.com/sql/
IIS	http://www.microsoft.com/ntserver/web/default.asp
Windows NT 4	http://www.microsoft.com/ntserver/nts/default.asp
Windows 2000	http://www.microsoft.com/windows/server/default.asp
Site Server installation guide (Windows NT)	http://support.microsoft.com/support/siteserver/install_ss3.asp
Site Server installation guide (Windows 2000)	http://support.microsoft.com/support/kb/articles/q241/8/33.asp

Microsoft has done a significant amount of performance tuning for their various .com sites. They have done a fairly good job of documenting performance expectations, tuning recommendations, and best practices.

Summary

Performance tuning a Web server farm for scalability and reliability is a critical task. Each element of the overall system must be planned for, examined, and carefully tweaked. Also, nothing can beat careful monitoring of server and database resources during peak loading times.

APPENDIX
A

Database Tables and Stored Procedures

This appendix provides a script listing of all tables and stored procedures utilized in the sample store developed in the book. Each is provided in alphabetical listing.

Tables

```
CREATE TABLE dbo.Attribute (
    idAttribute int IDENTITY (1, 1) NOT NULL ,
    chrAttributeName varchar (255) NULL ,
    idAttributeCategory int NULL ,
    CONSTRAINT PK___3__12 PRIMARY KEY  CLUSTERED
    (
        idAttribute
    )
)

CREATE TABLE dbo.AttributeCategory (
    idAttributeCategory int IDENTITY (1, 1) NOT NULL ,
    chrCategoryName varchar (255) NULL ,
    CONSTRAINT PK___5__12 PRIMARY KEY  CLUSTERED
    (
        idAttributeCategory
    )
)

CREATE TABLE dbo.Basket (
    idBasket int IDENTITY (1, 1) NOT NULL ,
    intQuantity int NULL CONSTRAINT DF_Basket_intQuantity_1__13 DEFAULT
(0),
    olddtCreated int NULL ,
    idShopper int NULL ,
    intOrderPlaced int NULL CONSTRAINT DF_Basket_intOrderPlaced11__12
DEFAULT (0),
    intSubTotal int NULL CONSTRAINT DF_Basket_intSubTotal_13__12 DEFAULT
(0),
    intTotal int NULL CONSTRAINT DF_Basket_intTotal_15__12 DEFAULT (0),
    intShipping int NULL CONSTRAINT DF_Basket_intShipping_12__12 DEFAULT
(0),
    intTax int NULL CONSTRAINT DF_Basket_intTax_14__12 DEFAULT (0),
    dtCreated datetime NULL CONSTRAINT DF_Basket_dtCreated_1__12 DEFAULT
(getdate()),
```

```
        intFreeShipping int NULL CONSTRAINT DF_Basket_intFreeShipping1__13
DEFAULT (0),
        CONSTRAINT PK___9__12 PRIMARY KEY  CLUSTERED
        (
            idBasket
        )
)

CREATE TABLE dbo.BasketItem (
        idBasketItem int IDENTITY (1, 1) NOT NULL ,
        idProduct int NULL ,
        intPrice int NULL ,
        chrName varchar (255) NULL ,
        intQuantity int NULL CONSTRAINT DF_BasketItem_intQuantity1__12
DEFAULT (0),
        idBasket int NULL ,
        chrSize varchar (50) NULL ,
        chrColor varchar (50) NULL ,
        CONSTRAINT PK___10__12 PRIMARY KEY  CLUSTERED
        (
            idBasketItem
        )
)


CREATE TABLE dbo.Department (
        idDepartment int IDENTITY (1, 1) NOT NULL ,
        chrDeptName varchar (255) NULL ,
        txtDeptDesc text NULL ,
        chrDeptImage varchar (255) NULL ,
        CONSTRAINT PK___1__12 PRIMARY KEY  CLUSTERED
        (
            idDepartment
        )
)

CREATE TABLE dbo.DepartmentProducts (
        idDepartmentProduct int IDENTITY (1, 1) NOT NULL ,
        idDepartment int NULL ,
        idProduct int NULL ,
        CONSTRAINT PK___6__12 PRIMARY KEY  CLUSTERED
        (
            idDepartmentProduct
        )
)
```

```
CREATE TABLE dbo.FreeShip (
    intFreeShip int IDENTITY (1, 1) NOT NULL ,
    dtStartDate datetime NULL CONSTRAINT DF_FreeShip_dtStartDate_3__10
DEFAULT ('1/1/1900'),
    dtEndDate datetime NULL CONSTRAINT DF_FreeShip_dtEndDate_2__10
DEFAULT ('1/1/1900'),
    CONSTRAINT PK_FreeShip_4__10 PRIMARY KEY  CLUSTERED
    (
        intFreeShip
    )
)

CREATE TABLE dbo.OrderData (
    idOrder int IDENTITY (1, 1) NOT NULL ,
    idShopper int NULL ,
    chrShipFirstName varchar (50) NULL ,
    chrShipLastName varchar (50) NULL ,
    chrShipAddress varchar (150) NULL ,
    chrShipCity varchar (150) NULL ,
    chrShipState varchar (50) NULL ,
    chrShipZipCode varchar (15) NULL ,
    chrShipPhone varchar (25) NULL ,
    chrShipFax varchar (25) NULL ,
    chrShipEmail varchar (100) NULL ,
    chrBillFirstName varchar (50) NULL ,
    chrBillLastName varchar (50) NULL ,
    chrBillAddress varchar (150) NULL ,
    chrBillCity varchar (100) NULL ,
    chrBillState varchar (50) NULL ,
    chrBillZipCode varchar (15) NULL ,
    chrBillPhone varchar (25) NULL ,
    chrBillFax varchar (25) NULL ,
    chrBillEmail varchar (100) NULL ,
    dtOrdered datetime NULL CONSTRAINT DF_OrderData_dtOrdered_12__12
DEFAULT (getdate()),
    chrShipProvince varchar (150) NULL ,
    chrShipCountry varchar (150) NULL ,
    chrBillProvince varchar (150) NULL ,
    chrBillCountry varchar (150) NULL ,
    idBasket int NULL ,
    intFreeShipping int NULL CONSTRAINT DF_OrderData_intFreeShipp1__13
DEFAULT (0),
    CONSTRAINT PK___11__12 PRIMARY KEY  CLUSTERED
    (
        idOrder
```

```
    )
)

CREATE TABLE dbo.OrderStatus (
    idOrderStatus int IDENTITY (1, 1) NOT NULL ,
    idOrder int NULL ,
    idStage int NULL CONSTRAINT DF_OrderStatu_idStage_14__12 DEFAULT
(0),
    dtShipped datetime NULL ,
    dtFulfilled datetime NULL ,
    dtProcessed datetime NULL ,
    txtNotes text NULL ,
    chrShippingNum varchar (30) NULL ,
    intProcessed int NULL CONSTRAINT DF_OrderStatu_intProcesse1__12
DEFAULT (0),
    CONSTRAINT PK___13__12 PRIMARY KEY  CLUSTERED
    (
        idOrderStatus
    )
)

CREATE TABLE dbo.PaymentData (
    idPayment int IDENTITY (1, 1) NOT NULL ,
    idOrder int NULL ,
    chrCardType varchar (50) NULL ,
    chrCardNumber varchar (30) NULL ,
    chrExpDate varchar (25) NULL ,
    chrCardName varchar (150) NULL ,
    CONSTRAINT PK___12__12 PRIMARY KEY  CLUSTERED
    (
        idPayment
    )
)

CREATE TABLE dbo.ProductAttribute (
    idProductAttribute int IDENTITY (1, 1) NOT NULL ,
    idAttribute int NULL ,
    idProduct int NULL ,
    CONSTRAINT PK___4__12 PRIMARY KEY  CLUSTERED
    (
        idProductAttribute
    )
)

CREATE TABLE dbo.Products (
```

```
    idProduct int IDENTITY (1, 1) NOT NULL ,
    chrProductName varchar (255) NULL ,
    txtDescription text NULL ,
    chrProductImage varchar (255) NULL ,
    intPrice int NULL CONSTRAINT DF_Products_intPrice_3__12 DEFAULT (0),
    dtSaleStart datetime NULL CONSTRAINT DF_Products_dtSaleStart_2__12
DEFAULT ('1 / 1 / 80'),
    dtSaleEnd datetime NULL CONSTRAINT DF_Products_dtSaleEnd_1__12
DEFAULT ('1 / 1 / 80'),
    intSalePrice int NULL CONSTRAINT DF_Products_intSalePrice_4__12
DEFAULT (0),
    intActive int NULL CONSTRAINT DF_Products_intActive_3__12 DEFAULT
(0),
    intFeatured tinyint NULL CONSTRAINT DF_Products_intFeatured_3__10
DEFAULT (0),
    dtFeatureStart datetime NULL CONSTRAINT DF_Products_dtFea-
tureStar2__10 DEFAULT ('1/1/80'),
    dtFeatureEnd datetime NULL CONSTRAINT DF_Products_dtFeatureEnd_1__10
DEFAULT ('1/1/80'),
    CONSTRAINT PK___2__12 PRIMARY KEY  CLUSTERED
    (
        idProduct
    )
)

CREATE TABLE dbo.RelatedProducts (
    idRelatedProduct int IDENTITY (1, 1) NOT NULL ,
    idProductA int NULL CONSTRAINT DF_RelatedPro_idProductA_1__12
DEFAULT (0),
    idProductB int NULL CONSTRAINT DF_RelatedPro_idProductB_2__12
DEFAULT (0),
    idRelationType int NULL CONSTRAINT DF_RelatedPro_idRelationT3__12
DEFAULT (0),
    CONSTRAINT PK___7__12 PRIMARY KEY  CLUSTERED
    (
        idRelatedProduct
    )
)

CREATE TABLE dbo.Shipping (
    idQuantityRange int IDENTITY (1, 1) NOT NULL ,
    intLowQuantity int NULL CONSTRAINT DF_Shipping_intLowQuantit3__12
DEFAULT (0),
    intHighQuantity int NULL CONSTRAINT DF_Shipping_intHighQuanti2__12
DEFAULT (0),
```

```
      intFee int NULL CONSTRAINT DF_Shipping_intFee_1__12 DEFAULT (0),
      CONSTRAINT PK___14__12 PRIMARY KEY  CLUSTERED
      (
         idQuantityRange
      )
)

CREATE TABLE dbo.Shopper (
   idShopper int IDENTITY (1, 1) NOT NULL ,
   chrFirstName varchar (50) NULL ,
   chrLastName varchar (50) NULL ,
   chrAddress varchar (150) NULL ,
   chrCity varchar (100) NULL ,
   chrState varchar (2) NULL ,
   chrZipCode varchar (15) NULL ,
   chrPhone varchar (30) NULL ,
   chrFax varchar (30) NULL ,
   chrEmail varchar (150) NULL ,
   dtEnteredold int NULL ,
   chrUserName varchar (25) NULL ,
   chrPassword varchar (25) NULL ,
   intCookie tinyint NULL CONSTRAINT DF_Shopper_intCookie_1__12 DEFAULT
(0),
   dtEntered datetime NULL CONSTRAINT DF_Shopper_dtEntered_1__12
DEFAULT (getdate()),
   chrProvince varchar (150) NULL ,
   chrCountry varchar (150) NULL ,
   CONSTRAINT PK___8__12 PRIMARY KEY  CLUSTERED
   (
      idShopper
   )
)

CREATE TABLE dbo.Tax (
   idState int IDENTITY (1, 1) NOT NULL ,
   chrState varchar (50) NULL ,
   intTaxRateOld int NULL ,
   fltTaxRate float NULL CONSTRAINT DF_Tax_fltTaxRate_1__13 DEFAULT
(0),
   CONSTRAINT PK___15__12 PRIMARY KEY  CLUSTERED
   (
      idState
   )
)
```

Stored Procedures

```
CREATE PROCEDURE sp_AddProdDept

@idProduct int,
@idDepartment int

AS

insert into DepartmentProducts(idProduct, idDepartment)
values(@idProduct, @idDepartment)
GO

CREATE PROCEDURE sp_AddProductAttribute

@idAttribute int,
@idProduct int

AS

insert into ProductAttribute(idAttribute, idProduct)
values(@idAttribute, @idProduct)
GO

/*  Returns the attributes in the database for the
    specifiec product.
*/
CREATE PROCEDURE sp_Attributes

/*  Pass in the ID of the product */
@idProduct int

AS

/*  select statement to return attributes for the product. */
select products.idproduct,
       attribute.idattribute,
       attribute.chrattributename,
       attributecategory.chrcategoryname,
       productattribute.idproductattribute

from products, productattribute, attribute, attributecategory

where
```

```
products.idproduct = @idProduct and
productattribute.idproduct = @idProduct and
productattribute.idattribute = attribute.idattribute and
attribute.idattributecategory = attributecategory.idattributecategory

order by chrcategoryname
GO


/*  Procedure to get the quantity of items
    in the basket */
CREATE PROCEDURE sp_BasketQuantity

/*  Pass in the ID of the basket */
@idBasket int

AS

/*  Select statement to sum up the quantity of items
    in the basket */
select quantity=sum(intQuantity)
from basketitem
where idBasket = @idBasket
GO

/* Stored procedure to total the prices of the
   items in the basket. */
CREATE PROCEDURE sp_BasketSubTotal

/*  Pass in the ID of the basket */
@idBasket int

AS

/*  Retrieve the price and quantity of the items
    in the basket.  The sum is then calculated.
*/
select subtotal=sum(intQuantity * intPrice)
from basketitem where idBasket = @idBasket
GO

/*  Checks the quantity of items in the basket for
    the specified product.
*/
CREATE PROCEDURE sp_CheckBasketItemQuantity
```

```
/*  Pass in the ID of the product and
    the ID of the basket
*/
@idProduct int,
@idBasket int

AS

/*  Retrieve the quantity value */
select intQuantity from basketitem
where idProduct = @idProduct and
      idBasket = @idBasket
GO

CREATE PROCEDURE sp_CheckFreeShip

AS

select * from FreeShip where getdate() >= dtStartDate and getdate() <=
dtEndDate
GO

/*  Clear the items in the basket */
CREATE PROCEDURE sp_ClearBasketItems

/*  Pass in the ID of the basket */
@idBasket int

AS

/*  Delete all items in the specified basket */
delete from basketitem where idBasket = @idBasket
GO

/*  Creates a new basket and returns the ID */
CREATE PROCEDURE sp_CreateBasket

/*  Pass in the ID of the shopper
    the basket will belong to.
*/
@idShopper int

AS
```

```
/*  Insert a new role into the basket and
    set the shopper ID
*/
insert into basket(idShopper) values(@idShopper)

/*  Retrieve the ID of the basket which will be in the
    @@identity variable value
*/
select idbasket = @@identity
GO

CREATE PROCEDURE sp_DeleteDept

@idDepartment int

AS

delete from department where idDepartment = @idDepartment
GO

CREATE PROCEDURE sp_DeleteOrder

@idOrder int

AS

declare @idBasket int

select @idBasket = idBasket from OrderData where
idOrder = @idOrder

delete from orderdata where idOrder = @idOrder
delete from paymentdata where idOrder = @idOrder
delete from OrderStatus where idOrder = @idOrder

delete from Basket where idBasket = @idBasket

delete from BasketItem where idBasket = @idBasket


GO

CREATE PROCEDURE sp_DeleteProdDept
```

```
@idDepartmentProduct int

AS

delete from departmentproducts where idDepartmentProduct = @idDepart-
mentProduct
GO

CREATE PROCEDURE sp_DeleteProduct

@idProduct int

AS

delete from products where idProduct = @idProduct
GO

CREATE PROCEDURE sp_DeleteProductAttribute

@idProductAttribute int

AS

delete from productattribute where idProductAttribute = @idProductAt-
tribute
GO

CREATE PROCEDURE sp_DeleteProductRelation

@idRelatedProduct int

AS


delete from RelatedProducts where
idRelatedProduct = @idRelatedProduct


GO

CREATE PROCEDURE sp_DeleteShippingRate

@idQuantityRange int

AS
```

```
delete from shipping where idQuantityRange = @idQuantityRange
GO

/*  Retrieve the shipping rates for the store */
CREATE PROCEDURE sp_GetShippingRate

AS

/*  Return all of the shipping values */
select * from shipping
GO

/*  Return the tax rate setting for the store.  */
CREATE PROCEDURE sp_GetTaxRate

/*  Pass in the state */
@chrState varchar(2)

AS

/*  Retrieve the tax rate for the specified state */
select fltTaxRate from tax where chrState = @chrState
GO

/*  Initialize the order status table for
    a new order */
CREATE PROCEDURE sp_InitializeOrderStatus

/*  Pass in the ID of the order */
@idOrder int

AS

/*  Insert the new order status and set the ID of
    the order */
insert into OrderStatus(idOrder) values(@idOrder)
GO

/*  Stored procedure to insert a new basket
    item */
CREATE PROCEDURE sp_InsertBasketItem

/*  Pass in the id of the basket, quantity, price
    product name, product price, ID of the product,
```

```
      size of the product and the color.
*/
@idBasket int,
@intQuantity int,
@intPrice int,
@chrName varchar(255),
@idProduct int,
@chrSize varchar(50),
@chrColor varchar(50)

AS

/*  Insert the item into the table */
insert into basketitem(idBasket, intQuantity,
                       intPrice, chrName,
                       idProduct, chrSize,
                       chrColor)

             values(@idBasket, @intQuantity,
                    @intPrice, @chrName,
                    @idProduct, @chrSize,
                    @chrColor)
GO

CREATE PROCEDURE sp_InsertDept

@chrDeptName varchar(255),
@txtDeptDesc text,
@chrDeptImage varchar(100)

AS

insert into department(chrDeptName, txtDeptDesc, chrDeptImage)
values(@chrDeptName, @txtDeptDesc, @chrDeptImage)

select idDepartment = @@identity
GO

/*  Stored procedure to insert the order data
    into the database.
*/
CREATE PROCEDURE sp_InsertOrderData

/*  All key values are inserted into the
    database.
```

```
*/
@idShopper int,
@chrShipFirstName varchar(150),
@chrShipLastName varchar(150),
@chrShipAddress varchar(150),
@chrShipCity varchar(150),
@chrShipState varchar(25),
@chrShipProvince varchar(150),
@chrShipCountry varchar(150),
@chrShipZipCode varchar(150),
@chrShipPhone varchar(150),
@chrShipEmail varchar(150),
@chrBillFirstName varchar(150),
@chrBillLastName varchar(150),
@chrBillAddress varchar(150),
@chrBillCity varchar(150),
@chrBillState varchar(25),
@chrBillProvince varchar(150),
@chrBillCountry varchar(150),
@chrBillZipCode varchar(150),
@chrBillPhone varchar(150),
@chrBillEmail varchar(150),
@idBasket int

AS

/*  Insert the data */
insert into orderdata(idShopper, chrShipFirstName,
                    chrShipLastName, chrShipAddress,
                chrShipCity, chrShipState,
                    chrShipProvince, chrShipCountry,
                    chrShipZipCode, chrShipPhone,
                    chrShipEmail, chrBillFirstName,
                    chrBillLastName, chrBillAddress,
                    chrBillCity, chrBillState,
                    chrBillProvince, chrBillCountry,
                    chrBillZipCode, chrBillPhone,
                    chrBillEmail, idBasket)

        values(@idShopper, @chrShipFirstName,
                    @chrShipLastName, @chrShipAddress,
                    @chrShipCity, @chrShipState,
                    @chrShipProvince, @chrShipCountry,
                    @chrShipZipCode, @chrShipPhone,
                    @chrShipEmail, @chrBillFirstName,
```

```
                              @chrBillLastName, @chrBillAddress,
                              @chrBillCity, @chrBillState,
                              @chrBillProvince, @chrBillCountry,
                              @chrBillZipCode, @chrBillPhone,
                              @chrBillEmail, @idBasket)

select idOrder = @@identity
GO

/*  Stored Procedure used to insert payment
    from an order.
*/
CREATE PROCEDURE sp_InsertPaymentData

/*  Pass in the order id, credit card type, credit
    card number, credit card expiration date and name
    of the customer on the card.
*/
@idOrder int,
@chrCardType varchar(100),
@chrCardNumber varchar(50),
@chrExpDate varchar(25),
@chrCardName varchar(150)

AS

/*  Insert the data into the paymentdata table */
insert into paymentdata(idOrder, chrCardType,
        chrCardNumber, chrExpDate,
        chrCardName)

        values(@idOrder, @chrCardType,
          @chrCardNumber, @chrExpDate,
          @chrCardName)
GO

CREATE PROCEDURE sp_InsertProduct

@chrProductName varchar(255),
@txtDescription text,
@chrProductImage varchar(100),
@intPrice int,
@intActive int

AS
```

```
insert into products(chrProductName, txtDescription, chrProductImage,
intPrice, intActive)
values(@chrProductName, @txtDescription, @chrProductImage, @intPrice,
@intActive)

select idProduct = @@identity
GO

CREATE PROCEDURE sp_InsertProductRelation

@idProductA int,
@idProductB int,
@RelationType int

AS

insert into RelatedProducts(idProductA, idProductB, idRelationType)
values(@idProductA, @idProductB, @RelationType)
GO

CREATE PROCEDURE sp_InsertShippingRate

@intLowQuantity int,
@intHighQuantity int,
@intFee int

AS

insert into shipping(intLowQuantity, intHighQuantity, intFee)
values(@intLowQuantity, @intHighQuantity, @intFee)
GO

/*  Utilized to insert a new shopper
    into the database.
*/
CREATE PROCEDURE sp_InsertShopper AS

/*  Insert the shopper into the database and
    set the first and last name to blank */
insert into shopper(chrusername, chrpassword)
            values('', '')

/*  Return the identity column ID of the shopper */
select idShopper = @@identity
```

```
GO

CREATE PROCEDURE sp_ManagerRetrieveProdSearch

@intStartProdID int,
@intRowCount int,
@chrSearchText varchar(100)

AS

set rowcount @intRowCount

select idProduct, chrProductName, intPrice
from products
where idProduct >= @intStartProdID and
      chrProductName like '%' + @chrSearchText+ '%'
GO

CREATE PROCEDURE sp_ManagerRetrieveProducts

@intStartProdID int,
@intRowCount int

AS

set rowcount @intRowCount

select idProduct, chrProductName, intPrice
from products where idProduct >= @intStartProdID
GO

/*  Stored Procedure to remove an item from
    the basket */
CREATE PROCEDURE sp_RemoveBasketItem

/*  Pass in teh ID of the basket and
    the ID of the basket item to be
    removed.
*/
@idBasket int,
@idBasketItem int

AS

/*  Delete the item from the database */
```

```
delete from basketitem
where idBasket = @idBasket and
      idBasketItem = @idBasketItem
GO

CREATE PROCEDURE sp_RetrieveAttributes AS

select * from attribute, attributecategory
where attribute.idattributecategory = attributecategory.idAttributeCat-
egory
order by attributecategory.chrCategoryName
GO

/*  Stored Procedure to retrieve the
    basket item from the database */
CREATE PROCEDURE sp_RetrieveBasketItem

/*  Pass in the ID of the basket */
@idBasket int

AS

/*  Retrieve the items for the specified basket */
select * from basketitem where idBasket = @idBasket
GO

/*  Retrieve the department data */
CREATE PROCEDURE sp_RetrieveDept

/*  Pass in the ID of the department */
@idDepartment int

AS

/*  Select all of the data on the
    department */
select * from department
where idDepartment = @idDepartment
GO

CREATE PROCEDURE sp_RetrieveDeptByProd

@idProduct int

AS
```

```
select * from department, departmentproducts
where departmentproducts.idProduct = @idProduct and
      department.iddepartment = departmentproducts.iddepartment
GO

/*  Stored Procedure to retrieve the products
    assigned to the specified department */
CREATE PROCEDURE sp_RetrieveDeptProducts

/*  Pass in the ID of the department */
@idDept int

AS

/*  Select the product data from the
    related products */
select * from products, departmentproducts

where products.idproduct = departmentproducts.idproduct and
      departmentproducts.iddepartment = @idDept
GO

/*  Stored procedure to retrieve all of
    the departments in the database */
CREATE PROCEDURE sp_RetrieveDepts AS

/*  Select all of the departments data */
select * from department
GO

CREATE PROCEDURE sp_RetrieveFeaturedProducts AS

select * from products where intFeatured = 1 and
getdate() >= dtFeatureStart and getdate() <= dtFeatureEnd
GO

CREATE PROCEDURE sp_RetrieveFreeShip AS

select * from FreeShip
GO

/*  Stored Procedure to retrieve the last
    basket for the shopper. */
CREATE PROCEDURE sp_RetrieveLastBasket
```

```
/*  Pas in the ID of the shopper */
@idShopper int

AS

/*  Select the basket data for all baskets
    assigned to the shopper and where the
    order was never finished.  We sort the
    data in descending order so that the
    last basket is returned first. */
select * from basket
where idShopper = @idShopper and
      intOrderPlaced =0 and intTotal = 0
order by dtCreated DESC
GO

CREATE PROCEDURE sp_RetrieveNonPurchFeatureProd

@idBasket int

AS

select * from products
where
    intFeatured = 1 and
    getdate() >= dtFeatureStart and
    getdate() <= dtFeatureEnd and
    products.idproduct Not In
    (select idProduct from basketitem where basketitem.idbasket =
@idBasket)
GO

/*  Retrieve orders for the shopper */
CREATE PROCEDURE sp_RetrieveOrders

/*  Pass in the ID of the shopper */
@idShopper int

AS

/*  Select the order data for the shopper.  To return
    all of the core order data we have to join the
    OrderData, OrderStatus and Basket tables.
*/
```

```
select * from OrderData, OrderStatus, basket
where @idShopper = @idShopper and
      OrderData.idOrder = OrderStatus.idOrder and
      basket.idBasket = OrderData.idBasket
GO

CREATE PROCEDURE sp_RetrievePaymentData

@idOrder int

AS

select * from paymentdata
where idOrder = @idOrder


GO

/*  Retrieve the product data */
CREATE PROCEDURE sp_RetrieveProduct

/*  Pass in the ID of the product */
@idProduct int

AS

/*  Select the product data */
select * from products
where idProduct = @idProduct
GO

CREATE PROCEDURE sp_RetrieveProductRelations

@idProduct int

AS

select * from relatedproducts, products
where idProductA = @idProduct and
      products.idProduct = relatedproducts.idProductb
GO

CREATE PROCEDURE sp_RetrieveProducts

AS
```

```
select * from products
GO

/*  Retrieve the profile based on email
    and password */
CREATE PROCEDURE sp_RetrieveProfile

/*  The email address and password
    are passed in */
@email varchar(255),
@password varchar(25)

AS

/*  Select the shopper data */
select * from shopper
where chrEmail = @email and
      chrPassword = @Password
GO

/*  Retrieve the shopper profile */
CREATE PROCEDURE sp_RetrieveProfileByID

/*  Pass in the shopper ID */
@idShopper int

AS

/*  Select the shopper data by shopper
    ID */
select * from shopper
where idShopper = @idShopper
GO

/*  Retrieve the receipt header by shopper ID
    and Order ID */
CREATE PROCEDURE sp_RetrieveReceiptHeader

/*  Pass in the ID of the shopper and
    the ID of the Order */
@idShopper int,
@idOrder int

AS
```

```
/*  Select the receipt header which requires
    joining the orderdata and basket tables
*/
select * from OrderData, Basket
where Orderdata.idOrder = @idOrder and
      OrderData.idShopper = @idShopper and
      OrderData.idBasket = Basket.idBasket
GO

/*  Stored Procedure to retrieve the
    receipt items.
*/
CREATE PROCEDURE sp_RetrieveReceiptItems

/*  Pass in the ID of the shopper and the
    Id of the order */
@idShopper int,
@idOrder int

AS

/*  Select the contents of the basketitem,
    basket and orderdata tables.
*/
select * from basketitem, orderdata
where orderdata.idshopper = @idShopper and
      orderdata.idOrder = @idOrder and
      basketitem.idbasket = orderdata.idbasket
GO

/*  Stored procedure to retrieve related
    products to the specified product.
*/
CREATE PROCEDURE sp_RetrieveRelatedProducts

/*  Pass in the ID of the product */
@idProduct int

AS

/*  Select the related products.  Note
    that cross sell related products are
    defined by a setting of 1. */
select * from relatedproducts, products
```

```
where   relatedproducts.idProductb = products.idproduct and
        relatedproducts.idProducta = @idProduct and
        idRelationType = 1
GO

CREATE PROCEDURE sp_RetrieveSaleProducts AS

declare @Cnt int

select @cnt = count(*) from products where getdate() >= dtSaleStart and
getdate() <= dtSaleEnd

select @Cnt, *  from products where getdate() >= dtSaleStart and get-
date() <= dtSaleEnd
GO

CREATE PROCEDURE sp_RetrieveTaxRates AS

select * from tax
GO

/*  Stored procedure to retrieve up sell products */
CREATE PROCEDURE sp_RetrieveUpSell

/*  Pass in the ID of the product */
@idProduct int

AS

/*  Select the up sell products.  Note the
    relationship is defined by a setting of 2.
    A setting of 1 indicates an cross sell. */
select * from relatedproducts, products
where products.idproduct = relatedproducts.idproductb and
      relatedproducts.idProducta = @idProduct and
      idRelationType = 2
GO

/*  Stored procedure to search for products based
    on passed in parameters. */
CREATE PROCEDURE sp_SearchProducts

/*  Pass in the search text, low price and
    high price */
@SearchText varchar(255),
```

```
@Low int,
@High int

AS


/*  Select products from the data base where the
    product name or description contain the search
    text.  And where the price falls in the given
    parameters. The products are ordered by the
    product name. */
select * from products
where (chrProductName like '%' + @SearchText+ '%' or
      txtDescription like '%' + @SearchText + '%') and
      (intPrice >= @low and intPrice <= @High)
order by chrProductName
GO


/*  Stored procedure to update the basket
    values */
CREATE PROCEDURE sp_UpdateBasket

/*  Pass in the ID of the basket, the total
    quantity, the order subtotal, the shipping
    value, the tax value, the order total and a
    flag indicating the order was placed. */
@idBasket int,
@intQuantity int,
@intSubTotal int,
@intShipping int,
@intFreeShipping int,
@intTax int,
@intTotal int,
@intOrderPlaced int

AS

/*  Update the basket */
update basket set
   intQuantity = @intQuantity,
   intSubtotal = @intSubtotal,
   intShipping = @intShipping,
   intFreeShipping = @intFreeShipping,
   intTax = @intTax,
   intTotal = @intTotal,
```

```
        intOrderPlaced = @intOrderPlaced
where    idBasket = @idBasket
GO

CREATE PROCEDURE sp_UpdateBasketItem

@idBasketItem int,
@chrName varchar(255),
@chrColor varchar(50),
@chrSize varchar(50),
@intQuantity int,
@intPrice int

AS

update BasketItem set
    chrName = @chrName,
    chrColor = @chrColor,
    chrSize = @chrSize,
    intQuantity = @intQuantity,
    intPrice = intPrice

where idBasketItem = @idBasketItem
GO

/*  Stored procedure to update the
    basket item quantity. */
CREATE PROCEDURE sp_UpdateBasketItemsQuantity

/*  Pass in the ID of the basket, the quantity
    and the ID of the product (basket item). */
@idBasket int,
@intQuantity int,
@idProduct int

as

/*  Update the basketitem table wit the new
    quantity for the product. */
update basketitem set intQuantity = @intQuantity
where idBasket = @idbasket and
      idProduct = @idProduct
GO

CREATE PROCEDURE sp_UpdateDepartment
```

```
@idDepartment int,
@chrDeptName varchar(255),
@txtDeptDesc text,
@chrDeptImage varchar(100)

AS

update department set
   chrDeptName = @chrDeptName,
   txtDeptDesc = @txtDeptDesc,
   chrDeptImage = @chrDeptImage
where idDepartment = @idDepartment
GO

CREATE PROCEDURE sp_UpdateFreeShip

@dtStartDate datetime,
@dtEndDate datetime

AS

Update FreeShip set dtStartDate = @dtStartDate, dtEndDate = @dtEndDate
GO

CREATE PROCEDURE sp_UpdateOrderData

@idOrder int,
@chrBillFirstName varchar(255),
@chrBillLastName varchar(255),
@chrBillAddress varchar(255),
@chrBillCity varchar(255),
@chrBillState varchar(25),
@chrBillZipCode varchar(25),
@chrBillPhone varchar(255),
@chrBillEmail varchar(255),
@chrShipFirstName varchar(255),
@chrShipLastname varchar(255),
@chrShipAddress varchar(255),
@chrShipCity varchar(255),
@chrShipState varchar(25),
@chrShipZipCode varchar(25),
@chrShipPhone varchar(255),
@chrShipEmail varchar(255)
```

```
AS

update orderdata set

    chrBillFirstName = @chrBillFirstName,
    chrBillLastname = @chrBillLastname,
    chrBillAddress = @chrBillAddress,
    chrBillCity = @chrBillCity,
    chrBillState = @chrBillState,
    chrBillZipCode = @chrBillZipCode,
    chrBillPhone = @chrBillPhone,
    chrBillEmail = @chrBillEmail,
    chrShipFirstName = @chrShipFirstName,
    chrShipLastname = @chrShipLastname,
    chrShipAddress = @chrShipAddress,
    chrShipCity = @chrShipCity,
    chrShipState = @chrShipState,
    chrShipZipCode = @chrShipZipCode,
    chrShipPhone = @chrShipPhone,
    chrShipEmail = @chrShipEmail

where

    idOrder = @idOrder
GO

CREATE PROCEDURE sp_UpdateOrderStatus

@idOrder int,
@intStage int,
@chrShippingNum varchar(100)

AS

update OrderStatus set
    idStage = @intStage,
    chrShippingNum = @chrShippingNum
where
    idOrder = @idORder
GO

CREATE PROCEDURE sp_UpdatePaymentData

@idOrder int,
@chrCardType varchar(100),
```

```
@chrCardNumber varchar(50),
@chrExpDate varchar(25),
@chrCardName varchar(150)

AS

update PaymentData set
    chrCardType = @chrCardType,
    chrCardNumber = @chrCardNumber,
    chrExpDate = @chrExpDate,
    chrCardName = @chrCardName
where
    idOrder = @idOrder
GO

CREATE PROCEDURE sp_UpdateProduct

@idProduct int,
@chrProductName varchar(255),
@txtDescription text,
@chrProductImage varchar(100),
@intPrice int,
@intActive int,
@intFeatured int,
@dtFeatureStart datetime,
@dtFeatureEnd datetime,
@intSalePrice int,
@dtSaleStart datetime,
@dtSaleEnd datetime

AS

update products set
    chrProductName = @chrProductName,
    txtDescription = @txtDescription,
    chrProductImage = @chrProductImage,
    intPrice = @intPrice,
    intActive = @intActive,
    intFeatured = @intFeatured,
    dtFeatureStart = @dtFeatureStart,
    dtFeatureEnd = @dtFeatureEnd,
    intSalePrice = @intSalePrice,
    dtSaleStart = @dtSaleStart,
    dtSaleEnd = @dtSaleEnd
where
```

```
   idProduct = @idProduct
GO

CREATE PROCEDURE sp_UpdateShippingRate

@idQuantityRange int,
@intLowQuantity int,
@intHighQuantity int,
@intFee int

AS

update shipping set
  intLowQuantity = @intLowQuantity,
  intHighQuantity = @intHighQuantity,
  intFee = @intFee
where
  idQuantityRange = @idQuantityRange

GO

/*  Stored procedure to update the shopper
    data */
CREATE PROCEDURE sp_UpdateShopper

/*  Pass in the key shopper data */
@chrFirstName varchar(150),
@chrLastName varchar(150),
@chrAddress varchar(150),
@chrCity varchar(150),
@chrState varchar(150),
@chrProvince varchar(150),
@chrCountry varchar(100),
@chrZipCode varchar(50),
@chrPhone varchar(25),
@chrFax varchar(25),
@chrEmail varchar(100),
@chrPassword varchar(25),
@intCookie int,
@idShopper int

AS

/*  Update the shopper data for the given
    shopper ID */
```

```
        update shopper  set
              chrFirstName = @chrFirstName,
        chrLastname = @chrLastName,
        chrAddress = @chrAddress,
        chrCity = @chrCity,
        chrState = @chrState,
        chrProvince = @chrProvince,
        chrCountry = @chrCountry,
        chrZipCode = @chrZipCode,
        chrPhone = @chrPhone,
        chrFax = @chrFax,
        chrEmail = @chrEmail,
        chrPassword = @chrPassword,
        intCookie = @intCookie
where   idShopper = @idShopper
GO

CREATE PROCEDURE sp_UpdateTaxRate

@fltTaxRate float,
@idState int

AS

update tax set fltTaxRate = @fltTaxRate
where idState = @idState
GO
```

INDEX

Note to the Reader: Throughout this index **boldfaced** page numbers indicate primary discussions of a topic. *Italicized* page numbers indicate illustrations.

A

Abandon method, 279
about.asp page, 622
abstraction, 644
Accept pipeline stage, 606, 639
Access, 28
Active check box, **374–375**
active flag, 371
Active Server Page option, 79
Active Server Pages (ASP), **16–17**
  backups for, 71
  in IIS, 16
  in Visual InterDev, 17
active setting, 395
ActiveX objects
  for Site Server, 600
  for Visual Basic 6, 18
ActiveX Data Objects (ADO)
  for databases, 91
  in ManageDept.asp page, **410–411**
  for projects, 227
  for relationships, 522
  for SQL Server, 18
Ad Server, 21, 645

Add New Product link, 365
add new product page, 369, *370*
Add option, 79
AddAttribute.asp page, 383, **401–402**
adding
  assignments of departments to products, **398–400**
  attributes, 118, **401–403**
  departments, **407–410**, *419*
  items to baskets. *See* AddItem.asp page
  products, **365–369**
  shipping ranges, **445–447**
AddItem.asp page, 142
  baskets in, **165–166**
  duplicate item checks in, **166**
  inserting items into baskets in, **167–168**
  product values in, **164–165**
  quantity checks in, **164**
  shopper IDs in, **163–164**
  updating baskets in, **167**
AddItem method, 603
AddLanguage method, 628
AddMessage method, 628
AddNewDept.asp page, **407–409**
AddNewProduct.asp page, 365, **367–369**

AddRelation.asp page, 524, **526–527**
addresses
    billing. *See* billing data
    e-mail. *See* e-mail and e-mail addresses
    IP, 65, 67, *69*
    shipping. *See* shipping data
AddShipping.asp page
    adding shipping ranges in, **446–447**
    connections in, **445–446**
    posting to, 439
AddUpgradeItem.asp page, 514, **518–519**
AdminFile object, 600
Adminsite object, 600
AdminWebServer object, 600
ADO (ActiveX Data Objects)
    for databases, 91
    in ManageDept.asp page, **410–411**
    for projects, 227
    for relationships, 522
    for SQL Server, 18
Advertising server component, **597**
American Diabetes Association Web site, 61
Analysis component, **597**
ANSI compliant code, 29
Application_OnEnd function, 116
Application_OnStart function, 116
Application Title setting, 226
application variables, 649
ASP (Active Server Pages), **16–17**
    backups for, 71
    in IIS, 16
    in Visual InterDev, 17
ASP Conventions link, 652

assignments
    of attributes, 119–120
    of departments to products, **375–377**
        adding, **398–400**
        deleting, **397–398**
    of SKUs, 402
at signs (@) in e-mail addresses, 222, 263
AttachFile method, 272
AttachUrl method, 272
Attribute table, **32–33**, 48, 656
Attribute Category table, **33**, 48, 656
attributes
    adding, 118, **401–403**
    assigning, 119–120
    building, **144–146**
    categories for, 119
    color, **378–379**
    deleting, **400–401**
    displaying, **382**, 483
    retrieving, **143–144**, **147–148**, **382–383**,
        388–389
    size, **381–382**
    table of, **379–380**
authentication, 72
availability of inventory, 35

B

B-to-B (business-to-business) market space, 4
backups
    scenarios for, 74
    server, **71**
bandwidth, 645

Basket.asp page, *182*
    checking for baskets in, **174–175**
    for Clock Tower site, 622
    displaying basket contents in, **175–176**
    for featured products, **537–539**
    forms in, **173–174**
    links in, **176–177**
    looping through basket items in, **178–179**
    retrieving basket contents in, **175**
    Submit button in, **180–181**
    subtotals in, **180**
    tables in, **177**
    up-sell products in, **510–512**
Basket table, **38–39**
    deleting orders from, 472
    in order searches, 458
    script for, 48–49, 656
Basket Items table, **39–40**
BasketItem table
    deleting orders from, 472
    in order searches, 458
    script for, 49, 656
baskets
    adding items to. *See* AddItem.asp page
    checking for and creating, **165–166**,
        174–175
    for Clock Tower site, **634–636**
    in database design, **38–40**, *38*
    deleting items from, **186–190**, *189–190*
    designing, **162**, *163*
    displaying. *See* Basket.asp page
    emptying, **190–192**, *192–193*
    and free shipping, **570**
    in Header.asp page, **122–123**

    number of items in, **255**
    product quantities in, **164**, **170**
    retrieving contents of, **126–127**, **175**,
        329–330, **333–334**
    subtotals of, **180**, **256**
    for up-sell products, 514, 519
    updating, **167**, **170–171**, **182–186**, *185–186*,
        495, **498–499**
    in ValidatePayment.asp page, **269**
Bcc property, 272
best practices
    database, **645–646**
        configuring and utilizing SQL Server,
            646
        database design, **647**
        redundancy and reliability in, **646–647**
    IIS, **647–648**
billing data
    in Clock Tower site, 621
    in OrderDetail.asp page, **479–481**
    in Payment.asp page, **243–250**
    in UpdateOrder.asp page, **490–491**
    in ValidatePayment.asp page, **258–259**,
        261–262, **266–267**
    in ValidateShipping.asp page, **224**
bitmapped images, 648
BizTalk tool set, 20
Body property, 272–273
BodyFormat property, 272
books online, 616
browsers, **22–24**, *23*
    in server management, **75**
    in Visual Basic 6, 18

browsing
departments, **130–140**, *133, 139*
products, **140–150**, *149–150*
browsing phase
description of, **7**
tools for, 24
built-in ASP objects, 16
business code processing, 643
business rule management tools, 10
business-to-business (B-to-B) market space, 4
Buy Now tool, 599

(

C-to-B (consumer-to-business) e-commerce, 4
caching, 649
cascading style sheets, 24
categories
for attributes, 119
for products, **34**
tools for, 10
Cc property, 272
CDONTS (Collaboration Data Objects for
Windows NT), 271
Certificate server, 15
certificates, SSL
backups for, 71
managing, 72
charges, displaying, **233–234**
checked attribute, 545
Checked keyword tag, 253
checkout phase
description of, **7**
tools for, 25

checkout process
approaches to, **198**
in Clock Tower site, 621
confirmation page, **278–279**, *280*
defining, **196–197**, *197*
Payment.asp page. *See* Payment.asp page
shipping and tax calculations in, **225–232**
shipping page. *See* Shipping.asp page
shopper profile process in, 198–200, *199*
tax and shipping data for, **201–202**
ValidatePayment.asp page.
See ValidatePayment.asp page
ValidateShipping.asp page, **220–225**
checksum calculations, 261
chrAddress field, 36
chrAttributeName field, 32
chrBillAddress field, 41
chrBillCity field, 41
chrBillEmail field, 41
chrBillFax field, 41
chrBillFirstName field, 41
chrBillLastName field, 41
chrBillPhone field, 41
chrBillProvince field, 41
chrBillState field, 41
chrBillZipCode field, 41
chrCardName field, 42
chrCardNumber field, 42
chrCardType field, 42
chrCategoryName field, 33
chrCCExpMonth field, 237
chrCCExpYear field, 237
chrCCName field, 237
chrCCNumber field, 237
chrCCType field, 237

chrCity field, 36
chrColor field, 39
chrCountry field, 36
chrDeptImage field, 30
chrDeptName field, 30
chrEmail field, 37
chrExpDate field, 42
chrFax field, 37
chrFirstName field, 36
chrLastName field, 36
chrName field, 39
chrPassword field, 37
chrPhone field, 36
chrProductImage field, 32
chrProductName field, 32
chrProvince field, 36
chrShipAddress field, 41
chrShipCity field, 41
chrShipEmail field, 41
chrShipFax field, 41
chrShipFirstName field, 41
chrShipLastName field, 41
chrShipPhone field, 41
chrShippingNum field, 43
chrShipProvince field, 41
chrShipState field, 41
chrShipZipCode field, 41
chrSize field, 39
chrState field
    in Shopper table, 36
    in Tax table, 46
chrUserName field, 37
chrZipCode field, 36
CIP (Commerce Interchange Pipeline)

for information exchange, 20
    for Microsoft Market, 616
city data in Clock Tower site, 634
class objects, 228
cleaning
    session variables, 279
    shipping data, **266**
clearing out baskets, 39
ClearItems method, 603
ClearOrderForm method, 603
client side HTML, 17
Clock Tower site, **615**, **620–621**, *620–621*
    commerce objects in
        data functions, **630**
        dictionary, **626–627**
        message manager, **627–628**
        order form, **632–636**
        page, **630–631**
        StandardSManager, **628–629**
    management interface pages for, **623–624**
    pipelines in, **636–639**, *638–639*
    shopping interface pages for, **622–623**
    SQL database for, **624–626**
clocktower_basket table, 625
clocktower_dept table, 625
clocktower_product table, 626
clustering, 646
code blocking, 650
code compilation
    of DLLs, 232
    in performance, 650
    in three tier architecture, 644
code heavy sections, 75
coffee-related products, 615

Collaboration Data Objects for Windows NT (CDONTS), 271
color attribute, **378–379**
columns, 646
COM (Component Object Model) objects and components
    in ASP, 16
    backups for, 71
    building, 225–226, *226*
    deploying, 232
    MTS for, 599
    for pipelines, 603
    for Site Server, 600
    in Visual Basic 6, 18–19
    in Windows NT Server 4, 14
Commerce Edition tools, 611, *612*
Commerce Host Administration snap-in, 613, *614*
Commerce Interchange Pipeline (CIP)
    for information exchange, 20
    for Microsoft Market, 616
Commerce Interchange tool, 598
commerce objects for Clock Tower site
    data functions, **630**
    dictionary, **626–627**
    message manager, **627–628**
    order form, **632–636**
    page, **630–631**
    StandardSManager, **628–629**
Commerce Server, 21, **597–598**, **600–603**
Commerce Server link, 652
CommitData method, 634
Communicator, 22

compilation
    of DLLs, 232
    in performance, 650
    in three tier architecture, 644
Component Object Model. *See* COM (Component Object Model) objects and components
componentizing processing, 603
ConfigurationCacheHelper object, 600
configuring
    databases, 73
    drive space, 74
    IIS, 65, *66*
    SQL Server, **646**
confirmation.asp page
    in checkout process, **278–279**, *280*
    session variables for, 267
confirmation receipts, **271–274**
Confirmed.asp page, **278–279**, 622
connection string map, 636
connections, database
    pooling, 646
    programming, 649
    requirements for, 61
    in subscription application, **99–100**
consumer-to-business (C-to-B) e-commerce, 4
content subscriptions, 617
content synchronization, 62
ContentBase property, 272
ContentLocation property, 272
controls in Visual Basic 6, 18
conversions, data type, 630–631
cookies, 36, 199–200
    checking for, 121

expiration dates for, 274, 313
in Payment.asp page, **253–254**
in ProfileDisplay.asp page, **304–305**
shopper IDs in, 122
in Shopper table, 54
in UpdateProfile.asp page, **313**
in ValidatePayment.asp page, 270, **274–275**
Cookies collection, 274, 313
copyright.asp page, 624
copyright notices, 127
core components, Site Server, **594–598**
country data
in Clock Tower site, 634
in Payment.asp page, **251–252**
in ProfileDisplay.asp page, **302–303**
in UpdateProfile.asp page, **308–310**
in ValidatePayment.asp page, **262–263**
in ValidateShipping.asp page, **221–222**
Create Profile function, 199
CreateShopperID method, 629
credit card data
CIP components for, 20
in OrderDetail.asp page, **482–483**
in Payment.asp page, **237–242**
in PaymentData table, 42
security for, 36
in subscription application, **84–85**
in ValidatePayment.asp page, **259–260,
268–269**
cross-sell products, 31
in Microsoft Press site, 616
relating, **508–510**
currency, formatting, 178, 630
current date
for featured products, 537, **539–540**
for free shipping, **569**

current status in order searches, **464–465**
custom installs, 611, *611*
customer/visitor phase
description of, **6**
tools for, 24
Cybercash tool, 261

D

data functions for Clock Tower site, **630**, 636
data loading in store foundation design,
117–120
data synchronization, 62
data table for subscription sample application, **78–79**
data type conversions, 630–631
data validation
payments. *See* ValidatePayment.asp page
in ProcessSub.asp page, **87–89**
shipping. *See* ValidateShipping.asp page
of states and provinces, **225**
database design, **647**
baskets in, **38–40**, *38*
in best practices, **647**
departments in, **29–30**, *30*
final design, *47*, *47*
order status in, **42–43**, *43*
orders in, **40–42**, *40*
products in, **30–35**, *31*
shipping tables in, **44–45**
shoppers in, **35–37**
SQL scripts for, **47–56**
SQL Server in, **28–29**
tax tables in, **46**

databases, 17
   abstraction for, 644
   best practices for, **645–646**
      configuring and utilizing SQL Server,
         646
      database design in, **647**
      redundancy and reliability in, **646–647**
   for Clock Tower site, **624–626**
   connections to
      pooling, 646
      programming, 649
      requirements for, 61
      in subscription application, **99–100**
   designing. *See* database design
   insertions into, **91–93**
      payment information, **267–269, 277–278**
      related products, **526–527**
   searches in, 156
   servers for, **62**
   setup for, **73–74**
   Visual InterDev tools for, 17
DataFunctions object, 600, 630
date_changed field, 625
dates
   for featured products, 537, **539–540,**
      544–546
   formats for, 580
   for free shipping, **569, 579–580**
   in order searches, **455–456, 460,** 463
   for product sales, 573
DBStorage object, 600, **633–634,** 651
DCOM (Distributed Component Object
      Model), 20
debugging tools in Visual InterDev, 17

declaring variables, 228, 649
Default.asp page
   building, **128–129,** *129*
   for Clock Tower site, 622–623
   for featured products, **535–537**
   for sale items, **556–558**
default connection strings, 636
Default Web Site Properties dialog box, 65,
      66–68
DefaultItemPrice component, 638
DefaultShipping component, 607
DeleteAttribute.asp page, **400–401**
DeleteDept.asp page, **416–417**
DeleteItem.asp page, 178, **187–188**
DeleteOrder.asp page, 467, **472**
DeleteProduct.asp page, **392–394**
DeleteRelated.asp page, **527–528**
DeleteShipping.asp page, 438, **444–445**
deleting
   assignments of departments to products,
      397–398
   attributes, **400–401**
   basket items, **186–190,** *189–190*
   departments, **416–418**
   orders, **467, 471–473**
   products, **392–394**
   relationships, **527–529**
   shipping ranges, **444–445**
   shipping rates, **438–439**
Dell Computers site, 19
Department table, 30, 50, **656–657**
DepartmentProducts table, **34,** 50, 657
departments
   adding, **407–410,** *419*

assignments to, **375–377**
  adding, **398–400**
  deleting, **397–398**
browsing, **130–140**, *133*, *139*
creating, **406–409**
in database design, **29–30**, *30*
deleting, **416–418**
dictionary entry for, 627
displaying, **375–376**, **403–406**, **412–413**, *418*
editing, 419, *420*
image files for, **413**
previewing, 420, *421*
products in, **34**, **134–137**, 390–392, *390–392*
retrieving, **130–131**, **133**, **135**, **138**, **377–378**, **387**, **406**, **414**
tools for, 10
updating, **411–412**, **414–416**
deployment package, 232
Dept.asp page, *133*, 622
  headers in, **130**
  images in, **131–132**
  retrieving departments in, **130–131**
dept_delete.asp page, 623
dept_description field, 625
dept_edit.asp page, 623
dept_id field
  in clocktower_dept table, 625
  in clocktower_product table, 626
dept_list.asp page, 623
dept_name field, 625
dept_new.asp page, 623
DESC option, 126
description field, 626
Design view for HTML pages, 79–80

designing
  baskets, **162**, *163*
  databases. *See* database design
  featured products, **534–535**
  related products, **506**
  sale features, **554–555**
  store manager, **340–343**, *340*, *342*
development environment, **64**, *65*
development management, **63–64**
device backup, 74
DHTML
  browser support for, 24
  in Visual Basic 6, 19
Dictionary object, 600, 602, **626–627**
Directory Security Pane, 72, *72*
displaying
  attributes, **382**, 483
  basket contents. *See* Basket.asp page
  charges, **233–234**
  credit card information, **482–483**
  departments, **375–376**, **403–406**, **412–413**, *418*
  free shipping information, **567–568**, **582–583**
  orders, **323–324**, **483**
  payment information, **481–482**
  product image files, **373–374**
  products, **371–373**
  profiles. *See* ProfileDisplay.asp page
  sale items, **560–562**, *564*
  shipping charges, **486–487**
  shipping rates, **436–437**
  subtotals, **486–487**
  taxes, **486–487**
  totals, **486–487**

distance shipping model, 44
Distributed Component Object Model
        (DCOM), 20
DLLs, compiling, 232
dots (.) in e-mail addresses, 222, 263
drive space, configuring, 74
DSN settings, 612–613, *613*
dtCreated field, 38, 48
dtEntered field, 37, 54
dtFulfilled field, 43
dtOrdered field, 41, 50, 460
dtProcessed field, 43
dtSaleEnd field, 32, 53, 573
dtSaleStart field, 32, 53, 573
dtShipped field, 43
dual processors, 642
duplicate item checks, **166**
dynamic values, 647

E

e-mail address field, 222
e-mail and e-mail addresses
        for confirmation receipts, **271–274**
        Microsoft Exchange Server for, 21
        in order history, 317, 320
        in order searches, 459
        in profiles, **286–291**
        for sending passwords, 293
        session variables for, 292
        for shopper profiles, 199, 325
        in ValidatePayment.asp page, **263**
        in ValidateShipping.asp page, **222**

e-mail protocol, 15
EDI (Electronic Data Interchange), 6
editing
        departments, 419, *420*
        HTML, 22
        pipeline components, 607, *608*
        profiles, 198
Electronic Data Interchange (EDI), 6
Electronics Boutique site, 28
EmailPassword.asp page, **289–291**
EmptyBasket.asp page, 180, **190–191**
emptying baskets, **190–192**, *192–193*
end dates
        for featured products, 537, **544–546**
        for free shipping, **569**, **579–580**
error.asp page, 623–624
error checking and handling
        in Clock Tower site, 632
        in Payment.asp page, **242–243**
        programming, 649
        in Shipping.asp page, **206**
        in subscription application, **89–90**
        in UpdateProfile.asp page, **310–311**
        in ValidateShipping.asp page, **223–224**
Error session variable, 206, 242, 264
Exchange Server, 21
exchanging information, CIP for, 20
expiration date
        of cookies, 274, 313
        of credit cards, 42, 237, **239–242**, 260,
                482–483
Expires property, 274

F

failover, 646

featured products
basket for, **537–539**
building and designing, **534–535**
dates for, 537, **539–540**, **544–546**
default page for, **535–537**
navigation bar for, **540–542**
retrieving, **537**
testing, **542–544**, *542–544*, **548–550**, *549–551*
updating, **545–548**
fees, shipping, 436
15 ASP programming tips link, 652
FileDocument object, 600
financial transactions, 9
firewalls, 62
first link in ListProducts.asp page, 354
FixedShipping component, 638
fltTaxRate field, 432
Footer.asp page, **127–128**, 623
FormatCurrency function, 178
formatting
currency, 178, 630
dates, 580
Header.asp page, **123–125**
forms
for Clock Tower site, **633–634**
in ProfileDisplay.asp page, **294**
for subscription application, **81–84**
free shipping
basket updates for, **570**
calculations for, **569**
dates for, **569**, **579–580**

displaying information for, **567–568**,
582–583
implementing, **565–568**
managing, **577**
navigation bar for, **578**
retrieving data for, 578, **580**
store manager for, **577–580**
testing, **571–572**, *571–572*, **586–587**, *586–587*
updating, **580–581**, **583–586**
FreeShip table, 657
FreeShipping session variable, 565
From property, 272
FrontPage 2000, 22
FrontPage Extensions, 16, 65
FrontPage option, 65
FrontPage Server Administrator, 67, *68*
FTP service, 15
fulfill order phase
description of, **9**
tools for, 25

G

General tab, 226, *227*
GetData() function, 50
GetDate() function, 48, 54, 569
global.asa file
for Clock Tower site, 622, 638
contents of, 69
creating, 116
for messages, 627
global variables, 650
groups, selling products in, 176

H

Handling pipeline stage, 606
hardware, system, **642**
Header.asp page
    baskets in, **122–123**
    for Clock Tower site, 623
    cookies in, **121**
    for featured products, **540–542**
    formatting, **123–125**
    for sale items, **558–560**
    shopper records in, **121–122**
headers
    for HTML pages, 80
    for receipts, **326–329**, **333**, **488**
hidden fields, 142
high quantities for shipping, 436
high variable in searches, **152–154**
histories, order
    initializing, **269**
    interface
        OrderHistoryDisplay.asp page. *See*
            OrderHistoryDisplay.asp page
        OrderReceipt.asp page. *See* Order-
            Receipt.asp page
        OrderStatus.asp page, **316–318**
        sp_RetrieveOrders stored procedure,
            324–325
        sp_RetrieveProfile stored procedure,
            325–326
    managing, **284–285**, *285*
home page, **128–129**, *129*
HTML
    browser support for, 24

client side, 17
editing tools for, 22
for subscription sample application, **79–85**,
    79
HTTP_REFERER variable, 232
HTTP service, 15

I

idAttribute field
    in Attribute table, 32, 48
    in Product Attribute table, 33
idAttributeCategory field
    in Attribute table, 32, 48
    in Attribute Category table, 33
idBasket field
    in Basket table, 38, 48
    in Basket Items table, 39, 49
idBasket session variable, 165
idBasketItem field, 39
idDepartment field
    in Department table, 30
    in DepartmentProducts table, 34
idDepartmentProduct field, 34
@@identity system variable, 126, 169, 277
idOrder field
    in OrderData table, 40, 50
    in OrderStatus table, 43
    in PaymentData table, 42
idOrderStatus field, 43, 51
idPayment field, 42, 51
idProduct field
    in Basket Items table, 39

in DepartmentProducts table, 34
in Product Attribute table, 33
in Products table, 32, 53
idProductA field, 34
idProductAttribute field, 33, 52
idProductB field, 34
idQuantityRange field, 45, 54
idRelatedProducts field, 34, 53
idRelationType field, 34
idShopper field
in Basket table, 38
in OrderData table, 40
in Shopper table, 36, 54
IDShopper variable, 116, 121
idStage field, 43, 51, 275
idState field, 46, 55
idSubscription variable, 102–103
IIS (Internet Information Server), **15–16**
backups for, 71
best practices, **647–648**
configuring, 65, *66*
with Visual Basic 6, 18
IIS link, 652
IIS 4.0 Tuning link, 652
IIS queue, 648
image_file field, 626
image_height field, 626
image_width field, 626
images
in Basket.asp page, 180
bitmapped, 648
in Dept.asp page, **131–132**
in ManageDept.asp page, **413**
in ManageProduct.asp page, **373–374**
in Products.asp page, **136–137**

Importance property, 272
Index Server, 15, 156
indexes, database, 647
Inetinfo process, 647
information resources, **652–653**
initializing
order histories, **269**
order status, **275**
InitManager method, 629
InitStorage method, 633
input fields for subscription application,
    81–84
InsertData method, 634
inserting
data into databases, **91–93**
payment information, **267–269, 277–278**
related products, **526–527**
items into basket. *See* AddItem.asp page
shoppers, 125–126
installing Site Server, **609–614**, *610–614*
Instr function, 222
intActive field, 32
intCookie field, 37, 54
interfaces, user. *See* user interface
internal corporate purchasing, 616
international options
in Shipping.asp page, **215–216**
support for, 198
international ordering, 8
Internet Explorer browser, 22, *22*
Internet Information Server (IIS), **15–16**
backups for, 71
best practices, **647–648**
configuring, 65, *66*
with Visual Basic 6, 18

intFeatured variable, 546
intFee field, 45
intFreeShipping field, 554, 582–584
intHighQuantity field, 45
intLowQuantity field, 45
intOrderPlaced field, 38
intPrice field
   in Basket Items table, 39
   in Products table, 32, 53
intProcessed field, 43, 51
intQuantity field
   in Basket Items table, 39, 49
   in Basket table, 38
intSalePrice field, 32, 53, 573
intShipping field, 39
intSubTotal field, 38
intTax field, 39
intTaxRate field, 46, 55
intTotal field, 39
inventory availability, 35
Inventory pipeline stage, 605–606
IP addresses, 65, 67, *69*
IsDate function, 87
Item Adjust Price pipeline stage, 605
item codes, 483
Item Price pipeline stage, 605
item quantity shipping model, 44
Items collection, 635

J

JavaScript
   browser support for, 24
   for components modules, 607

K

Key Manager interface, 72, *73*
keyword searches, 150
Knowledge Manager component, **597**

L

LDAP (Lightweight Directory Access Protocol), 20
like queries, 155, 459, 461
line item total, 483
links to products, **34–35**
list.asp page, 624
list_column.asp page, 624
list_no_rows.asp page, 624
list_price field, 626
list_row.asp page, 624
ListDepts.asp page
   connections in, **403–404**
   displaying departments in, **404–405**
   looping through departments in, **405–406**
ListProducts.asp page, **350**
   connections for, **350–351**
   links in, **354–355**
   list starting point in, **351**
   looping through products in, **353–354**
   retrieving number of products in, **352**
   searching in, **355–356**
   table in, **352–353**
load balancing, 62–63, **643**
load planning, **75**

loading
  considerations for, 73
  in store foundation design, **117–120**
  tax and shipping data, **201–202**
local variables, 650
Locale property, 630
Localhost IP addresses, 65
Login.asp page, **344–345**, *344*
login IDs, 613
login names, 647
logins
  for order history, **316–318**, *319*
  for profile interface, **286–288**, *288–289*
  for store manager, **343–345**, *344*
logos, 123
low quantities for shipping, 436
low variable in searches, **152–153**

M

mail. *See* e-mail and e-mail addresses
mail protocol, 15
MailFormat property, 272
Make tab, 226
ManageDept.asp page
  ADO record sets in, **410–411**
  displaying departments in, **412–413**
  image files in, **413**
  links to, 405
  security in, **410**
  updated departments in, **411–412**
ManageFreeShipping.asp page
  connections in, **578–579**

dates in, **579–580**
  security in, **577–578**
Management console, 16
ManageOrders.asp page
  dates in, **455–456**
  products in, **456**
  security in, **454–455**
ManageProduct.asp page
  Active check box in, **374–375**
  attributes in
    color, **378–379**
    displaying, **382**
    retrieving, **382–383**
    size, **381–382**
    table of, **379–380**
  for departments
    assignments, **375–377**
    listing, **375–376**
    retrieving, **377–378**
  header in, **370–371**
  images in, **373–374**
  for products
    displaying, **371–373**
    featured, **544–546**
    related, **522–525**
    retrieving, **371**
    sales, **573**
  select boxes in, **383–386**
manager.asp page, 624
ManagerMenu.asp page, **345–348**, *348*, **577**
ManageShipping.asp page
  connections in, **435–436**
  shipping rates in
    deleting, **438–439**

displaying, 436–437
looping through, 437–438
ranges, 440
retrieving, 436
Submit button in, 439, 441
ManageTax.asp page
includes in, 424
Submit button in, 428
tax data in
entering, 427–428
looping through, 425–426
retrieving current settings in, 425
updating, 426–427
manufacturer field, 626
marketing phase
description of, 5–6
tools for, 24
Marshalled_Order Field
in clocktower_basket table, 625
in VCTurbo and VCRocket, 651
Martha Stewart site, 19, 28
Membership and Personalization, 617
Membership Server, 20
memory
conserving, 645
for Site Server, 595
Merchant Information pipeline stage, 605
message manager object, 627–628, 636
Message Queue Server, 15
MessageManager object, 600
mgmt_footer.asp page, 624
mgmt_header.asp page, 624
MicroPipe object, 601
Microsoft Access, 28

Microsoft ActiveX Data Objects 2 Library, 227
Microsoft Developer Network (MSDN), 272, 646
Microsoft Exchange Server, 21
Microsoft FrontPage 2000, 22
Microsoft Internet Explorer, 609
Microsoft Management Console (MMC)
for process management, 65, *66*
for Site Server Administrator, 613, *614*
Microsoft Market site, 616
Microsoft Message Queue (MSMQ)
in CIP, 20
in IIS, 15
Microsoft Office, 22
Microsoft Press site, 616–617
Microsoft tool set
Active Server Pages/Visual Interdev, 16–17
browser issues, 22–24, *23*
Internet Information Server, 15–16
miscellaneous tools, 21–22
Site Server 3, 19–21
SQL Server, 17–18
SSL/Verisign certificates, 21
utilization of, 24–25
Visual Basic 6, 18–19
Windows NT Server 4, 14–15
Microsoft Transaction Server (MTS)
for COM components, 599
in IIS, 15
for resource conservation, 646
Microsoft Visual Studio, 22
Microsoft Wallet tool, 599
Microsoft Windows NT Server, 14–15, 594–595, 609

MMC (Microsoft Management Console)
   for process management, 65, *66*
   for Site Server Administrator, 613, *614*
money, formatting, 178, 630
Money method, 630
monitoring performance, 648
month of credit card expiration, **239–241**
MSCSQueryMap dictionary object, 627
MSDN (Microsoft Developer Network), 272,
   646
MSDN link, 652
MSMQ (Microsoft Message Queue)
   in CIP, 20
   in IIS, 15
MTS (Microsoft Transaction Server)
   for COM components, 599
   in IIS, 15
   for resource conservation, 646
MtsPipeline object, 601
MtsTxPipeline object, 601
multiple departments for products, **34**
multiple server support, **62–63**, *62–63*, 74

N

name field, 626
navigation and navigation bar, **176**
   in Clock Tower site, 621
   code for, **342–343**
   for featured products, **540–542**
   for free shipping, **578**
   in Header.asp page, 123–124
   for sale items, **558–560**, *563*
   in searching, **362–363**

navigation links, 124
NavInclude.asp page
   for free shipping, **578**
   for product management, **342–343**
Netscape Navigator browser, 22, *22*
new department link, 418
New tab, 67
NewDept.asp page, **406–408**
NewMail object, **271–273**
NewProduct.asp page, **365–367**
newsgroup support, 15
next-day shipping option, 45
next link in ListProducts.asp page, 354, 357
NNTP service, 15
No cookie profile scenario, 200
No previous profile scenario, 200
NOT IN operation, 539
number of basket items, **255**

O

Object tag, 650
ODBC DSNs
   backups for, 71
   for databases, 91
ODBC with SQL Server, 18
OLE DB provider, 18
1-800-Flowers site, 28
online content subscriptions, 617
operating system files, backups for, 71
OPPs (order processing pipelines), 598,
   603–604, *604*
   in Clock Tower site, **636–639**, *638–639*
   editors for, 607, *608*

Plan, **605–606, 637**
Product, **604–605**
Purchase, **606–607**
optimization
   programming practices for, **649–650**
   in three tier architecture, 644
   tuning for, 647
option boxes
   in Payment.asp page, **250–251**
   in ProfileDisplay.asp page, **300–302**
   in Shipping.asp page, **208–215**
Option Explicit statement, 228, 649
Order Adjust Price pipeline stage, 605
Order Check pipeline stage, 605
order form object, **632–636**
order history
   initializing, **269**
   interface
      OrderHistoryDisplay.asp page. *See*
         OrderHistoryDisplay.asp page
      OrderReceipt.asp page. *See* Order-
         Receipt.asp page
      OrderStatus.asp page, **316–318**
      sp_RetrieveOrders stored procedure,
         324–325
      sp_RetrieveProfile stored procedure,
         325–326
   managing, **284–285**, *285*
Order Initialization pipeline stage, 605
order process phase
   description of, **9**
   tools for, 25
order processing pipelines (OPPs), 598,
   603–604, *604*

in Clock Tower site, **636–639**, *638–639*
editors for, 607, *608*
Plan, **605–606, 637**
Product, **604–605**
Purchase, **606–607**
Order Subtotal pipeline stage, 606
Order Total pipeline stage, 606
order total shipping model, 44
OrderData table, **40–41**
   in order searches, 458
   script for, 50–51, 657
OrderDetail.asp page
   address information in, **477, 479–481**
   credit card information in, **482–483**
   displaying ordered items in, **483**
   for free shipping, **582–583**
   looping through orders in, **484–486**
   order IDs in, **478**
   payment information in, **481–482**
   security in, **476–477**
   Submit button in, **487–488**
   table in, **483–484**
   totals, tax, and shipping in, **486–487**
   updates in, **477–478**
orderform.asp page, 622
OrderForm object, 601–603
OrderHistoryDisplay.asp page
   connections for, **318–320**
   displaying orders in, **323–324**
   finishing up, **324**
   looping through orders in, **321–323**
   retrieving orders in, **320–321**
   tables in, **321**

OrderReceipt.asp page, **326**
  headers in, **326–329**
  looping through data in, **330–331**
  retrieving basket items in, **329–330**
  subtotals, shipping, tax, and totals in, **331–333**
  table in, **330**
orders
  checkout process for. *See* checkout process
  in database design, **40–42**, *40*
  deleting, **467**, **471–473**
  displaying, **323–324**, **483**
  histories of. *See* order history
  inserting data for, **275–277**
  pipelines for. *See* order processing pipelines (OPPs)
  retrieving, **320–321**, **324–325**
  reviewing. *See* OrderDetail.asp page
  searching for. *See* OrderSearch.asp page
  status of
    in database design, **42–43**, *43*
    initializing, **275**
    updates for, **473–475**, *475–476*
  tracking and reporting tools for, 10
  updating, **477–478**, **490–501**, *500–501*
OrderSearch.asp page
  connections in, **462**
  current status in, **464–465**
  dates in, **460**, **463–464**
  deleting orders in, **467**
  e-mail addresses in, **459**
  looping through return results in, **463**
  posting to, 455
  product name checks in, **461**

queries in, **457**
retrieving form values in, **457–458**
select boxes in, **466**
shipping tracking numbers in, **466**
shopper names in, **459–460**
SQL checks in, **461**
tables in, **458–459**, **462–463**
totals in, **463–464**
updating status in, **465**
OrderStatus.asp page, **316–318**
OrderStatus table, **42–43**
  deleting orders from, 472
  in order searches, 458
  script for, 51–52, 658

P

Package and Deployment Wizard, 232
Page object, 601, **630–631**
page structure, **120–121**, *120*
  header and footer pages, **121–128**
  home pages, **128–129**, *129*
passwords
  appropriate, 647
  in authentication, 72
  in Login.asp page, 344–345
  for order history, 316–317, 320
  in Payment.asp page, **254**
  for profiles, 199–200, 253–254, **286–291**, **304–305**, 325
  sending, **293**
  session variables for, 292
  for shoppers, 36

for Site Server, 613
in ValidatePayment.asp page, 270
Payment.asp page
    address defaults in, **252–253**
    billing address in, **243–244**
    billing address states in, **244–250**
    charges displayed in, **233–234**
    in Clock Tower site, 621
    cookies in, **253–254**
    country and province information in, **251–252**
    credit card information in, **237–238**
        expiration month, **239–241**
        expiration year, **241–242**
    error messages in, **242–243**
    for free shipping, **565–568**
    links to, **232–233**
    option boxes in, **250–251**
    passwords in, 254
    payment information in, **238–239**
    Submit button in, **254–255**
    subtotals in, **236–237**
    taxes and shipping in, **234–235**
    totals in, **235**
payment data
    displaying, **481–482**
    inserting into databases, **277–278**
    in Payment.asp page. *See* Payment.asp page
    retrieving, **488–489**
    updating, **492**, **497–498**
payment phase
    description of, **8**
    tools for, 25

Payment pipeline stage, 606, 639
PaymentData table, **42**
    deleting orders from, 472
    script for, 52, 658
peak loading, configuring, 73
performance
    monitoring, 648
    programming practices for, **649–650**
    in three tier architecture, 644
    tuning for, 647
periods (.) in e-mail addresses, 222, 263
Personalization & Membership component, **596**
Personalization Server, 20
phases
    checkout, **7**
    customer/visitor, **6**
    description of, **4–5**, *5*
    fulfill order, **9**
    marketing, **5–6**
    payment, **8**
    process order, **9**
    product browsing, **7**
    receipt, **8**
    ship order, **9**
    shopping basket, **7**
    tax and shipping, **7–8**
    tools for, **24–25**
    Web site visit, **6–7**
PipeContext object, 602
pipelines, order processing, 598, **603–604**, *604*
    in Clock Tower site, **636–639**, *638–639*
    editors for, 607, *608*
    Plan, **605–606**, 637

Product, **604–605**
Purchase, **606–607**
Plan pipeline, **605–606**, **637**
pooling database connections, 646
Predictor object, 601, 616
preview link, 392
previewing departments, 420, *421*
previous link in ListProducts.asp page, 354
prices
    displaying, 483
    for sale items, **560–562**
    in SKUs, 403
process order phase
    description of, **9**
    tools for, 25
processors, 642, 644
ProcessSub.asp page
    data retrieval in, **86–87**
    data validation in, **87–89**
    error information in, **89–90**
    inserting database data in, **91–93**
    testing, **94–95**, *95–96*
    thank you message and data recap in,
        90–91
ProdAddDept.asp page, 376, **398–399**
ProdInc session variable, 350, 359
Product.asp page
    building attributes in, **144–146**
    for Clock Tower site, 622
    cross-sell products in, **508–509**
    headers in, **140–141**
    retrieving attributes in, **143–144**
    retrieving products in, **141**
    for sale items, **560–562**

Submit button in, **146–147**
    tables in, **142–143**
product browsing phase
    description of, **7**
    tools for, 24
product_delete.asp page, 623
product_edit.asp page, 623
Product Info pipeline stage, 604–605
product information stage in VCTurbo and
        VCRocket, 651
product_list.asp page, 623
product_new.asp page, 624
Product pipeline, **604–605**
ProductAttribute table, **33**, 52, 658
products
    adding, **365–369**
    assignments to departments, **375–377**
        adding, **398–400**
        deleting, **397–398**
    attributes for. *See* attributes
    baskets for. *See* AddItem.asp page; baskets
    browsing, **140–150**, *149–150*
    categorizing, **34**
    in database design, **30–35**, *31*
    deleting, **392–394**
    in departments, **34**, **134–137**, 390–392,
        390–392
    dictionary entry for, 627
    displaying, **371–373**
    editing, 389, *389*
    featured, **544–546**
    image files for, **373–374**
    limits for sale items, 562
    linking, **34–35**

listing, **350–358**
in order searches, **456**
related. *See* related products
retrieving, **135–136**, **138**, **141**, **147**, **371**,
      386–387
searching for. *See* Search.asp page; Search-
      Products.asp page
tools for, 10
updating, **394–397**
Products.asp page
      images in, **136–137**
      record sets in, **134**
      retrieving departments in, **135**
      retrieving products in, **135–136**
Products table, **32**, 53, 658
Profile.asp page, **204**, **286–288**
ProfileDisplay.asp page
      addresses in, **303–304**
      cookies in, **304–305**
      country and province data in, **302–303**
      forms in, **294**
      option boxes in, **300–302**
      passwords in, **304–305**
      retrieving data in, **291–292**
      retrieving profiles in, **292–293**
      sending passwords in, **293**
      session variables in, **292**
      shopper values in, **294**
      states in, **295–300**
      Submit button in, **305**
      text boxes in, **294–295**
ProfileRetrieve session variable, 203–204
profiles, **35–37**, **286**, *286*
      checking for, **203**

defining process for, 198–200, *199*
displaying. *See* ProfileDisplay.asp page
login page for, **286–288**, *288–289*
passwords for, 199–200, 253–254, **286–291**,
      304–305, 325
in Payment.asp page, **253–254**
retrieval scenarios for, 200
retrieving, **217**, **292–293**, **306**, **325–326**
updating, **270–271**, **306–314**, *315–316*
programming, **649–650**
Project Explorer window, 79
Project menu, 226
Project Name setting, 226
projects
      ADO objects for, 227
      creating, 67
      in store foundation design, **115–117**
      types of, 226
promotions
      cross-sell products, 31
            in Microsoft Press site, 616
            relating, **508–510**
      featured products. *See* featured products
      sale features. *See* sale features
      tools for, 10
      up-sell products. *See* up-sell products
properties dialog box, 226, *227*
province data
      in Payment.asp page, **251–252**
      in ProfileDisplay.asp page, **302–303**
      in UpdateProfile.asp page, **308–309**
      in ValidatePayment.asp page, **264**
      in ValidateShipping.asp page, **223**
      validation for, **225**

Publishing component, **596**
purchase.asp page, 622
Purchase Check pipeline stage, 606, 639
Purchase pipeline, **606–607**, 638–639
Push component, **597**
PutShopperID method, 629

Q

quad processors, 642
quantities
  in baskets, **164**, **170**
  displaying, 483
  limiting, 562
queries in Search.asp page
  process of, **154**
  results of, **154–155**
query map
  in Clock Tower site, 636, 638
  in VCTurbo and VCRocket, 651
QueryMap object, 602
QueryProdInfoADO component, 638
queue saturation, 648
queues, **647–648**
Quick View for HTML pages, 79–80

R

RAID 5 systems, 642
RAM
  conserving, 645
  for Site Server, 595

ranges
  in searches, 151
  for shipping, 436, **440**
    adding, **445–447**
    deleting, **444–445**
RDS (Remote Data Services), 11, 22
real-time replication, 74
receipt phase
  description of, **8**
receipts, *334*
  headers for, **326–329**, **333**, **488**
  items on, **329–330**
  looping through data for, **330–331**
  retrieving, **489**
  subtotals, shipping, tax, and totals in,
    331–333
  table for, **330**
  updating, **493**
  in ValidatePayment.asp page, **271–274**
  in VCTurbo and VCRocket, 651
recommendation engines, 156
record sets
  in ManageDept.asp page, **410–411**
  in Products.asp page, **134**
redundancy, 642
  in database best practices, **646–647**
  in three tier architecture, 644
References dialog box, 226, *227*
registration process, 615
related products, **34–35**
  building relationships, **507**, *507*
  cross-sell, **508–510**
  deleting relationships, **527–529**
  designing, **506**

displaying, **522–523**

inserting into databases, **526–527**

selecting products for, **524–526**

testing, **529**, *529–530*

up-sell, **510–520**, *520–521*

RelatedProducts table, **34**, 53–54, 658–659

reliability

in database best practices, **646–647**

systems for, 642

Remote Data Services (RDS), 11, 22

remote server site management, 17

RemoveProdDept.asp page, 375, **397–398**

Replace command, 92

replication scenarios, 74

reports, **98–105**, *104–105*

Request object, 86

RequestQueueMax setting, 648

requirements

for database connections, 61

for Site Server, **594–595**

resources, **652–653**

retrieving

attributes, **143–144**, **147–148**, **382–383**, **388–389**

basket contents, **126–127**, **175**, **329–330**, **333–334**

billing data, **266–267**

departments, **130–131**, **133**, **135**, **138**, **377–378**, **387**, **406**, **414**

featured products, **537**

free shipping information, 578, **580**

number of basket items, **255**

orders, **320–321**, **324–325**

payment data, **488–489**

products, **135–136**, **138**, **141**, **147**, **371**, **386–387**

profiles, **217**, **292–293**, **306**, **325–326**

receipt headers, **333**, **488**

receipts, **489**

sale items, **558**

shipping rates, 229, **231**, **441**

shopper profiles, 199, **217**

subscription information, **86–87**

tax rates, 228, **231**, **425**, **429**

up-sell products, **512–513**

reviewing orders. *See* OrderDetail.asp page

RND function, 557

S

sale features

designing, **554–555**

free shipping. *See* free shipping

sale items

default page for, **556–558**, *563*

displaying, **560–562**, *564*

managing, **572–576**, *576–577*

navigation bar for, **558–560**, *563*

retrieving, **558**

saving

order forms, **633–634**

profile passwords, 253

subscription information, **102–103**

script editor, 17

Scriptor component, 607

scripts

for database design, **47–56**

for stored procedures, **660–663**
for subscription sample application, **86–93**
for tables, **656–659**
Search.asp page
    checking for results in, **151**
    checking for search requests in, **152–153**
    high values in, **153–154**
    low values in, **153**
    query process in, **154**
    query results in, **154–155**
    tables in, **151–152**
Search component, **596**
search variable, 152
searching
    in ListProducts.asp page, **355–356**
    for orders. *See* OrderSearch.asp page
    for products. *See* Search.asp page; Search-
        Products.asp page
    sites, **156**
SearchProducts.asp page
    connections in, **359**
    criteria in, **360–361**
    includes in, **358–359**
    links in, **361–362**
    navigation in, **362–363**
    posting to, 355
    search option in, **363**
    session variables in, **359–360**
Secure Sockets Layer (SSL)
    backups for, 71
    managing, 72
    requirements for, 61
    support for, **21**

security
    for credit card data, 36
    ManagerMenu.asp page for, **345–348**
    server, 62, **71–72**, *72–73*
    SSL and Verisign certificates for, **21**
    for store manager, **343–349**, *344*, *348*
    tools for, 10
    in Trey Research site, 617
    ValidateCheck.asp page for, **348–350**
    in Windows NT Server 4, 14
segmentation in three tier architecture, 644
select boxes
    in ManageProduct.asp page, **383–386**
    in order searches, 464
Select Features screen, 609, *610*
Select System DSN dialog box, 613, *613*
selected HTML keyword, 208
Send method, 272, 290
sending passwords, **293**
server farm design
    database servers, **62**
    multiple server support, **62–63**, *62–63*
    staging and development management,
        63–64
    Web servers, **60–61**
Server Too Busy message, 648
servers
    backups for, **71**
    browser considerations in, **75**
    database setup for, **73–74**
    development environment in, **64**, *65*
    load planning, **75**
    security for, 62, **71–72**, *72–73*
    setup for, **65–70**, *66–70*

SQL Server. *See* SQL Server
in three tier architecture, 644
ServerVariables collection, 232
service packs, 595
Session_OnEnd function, 116
Session_OnStart function, 116
session variables, **80**, 89
   clearing, 279
   for confirmation.asp page, 267
   for performance, 649
   in ProfileDisplay.asp page, **292**
   for province information, **223**
   in SearchProducts.asp page, **359–360**
   for state information, 80, 114
   timeouts for, 349
   in ValidatePayment.asp page, **264–265**
sessions, timeout setting for, 80, 349
SetLocalids method, 272
ship order phase
   description of, **9**
   tools for, 25
Shipping.asp page, **202–203**, *218–219*
   checking for baskets in, **203**
   checking for profiles in, **203**
   error checking in, **206**
   international options in, **215–216**
   links in, **204**
   option boxes in, **208–215**
   session variables in, **204–205**
   shipping addresses in, **206–208**
   Submit button in, **216–217**
   testing, **218**, *218–219*
shipping data
   CIP components for, 20
   cleaning, **266**

in Clock Tower site, 621
cost calculations, **225–232**
displaying, **486–487**
free. *See* free shipping
loading, **201–202**
in OrderDetail.asp page, **477**, **479–481**, **486–487**
in OrderReceipt.asp page, **331–333**
page for. *See* Shipping.asp page
in Payment.asp page, **234–235**
in ProfileDisplay.asp page, **303–304**
ranges for, **436**, **440**
   adding, **445–447**
   deleting, **444–445**
rates for
   calculating, **230**
   deleting, **438–439**
   displaying, **436–437**
   retrieving, 229, **231**, **441**
   updating, **441–444**
   tracking numbers in, **466**
   updating, **490–491**, **495**
Shipping function, 228, **230**, 234
shipping phase
   description of, **7–8**
   tools for, 25
Shipping pipeline stage, 606
Shipping session variable, 569
Shipping table, **44–45**, 54, 659
shop.asp page, 623
shopper_id field, 625
shopper IDs
   in AddItem.asp page, **163–164**
   in cookies, 122
Shopper Information pipeline stage, 604–605

Shopper table, **35–37**, 54–55, 659
shoppers
    in Clock Tower site, **629**
    in database design, **35–37**
    in Header.asp page, **121–122**
    inserting, 125–126
    in order searches, **459–460**
    profiles for. *See* profiles
    tools for, 10
    in VCTurbo and VCRocket, 651
shopping basket phase
    description of, **7**
    tools for, 25
shopping baskets. *See* baskets
Shopping function, 495
shopping interface pages for Clock Tower
    site, **622–623**
ShowAttributeList subroutine, 382
SimpleDBDS object, 601
SimpleList object, 601
SimpleUSTax component, 638
single processors, 642
single quotes (')
    in shipping data, 266
    in SQL Server, 92
Site Builder Wizard, 598–599
Site manager pages, 598
site name for Clock Tower site, 636
Site object, 602
Site Server, **19–21**
    Clock Tower site. *See* Clock Tower site
    Commerce Server objects in, 598, **600–603**
    core components, **594–598**
    enhancements to, **650–651**
    installing, **609–614**, *610–614*
    Microsoft Market site, **616**
    Microsoft Press site, **616–617**
    order processing pipelines in, 598, **603–604**,
        604
        editors for, 607, *608*
        Plan, **605–606**, 637
        Product, **604–605**
        Purchase, **606–607**
    requirements for, **594–595**
    Trey Research site, **617**
    Volcano Coffee site, **615–616**
Site Server installation guide, 652
Site Server link, 652
sites
    architecture of, **114**, *115*
    searching, **156**
    synchronizing, 74
siteutil.asp page, 624
size attribute, **381–382**
sku field, 626
SKUs
    assigning, 402
    in clocktower_product table, 626
    handling, **144**
    prices in, 403
SMTP server, 272
SMTP service, 15
source code control, 22
Source view for HTML pages, 79–80
SourceSafe program, 64
sp_AddProdDept stored procedure, **399–400**
sp_AddProductAttribute stored procedure,
    401–403

sp_Attributes stored procedure, 143, **147–148**, 378, **388**

sp_BasketQuantity stored procedure, 233, **255**

sp_BasketSubTotal stored procedure, 233, **256**

sp_CheckBasketItemQuantity stored procedure, 166, **170**

sp_CheckFreeShip stored procedure, 565, **569**

sp_ClearBasketItems stored procedure, **190–191**

sp_CreateBasket stored procedure, 165, **169–170**, 174

sp_DeleteDept stored procedure, **417–418**

sp_DeleteOrder stored procedure, **471–473**

sp_DeleteProdDept stored procedure, **397–398**

sp_DeleteProduct stored procedure, **394**

sp_DeleteProductAttribute stored procedure, **400–401**

sp_DeleteProductRelation stored procedure, **529**

sp_DeleteShippingRate stored procedure, **444–445**

sp_GetShippingRate stored procedure, 229, **231**, 436, **441**

sp_GetTaxRate stored procedure, 228, **231**

sp_InitializeOrderStatus stored procedure, 269, **275**

sp_InsertBasketItem stored procedure, **167–169**, 519

sp_InsertDept stored procedure, **409–410**

sp_InsertOrderData stored procedure, 267, **275–277**

sp_InsertPaymentData stored procedure, 268, **277–278**

sp_InsertProduct stored procedure, 367, **369**, *370*

sp_InsertProductRelation stored procedure, **526–527**

sp_InsertShippingRate stored procedure, **446–447**

sp_InsertShopper stored procedure, 121, **125–126**

sp_ManageRetrieveProducts stored procedure, **356–358**, *357–358*

sp_ManagerRetrieveProdSearch stored procedure, 360, **363–364**, *364*

sp_RemoveBasketItem stored procedure, **187–188**, 519

sp_RetrieveAttributes stored procedure, 382, **389**

sp_RetrieveBasketItem stored procedure, 175, **184–185**

sp_RetrieveDept stored procedure, **138**, 410, **414**

sp_RetrieveDeptByProd stored procedure, 375, **387**

sp_RetrieveDeptProducts stored procedure, **138**

sp_RetrieveDepts stored procedure, 130, **133**, 377, **387**, **406**

sp_RetrieveFeaturedProducts stored procedure, 535, **537**, 540

sp_RetrieveFreeShip stored procedure, 578, **580**

sp_RetrieveLastBasket stored procedure, 122, **126–127**

sp_RetrieveNonPurchFeatureProd stored procedure, 537, **539–540** sp_RetrieveOrders stored procedure, 320, **324–325**

sp_RetrievePaymentData stored procedure, 481, **488–489**

sp_RetrieveProduct stored procedure, 141, **147**, **386–387**, 513

sp_RetrieveProductRelations stored procedure, **525–526**

sp_RetrieveProducts stored procedure, **526**

sp_RetrieveProfile stored procedure, 292, **306**, 320, **325–326**

sp_RetrieveProfileById stored procedure, 204, **217**

sp_RetrieveReceiptHeader stored procedure, 327, **333**, 477, **488**

sp_RetrieveReceiptItems stored procedure, 329, **333–334**, 483, **489**, 493

sp_RetrieveRelatedProducts stored procedure, **508–510**

sp_RetrieveSaleProducts stored procedure, 556, **558**

sp_RetrieveTaxRates stored procedure, 425, **429**

sp_RetrieveUpSell stored procedure, **512**

sp_SearchProducts stored procedure, 154, **156–157**

sp_UpdateBasket stored procedure, 495, **499**, **569–570**, 584

sp_UpdateBasketItem stored procedure, 494, **498**

sp_UpdateBasketItemsQuantity stored procedure, 167, **170–171**, 184

sp_UpdateDepartment stored procedure, **415–416**

sp_UpdateFreeShip stored procedure, 580

sp_UpdateOrderData stored procedure, 491, **496–497**

sp_UpdateOrderStatus stored procedure, **473–475**

sp_UpdatePaymentData stored procedure, 492, **497–498**

sp_UpdateProduct stored procedure, **396–397**, **547–548**, **573–575**

sp_UpdateShippingRate stored procedure, **443–444**

sp_UpdateShopper stored procedure, 270, 312, **314–316**

sp_UpdateTaxRate stored procedure, **432–434**

spike loads, 73

splitting functions, 647

SQL database
    for Clock Tower site, **624–626**
    with Visual InterDev, 17

SQL Enterprise Manager, 28–29

SQL Executive service, 29

SQL scripts for database design, **47–56**

SQL Server, **17–18**, **28–29**
    backups for, 71
    configuring and utilizing, **646**
    DNS settings for, 612
    installing, 609
    single quotes in, 92
    for Site Server, 594

SQL Server link, 652

SSL (Secure Sockets Layer)
    backups for, 71
    managing, 72
    requirements for, 61
    support for, **21**

staging management, **63–64**
StandardSManager object, 601, 615, **628–629**
start dates
    for featured products, 537, **544–546**
    for free shipping, 569, **579–580**
start product session variable, 354
starter stores
    Clock Tower site. *See* Clock Tower site
    Microsoft Market site, **616**
    Microsoft Press site, **616–617**
    Trey Research site, **617**
    Volcano Coffee site, **615–616**
StartProd variable, 351, 354, 359
state data, session variables for, 80, 114
states
    data validation for, **225**
    in Payment.asp page, **244–250**
    in ProfileDisplay.asp page, **295–300**
    in shopping basket, 38
    in UpdateProfile.asp page, **308–309**
    in ValidatePayment.asp page, **262–264**
    in ValidateShipping.asp page, **223**
static Web pages, 648, 650
status of orders
    in database design, **42–43**, *43*
    initializing, **275**
    updates for, **473–475**, *475–476*
sticky applications, 6
store foundation design
    data loading in, **117–120**
    pages in, **112–114**
    project setup in, **115–117**
    site architecture in, **114**, *115*
store manager

designing, **340–343**, *340, 342*
    security for, **343–349**, *344, 348*
stored procedures
    importance of, 646
    for performance, 650
    script listings for, **662–686**
storefront management, **10–11**
strBody variable, 273
strError variable, 223
style sheets, 24
Subject property, 272–273
Submit button
    in Basket.asp page, **180–181**
    in ManageOrders.asp page, 456
    in ManageShipping.asp page, **439, 441**
    in ManageTax.asp page, **428**
    in NewDept.asp page, 407–408
    in OrderDetail.asp page, **487–488**
    in OrderSearch.asp page, 466
    in Payment.asp page, **254–255**
    in Product.asp page, **146–147**
    in ProfileDisplay.asp page, **305**
    in Shipping.asp page, **216–217**
    in Subscription.asp page, 85
SubReport.asp page
    database connections in, **99–100**
    links to, **103–104**
    saving displayed data in, **102–103**
    table in, **100–102**
    testing, **103–104**, *104–105*
Subscription.asp page
    credit card information in, **84–85**
    header information in, **80–81**
    input fields in, **81–84**

submit button in, **85**
testing, **94**, *94*
subscription sample application
  data table for, **78–79**
  form for. *See* Subscription.asp page
  managing. *See* SubReport.asp page
  script code for, **86–93**
  testing, **94–98**, *94–98*
subtotals
  of baskets, **180**, **256**
  displaying, **486–487**
  in OrderReceipt.asp page, **331–333**
  in Payment.asp page, **236–237**
  updating, **494–495**
synchronization
  with multiple servers, 62
  support for, 74
system architecture
  considerations in, **645**
  hardware, **642**
  load balancing, **643**
  three tier, **643–645**, *644*
system configuration
  server farm design
    database servers, **62**
    multiple server support, **62–63**, *62–63*
    staging and development management,
      63–64
    Web servers, **60–61**
  server management. *See* servers

T

T-SQL (Transact-SQL) language, **29**
tables, script listings for, **656–661**
Tax function, **228–229**, 235, 495
tax phase
  description of, **7–8**
  tools for, 25
Tax pipeline stage, 606
Tax table, **46**, 55, 659
taxes
  calculating, **225–232**
  CIP components for, 20
  displaying, **486–487**
  with free shipping, 567–568
  managing, **424**
  in OrderReceipt.asp page, **331–333**
  in Payment.asp page, **234–235**
  rates for
    for Clock Tower site, 638
    entering, **427–428**
    loading, **201–202**
    looping through, **425–426**
    retrieving, 228, **231**, **425**, **429**
    updating, **426–427**, **429–434**, *433–435*
  updating, **495**
TaxShip.asp page, **230**
TaxShip.cls file, **228–229**
TCP/IP networking, 14
team project development, 17
TechNet link, 652
templates for HTML pages, 79

testing
  code heavy sections, 75
  featured products, **542–544**, *542–544*,
    548–550, *549–551*
  free shipping, **571–572**, *571–572*, **586–587**,
    586–587
  order search system, **467–470**, *468–471*
  order updates, 475, *475–476*, 499, *500–501*
  payment page, 256, *257–258*
  profile updates, 315–316, *315–316*
  related products, 529, *529–530*
  Shipping.asp page, **218**, *218–219*
  shipping manager interface, 447
  SubReport.asp page, **103–104**, *104–105*
  subscription sample application, **94–98**,
    94–98
text boxes, **294–295**
thank you message, 90, 97, *98*
threads, **647–648**
three tier architecture, **643–645**, *644*
timeouts for sessions, 80, 349
titles in Header.asp page, 123
To property, 272–273
totals
  displaying, **486–487**
  with free shipping, 567–568
  in order searches, 463
  in OrderReceipt.asp page, **331–333**
  in Payment.asp page, **235**
  updating, **495**
tracking numbers, **466**
Transact-SQL (T-SQL) language, **29**
Transaction Server
  for COM components, 599

  in IIS, 15
  for resource conservation, 646
Trey Research site, **617**
two-day shipping option, 45
txtDeptDesc field, 30
txtDescription field, 32
txtNotes field, 43

U

Ulla Popken site, 19
unstructured searches, 156
up-sell products, 31. *See also* **related products**
  in AddUpgradeItem.asp page, **518–519**
  in Basket.asp page, **510–512**
  relationships for, **506**, *507*
  retrieving, **512–513**
  in UpgradeProduct.asp page, **513–518**
UpdateBasket.asp page, **182–186**, *185–186*
updated department data, **411–412**
UpdateDept.asp page, 411, **414–416**
UpdateFreeShipping.asp page, **581**
UpdateOrder.asp page
  basket updates in, **495**
  billing and shipping information in,
    490–491
  for free shipping, **583–586**
  looping through data in, **493–494**
  payment data in, **492**
  posting to, 477
  receipt items data in, **493**
  retrieving data in, **490**
  subtotals in, **494–495**

totals, shipping, and taxes in, **495**
updating data in, **491–492**
UpdateProduct.asp page, **394–396**
  for featured products, **545–547**
  posting to, 371
  for product sales, **573–574**
UpdateProfile.asp page
  checking for blank fields in, **308**
  cookies in, **313**
  country data in, **308–310**
  database connections in, **312**
  error checking in, **310–311**
  finishing up, **313–314**
  retrieving data for, **306–308**
  state and province data in, **308–309**
  updating profiles in, **312–313**
UpdateShipping.asp page
  connections in, **441–442**
  looping through shipping rates in, **442–443**
  posting to, 436
  updating shipping rates in, **443**
UpdateStatus.asp page, 465, **473–474**
UpdateTaxes.asp page
  looping through tax data in, **430–432**
  posting to, 426
  retrieving tax data in, **429–430**
  updating tax data in, **432**
updating
  baskets, **167, 170–171, 182–186,** *185–186,*
    495, 498–499
  billing information, **490–491**
  departments, **411–412, 414–416**
  featured products, **545–548**
  free shipping, **580–581, 583–586**

order status, **473–475,** *475–476*
orders, **477–478, 490–501,** *500–501*
payment data, **492, 497–498**
products, **394–397**
profiles, **270–271, 306–314,** *315–316*
shipping information, **490–491, 495**
shipping rates, **441–444**
support for, 74
tax rates, **426–427, 429–434,** *433–435*
taxes, **495**
UpgradeProduct.asp page
  connections in, **513**
  links to, 511
  up-sell products in, **513–518**
upgrading products, 34
URLShopperArgs method, 631
user interface
  browsing in, **129–130**
    departments, **130–140,** *133, 139*
    products, **140–150,** *149–150*
  page structure in, **120–121,** *120*
    header and footer pages, **121–128**
    home pages, **128–129,** *129*
  programming the, **535–544**
  searching in
    checking for results in, **151**
    checking for search requests in, **152–153**
    high values in, **153–154**
    low values in, **153**
    query process in, **154**
    query results in, **154–155**
    tables in, **151–152**
  store foundation design
    data loading in, **117–120**

pages in, **112–114**
project setup in, **115–117**
site architecture in, **114**, *115*
usernames
  in authentication, 72
  in Login.asp page, 344–345
  for order history, 316
  for shoppers, 36
util.asp page, 623
utilizing SQL Server, **646**

V

ValidateCCNumber component, 639
ValidateCheck.asp page, **348–350**
ValidatePayment.asp page, **569**
  billing data in, **258–259**, **261–262**
  cleaning shipping data in, **266**
  cookies in, 270, **274–275**
  country and state data in, **262–264**
  credit card data in, **259–260**, **268–269**
  database insertions in, **267–269**
  e-mail addresses in, **263**
  e-mail confirmation receipts in, **271–274**
  final basket data in, **269**
  order histories in, **269**
  province data in, **264**
  retrieving data for, **258–259**, **266–267**
  session variables in, **264–265**
  updating shopper profiles in, **270–271**
ValidateShipping.asp page
  billing information in, **224**
  country information in, **221–222**

e-mail addresses in, **222**
error checking in, **223–224**
Error session variable in, 206
retrieving data for, **220–221**
session variables in, **223**
state and province information in, **223**
value checking methods, 630–631
Value property, 272
VANs (Value-Added Networks), 20
variables
  benefits of, 86
  declaring, 228, 649
  in performance, 650
  session. *See* session variables
VBScript language
  in ASP, 16
  for components modules, 607
VCRocket, **650–651**
VCRocket link, 652
VCTurbo, **650–651**
Verisign certificates, **21**
version management, 22
Version property, 272
virtual Webs, 69
Visual Basic 6, **18–19**, 226, *226*
Visual C++, 22
Visual InterDev tool, **16–17**
  in development environments, 64
  for HTML pages, 79
  for IP addresses, 67, *69*
  with SQL Server, 28
Visual J++, 22
Visual Modeler, 22

Visual Source Safe, 22
 in development environments, 64
 with Visual InterDev, 17
Visual Studio
 for Site Server, 595
 for SQL Server, 28
Volcano Coffee site, **615–616**

W

Wallet tool, 599
warm backups, 74
Web applications, connecting to, 69, *70*
Web servers, **60–61**
 setup for, **65–70**, *66–70*
 in Windows NT Server 4, 14
Web site visit phase
 description of, **6–7**
 tools for, 24
weight shipping model, 44
WIN INET tools, 18
Windows 2000, 15
Windows 2000 link, 652
Windows NT 4 link, 652
Windows NT 4 option pack, **15–16**, 609

Windows NT Challenge/Response, 72
Windows NT Server 4, **14–15**, 594–595, 609
WYSIWYG HTML editing tools, 22

X

xt_data_add_update.asp page, 624
xt_data_delete.asp page, 624
xt_orderform_additem.asp page, 622, 631
xt_orderform_clearitems.asp page, 622
xt_orderform_delitem.asp page, 622
xt_orderform_editquantities.asp page, 622
xt_orderform_prepare.asp page, 622
xt_orderform_purchase.asp page, 623

Y

year of credit card expiration, **241–242**

Z

zip codes, look-up data for, 225

SYBEX BOOKS ON THE WEB

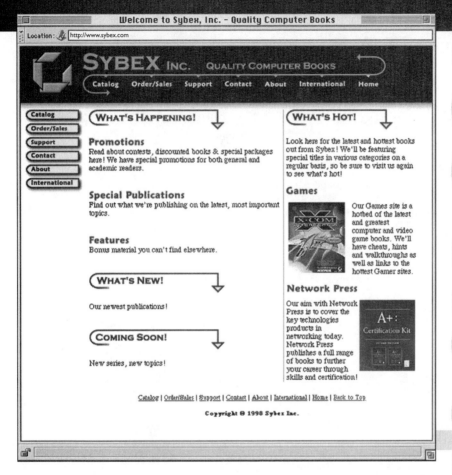

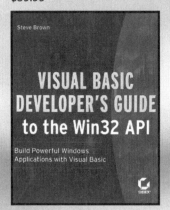